Pragmatics and
the English Language

PERSPECTIVES ON THE ENGLISH LANGUAGE

Series Editors: Lesley Jeffries and Dan McIntyre

Published titles

PRAGMATICS AND THE ENGLISH LANGUAGE
Jonathan Culpeper and Michael Haugh

THE LANGUAGE OF EARLY ENGLISH LITERATURE: FROM CÆDMON TO MILTON
Sara M. Pons-Sanz

DISCOURSE AND GENRE: USING LANGUAGE IN CONTEXT
Stephen Bax

STUDYING THE HISTORY OF EARLY ENGLISH
Simon Horobin

CRITICAL STYLISTICS: THE POWER OF ENGLISH
Lesley Jeffries

ENGLISH LITERARY STYLISTICS
Christiana Gregoriou

STUDYING LANGUAGE: ENGLISH IN ACTION
Urszula Clark

THINKING ABOUT LANGUAGE: THEORIES OF ENGLISH
Siobhan Chapman

DISCOVERING LANGUAGE: THE STRUCTURE OF MODERN ENGLISH
Lesley Jeffries

Forthcoming title

STUDYING DIALECT
Rob Penhallurick

Perpectives on the English Language

Series Standing Order
ISBN 978–0–333–96146–9 hardcover
ISBN 978–0–333–96147–6 paperback
(*outside North America only*)

You can receive future titles in this series as they are published by placing a standing order. Please contact your bookseller or, in the case of difficulty, write to us at the address below with your name and address, the title of the series and one of the ISBNs quoted above.

Customer Services Department, Macmillan Distribution Ltd, Houndmills, Basingstoke, Hampshire, RG21 6XS, UK

Pragmatics and the English Language

Jonathan Culpeper
Lancaster University, UK

and

Michael Haugh
Griffith University, Australia

palgrave
macmillan

First published 2014 by
PALGRAVE MACMILLAN

Palgrave Macmillan in the UK is an imprint of Macmillan Publishers Limited, registered in England, company number 785998, of Houndmills, Basingstoke, Hampshire RG21 6XS.

Palgrave Macmillan in the US is a division of St Martin's Press LLC, 175 Fifth Avenue, New York, NY 10010.

Palgrave Macmillan is the global academic imprint of the above companies and has companies and representatives throughout the world.

Palgrave® and Macmillan® are registered trademarks in the United States, the United Kingdom, Europe and other countries

ISBN: 978–0–230–55173–2

This book is printed on paper suitable for recycling and made from fully managed and sustained forest sources. Logging, pulping and manufacturing processes are expected to conform to the environmental regulations of the country of origin.

A catalogue record for this book is available from the British Library.

A catalog record for this book is available from the Library of Congress.

Printed in China.

Contents

List of Tables

List of Figures

Series Editors' Preface

We are delighted to introduce another new volume in the Perspectives on the English Language series. The first phase of this series produced three basic core books which cover the essentials for those studying English Language at undergraduate level and this core was followed by a second phase of books dealing with specific topics in linguistics as applied to the English Language. The core books (Jeffries 2006, Clark 2006 and Chapman 2007) remain at the centre of the series, establishing some common ground in terms of the descriptive apparatus, the social variation and the philosophical approaches to English. We now also have a growing range of texts dealing with some of the major themes of linguistics but applied specifically to English. These include literary linguistics (Gregoriou 2008), discourse analysis (Bax 2010), critical stylistics (Jeffries 2010), the development of early English (Horobin 2009) and the language of early English literature (Pons-Sanz 2014).

We aim for our books to share the linguistic/scientific principles of rigour and replicability in their approach to linguistic data, and we are proud of their accessibility, without any consequential over-simplification of material or treatment. The level of these books is intended to be appropriate for undergraduates studying these topics as part of an English Language or joint degree including English Language. However, students or researchers at higher levels, but new to the particular topic, should find that they work as a good starting point for their reading, as the volumes produced during this second phase are all research-led and address theoretical as well as descriptive issues.

The next phase of development of the series will include books which continue to broaden the range of topics as well as being based on cutting-edge research. The clarity and accessibility will continue to be an important aspect of the series, as will the scientific principles mentioned above. We also aim to produce a still higher level of book, modelled on the monograph, but written for students as well as researchers. This will complete the link between teaching-only textbooks and research monographs which we see as a false dichotomy in any case.

This volume on the pragmatics of English brings together two significant researchers in the field who take the reader from the basics of referential meaning through to the most recent questions of whether pragmatics is concerned mainly with the language users' meaning (first-order) or the analysts' meaning (second-order). Thus, although this book starts out with few assumptions about the background knowledge of the reader, it manages to introduce not only the main pragmatic features of English(es) but also debate the theoretical questions that currently concern those working in this field. Though pragmatics as a sub-discipline of linguistics has tended to illustrate its constructs using English examples, there has so far been no accessible general treatment of the pragmatics of the English Language itself. This book puts that omission right.

Lesley Jeffries and Dan McIntyre

Acknowledgements

In the making of this book, we have racked up debts. We cannot thank enough the people who patiently read through the first draft, warts and all, namely, Geoffrey Leech, Judith O'Byrne and the four reviewers procured by Palgrave Macmillan (especially, the heroic reviewer 4). Their commentary has saved us from howlers and infelicities, and enabled us to enhance innumerable aspects of the book. Any deficiencies that remain are, of course, our responsibility. We would also like to thank the people at Palgrave Macmillan for their support: Kitty van Boxel for helping in the early stages, Aléta Bezuidenhout for her careful eye in the closing stages, and Paul Stevens for his considered direction. Finally, we would like to thank John Heywood for his invaluable help with the index.

Example 4.1 is reproduced by permission of Universal UClick.

Examples of usage taken from the British National Corpus (BNC) were obtained under the terms of the BNC End User Licence. Copyright in the individual texts cited resides with the original IPR holders.

Figure 7.1 is reproduced from Watts (2005: xliii) by permission of De Gruyter.

Example 8.1 is reproduced from the *Brisbane Sunday Mail* by permission of Rory Gibson.

Transcription Conventions

[ ]	overlapping speech
(0.5)	numbers in brackets indicate pause length
(.)	micropause
:	elongation of vowel or consonant sound
-	word cut-off
.	falling or final intonation
?	rising intonation
,	'continuing' intonation
=	latched utterances
<u>underlining</u>	contrastive stress or emphasis
CAPS	markedly loud
° °	markedly soft
.hhh	in-breathe
Hhh	out-breathe/laughter
↓ ↑	sharp falling/rising intonation
> <	talk is compressed or rushed
< >	talk is markedly slowed or drawn out
( )	blank space in parentheses indicates uncertainty about the transcription
(( ))	double brackets indicates extra contextual or non-verbal information

1 Introduction

1.1 Introduction

Meaning can kill you. In the UK in 1952, Derek Bentley and Christopher Craig broke into a warehouse. Craig was armed with a revolver. They had been seen entering, and the police were called. One police officer managed to grab hold of Bentley. At this point, witnesses claimed that Bentley said: *Let him have it, Chris*. Craig fired, but only grazed the police officer. Nevertheless Bentley was arrested, while Craig managed to get away. Upon the arrival of more police officers, Craig was apprehended, but not before shooting one of them dead. Craig and Bentley were charged with murder, which for Bentley carried the possibility of the death sentence (Craig was underage). Much of the court case, and the subsequent appeals, focused on the ambiguity of the words Bentley had spoken. Do they mean "let the police officer have the gun, Chris", or do they have the more idiomatic meaning "shoot the police officer, Chris" (presumably derived by metonymy from "let the police officer have a bullet, Chris", assuming *it* refers to a bullet)? The judge and jury decided on the latter, and Bentley was sentenced to death and hanged. The fact that they made this decision perhaps reflects the cursory way in which ambiguities and indeterminacies of meaning are generally treated. The folk belief is that language fixes meanings, and their recovery is easy – you just need to know the code. In fact, humans determine meanings, and their recovery is far from easy – certainly not just a simple matter of decoding. In 1998 the Court of Appeal overturned Bentley's conviction. The judge, Lord Bingham, made it clear that the summing up of the original judge, Lord Goddard, had not given adequate attention to the possible ambiguity of the *Let him have it, Chris*, or even whether he had actually said it (R v. Derek William Bentley 1998, paragraphs 74 and 86). In fact, scholars of traditional linguistics would not fare much better in accounting for Bentley's utterance. Phonology, morphology, syntax and even semantics would have little to contribute to our understanding of why Bentley's utterance was ambiguous, part of which is understanding to whom or what *him* and *it* are referring, and also understanding the presence of literal and non-literal meanings. In contrast, such issues lie at the heart of pragmatics. Let us begin this chapter by working through some examples illustrating issues which are pertinent to pragmatics. After this, we will briefly outline our view of pragmatics, and then conclude by introducing the chapters of this book.

1.2   Meanings in context

1.2.1   Beyond the linguistic code

It is a truth universally acknowledged that a single person in possession of a fine dictionary must be able to access the correct meaning of a piece of language. The previous sentence was intended to be ironic, but alas many people would not understand it as such. People place great reliance on dictionaries to decode language and expose its meanings. But how far will this actually get us in understanding the language people use? Let us work through some of the problems that one encounters. In doing so, we will simultaneously explore a number of jokes, not least because jokes often exploit the construction of meaning.

The assignment of sense

Polysemy, when a lexeme has multiple related senses, is a normal feature of many words (in this book, technical terms relating to pragmatics are emboldened and defined; they are also listed in the index). The English word *set*, for example, has 36 senses listed in the *Collins Cobuild Dictionary of the English Language* (1987), plus various usages in expressions. There is also the issue of **homonymy**, two or more different lexemes with the same form. For example, in the sentences *Catch the ball* and *We're going to the ball*, the senses of *ball* are not the same. Note that when you read those sentences, you assign a sense that fits the understanding you construct in your head. People can, of course, exploit your assignment of sense. Consider this joke:

> [1.1]   A: Why can't a man's head be twelve inches wide?
> B: Er ... don't know.
> A: Because if it was, it would be a foot.

Here, the words *twelve inches wide* prime your mind to expect an answer relating to measurement (even if you had no knowledge of the notion of "inch", you might well infer that it is the unit of measurement given that the number twelve is applied to the width of something). Indeed, A's solution to the joke does relate to measurement: twelve inches on one scale of measurement are equivalent to a foot on another. However, this does not easily fit the meaning speaker A is constructing. If twelve inches is the same as a foot, then why can it not be the width of a man's head? The solution is in another meaning of *foot*, namely, the part of your leg below the ankle. And of course a *head* is not a *foot*. This joke exploits the polysemic word and the target's assignment of sense; it is a pun. This joke is lost on people who are not familiar with imperial measurements. For them, the most readily accessible meaning of the word *foot* is likely to be that it is the part of the body below the ankle. The humour falls flat.

The assignment of structural meaning

Although certainly not as frequently an issue as sense assignment, there will be occasions when the structure of a sentence offers more than one meaning. A classic example, and one grammarians love poring over, is *Can you see the man with the telescope?* Is the question about seeing the man with the aid of a telescope (in which case, *with the telescope* is an (instrumental) adverbial working with the verb *see*), or about seeing the man who has a telescope (in which case, *with the telescope* is a prepositional phrase post-modifying the head noun *man*)? Consider this joke:

[1.2]   Q: How do you make a cat drink?
         A: Easy, put it in a liquidiser.

The joke exploits the two different ways in which you can parse the question. In one, *drink* is the main verb of the embedded noun clause *a cat drink*; in the other, *drink* is the head noun of the noun phrase and pre-modified by *cat*. However, part of the success of this joke, just as with the previous joke, relies on the target understanding the sentence in the first way, at least initially. That we are predisposed to do this is not surprising, because this interpretation fits a plausible, non-extraordinary scenario of one's cat being dehydrated. In contrast, a "cat drink" as a kind of beverage is bizarre. The realisation in one's mind of the alternative reading is how the joke works. Incidentally, the joke is more likely to fall flat if it is spoken and heard rather than written and read. The different grammatical parsings would sound different: they have different prosodies (try saying them to get an idea of this).

The assignment of reference

In the previous examples, the words and structures flag potential meanings from which we can choose, a choice we make on the basis of how we understand the context. However, some linguistic expressions – notably, **refer-ring expressions** – do not carry with them multiple senses from which we select, but rely to a greater extent on the target enriching their meaning with information drawn from the context. This is a matter of **reference**. Consider this joke:

[1.3] A man and a friend are playing golf one day. One of the guys is about to chip onto the green when he sees a long funeral procession on the road next to the course. He stops in mid-swing, takes off his golf cap, closes his eyes, and bows down in prayer. His friend says: "Wow! That is the most thoughtful and touching thing I have ever seen. You are truly a kind man."

The other man replies, "Yeah, well, we were married thirty-five years."

Clearly, the success of the joke relies on one working out the **referent** (what is referred to) of the word *we*. Given the subsequent use of the word *married*, we work out that *we* refers to a married couple consisting of the man and his wife, for whom the funeral procession is being held. The realisation that the man playing golf is the husband of the person whose funeral it is and that he is not part of the *long funeral procession* clashes with previous thoughts that this man is *thoughtful* or *kind*.

The assignment of utterance meaning

Having assigned relevant senses to words and worked out the relevant refer-ents of referring expressions, you may think that we are home and dry. This is not the case, as the following joke illustrates:

[1.4] I was coming back from Canada, driving through Customs, and the guy asked, "Do you have any firearms with you?" I said: "What do you need?"

What this joke illustrates is that the whole utterance *Do you have any firearms with you?* can have more than one meaning: is it an enquiry about whether the driver has firearms or a request for firearms? The difference between the two relates in part to understandings of what the speaker is trying to do, and what they are trying to do is a matter of **speaker intention**. Of course, the humour lies in the fact that the reader expects the former meaning, not least because they know that the driver is in *Customs*, a place commonly associated with searches for firearms and other dangerous weapons or devices, yet the person driving the car answers as if it were the latter.

Collectively, these different levels of meaning and assignment illustrate the fact that dictionaries do not get us very far in understanding the full meaning of language used in context. This is not to say that they are of no use. Indeed, they are useful in identifying a limited number of potential senses. But we still need to work out which sense is relevant, and much more besides. Speakers of utterances use language to flag potential meanings – that is, meanings which they think are likely to be understood in a particular context; while hearers infer potential meanings – that is, meanings which they think are likely to have been meant in a particular context. Meaning in interaction involves both speakers and hearers (we adopt the traditional labels "speaker" and "hearer" here; in section 5.2 we explain their limitations). **Interactional meaning** is what the speaker means by an utterance and what the hearer understands by it (which could, of course, be two different things), and how these emerge and are shaped during interaction. We will have more to say about interactional meaning in every chapter of this book.

Jokes, as we saw, often exploit the fact that meanings cannot be straightforwardly decoded from words and structures. Many deploy a "garden path" tactic; that is to say, you are led into expecting one thing, only to find that it is another thing. That clash between what we expect and what we discover is the trigger for the potential humour. This is accounted for by an important theory in humour studies, namely, **Incongruity theory**, a theory that has evolved in various guises since Aristotle. Immanuel Kant, for example, comments: "Laughter is an affectation arising from the sudden transformation of a strained expectation into nothing" ([1790] 1951:172). More specifically, note that the jokes exploit interactional meaning: they exploit how understandings of the joke unfold in the interaction between not just the characters in the joke, but also the author of the joke and the reader. Clearly, the **discourse situation** – the configuration of discourse roles (e.g. authors, mouthpieces, addressees, overhearers; see section 5.2) relating to a particular interaction – needs to be taken into consideration.

1.2.2   The scope of pragmatics

Views about what the field of pragmatics encompasses and what its main thrust should be are controversial. Two principal camps can be identified, one involving a relatively **narrow view** and the other a relatively **broad view**.

The narrow view: syntax, semantics and pragmatics

Many notions in pragmatics can be seen in the work of early writers like Plato and Kant, but especially in that on **pragmatism** by the American philosopher Charles Sanders Peirce (1839–1914). However, it was another American philosopher, Charles Morris (1901–1979), drawing on Peirce's work along with that of Rudolph Carnap, who provided a point of departure for the field of pragmatics. In his *Foundations of the Theory of Signs* (1938: 6–7), he argues for the following three-way distinction:

- Syntax (or syntactics) = mono relationship (relationships between linguistic signs)
- Semantics = dyadic relationship (relationships between linguistic signs and the things in the world that they designate)
- Pragmatics = triadic relationship (relationships between linguistic signs, things they designate, and their users/interpreters)

This has provided linguists with a way of understanding how pragmatics relates to other key areas of linguistics.[1] Specifically, it distinguishes pragmatics as the area that deals with context, but also makes clear that it has some aspects in common with syntax and semantics. Morris seems to take a "micro" view of context, mentioning just users and interpreters, and not, for example, social relations or situations. Indeed, this kind of micro context has characterised foundational works in pragmatics such as Grice's (1975) Conversational Implicature or Sperber and Wilson's ([1986]1995) relevance theory, with their focus on users' intentions and interpreters' inferences.

Pragmatics in this view is often seen as another component in a theory of language, adding to the usual phonetics, phonology, morphology, grammar/ syntax and semantics. Sometimes the objective is to get pragmatics to "rescue" other more formal areas of linguistic theory. This is especially true of scholars whose main interest is not pragmatics: they can dispose of problematic areas into the "pragmatics dustbin", leaving their theories unsullied by contextual ambiguities, indeterminacies and the like. Scholars whose main interest is pragmatics are often set on bringing formal order to these contextual meanings, a case in point being Searle's work on speech act theory (e.g. 1969). Although such efforts encounter many problems, as we shall see in the case of speech act theory, for example, in Chapter 6, many insights can be gained from their attempted solution.

This view of pragmatics is usually identified as the Anglo-American view. The topics typically discussed within it include reference, deixis, presupposition, speech acts, implicature and inferencing – all of which will be extensively treated in the following chapters.

The broad view: pragmatic functions

What is often identified as the Continental European view of pragmatics does not exclude the kind of topic areas discussed in the Anglo-American view, but

---

[1] Morris himself was not, in fact, articulating a theory of language. He did not see these divisions as a matter of dividing up language but dividing up semiotics – the science of signs (e.g. words, gestures, pictures) and how they are organised, used to signify things and understood.

it encompasses much beyond them and has a rather different perspective – in fact, it might be considered in terms of a particular perspective on language. In this view pragmatics is the superordinate field, with disciplines such as linguistics, sociology and psychology as sub-fields. Thus, the range of topic areas is potentially huge. Moreover, pragmatics is not simply about adding a contextual dimension to a theory of language, but a "general cognitive, social, and cultural perspective on linguistic phenomena in relation to their usage in forms of behaviour" (Verschueren 1999: 7). The first part of this quotation indicates that pragmatics is not simply sited within linguistics, but could equally be within cognitive, social or cultural fields of study. The final part of this quotation indicates that pragmatics does not look at linguistic phenomena *per se*, but only at linguistic phenomena in actual usage (the abstract patterns that characterise many areas of linguistic theory are not to be found here). And finally, note that the last word of the quotation broadens the object of analysis to behaviour, which is to say, what people *do*, whether with language or something else (e.g. a gesture), in social contexts. In practice, this view of pragmatics emphasises a socio-cultural perspective on the functioning of language. Superficially, the narrow and broad views seem to share an interest in cognition, but there is a difference of emphasis. As mentioned above, the cognitive intentions and inferences involved in generating a speaker's meaning or reconstructing a hearer's understanding of it characterise the narrow view. The broader view would not eschew these, but would often encompass broader cognitive notions, such as the way knowledge about situations, social institutions, cultures and so on might influence and be influenced by language.

Regarding our examples in section 1.2, this broad pragmatic view would not ignore the indeterminacies noted and how they might be resolved, but considerably more discussion would be devoted to the fact that they involved jokes. How does the joke work? How is it processed in the mind? Why is it being told here? What are its social functions? What influences whether it is successful or not? (The cat drink joke could well be abhorrent to cat lovers!) Note, of course, that a distinguishing feature of this view is that it is relatively "macro" in its approach to context.

It is important, however, that one should not over-emphasise differences between the Anglo-American and the Continental European views. A topic such as **politeness**, as discussed in Chapter 7, has a foothold in both, as it seeks to explain both some aspects of linguistic structure and some aspects of social function and context. Moreover, one could argue that any comprehensive analysis of linguistic data should do both, as indeed this book attempts to do. More micro linguistic issues are informed by dynamic two-way inter-relations with more macro socio-cultural issues; conversely, more macro issues of socio-culture are informed by dynamic two-way inter-relations with more micro linguistic issues. In fact, we would argue for the importance of bridging the micro and macro and not neglecting the middle ground.

1.3   The pragmatics of English

Referring to a "grammar of English" is not uncommon, and a "phonology of English", a "morphology of English" or a "semantics of English" all sound plausible. But what about a "pragmatics of English"?

A preliminary and not inconsiderable problem in thinking about the possibility of a pragmatics of English is to get a grasp on what "English" is. The "English language" is not in itself a neatly identifiable entity. Consider the view "English is the language of England". Historically, the roots of English are not in England at all, but in the old Germanic dialects of what is now north-western Germany. Once it became established in Britain, roughly 450 BC onwards, it was relatively restricted geographically: in the 16th century there were approximately three million speakers of English, nearly all indeed based in England. However, today there are well over 300 million native speakers of English – speakers in the USA, Canada, Australia, New Zealand, South Africa and so on. Strictly speaking then, we should now be talking about "Englishes". And we should not forget to mention a further 300 million regularly speaking English as a second language (i.e. in addition to their native language), and the huge number of people learning it as a foreign language, mainly to communicate with other non-native speakers of English (it is even said that there are more Chinese people learning English than there are native speakers of English in the USA!). Thus, most English is produced, heard and read outside England. One might argue that English has a common core of words and structures that are recognised as being English. The problem here is that not everybody would recognise the same things as being English. Even within England today there are dialectal differences that make identifying that common core difficult. One might appeal to some notion such as Standard English, claiming it represents the common core. But whose standard English are we talking about – British, American, Australian? And there is the issue of what is meant by standard. Appeals to such notions frequently slide from talk of a uniform set of features to talk of a set of features which a particular group considers best. Answers to that question typically involve the social evaluation of language (e.g. British people tend to think that the British standard is best). All these issues present a problem: if we cannot agree about what constitutes English, how can we study it? To study anything requires that there be an object to study. The answer is simply to accept that there is variation in English and there are various views as to what counts as English. We should try to accommodate this variation and those views in our descriptions rather than obliterating them. In this light, aiming at a "pragmatics of English" is not viable. What one stands a better chance of contributing to, however, is a "pragmatics of Englishes".

There has been a significant step forward towards a pragmatics of Englishes, namely, Anne Barron and Klaus P. Schneider's *The Pragmatics of Irish English* (2005). This seems to be the first book to focus exclusively on the pragmatics of a national variety of English. Sociolinguists and dialectologists have contributed to descriptions of Englishes (see, for example, Trudgill and Hannah's popular *International English: a Guide to the Varieties of Standard English*, 2002). But such descriptions avoid delving into anything pragmatic (except perhaps brief mentions of features such as tag questions or terms of address and their functions in context). Barron and Schneider's (2005) volume aims to plug this gap. They bring together a number of empirical studies examining Irish English in various contexts and taking account of socio-cultural norms of interaction. They cover a wide range of pragmatic phenomena, including discourse markers, silence, mitigation, speech acts (responding to thanks, offering), politeness and politeness strategies. Relative indirectness turns out to be a feature of Irish English. Schneider and Barron suggest that their volume could be seen as the beginning of a new discipline, **variational pragmatics**, which they suggest lies at the interface of pragmatics and dialectology.

Barron and Schneider's volume is a landmark. By assembling a group of relevant studies, it begins to fill a descriptive gap. Moreover, it stimulated the production of further studies, many of which will be mentioned in the course of this book. Of course, there is much still to be done. For example, they did not consider the complete range of speech acts, of discourse markers, and so on. Also, one might argue that the book does not quite have the broad scope that one might envisage for a pragmatics of Englishes. The following are some of the areas that one might consider:

1. Metapragmatics. This focuses on the language used in a particular English to talk about pragmatic phenomena, and also how such language interacts with the phenomena it talks about. It could include, for example, metapragmatic labels (e.g. speech act labels such as *request, threat, compliment*) or metapragmatic comments (e.g. "that was an order", "that was rude"). Such labels and comments can provide insights into beliefs about and the attitudes towards pragmatic phenomena, as well as the real effects that having those beliefs/attitudes can have on English, its social contexts and the people who speak it.

2. Pragmatic forms. This focuses on the nature of the pragmatic forms (forms that conventionally carry pragmatic meanings) of a particular English. For example, *could you tell me the time?* is so conventionalised as a request that it would seem perverse to respond to the literal meaning with *yes* or *no*.

The notion of "forms" here should be taken broadly – it can vary from a grammatical particle to a genre, and it can include forms of non-verbal behaviour.

3. Pragmatic functions. This focuses on the nature of the pragmatic functions of a particular English, for example, its range of speech acts and how individual speech acts perform particular functions.

4. Pragmatic contexts. This focuses on the nature of the pragmatic contexts of a particular English, that is to say, the nature of the contexts within which pragmatic forms and functions interact, for example, how a job interview, a service encounter or family mealtime interaction is constituted by particular pragmatic forms and functions.

5. Pragmatic variation. This focuses on how metapragmatics, pragma-forms, pragma-functions and pragma-contexts vary. Three dimensions of variation are important: (1) **inter-English variation** (similarities or differences amongst Englishes), (2) **intra-English variation** (similarities or differences amongst the sub-varieties of a particular English), and (3) **diachronic variation in English** (similarities or differences amongst the historical periods of a particular English, including how pragmatic phenomena have evolved both within a particular English and across Englishes).

We have listed these areas separately for expository convenience, but they, of course, all interact with each other.

1.4   This book

This book does not undertake the considerable project of describing the pragmatics of a particular English. Instead, it is a pragmatics book that is oriented towards a pragmatics of Englishes. As a pragmatics book, it covers an array of typical pragmatic topics, varying from the more formal to the more socio-cultural. In order, the chapters focus on referring expressions, information structure, pragmatic meaning (including conversational implicature), pragmatic acts (including speech acts), interpersonal pragmatics (including politeness) and metapragmatics. The keystone of our vision of pragmatics for this book is integration. The locus of integrating different perspectives in pragmatics is interaction. Every chapter in this book works towards a focus on the dynamics of pragmatic interaction. To an extent, we are taking the road carved out by Jenny Thomas in her book *Meaning in Interaction* (1995), though that book does not have the broad scope of ours or pursue interactional aspects to the same extent. We could also point to the work of Herbert Clark (e.g. 1996) and its influence in shaping approaches to interactional pragmatics. In our view, interaction is where pragmatic phenomena happen and so deserves special attention. With respect to theory, repeatedly in this book we describe the dynamic tension between what might be broadly called first-order and second-order perspectives on pragmatics. A first-order perspective is that of the participants themselves, the ones who are using language to mean and do things. A second-order perspective is that of the analyst, including ourselves, the writers of this book, and you the readers. Pragmatics, especially of the narrow Anglo-American kind, was traditionally rooted primarily in a second-order perspective, but has more recently seen a shift towards a first-order perspective, driven in part by pragmatics of the broad European kind. In tune with what we stated at the end of section 1.2.2, we advocate neither perspective exclusively, but seek a middle ground. In other words, we advocate an approach to theorising in pragmatics that not only respects both user and observer perspectives (or at least attempts to), but also bridges them (or at least attempts to). A particular characteristic of our approach is that it is strongly empirical; it informs and is informed by engagement with the data. To give it a label, we refer to this approach as **integrative pragmatics**.

As an English language book, our book does not attempt to be a systematic description of any particular English, but rather to show how pragmatic phenomena and concepts can be related to various Englishes. Every chapter is infused with examples and case studies. A major function of our Reflection boxes is to describe pragmatic variation in English (sometimes characteristics that are shared across a number of Englishes, sometimes specific to a particular English). Reflection boxes are also used to extend particular topics, to add theoretical detail, to describe a specific related phenomenon, and so on. In some ways, one might describe our book as a pragmatics book that is knowingly ethnocentric. In this respect we should note the 2009 special issue (vol. 41) of the *Journal of Pragmatics* entitled "Towards an Emancipatory Pragmatics". In the introduction to the special issue, the editors state (Hanks et al. 2007: 1–2):

> It is our shared conviction that pragmatics as an analytic enterprise has been dominated by views of language derived from Euro-American languages and ways of speaking. Speech acts defined in terms of standard illocutionary forces and felicity conditions, implicatures explained on the basis of the Gricean cooperative principle and maxims, politeness defined in terms of a universal notion of "face", and the very idea that speech is driven by the exchange of information are all examples of the problem. While these research traditions have enriched the field of pragmatics, they also have tended to rely uncritically on the common sense of speakers of modern Western languages, with the attendant premises of individualism, rationality, and market economy. That is, while they are presented as

general models of rational language use, they in fact rely heavily on the native common sense of their authors and practitioners.

Unlike most introductory pragmatics books which give the impression that the pragmatic phenomena they discuss are general, applicable to many languages and cultures, we call a spade a spade – this is a book about pragmatics and the English language.

2 Referential Pragmatics

2.1 Introduction

Leech (1983:11) briefly mentions the label for the area that we will discuss in this chapter, namely, **referential pragmatics**. He defines it as "the assignment of reference to referential expressions in a given utterance" (ibid.). The notion of reference briefly popped up in the previous chapter. Let us explore the area through an example. Consider this statement:

[2.1]   The Palgrave editor visited me in my office today.

The Palgrave editor is who exactly? There are several such editors who work for the publisher Palgrave, and there have been many such editors – which one are we talking about? This is a **referring expression** directing the reader to pick out a specific person from the context. Similarly, "my office" is directing the reader to pick out a particular place. Again, the reader will have to work out which office is being talked about. What of *me* and *my*? Clearly, they refer to the author of this statement, and it is up to the reader to work out who that author is. Similarly, *today* refers to the time period in which the author was writing, and we would need to work out when that is. All these expressions involve working out connections with context; they are referring expressions. In a very general sense, all expressions used in relation to something out there in the world – a world which includes the discourses we create – can be said to involve reference to something. **Reference**, broadly conceived, is a topic of special interest in semantics and philosophy. This kind of very general relation is not our focus here (for more on this, see Frege's classic [1892] 1952 work on sense and reference). We are interested in expressions, such as those in our example, whose meaning will seem inadequate without the interpreter having made a connection with a specific part of a specific context – a **referent**. The fact that those expressions involve a referent, an entity to which they refer, means that all referring expressions presuppose the existence of an entity. We will use the term **referring** to denote the narrower, more dynamic – indeed pragmatic – usage of expressions that connect with context, both drawing meaning from it and shaping it. Note that referring expressions do not in themselves refer to entities, but are used and interpreted by participants as doing so – that is what makes them pragmatic.

One key issue when considering referring expressions is, naturally, what specific aspect of context the speaker is referring to. In pragmatics, there are at least three key dimensions involved in referring. Consider, for instance, the following excerpt from the film *Four Weddings and a Funeral*, which starts when Charles attempts to introduce himself to another guest at the wedding:

[2.2]   Charles: How do you do, my name is Charles.
        Guest: Don't be ridiculous, Charles died 20 years ago!
        Charles: Must be a different Charles, I think.
        Guest: Are you telling me I don't know my own brother?
        Charles: No, no.

(Four Weddings and a Funeral, 1994,
director: Mike Newell, writer: Richard Curtis)

We can identify at least three different forms of referring going on in this rather "confused" interaction. First, we have both Charles and the guest referring to themselves and the other through various pronouns, including *I* and *you*. These involve pointing to a specific referent in the *extralinguistic* context and, most importantly, indicating how this referent relates to some point of reference (here the speaker). This is traditionally termed **deixis**. Second, there is some confusion (on the guest's part at least) as to whether *Charles* (when saying *my name is Charles*) refers to a person the guest already knows, or one he is getting to know at that very moment, or what we might term *epistemic* aspects of context. In this case, the speakers are referring to (here different) assumptions about who they think the other person has in mind. When the speaker assumes that the hearer knows the specific referent in mind, this comes under scope of **definiteness**, while when the speaker doesn't make such an assumption, it is a matter of **indefiniteness**. The crux of the guest's confusion here is the guest has his brother in mind when *Charles* is referred to, and consequently thinks that Charles does as well. Third, some expressions they use are used to refer back to things they have said earlier. For instance, when the guest utters *my own brother*, he is referring back to his previous reference to *Charles* who *died 20 years ago*. Instances where speakers are referring back to what has been earlier referred to in previous talk, or what might be termed *linguistic* aspects of context or **co-text**, comes under the scope of **anaphora**. In this chapter, we will be explaining in more detail the pragmatics of these three forms of referring.

Supplying a list of English referring expressions is not straightforward, however, as debates rage over where to draw the line with respect to what is referring and what is not. Let us first briefly consider the extremes. All scholars would agree that verbs and prepositions are not referring expressions. Consider our example [2.1] above: the verb *visited* and the preposition *in* were the only items we did not claim to be referring expressions. To understand them, you do not need to pick out a specific visit or a specific spatial relation with respect to the office (we ignore here the fact that *visited* carries a past tense marker). The other extreme is more controversial. Many, if not all, scholars would agree that the demonstrative *this* is a referring expression of some kind. But there are other possible candidates for referring expressions too. Table 2.1 lists English referring expressions that are thought to be so by many scholars.

In broad terms, the categories of Table 2.1 are ordered from those whose meaning is more descriptive, more encoded in the abstract sense of the expression, to those whose meaning is more contextual, more dependent on a relationship with a specific contextual aspect. The former is more semantic and the latter more pragmatic. *The book*, a definite expression, has some descriptive meaning in the abstract, as the noun *book* denotes the concept of a book, although we do not know which particular book is being referred to; *this*, a deictic expression, has very little descriptive meaning in the abstract, although we may suppose that it concerns something relatively close in some way to the speaking voice (compare with *that*). The organisation of this chapter is based on this table. First, we attend to the extremes of the table, definite expressions followed by deictic expressions, and then anaphoric expressions in the middle. In the final section, we take a more interactional view of how referring expressions are used and understood.

Table 2.1 Categories of English referring expressions

Category		Examples	
Definite expressions	Definite noun phrases	the book(s), Jonathan's course(s), my example, etc.	More semantic
	Proper nouns	Michael, Smith, Professor Leech, etc.	↕
Anaphoric expressions		he, it, they, herself, etc.	
Deictic expressions		this, that, I, here, now, tomorrow, etc.	More pragmatic

2.2 Definite expressions

Definite expressions encode some semantic meaning in their nominal elements. For example, as mentioned above, *book* in the definite expression *the book* relates to whatever mental representation you have for the concept of a "book". Moreover, Frege ([1892]1952) noted that a definite expression not only denotes something but also implies that it exists (we will pick up on this in our discussion of presuppositions in section 3.2.2). Russell (1905), however, argued that the key issue with expressions such as *the book* is not just that they imply existence but that generally they indicate uniqueness (a particular book, in our example). For Russell, definite expressions do not refer directly to something; it is simply a matter of finding a true match between the semantic descriptive content of the expression and any candidates for a match in the world. Others (such as Strawson 1950) argue, from a more pragmatic perspective, that it all depends on the use of the expression in context. For example, the semantics of *the book* in a de-contextualised sentence such as *pass the book* may signal that a unique book is involved, but you are unlikely to know exactly which book is being referred to. In contrast, if somebody arrived in the room where you are right now and said the same to you, you may be led into thinking not only that a unique book is involved but also that they refer to the very book you are now reading. And, if they arrived when you were reading in bed, you might think that they refer to your bedtime novel. A starting point is to say that definite expressions are primarily used to invite the participant(s) to identify a particular referent from a specific context which is assumed to be shared by the interlocutors (we air this issue further below, especially in section 2.5).

There are various ways in which languages can signal definiteness. The paradigm method in English is the **definite article** *the,* the most frequent word in written and spoken English (Leech et al. 2001: 181 and 144). Like other noun phrase **determiners**, such as possessive determiner pronouns (e.g. *my/your/our/their book*), demonstratives (e.g. *this/that book*), or s-genitives (e.g. *Jonathan's book*), definite articles "determine" the definiteness of the noun phrase. Compare the sentences in [2.3]:

[2.3] (a) The book you're reading is great.
        (b) A book you're reading is great.

You are likely to interpret (a) as referring to the book you are currently reading (apologies for the immodesty!). But with (b), it could be about any book you are currently reading (this book, other course books, the novel you read when you go to bed, etc.). (b) contains the indefinite article *a*, contrasting with the definite article *the*. Apart from noun phrases with determiners, pronouns (e.g. *I, you, she, it*) can express definiteness in English, as can proper nouns, a topic we will discuss below.

Reflection: The development of *the* in English

The earliest stages of English had no definite article, nor did it have a contrasting indefinite article. Speakers and writers in Old English (approximately 500 to 1100) deployed the demonstrative form *se*, from which *the* seems to have developed, for some of the functions undertaken by today's *the*. *Se* is the nominative masculine form of the demonstrative and may not ring any present-day demonstrative bells, but the nominative and accusative neuter form is *þæt* (the first letter of this word represents the sound later represented by <th>) from which, as is plain to see, is derived the present-day demonstrative *that* (e.g. *pass me that sandwich, please*). Let us look at an example (demonstratives are underlined):

[2.4]   Hēr Ōswald, <u>se</u> ēadiga arcebiscop, forlēt <u>þis</u> life
         ond gefērde <u>þæt</u> heofonlīce; ond Æðelwine ealdorman
         gefōr on <u>þām</u> ilcan gēare. (The year 992, Anglo-Saxon Chronicle,
         Laud MS)[1]

         [Here Oswald, <u>the/that</u> blessed archbishop, gave up <u>this</u> life
         and reached <u>that</u> heavenly (life); and alderman (=elderman/
         nobleman) Æthelwine departed (this life) in the/<u>that</u> same year]

As one can see from the present-day translation, there are two points where the Old English demonstrative can be rendered by either present-day *the* or *that*. Both signal definiteness, that is, they invite participants to identify a particular entity (i.e. a particular archbishop; a particular year). Today, the difference between *the* and *that* in these contexts is that *that*, unlike *the*, is used to focus the target's attention on something. But in Old English this use is not so clear. Incidentally, the other instance of *that* in "that heavenly (life)" is not the same. In this case, it involves a deictic contrast with the previous demonstrative, *this*, such that the referent moved from the relatively close state of "this life" to the relatively faraway state of "that heavenly life". We will discuss deictic matters more fully in section 2.3, but the point to note here is that the Old English demonstrative *se*, along with its various forms, was deployed in a range of functions, including those for which we would regularly use the word *the* today.

Over time, then, a demonstrative form has developed into the definite article the English language has today. Note, with particular reference to Table 2.1, it has moved from the relatively contextual, extralinguistic category of deictic expressions to the relatively abstract, linguistic category of definite expressions; in other words, from more pragmatic to less. English is not alone in the way its definite article developed. Definite articles in Romance languages (e.g. French, Italian, Spanish), such as *le, il, el, lo, la*, have developed from the Latin

---

[1] The Old English text is taken from Quirk et al. (1975: 12); the translation is ours.

demonstrative *ille/illa* (masculine/feminine), although there are complexities for specific dialects of these languages (cf. Klein-Andreu 1996).

Although the categories in Table 2.1 do not always represent continuous links in a chain, if a particular item develops functions outside its initial category, they are usually functions that belong to a less contextually-determined category – they rely less on a specific context for a particular meaning and instead have the "same" meaning for a range of contexts, that is they are more abstract (it is a matter of controversy as to whether this is true of all languages; see Frajzyngier 1996, for some counter evidence). Thus, not only are definite expressions often developed from deictic expressions, but anaphoric expressions are often developed from deictic expressions, and proper nouns sometimes develop into common nouns (hence, **eponymic** nouns, such as *wellingtons, cardigan, sandwich, sadism* and *atlas*). This movement is consistent with what has, in historical linguistics, been referred to as **grammaticalisation**:

> As a lexical construction enters and continues along a grammaticalization pathway, it undergoes successive changes in meaning, broadly interpretable as representing a unidirectional movement away from its original or concrete reference and toward increasingly general and abstract reference. (Pagliuca 1994: ix)

Pagliuca's statement makes the connection with a movement away from meanings anchored in a concrete context towards the abstract.

Reflection: Marking definiteness

Many European languages are like English in having a separate word (or words) marking definiteness. Other languages, such as the Scandinavian languages Danish, Norwegian, Swedish and Icelandic and the Semitic languages Hebrew, Arabic and Kurdish, use an affix rather than a separate word. Yet other languages, such as Latvian, Xhosa and Indonesian, regularly deploy a demonstrative (e.g. *this, that*) for this purpose. English can also use a demonstrative to signal definiteness (try substituting *this* or *that* for *the* in sentence [2.3(a)] above), but it is not regularly deployed just to mark definiteness in the way that *the* is. Still other languages, such as Chinese, Japanese and Russian (and many other Slavic languages), use none of these resources to mark definiteness. This is why, of course, a distinctive feature of English spoken by speakers of these languages is the lack of the definite article (consider this sentence written by a Japanese pragmatics student: *It is principle of conversation*). Indeed, some research on marking definiteness in English in interactions where all the participants are "non-native" speakers, has suggested that dropping the definite article in some instances where it would be required in "standard" forms of English, and inserting it where it would not normally be grammatically required, is a feature of English as a lingua franca (see, for instance, Seidlhofer 2001).

It is not the case that any one form, such as the examples of definite expressions in Table 2.1, will always have a referring function, which, incidentally, is partly why these are pragmatic, not semantic, issues. Consider this sentence:

[2.5]   Bus and train are much the same price at the moment though it's quicker to take the bus.

>   (*BNC*, popular lore, periodical *Outdoor Action*)

This is not likely to be referring to a particular bus but to any vehicle with the attributes of a bus. It is a non-referential, descriptive usage of a definite expression, as opposed to a referential usage (this distinction was labelled **attributive** versus **referential** by Donnellan 1966). Here, we are talking about buses as opposed to any other mode of transport: the definite expression invites the interpreter to work out the more general category (transport) of which this is a specific sub-category (buses). So, in this case, the definite expression is not used to signal an act of identification but a distinction between the specific and the general. Additionally, we might note here that *in*definite expressions can also refer. Consider this sentence:

[2.6]   Suddenly, a small single-decker bus appeared at a corner not far away.

>   (*BNC* ADM 884, non-academic social science,
>   the book *Jaunting through Ireland*)

Clearly, we are referring to a particular, identifiable bus in a particular context, despite the fact that an indefinite article is used. Compare this with a non-referring usage of an indefinite expression, such as:

[2.7]   Too shy to board a bus: as a solitary student in London, he walked miles around the streets, sharpening his observation.

>   (*BNC* A8F 665, newspaper, *The Guardian*)

In section 2.5, we will examine the functions of referring expressions, including definite expressions, more closely.

We use **proper nouns** to invite hearers to identify the unique individual (or set of individuals) we are talking about. Proper nouns inherently identify a unique individual (or set of individuals); they have definiteness built in (and thus appear as a sub-category of definite expressions in Table 2.1). This fact may partly explain why, in English, one would not normally put a definite article before a proper noun: *the Jonathan* or *the Michael* sounds decidedly odd (except in limited contexts such as *that's not the Jonathan I was talking about*; see also the reflection box below). However, this is not a full explanation, because some other languages *do* allow a definite article before a proper noun. For example, in some dialects of Italian definite articles are systematically used before personal names (e.g. *la Maria*) and, in Italian generally, they are used before names of countries (e.g. *la Germania*).[2] This is not as bizarre as it may seem to the native English speaker. A century ago, Russell (1910–1911) argued that proper nouns are not just empty shells used to refer to a particular individual, but are associated with a descriptive content which determines what they refer to, somewhat like definite common noun phrases such as *the book*.

Reflection: Proper nouns and meaning

Whether one agrees that proper nouns work through associated descriptive content or not (and this is indeed controversial), there is no doubt that proper nouns are not the purest of referring expressions. They are not devoid of all abstract semantic meaning; they have rich connotations, with the line between connotative and denotative sense being fuzzy. Kasof (1993: 140), having reviewed a vast quantity of research (most of it North American) and conducted studies of his own, concludes that both first names and surnames "differ in attractiveness and connote impressions of the name bearer's age, intellectual competence, race, ethnicity, social class, and other attributes". It is not difficult to understand how these different associations have developed: at different times different names have been fashionable, and different social groups have preferred particular names. For example, the names *Kevin* and *Tracey*, though popular in the mid-eighties, have experienced rapid decline (see figures in Dunkling 1995), presumably because they became strongly associated with the young, moneyed, working class people of late Thatcherite Britain.

While some scholars (e.g. Kripke 1972) may argue, with some reason, against the descriptive content view, saying that proper nouns directly refer without any mediating semantic content, proper nouns clearly do have connotations that assist not only in the assignment of reference in context but also in the overall interpretation. For example, a tutor, writing to summon an elusive student, may sign the communication *Jonathan Culpeper* as opposed to *Jonathan*, in order to crank up the level of formality and thus strengthen the request/order.

The general and important point here, that each proper noun has its own semantic colouring which feeds into interpretive processes in interaction, is true of all referring expressions. Also, it is important to note that no one proper noun form is necessarily performing a referring function all the time. For example, Mick may be thought of as a proper noun (a popular short form of Michael), but it is a common noun in this sentence: "When he first came in

---

[2] Actually, we have some north-west Italian dialects in mind, and those dialects, oddly enough, allow definite articles before female personal names but not male.

I offered him a drink out of courtesy and I think he thought I was taking the mick out of his drinking in the past" (*BNC* AT1 1224; part of a biography).[3] Indeed, proper nouns evolving into common nouns (so-called **eponyms**) is a regular method of word-formation.

2.3   Deixis

We now turn to **deixis**, the category at the bottom of Table 2.1; we will discuss anaphora in the section following this one. Deixis relies heavily, though not completely, on the extralinguistic context to supply the referent, and not semantic elements within the deictic expression itself. It may be helpful to note here that the word *deictic* is borrowed from the Greek δεικτικ-ός (deiktikos), meaning "able to show, showing directly". Deixis involves connections between a reference point and aspects of the situation in which the utterance takes place; deictic expressions invite participants to work out particular connections. When somebody telephones another and says *it's me*, they invite the interlocutor to work out, on the basis of oral characteristics, that *me* refers to the speaker. Occasionally, of course, the speaker's assumptions that the interlocutor can work out who is speaking turn out to be wrong, and the interlocutor has to ask explicitly who it is (something which is potentially embarrassing, because the speaker assumed that you were sufficiently familiar with them to identify them). Consider another example, this time provided by Charles Fillmore (1997: 60):

[2.8]   The worst possible case I can imagine for a totally unanchored occasion sentence is that of finding afloat in the ocean a bottle containing a note which reads, "Meet me here at noon tomorrow with a stick about this big."

Who is *me*? Where is *here*? When is *tomorrow*? And how big is *this*? Examples such as this neatly illustrate how one's understanding depends on making connections between a reference point – that is, a **deictic centre** or anchorage point – from which the speaker positions their discourse and a particular context. If we cannot make these connections, we end up with very limited understanding.

The deictic centre is generally the I-here-now of the speaker, or, more accurately, of the speaking voice in the particular situation. The speaking voice could be that of, for example, an individual, a group of people, or a character in a book. Deictic expressions signal a perspective relative to a particular deictic centre (e.g.

---

[3]   "To take the mick(ey)" is a colloquial, idiomatic expression in British English meaning to make fun of somebody.

your "you" is my "I"; your "here" is my "there" etc.). In conversation, the deictic centre obviously flips back and forth according to who is speaking. The deictic centre can also be projected. If somebody rings you up and invites you over for some coffee, you may reply: *I'll come over in a few minutes. Come* is a deictic verb, as it suggests the movement of something in the context towards the deictic centre. In this case, the deictic centre is not that of the speaker but that of the addressee. This is a case of **deictic projection**: the speaker projects the deictic centre onto the addressee and speaks from the point of view of the addressee.

A key point about deictic expressions is that they interface with grammatical systems. This feature is brought out in Levinson's (1983: 54) definition of deixis:

> Deixis concerns the ways in which languages encode or grammatical-
> ise features of the context of utterance or speech event, and thus also
> concerns ways in which the interpretation of utterances depends on the
> analysis of that context of utterance.

Expressions such as *I*, *me* and *my* are most clearly part of grammatical systems (we shall see in a moment how the context of utterance has not always been grammaticalised in the same way in earlier periods of English). Table 2.2 displays the types of deixis traditionally identified and their associated expressions.

Of course, deictic expressions can be used non-deictically. Consider the underlined items in these sentences:

[2.9]   Read the small print; <u>you</u> never know what <u>you</u> may find.

> (*BNC* CTX 1117, popular lore,
> the magazine *What Personal Computer*)

Now <u>there</u> is another way of advertising and with Harrogate not coming off, I must say I'm quite keen on this.

> (*BNC* J9P 250, public speech,
> charity committee meeting)

Expressions such as <u>*I*</u>, <u>*me*</u> and <u>*my*</u> are most clearly part of grammati-cal systems

> (sentence used a few lines above)

Here, *you* is a generic usage, not referring to anyone in particular (it is similar to "one never knows"); *there* does not pick out a particular location, but is a case of "existential *there*", that is to say, a kind of dummy subject which occurs in clauses about the existence or occurrence of something; finally, *I*, *me* and *my* do not refer to the speaker, as they are (metalinguistic) mentions of the pronoun rather than uses of them. As Fillmore (1997) points out, even demonstratives, a category that seems to be the purest category of deictic items, in fact have both deictic and non-deictic usages. **Gestural** usages, such as *this foot*, are supported

Table 2.2 Deixis types and English expressions

Deixis type		Examples of English deictic expressions
Personal	(a) Participants	I, you, we, etc.
	(b) Social relationships	Geoff, Mr Leech, Professor Leech, Sir, Madam, your grace, etc.
Spatial		this, that, here, there, come, go, opposite, away, etc.
Temporal		now, then, today, next week, [tense], recently, soon, etc.
Discourse		that chapter, this means that…, in the next chapter, etc.

by a gesture like pointing; they are deictic. **Symbolic** usages, in contrast, rely on general spatio-temporal knowledge; they could be accompanied by a gesture, but would still be understood without. For example, in this newspaper head-line *Technology: Let's make this country the best* (*The Guardian*, 1/9/13), it will be obvious to most UK-based Guardian readers that *this country* refers to the UK, without gestures. The converse is also true: typically non-deictic expressions can be used deictically. For example, *he* or *she* would not normally be discussed as deictic expressions, as they are typically anaphoric, referring back to some-thing mentioned previously in the discourse rather than connecting with the extralinguistic context (we will discuss anaphora in the following section). But it is not too difficult to imagine a context in which they clearly have a deictic referring function. Consider a (reconstructed) conversation during which a parent brings a crying baby into the room and an interlocutor says:

[2.10]   So, he's the one making all the noise!

We should also keep in mind the fact that items within categories, such as those of Table 2.1, vary with respect to the degree to which they are semanti-cally descriptive and contextually pragmatic. For example, *here* indicates the speaker's spatial deictic centre, but *come* also encodes the meaning of locomo-tion towards it.

Let us elaborate on the particular categories of Table 2.2. **Personal**, as a deictic category, refers to the identification of three discourse roles in the speaking situation: the speaker (the first person), the hearer (the second person), and the party being talked about (the third person). Person is a hugely important grammatical category. First, second and/or third person is marked or implicit in all utterances. An indication of its importance in English is in the fact that the second most frequent word in spoken English is *I* and the third is *you* (Leech et al. 2001: 144) (as we noted earlier, the most frequent is *the*). **Personal deixis** invites participants to identify the relevant discourse role(s) in the context. Person markers are not devoid of encoded meaning. In fact, they rarely encode person alone, but also have other grammatical distinctions. In English, these are number (e.g. *I* vs. *we*), gender (e.g. *he* vs. *she*) and case (e.g. *she* vs. *her*). Note here that *deictic* person markers are typically the first and second persons, not the third. Third person forms are generally anaphoric, that is, not extralinguistic but referring back to the linguistic co-text of the utterance, though, as illustrated in the previous paragraph, third person forms can be used deictically.

Reflection: Person markers in the history of English

English used to have a somewhat different system of grammaticalised expressions available for deictic purposes. Regarding personal pronouns, one notable difference concerned number. While today we can use most personal pronouns to distinguish number, insofar as the referent is singular or plural (e.g. *I* vs. *we*), in Old English there were also the remnants of the "dual" forms of the first and second person pronouns. Thus, *wit* meant we-both, and *yit* meant you-both (this, of course, would also have implications for what at that time counted as plural in this grammatical system – it would have been more than two, whereas today it is more than one).

However, the area of radical change concerns the second person pronouns. Elizabethan English, for example, offered a choice between two sets of pronominal forms for the second person: the forms *ye, you, your, yours* and *yourself* (the you-forms), and the forms *thou, thee, thy, thine* and *thyself* (the thou-forms). In Old English, *you* generally used the first set for a plural referent and the second for a singular. But by Middle English the variant chosen could have significant social implications. These items had taken on a stronger social deictic role, rather than just personal. The usage of these sets is a matter of great controversy. Brown and Gilman (1960) predicted that high status social equals used you-forms to each other, low status social equals used thou-forms to each other, high status individuals used thou-forms to lower status, and low status individuals used you-forms to higher status. These predictions fit the usage of Middle English reasonably well. One can see a certain similarity in the way you-forms and thou-forms were used in this period of English with the way, for example, *tu* and *vous* are used in today's French or *du* and *Sie* in German. However, these predictions become more and more unreliable as we move towards the 17th century. The meanings of any particular usage had increasingly to be inferred from the specifics of context. Take this brief extract from the *Merrie Tales of Skelton* (1567) as an example. In this tale Skelton, a parson, tries to persuade a cobbler to go to war.

[2.11] Neybour, you be a tall
man, and in the Kynges warres
you must bere a standard.

Generally, in this tale Skelton uses *thou* to the cobbler. This fits the theory, which predicts a high status participant using *thou* to a lower status participant. But here, despite the difference in social status, Skelton uses *you* to the cobbler. Why he does so is a pragmatic issue, not simply a matter of correlating usage and status. Here, Skelton is trying to be persuasive; using *you* lends a note of respect.

Ultimately, the thou-forms have become obsolete, except in some areas of Yorkshire and Lancashire (and some religious contexts). The fact that English second person pronouns have now been reduced to a single set of forms based on *you*, without any encoded meanings regarding number or social position, marks English out as distinct from many languages, especially European. By way of a postscript, it is worth noting that some dialects of English have relatively recently developed the plural form *yous*, Liverpool English is a case in point, and this expression has been identified as characteristic of at least some Australian and Irish speakers of English (Horvath 1985). In some dialects of American English, particularly in the South and Texan regions of the US, other second person plural forms, such as *y'll* ("you all") and *yinz* ("you ones"), can be found.

In Table 2.2, we have split personal deixis into two sub-categories, one pertaining to participant marking and the other pertaining to social relationship marking. The latter sub-category is often referred to as **social deixis**. There is absolutely no hard and fast distinction between these two sub-categories (see Marmaridou 2000: 79). The history of you-forms and thou-forms in English is a case in point. Today, English relies largely on **vocatives**, expressions usually used to address people, to mark social relationships, especially in the form of noun phrases (usually comprised of proper nouns and/or titles). Note, of course, the overlap here with the discussion of proper nouns in section 2.3. However, remember that we are focusing on deictic *uses* of proper nouns (compare the deictic *Geoff, come here* with the non-deictic *Geoff came here*). A summary of social deictic expressions in present-day British English with very brief indications regarding context of usage and the proportion of uses accounted for by each type (expressed as a percentage) is as follows (from Leech 1999: 109–113 and Biber et al. 1999: 1111–1113):

Endearments (e.g. (my) darling, love, sweetie). Typical address between close female family members, sexual partners and "favourite" people (5%).

Family (kinship) terms (e.g. mum(my), dad(dy), ma, pa, grandma, granny, grandpa, granddad). Typical address to family members of an older generation (10%).

Familiarisers (e.g. guys, mate, folks, bro). Typical address between males signalling solidarity (15%).

First names (a) Typical address between friends and family members, as well as other (even casual) acquaintances (35%). (b) A sub-group of first names is familiarised first names, shortened first names and/or with the pet suffix -y/-ie (e.g. Marj, Tom, Jackie) (30%).

Title and surname (e.g. Mrs Johns, Mr Graham, Ms. Morrisey). Typical means of marking a more distant and respectful relationship (below 2.5%).

Honorifics (e.g. sir, madam, ma'am). Relatively rare in English, they may occur in situations such as formal service encounters, where there is a markedly asymmetrical relationship between speakers (below 2.5%).

Other See below (below 5%).

Although relatively rare, there is a wide range of "Other" forms, limited only by one's creativity. Biber et al. (1999: 1109–1110) provide some illustrations (from the Longman Corpus of English):

[2.12]   Hello <u>lazy</u>!
Oh, make your bloody mind up <u>boy</u>!
Come on <u>you reds</u>, come on <u>you reds</u>, come on <u>you reds.</u>
<u>Those of you who want to bring your pets along</u>, please sit in the back of the space ship.

As might have been observed from the above summary, social deictic expressions mark not only social relationships but also, amongst other factors, settings and in particular their degree of formality. A good example of social deixis restricted to a particular setting is the use of surnames only in more traditional schools – notably, British public schools – not just by teachers to pupils but also, to an extent, between pupils themselves.

Reflection: Social deixis across languages

Person marking varies hugely from language to language. Consider, for example, that Fijian is said to have 135 person forms, whereas Madurese, an Austronesian language, has only two (Siewierska 2004: 2). One of the reasons for this is that person marking interacts with the socio-cultural contexts of the particular language. As Mühlhäusler and Harré (1990: 207, quoted in Siewierska 2004: 214) comment, "pronominal grammar provides a window to the relationship between themselves and the outside world". Obviously, this fact is most salient with respect to social deixis. Non-singular second person marking when addressing a single person is often a way of signalling social distance, deference (particularly in the context of an age differential) or formality, as was the case, at least to some extent, with the you-forms in earlier periods of English, and is still the case in many European languages (e.g. French, German, Spanish, Greek, Danish, Swedish, Russian, Czech). Non-singular person marking is also used for single referents in many other languages, but not necessarily for the same social reasons. Some languages achieve such social functions with the use of the third person. For example, in Italian one uses the third person feminine singular *lei*, and in German the third person plural *Sie*. Such person marking phenomena are part of **linguistic honorifics**, conventional systems of forms that "honour" (i.e. express deference to) a participant (usually but not necessarily the addressee) in some way. Such forms include not only person markings, but also forms of address, various affixes, clitics and particles, and choice of vocabulary. Present-day English does not have a rich honorific system, being now largely confined to forms of address, as noted above. Other languages, particularly those of East and South-East Asia (e.g. Thai, Japanese, Nepali, Korean) have remarkably rich systems. In Thai, there are said to be 27 forms used for the first person, 22 for the second and eight for the third. These are used according to, amongst other things, social status, intimacy, age, sex and kinship, and to reflect deference or assertiveness (see Cooke 1968, quoted in Siewierska 2004: 228).

Person markers, as we have seen for all referring expressions in this chapter, are not always used in such a way that their encoded meaning matches their usage. Mismatches are often deployed for the purpose of generating local social meanings. Consider, for example, the range of possible referents for the English form *we* (based on the list given in Siewierska 2004: 215):

[2.13]   (a) We (= I) are not interested in the possibility of defeat. [Queen Victoria on the Boer War, 1899]

(b) We (=not I but you) want to eat our (=your) din dins now. [Carer talking to patient]

(c) We (=she or he) had wet panties again in playgroup. [Mother talking about her child]

(d) We (=I individually, and I individually, etc.) solemnly swear ...

(e) Shall we (=I or you) book for just the two of us (=me and you) then?

(f) We (=I and he) will join you the moment John arrives.

(g) We (=I and they) are underpaid and overworked.

(h) We (=you, you, and you, etc. addressees) will hear in this presentation ...

Some of these mismatches have become well established. (a) is of course the **royal-we** (pragmatically "I"), a more recent example of which are the words of Margaret Thatcher upon discovering that she had become a grandmother in 1989: *we have become a grandmother.* The royal-we might be said to be a case of self-deference: the speaker is the honorific focus. (b) is a typical usage of the **exclusive-we** (pragmatically not "I"), where the avoidance of the pronoun *you* in requests or commands lends a veneer of politeness (see Wales 1996, for a full discussion of *we* and other English pronouns).

As can be seen from Table 2.2, a category of deictic expressions can express spatial relations. As far as English is concerned, **spatial deixis** typically expresses a relationship relating to distance between the deictic centre of the speaker and a referent. English has a **proximal/distal** (as in near/far) contrast, as might be illustrated by items such as *here/there* and *this/that*. However, usage of these items, particularly the final set of demonstratives, is not always restricted to physical spatial relations. In the extract from Shakespeare below, John of Gaunt laments the fact that England is not what it was; England has been sold out by Richard II, the current king, in pursuit of his own glory. The contrast is between proximal *this England*, near in time, and distal *that England*, further away in time.

> [2.14]   This royall Throne of Kings, this sceptred Isle
> This earth of Maiesty, this seate of Mars,
> This other Eden, demy paradise,
> This Fortresse built by Nature for her selfe,
> Against infection, and the hand of warre:
> This happy breed of men, this little world,
> This precious stone, set in the siluer sea,
> Which serues it in the office of a wall,
> Or as a Moate defensiue to a house,
> Against the enuy of lesse happier Lands,
> This blessed plot, this earth, this Realme, <u>this England</u>,
> [...]
>
> Is now Leas'd out (I dye pronouncing it)
> Like to a Tenement or pelting Farme.
> England bound in with the triumphant sea,
> Whose rocky shore beates backe the enuious siedge
> Of watery Neptune, is now bound in with shame,
> With Inky blottes, and rotten Parchment bonds.
> <u>That England</u>, that was wont to conquer others,
> Hath made a shamefull conquest of it selfe.
>
> (*Richard II*, Act II, Scene I; First Folio 1623)

We might also briefly note that sometimes the issue is one of focusing the target's attention. Thus, while *here* in *Here she is!* might well convey the fact that somebody has arrived in the vicinity, it also draws attention to that fact; and *that* in *I'd like that one* (said of several items all the same distance from the speaker) focuses the target's attention on one particular item.

Reflection: Spatial deixis and comparisons with today's English

Today, English deictic spatial expressions are part of a two-term system. However, English used to have a three-term system. In addition to the adverbs *here* and *there*, English had the expression *yonder*, and, in addition to the demonstratives *this* and *that*, it had the expression *yon*. For example, Geoffrey Chaucer writes around 1386 *Whos is that faire child that stondeth yonder?* (*Man of Law's Tale*). These items were used for entities at some distance from the deictic centre but still within sight; they are a kind of medial stage between proximal and distal. Modern Spanish is an example of a language with a three-term system (*este, ese* and *aquel*) based on similar lines.

Other languages differ from English with respect to the number of terms used and the kind of relationship captured. Modern German is a case in point. While modern spoken German has an adverb contrast with *hier* ("here") and *dort* ("there"), it does not have a demonstrative contrast of the type achieved in English by *this* and *that*. Demonstratives occurring with nouns are comprised of *dieser* and stressed *der, die, das*. The unstressed latter items are usually considered definite articles. However, as Diessel (2008) points out, what makes all these items demonstrative-like rather than definite article-like is their pragmatic function: "like distance-marked demonstratives, these expressions are commonly used to focus the hearer's attention on entities in the surrounding situation, which is not what speakers usually do with definite markers". Readers will note some similarity here with Old English, as discussed above. Some languages mark even more degrees of distance. Malagasy apparently uses seven demonstrative adverbs and six demonstrative pronouns to mark increasing degrees of distance from the speaker (Anderson and Keenan 1985: 292–294).

English has a spatial deictic system based on degrees of distance between the speaker as deictic centre and the referent. Some languages have a different kind of relationship as their basis, one that is less egocentric and not based on degrees of distance. Japanese is an example of the language that factors in nearness (or not) of the referent to the speaker, the hearer and the speaker and hearer. Thus, it has *kono* (near the speaker), *sono* (near the hearer) and *ano* (away from the speaker and hearer) (Kuno 1973: 27, cited in Diessel 2008). If one remembers the notion of deictic projection, as introduced above, one can see how this might work: for example, with *sono* the speaker projects the deictic centre onto the hearer. Such deictic systems have been described as person-based systems as opposed to distance-based systems (Anderson and Keenan 1985). Finally, we briefly note here that some Austronesian languages do not take any speech participants as deictic centres but orientate towards absolute geographical location points, such as seaward versus landward, or even simply co-ordinates like north, south, east and west.

The final category in Table 2.2, **temporal deixis**, concerns expressions which can convey relations over time. As far as English is concerned, they typically express a relationship between a deictic centre and the time of the speaker's utterance. *Now* refers to a span of time encompassing the speaker's utterance; the use of the present tense as opposed to the past can mark the speaker's current time of speaking (and auxiliary verbs such as *will*, *shall*, *going to*, etc. can mark some point in the future); *tomorrow*, *next week*, *yesterday*, *ago*, etc. indicate a span of time in relation to the speaker's current utterance.

Deictic expressions, as we have seen, are usually taken as referring to entities in the extralinguistic world. Some scholars have also distinguished **discourse** or **textual deixis**, which involves making a connection with a segment of discourse. Consider these (reconstructed) words said by a tutor at the end of a lecture in the UK:

[2.15] <u>That</u>'s the end. But don't rush off just yet. As I said at the beginning, I have some announcements. <u>Here</u> they are. [Then displays and reads announcements on a Powerpoint slide]

That points back to the preceding discourse (i.e. the lecture); *here* points to upcoming discourse. Given that we are now dealing with textual links, this category of deixis is not so pure. It also overlaps with the notion of anaphora, which we will discuss in the following section, though it is in principle distinguishable on some counts, as we will note.

2.4 Anaphora

Anaphoric expressions refer to a previously expressed textual unit or meaning, the so-called antecedent. Anaphora, in the context of linguistics, is generally understood to refer to "a relation between two linguistic elements, wherein the interpretation of one (called an anaphor) is in some way determined by the interpretation of the other (called an **antecedent**)" (Huang 2000: 1). It may be helpful to know that the term **anaphora** is derived from the Greek word αναφορα, meaning "carrying back". Here is an example:

[2.16] A: Should Michael peel the potatoes on the board?
B: Yes, <u>he</u> can <u>do</u> <u>them</u> <u>there</u>.

The anaphoric expressions in B's utterance and their antecedents are as follows: *he* (*Michael*), *do* (*peel*), *them* (*the potatoes*) and *there* (*on the board*). The fact that both the anaphoric expressions and their antecedents refer to the same entities – they are **co-referential** – is a characteristic of many anaphora, but not of deixis. This is not to say that there is no overlap with deixis. Readers will have noted that the form *there* is also used as a deictic expression. Indeed, in B's utterance one could imagine a scenario in which *there* is used not only to refer back to *on the board* but to pick out deictically the particular board to be used (the speaker could simultaneously point). Expressions functioning anaphorically comprise most frequently third person pronouns (e.g. *he*) and repeated or synonymous noun phrases (e.g. B in the above example could have repeated "the potatoes"), but also, for example, other definite noun phrases (including pronouns, demonstratives such as *those*, proper nouns), pro-forms (e.g. *do*) and adverbs (e.g. *there*). To this list we might add the absence of an expression where it is expected, a "gap" in the syntax. A typical example is the absence of the second finite verb in co-ordinated structures, such as: *She took kindly to him, and he* [took kindly] *to her* (*BNC* G0M 1282, prose fiction, the novel *The Holy Thief*). Needless to say, the resources available for expressing anaphoric reference vary from language to language. For example, some languages (e.g. Salt-Yui, a Papuan language) lack third person pronouns, deploying full nominal expressions instead (Siewierska 2004: 6, who cites Irwin 1974).

As one might guess, even typical anaphoric expressions are not always anaphoric and do not always refer, at least not straightforwardly. Consider these examples, all of which concern the third person singular pronoun:

[2.17] (a) **It**'s not looking good. [Said looking at the dark clouds in the sky]
  (b) What time is **it**? [An off-the- cuff remark]
  (c) I think **it**'s wonderful, the strives are to be made in medicine ... [*BNC* FLG 101, TV discussion]
  (d) Kill **it**, cook **it**, eat **it** [The title of a BBC documentary on the sources of food]

It in (a) has no textual antecedent. It is not anaphoric but most obviously a deictic usage: it points to the particular state of the sky. Halliday and Hasan ([1976] 1997) label uses that rely on something outside the text for their interpretation **exophoric**, a category which contrasts with **endophoric**, which includes uses that rely on something inside the text. *It* in (b) is similar to (a),– it has no textual antecedent. However, although it also involves the extralinguistic context, and thus is exophoric, it is not picking out something specific in the situational context in which it is said, as would be the case with deixis. Instead, it is an empty or dummy subject referring to an aspect of the context of the utterance that can readily be inferred. Dummy subjects (or objects) such as this are often used to refer to very general contextual aspects of utterance, notably, relating to time, distance (e.g. *how far is it to Lancaster*) or weather (e.g. *it's nice and warm*) (Biber et al. 1999: 332). Halliday and Hasan (1997) label such uses **homophoric**. *It* in (c) is similar to an anaphoric usage, but in this case it is referring forward to the textual segment *the strives are to be made in medicine* (by the unusual noun "strives" the speaker presumably means the things that can be successfully striven for). Such uses are termed **cataphoric** (Halliday and Hasan 1997). Finally, the point of interest regarding (d) is that each instance of *it* is co-referential, that is, each refers to the same entity. Except that they do not quite. The animal that is killed is not identical to the animal that is cooked and is eventually eaten. But of course, the point of this title is to make it clear that we are anaesthetised to the realities of eating meat by the fact that we only encounter "it" as prepared food in supermarkets.

Reflection: Anaphoric and other referring expressions – their variation across English written registers

Biber et al. (1998: chapter 5) explore the usage of referring expressions, particularly anaphoric expressions, across different registers, using the corpus-based methodology (see also Biber et al. 1999: 237–240, for similar findings). More specifically, they examine referring expressions (noun phrases and pronouns) across two spoken registers, conversation and public speeches (though we will not report the results of public speeches here) from the London-Lund corpus, and two written registers, news reportage and academic prose, from the LOB corpus. They found an uneven distribution of referring expressions. News reportage had the largest number (63 per 200 words), then conversation (61) and finally academic prose (51). To understand these differences better Biber et al. then looked at the distribution according to type of referring expression, retrieving frequencies across the registers for exophoric pronouns, anaphoric pronouns and anaphoric nouns. They discovered that exophoric referring expressions made up over half of the referring expressions in conversation, whereas they were almost non-existent in the written registers, news and academic prose. Those written registers were dominated by anaphoric nouns. In other words, people, not surprisingly, regularly refer to aspects of their immediate extralinguistic context in conversation, whereas in the written registers they refer to aspects of the (previous) text.

They also looked at the average distance between the referring expression and the antecedent in the various registers (the distance was defined as the number of intervening noun phrases). Some large differences emerged. The averages are: conversation (4.5), academic prose (9.0) and news reportage (11.0). That referring expressions occur much closer to their antecedents in conversation can be partly explained by the fact that conversation is conducted online with all the mental processing pressures that implies – referring expressions with short distances to their antecedents are easier to understand. But this finding is also a consequence of the referring expression type. Exophoric referring expressions do not have intervening textual material: they refer directly to their referents.

2.5 Using and understanding referring expressions in interaction

2.5.1 Referring expressions and context

The following is the beginning of Ken Kesey's novel *One Flew over the Cuckoo's Nest* ([1962] 2003: 1):

[2.18] They're out there.

This is a creative way to begin a novel; it creates psychological prominence. We have the outline of a puzzle here, but not the pieces with which to complete it. We know that some group of people (*they*) are located in some space away from where the speaker/writer is (*out there*). The referring expressions begin to build the point of view of one particular character, the protagonist, who is incarcerated in a mental institution. It flags the kind of context that needs fleshing out. This helps achieve the dramatic purpose of the novelist.

Let us look at another literary example. This is the first stanza of W.H. Auden's poem *Funeral Blues* (*Stop all the Clocks*) ([1936]1976):

[2.19] Stop all the clocks, cut off the telephone,
        Prevent the dog from barking with a juicy bone,
        Silence the pianos and with muffled drum
        Bring out the coffin, let the mourners come.

As we pointed out in section 2.2, definite noun phrases presuppose the existence of their referents, and can be used to invite the participant(s) to identify a particular referent from a specific context which is *assumed to be shared*. Thus, the definite noun phrase in *The book you're reading is great* (example [2.3 (a)]) may be taken as identifying the book the speaker sees you reading, rather than, say, the one you read when you go to bed, because you both share (e.g. through physical co-presence, visual contact) that specific context. However, the definite noun phrases in the Auden poem are not like this. They presuppose the existence of *clocks, telephone, dog, pianos, coffin* and *mourners*, but in doing this they also construct the context in which the particular referents can be identified. They do not passively rely on a specific shared context for interpretation; rather, they construct a specific shared context in which they can be interpreted. These items construct a particular fictional world. More particularly, the items *coffin* and *mourners* in the final line trigger the contextual **frame** or **schema** of a funeral by virtue of the fact that they are stereotypical components of that contextual frame (see section 3.2.1, for a discussion of schemata and background knowledge in general). Thus, they suggest the frame in which they can be identified as particular components, as opposed to simply being identified as particular components within a given frame.

It is not surprising that literary-linguistic scholars have focused on how referring expressions in literature contribute to the creation of fictional worlds (e.g. Semino 1997). In fact, it is normal in all kinds of interaction for people to rely on information from context to interpret referring expressions and also to use referring expressions to help construct the contexts in which they are interpreted. It is a two-way street. Note that this is a radical departure from the traditional approach to referring expressions, which focuses on the context fleshing out the referring expression and not the referring expression signalling the context of which it is a part. An excellent example of the latter, cited by Epstein (1999: 58), appears in a newspaper. In this example, a sports commentary writer reflects on the city of Los Angeles's loss of two professional football teams who used to play there:

[2.20]   So we lost the Rams and the Raiders. Lost our innocence. But hold **the flowers**. Put away **the handkerchiefs**. Stop **the sobbing**. We still have the Rose Bowl, haven't we? (original emphasis)

Like the poem above (and probably partly inspired by it), the definite noun phrases *the flowers*, *the handkerchiefs* and *the sobbing* refer to stereotypical components of the frame of the funeral. The funeral frame itself is not mentioned prior to the usage of these definite noun phrases. As Epstein (1999: 58) comments, "the frame itself need not be directly evoked at all ... but can be activated simply by mentioning some of its salient elements".

In section 2.2, we wrote that "definite expressions are primarily used to invite the participant(s) to identify a particular referent from a specific context which is assumed to be shared by the interlocutors". The use of "primarily" was judicious because the uses of referring expressions discussed in this section – creating psychological prominence, expressing viewpoint or triggering frames – do not fit well the idea of identifying particular referents from items in a given category. Epstein (1999) suggests that thinking in terms of "accessibility" is preferable, and we will expand on this notion in the following section.

2.5.2   Referring expressions and accessibility

Prince (1981) and Ariel (1988, 1990) propose that different types of referring expressions are used by producers according to their assumptions about how accessible the referent is in the mind of the target. Ariel (1988) proposes an Accessibility Marking Scale, along which referring expressions are ranked according to degrees of accessibility. Thus, at one end producers use zeros (gaps), pronouns and demonstrative pronouns for highly accessible referents, while at the other end they use long definite expressions and full names to refer to less accessible referents. For example, in saying *have you got it with you?* the producer assumes that the referent of *it* is highly accessible to the target, one does not have to spell it out. In contrast, in saying *have you got your classic car with you?*, the producer assumes that the referent is less accessible to the target and so the fuller *your classic car* is required. The accessibility of referents is said to be determined by four factors: the saliency of the referent, the recency of a previous mention, the number of other referents competing for the role of antecedent, and the degree of cohesion between the units that the expression and its antecedent occur in.

Gundel et al.'s (1993) Givenness Hierarchy ranks referring expressions along a scale according to the assumed **cognitive status** of the associated referents for the target. Cognitive status refers to the assumed attention state of the referent (e.g. something in focus right now, something in memory but not currently active, something completely unknown). However, unlike the Accessibility Marking Scale, the thrust of the Givenness Hierarchy is that particular referring expressions provide information to the target addressee about where in memory (or not in memory at all) the representation of the referent is expected to be found. For example, using the pronoun *it* (indeed, any unstressed third person pronoun) to refer to a classic car signals to the target that they do not need to search widely for the referent classic car, but that it is in focus, as in currently activated in short-term memory and the centre of attention (e.g. it is the immediate topic of conversation). In contrast, *a classic car* signals merely that the target knows the category "classic car" described by the expression – they can identify the type. Somewhere in between would be, for example, the expression *that classic car*, which signals that the target is familiar with the referent: they not only know the category but are able to identify the specific intended referent because they have a representation of it in memory.

Each type of referring expression is conventionally associated with a particular cognitive status; any use of that expression signals a particular cognitive status which the target can then take account of in their search for an interpretation. The cognitive statuses discussed in the work of Gundel and colleagues are as follows:

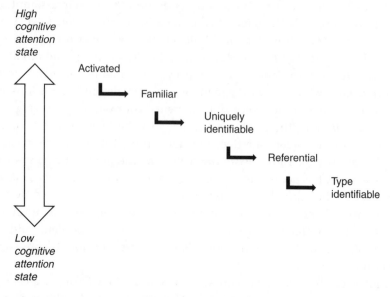

Figure 2.1   The cognitive statuses of referring expressions (solid black arrows can be taken to mean "and thus also", i.e. entailing)

A key point to note about these cognitive statuses is that they are not mutually exclusive. The statuses are related such that a particular cognitive status entails lower statuses. For example, an item that is in focus is necessarily activated, familiar, uniquely identifiable, and so on. The importance of this scale, Gundel and colleagues argue, is that it is a basis for implicational meanings, via Grice's (1975) Maxim of Quantity (to be discussed in Chapter 4), whereby using a form with a weaker status implicates that a stronger status does not obtain. Thus, saying *a classic car* implicates that the speaker believes that the addressee cannot uniquely identify the referent; whereas saying *that classic car* implicates, for instance, that the speaker believes that the referent is not in focus (i.e. activated in short-term memory and the centre of current attention).

Let us briefly illustrate some of these issues with the following joke:

[2.21]   Voice on the phone: Hello? Is that the maternity hospital?
    Receptionist: Yes.
    Voice on the phone: Can you send an ambulance round, the wife
              is about to have a baby.
    Receptionist: Is this her first baby?
    Voice on the phone: No. This is her husband.

At the heart of the joke are the differing understandings arising from the demonstrative *this* in the second utterance of the receptionist. Most likely for the receptionist (and indeed the reader) the referent of *this* has activated status, as the baby was mentioned in the immediately previous sentence, though it was not the topic (hence it was not in focus). In the receptionist's second utterance, *her first baby* is the topic, and thus it is brought into focus. According to the Givenness Hierarchy, we might have expected a husband to reply "no, it's not her first baby" or "yes, it's her first baby". However, the husband constructs a radically different understanding, namely, that *this* refers to the identity behind his voice. To sustain this, we must assume that he thinks that the receptionist thinks that *this* refers to the voice on the phone and that the voice is that of *her first baby* (i.e. in some bizarre world, the first baby is telephoning to ask for an ambulance!). In this scenario, *this* merely has the status of being referential, that is, referring to a particular voice, but not one that is even uniquely identifiable. This, of course, is completely improbable, because their respective identities have in fact been established (the social deixis of *the wife* implies that he is the husband): they at least have the cognitive status of activated.

The Givenness Hierarchy usefully throws light on how the choice of referring expression works. It is not, however, a complete account of referring expressions. It is based on the notion of **givenness**, understood as assumptions about accessibility for the target (we elaborate more on givenness in the following chapter). However, in section 2.5.1, we saw pronouns used in contexts where the referents' accessibility was not the only issue: it was not simply a matter of where to access something in one's mind. Epstein (1999), whose work is focused on the definite article *the*, was very aware of this, and hence defined accessibility simply as being "available for interpretation" (1999: 67). He concludes from his analyses of real data that "the article seems to be an instruction which prompts the addressee into making the appropriate conceptual constructions for interpreting the nominal in discourse" (ibid.). In other words, such prompts go beyond helping identify where in the mind to access a referent. A prompt can introduce new referents, and do so in such a way that facilitates interpretation of the discourse by, for example, creating psychological prominence, expressing a viewpoint or triggering frames.

2.5.3   Referring expressions and common ground

Again, recollect our statement that "definite expressions are primarily used to invite the participant(s) to identify a particular referent from a specific context which is assumed to be shared by the interlocutors". The idea of "assumed to be shared" is crucial in pragmatics. Note, for example, that the baby joke [2.21], is difficult to explain without reference to the notion of **common ground** (also broadly referred to as, for example, "mutual" or "shared" "knowledge", "assumptions" or "beliefs"). Specifically in the joke, the idea of making assumptions about people's assumptions arose ("we must assume that he thinks that the receptionist thinks that *this* refers to the voice on the phone and that the voice is that of *her first baby*").

Herbert Clark and his colleagues (see Clark 1996; Clark and Marshall 1981) have made important contributions to the understanding of common ground. To illustrate the issues, consider that the first author of this book is a closet petrolhead. Most of his colleagues in the world of academia would not know a connecting rod from a crankshaft. Consequently, if a conversation shifts to cars, he makes the assumption that they do not both have this background knowledge. Conversely, it is more than likely – given that his interests are hidden – that they make the assumption that he also lacks knowledge in this area. And conversations are tailored accordingly (e.g. cars are distinguished according to colour and fuel consumption rather than whether their engines incorporate pushrods or overhead camshafts). Note what is happening here: assumptions are being made on both sides about what knowledge is common to both parties, that is, about common ground. Importantly, one makes assumptions about what assumptions are being made about what knowledge is in common: he assumes that his colleagues assume that they both know very little about cars. This is important because deciding what to say will, in part, depend on your assumptions about what you think the other(s) think you both know. One could make further assumptions about those assumptions about the knowledge you have in common:

> He assumes that
> his colleagues assume that
> he assumes that
> they both know very little about cars.

And further levels could be added. Of course, this **infinite recursion** of assumptions is not the stuff of psychological reality – people would become mentally exhausted. Psycholinguistic research is not very precise about how many levels of assumptions are deployed in communication, some suggests we do not go beyond three, others suggesting at most six (see the research cited in Clark 1996: 100 and Lee 2001: 30). There is, in fact, another way of affording insights into this phenomenon, and that is by inspecting interactions themselves. People can check that assumptions about common ground are correct or repair understandings that appear to be based on erroneous assumptions about common ground (see the following section and also section 3.4.2, for further discussion and illustration). Recursion or reflexivity in pragmatics is a topic to which we will return in section 8.2.

Common ground can be seen as a subset of background knowledge, the subset that is relevant to communication because it is believed to be in common amongst the participants involved. Note here that we are more accurately talking about background assumptions and beliefs which are held with varying degrees of certainty rather than "knowledge".[4] On what basis might we suppose something to be common ground? One such basis concerns socio-cultural knowledge. We assume common information about: the practices and conventions of our cultures and communities (consider the shared information in academia); physical and natural laws; and experiences involving others. Another basis concerns personal experiences with other people. We assume common information about: whether others are co-present at an event or not; the kind of relations amongst us (friend/strangers, more powerful/less powerful); particular events; and particular discourses (see Clark 1996: 100–116, for an extensive elaboration of these bases). The fact that common ground involves, amongst other things, shared knowledge of particular discourses is important in a number of respects. Everything that is said in a discourse potentially constitutes part of the common ground for those participants party to the discourse, along with the other happenings that accompany that conversation (like the actions of participants, visual appearances, sounds). Discourse, of course, is dynamic, and, if it is, amongst other experiences, feeding common ground, then common ground is dynamic too – another issue to which we will return in the following section, as well as in section 3.4.2.

People tailor their referring expressions according to assumptions about common ground (cf. Clark and Wilkes-Gibbs 1986; Wilkes-Gibbs and Clark 1992). A definite noun phrase, a deictic expression or an anaphoric expression invites an interlocutor to interpret something in a particular way, often to pick out a particular referent in common ground. Whether or not your interlocutor will be able to do this is a calculated gamble based primarily on one's understanding of the common ground that pertains. If you say *can you repeat that please*, you assume that your interlocutor will understand what your deictic *that* is referring to (e.g. the specific portion of discourse that you have both shared), or if you say *can you pass me that*, you assume that your interlocutor can understand that your deictic *that* is referring to the pepper mill she has just been using in front of you.

---

[4] It goes without saying that one can never "know" anything for sure (knowledge is simply what is assumed until it is disproved) and that one can never truly share knowledge (we cannot copy the contents of our heads). Sperber and Wilson (1995) make much of this, saying that we should really be talking about knowledge as what can be potentially known, and about shared knowledge as what can be potentially shared about what is potentially known (see also Lee 2001).

Reflection: Recognitional deixis or thingamy

A specific phenomenon that it is strongly dependent on common ground concerns nominal expressions such as *thingamy, thingamajig, thingamabob, whojar, whatsit, what's-his-name, what-d'you-call-it,* and *you-know-what.* Such expressions, unlike the definite noun phrases discussed earlier, provide little descriptive information to help one work out what is being talked about. Yet, in the shared context of a dinner, an expression such as *thingamy* is likely to be taken as a reference to the pepper mill on the table, and was equally likely to have been used in the expectation that this reference would be assigned. Recognitional deixis is a label coined by Enfield (2003) for such items. It acknowledges that they behave like deictic expressions picking out items relative to the speaker's here and now, but also that they rely heavily on common ground to be successfully "recognised".

Why might we use such words? Consider these examples of recent usage of *thingamy* taken from the Oxford English Corpus:

[2.22]   **Society** Anyway back to the point – Mandela has little to do with this US vs. Iraq *thingamy* and it means that he can speak out in a way that many others can't but he's terribly involved in the whole Zimbabwe *thingamy* and it means that he can't speak about that.

Weblog I partook of the lambshank and Ma had the beef *thingamy.*

Weblog This is because some sort of technical *thingamy* happened with our hosting *thingamy.*

Although you do not have access to the full context, it is quite easy to see that they are often used in contexts where specialised lexis would be required (e.g. technical items or specialised cuisine), or where there may be difficulty in identifying an appropriate word (e.g. dealing with the sensitivities of a diplomatic wrangle), or where there are restrictions on the obvious term (e.g. labelling a cleaning product without actually using the trademark name). In context, it is highly likely that these will present few difficulties, because the participants have a common ground. Additionally, it is not the case that such expressions present participants with no descriptive information at all; in fact, they offer constraints on interpretations. This point is spelt out by Enfield (2003). He suggests, for example, that the speaker's message in using *what's-his-name* could be defined as: someone (male); I can't say this person's name now; by saying *what's-his-name* I think you'll know who I'm thinking of (2003:105). This contrasts with, for example, *you-know-what,* which "may have both 'avoidance' and 'conspiratorial' functions, whereby a speaker deliberately avoids saying a certain word, either to prevent potentially overhearing third parties from understanding, and/or to create exclusive air between interlocutors" (2003:106).

2.5.4   Referring expressions in interaction

Thus far in section 2.5 we have raised a number of issues that are key to interaction, including the idea that (1) referring expressions are not simply enriched by context but can also help construct it; (2) the choice of referring expression is influenced by the speaker's assumptions about the degree to which the referent is in the target's mind (i.e. its cognitive status) (see also Isaacs and Clark 1987, for experimental evidence); and (3) the choice of referring expression is influenced by assumptions about the common ground that pertains between specific interlocutors (see also Brennan and Clark 1996, for experimental evidence). All these go beyond our initial idea of inviting a participant to pick some particular referent out of a specific context. This section briefly explores two further notions at the heart of interaction. One is that the process of choosing and enriching referring expressions is dynamic (it is worked out in the course of interaction), and the other is that that process is emergent (it is not predetermined by certain combinations of referring expression and context).

As we noted in the previous section, shared discourse plays a role in feeding common ground. Here we see the participants using discourse to establish common ground. Example [2.23] illustrates how what is being referred to, the referent, emerges in the interaction, and how the two interlocutors collaborate in working it out.

[2.23] **Ivy**   I am told that she's going to live next door to the, where she used to live
the doctor's house er er <-|-> unless <-|->
PS22J <-|-> <unclear> <-|->
Ivy   that's pulled down, you know almost opposite the United Reform Church.
PS22J Which house is that?
Ivy   Well there you, I don't know what it's like now but they u--
PS22J It's not quite opposite, is it?
Ivy   Er
PS22J It's more or less opposite where your father's shoe shop was.
Ivy   Oh, is it? Oh
PS22J You mean the big red brick one next door to the doctor's surgery?
Ivy   Er i-- er, yes <unclear> the doctor <unclear> just there.
PS22J Yeah that's it I <unclear> <-|-> how <-|->
(*BNC* HDK 356–367, dialogue between two women, leisure context)

Clearly, Ivy wants to specify where the referent of *she* is going to live, but is having difficulty. Note the incomplete definite noun phrase "next door to the". Together they work it out through spatial deixis (*next door* twice, *opposite* three times), mapping out the location through questions and answers. The eureka moment comes with PS22J's hugely descriptive definite noun phrase *the big red brick one next door to the doctor's surgery*, assisting Ivy in identifying the location. And when Ivy confirms the referent of this noun phrase, PS22J switches to anaphoric *it*.

A key scholar to have explored conversational interaction and referring expressions, specifically anaphora, is Barbara Fox (1987, 1996). Fox (1987: 16) argues that there is a continuous interaction amongst the following three steps of reasoning:

1. Anaphoric form X is the "unmarked" form for a context like the one the participant is in now.
2. By using anaphoric form X, then, the participant displays a belief that the context is of a particular sort.
3. If the participant displays the belief that the context is of a particular sort, then the other parties may change their beliefs about the nature of the context to be in accord with the belief displayed.

Just as we have been discussing above, for Fox (1987: 17) "anaphoric choice at once is determined by and itself determines the structure of the talk". Also note that "change" is built in, as beliefs about context change then what counts as unmarked changes for the selection of the next form. What this means, then, is that the usage of referring expressions and what counts as their referents in context is not only a two-way street but a street whose direction is constantly shifting as it is mapped out by its traffic, or, to put it another way, the meanings of referring expressions emerge in a dynamic fashion as the interaction progresses.

Fox (1987: 18–19) suggests that the basic pattern in non-story conversation is that first mentions of a referent in a sequence are done with a full noun phrase, and thereafter a pronoun is used to display an understanding that the sequence is not closed (conversely, using a full noun phrase displays an understanding that it is closed). However, what counts as a sequence varies from genre to genre. As we have seen in the reflection box on variation across English written registers, the usage of referring expressions varies hugely across genres, so what will count as unmarked will vary. Moreover, note that this is a "basic" pattern; participants can exploit it. One context in which this can happen is disagreement. Note the final line of this example from Fox's data (Fox 1987: 62):

[2.24]   R: Those'r Alex's tanks weren't they?
         V: Podn' me?
         R: Weren't – didn' they belong tuh Al//ex?
         V: No: Alex ha(s) no tanks Alex is tryintuh buy my tank

Here, the use of a proper noun *Alex* instead of the pronominal *he* is geared towards attracting the attention of the first speaker to the fact that her or his assumptions about Alex are incorrect. Moreover, Downing (1996: 136) observes that proper nouns can be usefully deployed in contexts "where the speaker wishes to display his or her authority to speak about a particular referent, as is common in disagreement contexts", and this fits here.

Reflection: The use of *mate* in interactions amongst Australian speakers of English

We earlier mentioned in passing that "familiarisers", such as *mate*, are often used in British English as a means of signalling solidarity amongst males. However, recent work by Rendle-Short (2009) indicates that amongst Australian speakers of English, at least, younger females are now also using the term *mate* as an address term. Rather than being seen as a term used primarily by men to show "equality or egalitarianism", it is perceived as a "friendly and fun" term used to show intimacy. This indicates that the use and perception of socially deictic expressions can change over time, or at least they can change across generations of speakers of English.

Rendle-Short (2010) also illustrates in a follow-up study how the sequential placement of *mate* contributes to the understanding of participants about its function and implications in a particular context. It was found in her study that *mate* very often occurs after an assessment, agreement, acknowledgement or appreciation. In the following interaction, for instance, a father congratulates his son (a positive assessment) followed by the address term *mate*:

[2.25] Son: oh Dad. (0.2) I'm in. I'm in.
        Father: o::h well do::ne mate. (0.3) well done.
        Son: oh it's 'cos of you:: mate. you and the kids.
        Father: na:: mate. you did this. good on ya.
                                        (adapted from Rendle-Short 2010: 1206)

The son's appreciation in the following turn (*it's 'cos of you*) is also followed by *mate*. In such post-positioned contexts it is used to signal "open friendliness". However, in rejecting the acknowledgement, the father subsequently uses *mate* in the middle of his turn rather than it being post-positioned. In this case, the use of *mate* mitigates the force of this disagreement. We can see, then, that the sequential positioning of a referring expression can contribute, at least in part, to the interpretation of its particular function. We will return to consider the issue of sequentiality and speech acts in Chapter 6.

2.6   Conclusion

While it is clear that no referring expression is devoid of semantic meaning (*he* has the sense of something singular and usually male; the pro-form *do* of some kind of action etc.), definite expressions, deictic expressions and anaphoric expressions depend in large part for their full meaning on both the hearer working out the relevant referents, the speaker choosing referring expressions to nudge the target's understanding in the relevant direction, and both the speaker and the hearer collaborating in these processes. This is why they are both a semantic and a pragmatic phenomenon. We should also remember that referring expression forms do not always refer (*it*, the second word of this paragraph, for example, is not referring). We need to work out when they do and when they do not. The converse is also the case: sometimes non-referring expressions refer. Our final section, 2.5, focused on the uses and understandings of referring expressions in interaction. We pointed out that referring expressions are not simply empty slots filled with contextual information. Those referring expressions can, and often do, trigger the relevant contextual information with which they are filled. They can be used for a range of functions, including the expression of psychological prominence or a particular viewpoint. We discussed how speakers select particular referring expressions according to their assumptions about the degree to which the referent is in the target's mind's eye. In turn, hearers interpret those referring expressions in part by taking into consideration what is implied by the speaker's particular selection. We also introduced common ground and its role in influencing the selection of referring expressions and retrieval of referents. Finally, we focused on the dynamic and emergent characteristics of referring in interaction, including the exploitation of referring expressions, for example by choosing less obvious referring expressions to signal a particular interpersonal meaning such as relative power.

As far as English is concerned we have shown how, especially in our reflection boxes, some features that are common to many Englishes, such as the definite article, do not appear in other languages, and even within English English may have been different in the past. We have not only touched on contrasts with other languages, but also variation amongst Englishes and within a particular English. We also considered variation within speech and in writing. Apart from the obvious conclusion that discussions of workings of referring expressions cannot be based on data sets consisting just of English referring expressions, we should note that the way in which those expressions vary is a particular source of interest in its own right, whether it is accounting for changes from demonstratives to definite articles in terms of grammaticalisation, differences amongst written genres, or the role that referring expressions undertake in cueing their own interpretive frames. In fact, to fully understand the phenomena constituted by referring expressions we need to understand that variation.

3 Informational Pragmatics

3.1 Informational pragmatics

Why might a courtroom utterance such as *About how fast were the cars going when they smashed into each other?* sound as if the idea that the cars smashed into each other is being taken for granted? And why might an utterance such as *this book on pragmatics, let's hope it's good* sound different from *let's hope this book on pragmatics is good*? Answers to such questions flow from the study of informational pragmatics, an area that is concerned with "(a) how to segment the message into units; (b) how to assign degrees of prominence or subordination to different parts of the message; and (c) how to order the parts of the message" (Leech 1983:64). It is all about information packaging. Our term **informational pragmatics** is inspired by Leech's discussions of "textual rhetoric" (some scholars refer to this area of pragmatics as **discourse pragmatics**). Although the label "textual" is, as Leech acknowledges, inspired by Halliday's (e.g. 1973) work on language functions (just as is the use of "interpersonal" in "interpersonal rhetoric"), the notion of textual rhetoric is pitched as analogous to Grice's (1975) Cooperative Principle, which we will discuss in the following chapter. According to Leech (1983: 60), textual rhetoric helps

> to determine the stylistic form of the text in terms of segmentation, ordering, etc. ... [it] is based on speaker-hearer cooperation, a textually "well-behaved" utterance being one which anticipates and facilitates H's task in decoding, or making sense of, the text.

What we like about this definition is that it explicitly flags up the fact that constructing a text involves both the speaker and hearer, something that ties in with our interactional focus. Leech did not himself follow up the notion of textual rhetoric with further publications, but the substance of what he was talking about has been pursued under the heading of "information structure" in particular (Lambrecht's substantial 1994 study is of note). We have adopted the label informational pragmatics. We do not use the label information *structure* because that label suggests a different focus. Our focus is not on structure *per se*, something that would suggest a study in grammar, but structure insofar as it mediates communicative meanings in context, something that would suggest a study in pragmatics. One aspect this chapter has in common with textual rhetoric and information structure is that, linguistically, it focuses in particular on what is happening within the span of a sentence. This is, of course, a key point of departure from the previous chapter, where the linguistic focus was on short expressions.

This chapter is structured according to a distinction between information that is in the background and information that is in the foreground. As we explain in the next section, this is a tricky distinction, as it can be characterised in a number of different ways. The following two sections examine backgrounded information, specifically background assumptions (in relation to schema theory) and then presuppositions. In the next two sections, we examine foregrounded information, specifically the notion of salience (in relation to foregrounding theory) and then elements that constitute the focus. In our concluding section, we discuss informational grounding in an interactional perspective. Here we also reprise the notion of common ground, which we first introduced in section 2.5.3.

3.2   Informational ground: background and foreground

One general way of approaching the issue of background and foreground is to adopt a notion that arose out of the Gestalt psychology of the 1930s and 1940s, namely, the issue of **figure** and **ground** in visual perception. A picture will typically have **foregrounded** elements, the figure, and **backgrounded** elements, the ground. The perception of one is influenced by the other. In fact, what fascinated researchers such as Edgar Rubin, a Danish psychologist, were pictures whose figure and ground could be reversed and a new interpretation derived. This is illustrated by his famous vase picture published in *Synsoplevede Figurer* (Visually Experienced Figures) (1915), many variants of which have been produced.

In one interpretation, one sees a vase; in another interpretation, one sees two heads in profile. Moreover, in one interpretation the vase is the figure, but in the other it is the ground. This means that one cannot perceive the picture as a vase and two faces simultaneously. How might this work in language?

Some approaches (e.g. Chafe 1976) address the issue in terms of **given** information and **new**. These correspond to background and foreground respectively. In fact, we already met such issues in section 2.5.2, where the notion of

Source: John smithson (2007), Wikimedia Commons.
Figure 3.1   A figure/ground vase picture

givenness was aired in reference to Gundel et al.'s (1993) Givenness Hierarchy, a subtle view of the distinction between given and new information expressed in cognitive terms. You may recollect that they propose a scale to do with whether referents are in the foreground or background in terms of the knowledge and attention state of the addressee. Thus, something which the discourse has brought into focus right now, something which is active in the mind, something which is in memory but is not currently active and something completely unknown would all have different cognitive statuses. Generally speaking, cognitive status concerns the extent to which something is cognitively foregrounded in the minds of participants. Consider this question and its possible answers:

[3.1]   What model is your car?
  – My car is an Outback.
  – It's an Outback.
  – An Outback.

The answers progressively pare down the information they express to the bare essentials, the new information that answers the question, namely, *an Outback*. In the first answer, *my car is* repeats material from the question, information that is already given in the discourse. It is thus not surprising that the second answer can use a pronominal form and the third can omit the given information altogether.

For reasons of economy, the third or the second answer sound much more like what one would actually get in naturally occurring conversation. Of course, there is no requirement of actually saying the item in the previous discourse for something to be taken as given. Consider these possible exchanges said at a car club meeting:

[3.2]   What model is yours?
   – My car is an Outback.
   – It's an Outback.
   – An Outback.

In example [3.1], the discourse of the question brought the notion of the car into focus. In [3.2], the question does not bring the car into focus, but it is said in a context in which it can be readily assumed that all participants have cars. This assumption is given information. Hence, again, only *an Outback* supplies new information and the third answer takes full advantage of possible economies (arguably, one could also ditch the indefinite article).

In fact, the third answers in [3.1] and [3.2] are in tune with the discourse of example [3.3] (punctuation as per original; we have numbered the turns for ease of reference). Here, a member of a car bulletin board reconstructs a conversation he had at a car scrapyard, where he was searching for a particular part.

[3.3]   1 "what are you looking for"
         2 "95–98 subarus"
         3 "what kind of part"
         4 "the manifold absolute pressure sensor and the pressure source solenoid valve for a 95–98 subaru"
         5 "what model"
         6 "any"
         7 "what model is your car"
         8 "outback"
         (http://www.ultimatesubaru.org/forum/topic/53078-p1102p0106/)

Turns (5)–(6) support the point we were making above: there is no need for the answer in (6) to include "model", as that is discourse-old (cf. *any model*). Moreover, there is no need for the question to specify "what model of car", because in that context it can readily be assumed that "model" pertains to cars. So why does the scrap dealer say: *what model is your car* (line 7). This relates to the kind of interactional issues aired in section 2.5. Throughout this discourse it seems that each participant has different knowledge in mind, including different understandings of common knowledge. The scrap dealer "knows" that the customer is looking for a specific part for a specific model of a specific car and, further, that that part is for the car that the customer owns, which is why he tries to flush out the model of his car at the end. The customer, on the other hand, "knows" that the scrap dealer will not know much about the parts mentioned in (line 4) and hence, in (line 2), merely supplies the car year and make, knowing that all models of that make and year have the relevant part. Overall, then, each participant has a different conception concerning what is given. Each vies for power: the power of the expert, the one who "knows". This conversation was posted on the car bulletin board in order to illustrate the stupidity of car scrap dealers and why it is not worth trying to get parts from them.

There is an alternative perspective on the background/foreground distinction. Some grammarians, realising that sentence structure reflects the way people communicate information, adopted semantic notions that echo this distinction. It seems that the Prague School linguists of the early- to mid-20th century were amongst the first to propose a two-part structure in which the parts are connected by their "aboutness" relation (Fried 2009: 291). **Topic** (sometimes called theme or ground) refers to what is being talked about in the sentence, while **focus** (sometimes called comment or rheme) refers to what is being said about the sentence topic. The precise terms used and how they are defined is variable. Structural features are an important part of the definitions in work on grammar, for example by Chomsky (1965) and Halliday (e.g. 1994), and are briefly alluded to in work positioned on the interface between grammar and pragmatics (e.g. Lambrecht 1994). Regarding the topic, structural characteristics in English include: the nominal part of a clause; the constituent in the leftmost position (or occasionally the rightmost position); the subject; the thing which the proposition expressed by the sentence is about; and also the constituent lacking the focal accent. The focus, as one can guess, involves the aspects not covered by the topic (e.g. the verbal part plus its complement, the body of the clause, the predicate). Let us revisit part of [3.2] above:

[3.4]   [My car]$_{TOPIC}$ [is an Outback]$_{FOCUS}$

My car is indeed a nominal part of the sentence, in leftmost position and the subject. In contrast, *is an Outback* is indeed the verbal part of the clause plus its complement, the predicate. Note a further characteristic of such structures: the definite noun phrase *my car* **presupposes** information assumed to be known (namely, that a car of mine exists), whereas the remainder of the sentence **asserts** the new information about the car. This represents yet another way of conceiving of the background/foreground distinction. We will be looking closely at presuppositions in section 3.3.2.

There is overlap between **cognitive givenness/newness**, concerning the status of information in the mind (e.g. whether it is old/new, the focus of attention etc.), and **semantic givenness/newness**, concerning the presentation of information in the sentence, especially how one part is about another part. This is not surprising, it facilitates the target's processing if one starts with a topic containing easy to access, old information, which can then act as a background context for the focus containing the new information. Also, it comes as no surprise to observe that there is a connection between definiteness and topic. Recollect that in section 2.2 we defined definite expressions as items primarily used to invite the participant(s) to identify a particular referent from a specific context, which is assumed to be shared by the interlocutors. That "assumed to be shared information" is the subset of given information relating to common ground. However, there are occasions where there is little or no overlap between cognitive and semantic givenness. We will consider some of these in section 3.4.2. Before leaving the notion of semantic givenness, we should emphasise that the term "topic" here should not be confused with **discourse topic**. The key difference is that discourse topic pertains to what a discourse is about, and a discourse could contain one or more sentences, whereas semantic topic generally pertains to a portion of information within a sentence. In the previous examples the discourse was clearly about cars and knowing this assisted in the selection of referents. There are occasional exceptions where a whole sentence can be construed as both a semantic topic and a discourse topic, but this is relatively rare. We will return to the notion of discourse topic in the following section, specifically when we discuss context models.

Let us take stock. Some of the relevant characteristics of backgrounded and foregrounded information, broadly arranged from the more cognitive to the more linguistic, are captured in Table 3.1.

Table **3.1** Characteristics of backgrounded and foregrounded information in discourse

Background	Foreground
Participant-old information (i.e. information already known by a participant)	Participant-new information (i.e. information not already known by a participant)
Non-active information (i.e. information not currently active in a participant's mind)	Active information (i.e. information currently active in a participant's mind)
Discourse-old information (i.e. previously mentioned in the discourse)	Discourse-new information (i.e. not previously mentioned in the discourse)
Information that is presupposed by the sentence	Information that is asserted by the sentence
Information that is the topic of the sentence	Information that is the focus of the sentence

We have already touched on matters relating to the first three characteristics in section 2.5.2, where we discussed some cognitive aspects of understanding referring expressions. We will periodically connect with and elaborate the characteristics of Table 3.1 further during this chapter.

3.3   Informational background

3.3.1   Background assumptions

The importance of old or prior knowledge (assumptions) in understanding cannot be overestimated. We use such knowledge to enrich our understanding of what people say, make what they say cohere and even make predictions about what they are going to say. Unfortunately, in pragmatics the way in which we use such knowledge has generally been underestimated, something which stands in contrast with work in the cognitive sciences. Pragmatics has been focused on the kind of **pseudo-logical inferencing** to be discussed at length in the following chapter (notably, Grice's Cooperative Principle, 1975), which is characterised by mechanisms for drawing conclusions from premises. But a large part of meaning is understood through known associations, that is **associative inferencing** or knowledge-based inferencing. For example, if you know that that kind of utterance X, said by that kind of speaker Z, in that kind of context Y, usually has that kind of meaning W, you may simply arrive at the meaning on the basis of what usually happens. Thus the utterance *how are you?* said in a doctor's surgery to a patient is usually taken as a question eliciting information about symptoms and so on; whereas the same utterance said in an everyday context to an acquaintance is usually taken as phatic talk requiring a suitably phatic response (often in British English a repetition of *how are you?*). These scenarios do not require one to take the utterance and context as premises and then deploy a mechanism for calculating an implied bit of meaning. The important role of associative inferencing has been recognised by Recanati (2004) and championed by Mazzone (2011). It is important because it accounts for much of the inferencing we do. People are "cognitive misers" (Taylor 1981) and associative inferencing represents a less cognitively effortful way forward.

To understand how knowledge works, we need a theory of knowledge. The leading theory is **schema theory**, though that precise label may not be the one used ("frames", "scripts" and "scenarios", have been used in the literature, each within a somewhat different tradition and with a somewhat different emphasis).[1] Schema theory has been formulated by cognitive psychologists and researchers from other fields (e.g. Bartlett [1932] 1995; Neisser 1976; Schank and Abelson 1977). It has been used to account

---

[1] Today, cognitive psychologists may not always use the label schema theory or the other labels mentioned, but the essentials of schema theory live on in discussions of various connectionist models.

for how people comprehend, learn from and remember meanings in texts. Essentially, the idea is that knowledge is retrieved from long-term memory and integrated with information derived from the utterance or text, or indeed context, to produce an interpretation. The term "schema/schemata" refers to the "well integrated chunks of knowledge about the world, events, people, and actions" (Eysenck and Keane 2000: 352). They are usually taken to be relatively complex, higher-order, clusters of concepts, with a particular network of relationships holding those concepts together, and are assumed to constitute the structure of long-term memory. What have schemata got to do with inferencing? Schemata enable us to construct an interpretation that contains more information than we receive from the language itself. We can supply or infer extra bits of information – default values – from our schematic knowledge.

Andersen et al. (1977) conducted an experiment that conveniently illustrates how this inferencing might work. They asked people to read the following fictional passage:

[3.5]   Rocky slowly got up from the mat, planning his escape. He hesitated a moment and thought. Things were not going well. What bothered him most was being held, especially since the charge against him had been weak. He considered his present situation. The lock that held him was strong but he thought he could break it. He knew, however, that his timing would have to be perfect. Rocky was aware that it was because of his early roughness that he had been penalised so severely – much too severely from his point of view. The situation was becoming frustrating; the pressure had been grinding on him for too long. He was being ridden unmercifully. Rocky was getting angry now. He felt he was ready to make his move. He knew that his success or failure would depend on what he did in the next few seconds.

The key problem here is trying to work out the discourse topic. To begin with, who is Rocky? The text tells us about, for example, his spatial circumstances (he is on a *mat* and *held* by *the lock*), his goal (*planning his escape*), his evaluation of the situation (*things were not going well*), his history (*his early roughness, the pressure had been grinding on him for too long*), his evaluation of his plan to achieve his goal. (*He felt he was ready to make his move. He knew that his success or failure would depend on what he did in the next few seconds.*) We also, of course, learn that Rocky is his name, connoting that he is male (and quite possibly North American rather than British). But the text does not actually tell us who Rocky is or even where he is. Note that many of the clues are in referring expressions, especially definite noun phrases (*Rocky, the mat, his escape, the charge, his present situation, the lock* and so on). We discussed this very phenomenon in section 2.5.1, where we argued that referring expressions do not passively rely on a specific shared context for interpretation (i.e. common ground), but produce or trigger a specific shared context in which they can be interpreted – they trigger a schema by virtue of the fact that they are stereotypical components of that schema.

People understanding language generally try to activate a schema that will provide a scaffold for interpreting the incoming linguistic information. The alternative – keeping all the separate bits of information in the cognitive air – would be mentally taxing, to say the least, and would not constitute an understanding of the passage. Once activated, a schema gives rise to expectations (i.e. default values) – these expectations are knowledge-based associative inferences. Andersen et al. (1977) discovered that most of their informants thought that the discourse topic of the passage concerned a convict planning his escape from prison. Accordingly, referring expressions such as *Rocky*, the pronouns (e.g. *he*, *his*) and the definite noun phrases (e.g. *the situation*) could be assigned suitably coherent referents (e.g. convict, prison cell). Further, informants could disambiguate words such as *charge* or *lock* to fit the default values of that schema: the *charge* is a legal charge; the *lock* is the lock on the door. A door has not in fact been mentioned, let alone a prison cell, but these can be readily inferred, thereby enriching the interpretation. However, one group of people had an entirely different interpretation of the discourse topic. Men who had been involved in wrestling assumed that it was about a wrestler caught in the hold of an opponent. Thus, for example, *charge* is a physical charge by the opponent; the *lock* is a hold (possibly headlock) the opponent has on him.

Most informants gave the passage one distinct interpretation and reported being unaware of other perspectives while reading. The particular schema (or schemata) deployed in interpretation depends upon the experiences, including cultural experiences, of the interpreter. A person's experiences constitute the basis of their schemata. Fredric Bartlett's (1932[1995]) early pioneering work in schema theory was partly designed to explore cultural differences in interpretation (see also the experiment by Steffenson et al. 1979). Schema theory has been used more recently in the context of **cross-cultural pragmatics** (e.g. Scollon & Scollon 1995). For example, we have schemata or, to use Schank and Abelson's (1977) term, scripts about typical sequences of actions in particular contexts. But these vary culturally. For example, in a coffee bar in the UK it is usual to get your food (or order your food and then get it) before paying and then receiving a receipt. In contrast, in Italy it is usual to say what you want, pay for it, get a receipt and then get your food (sometimes having ordered it from a different person). A recipe for cross-cultural trouble!

Reflection: Category labels in block language

Block language refers to varieties of written English – such as headlines, book titles, labels, notices, lists and some types of postcard, advertisement, instructional manual – where "communicative needs strip language of all but the most information-bearing forms" (Biber et al. 1999: 263). This phenomenon is usually mentioned in grammar books, because it is characterised by reduced syntax – non-sentences consisting of a noun, noun phrase or nominal clause, the omission of closed-class items, such as forms of the verb *to be*, the articles, pronouns and generally whatever can be understood from the context (Quirk et al. 1985: 845–848). Consider this personal advertisement from a newspaper:

[3.6]   LONDON MAN, 32, SMART, non smoker. Accountant but Left interests and outlook. Looking to meet attractive, optimistic woman.

(New Statesman, 26 August 1994)

We might rewrite this more fully thus:

I am a London man, 32 years old, smart and a non smoker. I am an accountant, but I have Left interests and outlook. I am looking to meet an attractive, optimistic woman.

As can be seen, the use of capitals, or in some cases bold, is another characteristic of block language. But what we are specifically interested in here is the use of category labels inviting associative inferencing. The occupational term *accountant* places the advertiser within a particular social group, that is people whose occupational role is accountancy. People frequently perceive others as members of social groups rather than as individuals, and these groups are assumed to provide the basis for cognitive categories. However, if – as in the schema theory view – cognitive categories or concepts are organised as structured networks, then the word *accountant* primes the activation of other social information which is part of the network. The problem for the advertiser is that, although *accountant* might appear merely to denote a particular social role, for some people *accountant* is schematically linked to politically right-wing group membership and to particular personal interests (e.g. materialistic interests). These schematic links arise as a result of experience; certain kinds of people have tended to fill certain social roles. So, the writer has to block schematic associative inferences that are not wanted. This he does through the formal device *but*, a conjunction that carries the conventional implicature (Grice 1975; this phenomenon is discussed in the following chapter) that an expectation generated by the preceding text does not apply.

3.3.2 Presuppositions

We have, in fact, already met the most frequent kind of presupposition in English, namely, that achieved through definite noun phrases (NPs) like *the book* or *Michael* (see section 2.2). The primary idea is that such referring expressions invite participant(s) to identify a particular referent from a specific context which is assumed to be shared by the interlocutors, but that idea could not work if those referents were not assumed to exist. **Presuppositions** are assumptions that are typically taken for granted in a conversation – they are often part of the common ground – and are conventionally associated with particular linguistic expressions. The term presupposition should not be confused with its everyday usage, where it is taken as near enough synonymous with the term **assumption**, meaning that something is taken as being true without any explicit evidence, as illustrated by [3.7]:

[3.7] Last year was odd for me, musically – a year where all my naïve <u>presuppositions</u> about pop music were questioned by a new wave of rock criticism.

Stylus Magazine, http://ww w.stylusmagazine.com/
reviews/broken-social-scene/beehives.htm

This is not to say that the everyday notion of assumptions is not within the scope of pragmatics; we dealt with it in the previous section. However, the technical usage of the term presupposition is more restricted. For example, Levinson (1983: 168) writes that it pertains to "certain pragmatic inferences or assumptions that seem at least to be built into linguistic expressions and which can be isolated using specific linguistic tests". We will examine both those linguistic expressions and some of those tests in this section.

Much of the literature on presuppositions has been written by language philosophers (e.g. Gottlob Frege, Peter Strawson) or semanticists (e.g. Lauri Karttunen, Paul and Carol Kiparsky) (see the references in Beaver 1997). As much of this literature is populated by analyses of decontextualised constructed sentences, often sentences that people are never likely to use, it would not seem promising for a fruitful discussion of the distinctive or variational pragmatic characteristics of the English language. However, there are two areas that can be usefully explored: (1) the particular array of linguistic forms used in English for presuppositions; and (2) the particular contexts in which presuppositions appear, along with presuppositional functions in those contexts.

The kind of presupposition exemplified by *the book* and *Michael* in the first sentence of this section is an **existential presupposition**. These arise when the speaker seems to assume, and invites the hearer to assume, the existence of the entity to which they refer. Such presuppositions are discussed in early work by, for example, Frege (e.g. 1892), Russell (1905) and thoroughly by Strawson (1950). The classic, and somewhat bizarre, example Russell, Strawson and many others discuss is: *The king of France is bald*. They were fascinated by the fact that the sentence is not simply true or false according to the baldness of the king. The additional issue is that it presupposes the existence of a king of France, which we know not to be the case in this modern age. Later scholars broadened the notion to include other kinds of presupposition. Consider this example: *We are glad to have written this chapter*. Being *glad* about something presupposes that that something truly happened (i.e. it is true that we wrote this). This is a **factive presupposition**. The classic work on factivity, Kiparsky and Kiparsky (1970), discusses verbs (e.g. *regret, know, realise*) that presuppose the truth of their complements (the complement of our example being: *to have written this chapter*). Some verbs, such as *believe, suppose, intend* and *claim*, seem to push the truth status of their complements into a twilight zone where we are not sure about whether they are true or not. Hence, *we believe we have written this chapter* leaves the truth of whether we wrote it lingering in the air. These verbs trigger **non-factive presuppositions**. Some other structures do the opposite of factive presuppositions, that is, they presuppose that some proposition is not true. An example might be *If the computer had crashed, we might have lost our book manuscript*. Fortunately, this sentence does not report a calamity, because the presupposition triggered by the conditional structure suggests that the state of affairs in the first clause is not true – this is a **counterfactive presupposition**. With all these types of presupposition the presupposition is conventionally associated with particular linguistic forms – a definite noun phrase (*the book*), a particular emotive verb expression (*are glad*) and so on. Such linguistic forms are called **presuppositional triggers**. They invite a pragmatic inference to be made; that is, they invite the hearer to supply the assumptions associated with the linguistic form in its context of use.

Table 3.2 summarises the types of presupposition and presuppositional triggers that are generally discussed in the literature (see, in particular, Levinson 1983: 181–184, also Beaver 1997: 943–944). It should not be taken as a complete list, not least because there is disagreement in the literature about types of presupposition, presuppositional triggers and whether particular items are presuppositions at all. It is also worth noting, especially with regard to the items listed under "other", that there is some leakage into the category of conventional implicatures (see Karttunen and Peters 1979), which will be discussed briefly in sections 4.2.2.

Table 3.2 Types of presupposition and presuppositional triggers in English

Type	Presuppositional trigger	Example	Presupposition
Specific existential	A definite noun phrase (a definite article, demonstrative, possessive pronoun or s-genitive followed by a noun phrase, or a proper noun)	My car is red	>> There is a car which is mine
Non-specific existential	WH-questions (i.e. questions beginning who, what, when, why, where or how)	Who drove fast?	>> There is somebody who drove fast
	Cleft (or pseudo-cleft) sentences	It wasn't me that drove fast	>> There is somebody who drove fast
Factive	Factive emotive verbs (e.g. regret, be sorry, be glad)	I regret driving fast	>> I drove fast
	Factive epistemic verbs (e.g. realise, know, be obvious)	I realise that I was driving fast	>> I drove fast
Non-factive	Non-factive verbs (e.g. believe, suppose, imagine, dream, claim)	I claimed that I was driving fast	>> I may or may not have been driving fast
Counterfactual	Counterfactual conditionals	If I had been driving fast, I might have crashed	>> I was not driving fast
Other	Implicative verbs (e.g. manage, forget to, happened to)	I managed to drive fast	>> I tried to drive fast
	Change-of-state verbs (e.g. stop, begin, enter, come, go)	I stopped driving fast	>> I had been driving fast
	Iteratives (adverbs and verbs) (e.g. again, returned, repeat)	I drove fast again	>> I had been driving fast
	Temporal clauses (subordinate clauses beginning when, before, while, since, after, etc.)	When I drove fast, I skidded	>> I had been driving fast

Reflection: Presuppositional resources in other languages and change-of-state verbs

As briefly noted in Table 3.1, English has at its disposal a group of full lexical verbs that presuppose a state or situation that contrasts with the one they express. Thus, for example, if one *stops* something, it presupposes that something had started. There are two main groups of such verbs, one relating to the beginnings of such states (e.g. *begin, start, commence, get underway*) and one relating to the endings of such states (e.g. *stop, finish, terminate, break off*). However, other languages can achieve similar presuppositions through grammatical **aspect**.

Aspect refers to the completeness or wholeness of an action, event or state – hereafter in this box, the situation. It is not to be confused with grammatical tense, which refers to the location of the situation in time. English uses certain combinations of auxiliaries and participles to express a contrast between the perfect and imperfect aspect. For instance, *he had washed the dishes* means that the situation of washing the dishes is complete, whereas *he was washing the dishes* means that the situation of washing the dishes is ongoing. Aspect presents the speaker's perspective on the situation and not some kind of absolute reality. So it is perfectly possible to talk about situations that are not complete at a particular point in the past (e.g. *he was washing the dishes*), even though they are now complete at the point when the speaker talks about them.

The point of relevance for us here is that other languages can express other aspectual meanings through the grammar of verbs. "Ingressive", "inceptive" or "inchoative" aspect, broadly understood, involves an inflection, affix, auxiliary verb or grammatical particle placing a focus on the beginning of a situation. Let's imagine English had an inflection "begin", then the sentence *he was wash-begin the dishes* would express the meaning "he was just beginning to wash the dishes". "Egressive", "cessive" or "terminative" aspect, broadly understood, involves an inflection, affix, auxiliary verb or grammatical particle placing a focus on the ending of a situation. Let's imagine English had an inflection "end", then the sentence *he was wash-end the dishes* would express the meaning "he was just ceasing to wash the dishes".

A genuine ingressive example from another language would be the case of the prefix *za-* and the role it plays in certain Slavic languages, notably Russian, Ukrainian, Belarusian and Bulgarian (cf. Dickey 2000). Thus, in Russian *zapetj* means "to begin singing", *zaplakat* "to begin crying" and so on. Another example would be the inflection *–sco* in Latin, thus giving, for example, *pallesco* "to begin to turn pale" or *nigresco* "to begin to turn black" (cf. Kennedy 1985). The key point is that such aspectual resources presuppose a state or situation that contrasts with the one they express. If one expresses the sense "to begin singing" or "to begin to turn pale" employing aspectual resources, one presupposes that the target was not already singing or already pale.

Presuppositional triggers do not determine presuppositions, but rather have the potential to trigger an inference about what is presupposed. What is presupposed is **defeasible**, which means that what is inferred can be cancelled or suspended in particular contexts. But what are those contexts? Consider a negative version of our earlier sentence: *we are not glad to have written this chapter*. Here, the presupposition that we have truly written the chapter is not cancelled. The ability of presuppositions to survive the negative counterpart of a positive sentence is seen as a key test of presuppositions, the **constancy under negation** test. One reason why what is presupposed generally survives such negation is that a presupposition is not, generally, what is asserted by the sentence (a point made as early as Frege 1892: 69, quoted in Atlas 2004: 31). What is asserted is often new information (the figure); presuppositions are often old information (the background) (we will return to this point in section 3.4). Thus, in *we are/are not glad to have written this chapter*, we assert our gladness or lack of it in having written this chapter, but we always presuppose that we truly have written it.

However, there are also more indirect kinds of negation that can cancel presuppositions. Consider example [3.8]:

[3.8]   Do not seek the because — in love there is no because, no reason, no explanation, no solutions.

(Anaïs Nin (1990: 90), *Henry and June:*
From the Unexpurgated Diary of Anaïs Nin)

The because is a definite NP, triggering the presupposition that a "because" exists. Note that the fact it appears in a negative sentence (*Do not seek* ...) does not cancel this presupposition (cf. constancy under negation). However, *in love there is no because* does cancel it. This particular kind of indirect negation has been termed **metalinguistic negation** (e.g. Horn 1985). Metalinguistic negation is a somewhat controversial notion, but generally such constructions invite the reader/listener to reflect back on a previous utterance and correct their default understanding of it in the light of some objection. Note that it is not simply a matter of contradicting what was previously said. This is why metalinguistic negation would not work with a positive version of the first clause. *Seek the because – in love there is no because* results in contradiction,– it seems to be incoherent nonsense (if the two parts were said by different speakers in a dialogue, it is more plausible). With the negative version, as in [3.8], the second part clarifies the negation of the first: don't seek the because, because in love there is no because.

The survival or otherwise of presuppositions in the context of complex sentences has been the subject of much debate and is referred to as the **projection problem** (Karttunen 1973). This refers to the question of whether the presuppositions of an embedded clause "project" up, or survive, at higher levels of a sentence. In some instances this question arises due to the way in which presuppositional triggers can interact. Example [3.9], reporting what the captain of the ship Costa Concordia said about its sinking, is a case in point.

[3.9]   He claims that the rocky reef that the ship hit on the night of Jan 13 2012 was not marked on his nautical charts.

(*www.telegraph.co.uk,* September 2013)

Consider the embedded clause in isolation: "The rocky reef that the ship hit on the night of Jan 13 2012 was not marked on his nautical charts." Here, the definite NPs, *the rocky reef,* etc. and *his nautical charts,* trigger existential presuppositions – assumptions that these things exist. But the presence of the main verb, *claims,* a non-factive verb, introduces a rather non-committal stance; we are not sure whether the rocky reef, etc. and nautical charts exist. Of course, generally it is the case that if presuppositions in such complex sentences are considered in the context of the broader discourse and background knowledge, it is quite clear how one should take them (there was ample evidence, not least from TV footage, that the ship was on a rocky reef, and we can readily assume that a ship's captain would have nautical charts). Cases where a presuppositional clash remains are thus likely to be taken as bizarre or humorous. Consider this apparently real question asked in a US courtroom trial:

[3.10]   Question: Now, doctor, isn't it true that when a person dies in his sleep, in most cases he just passes quietly away and doesn't know anything about it until the next morning?

http://www.jacanaent.com/Library/Humour/
Courtroom%20Quotes.htm

Dies could be taken as a change-of-state verb, presupposing that the person is not alive, just as *passes ... away* could be taken as a change-of-state phrasal verb meaning that the person has moved away from life, thus presupposing that life is not now their state. *Until* introduces a temporal clause presupposing that he did know something about it the next morning. Of course, in our normal world view we assume that people who die are no longer sentient and thus could not know anything about it the next morning. The humour in this question then, and the reason it was posted on the web, is precisely the bizarre presuppositional incongruity created by the different presuppositional triggers.

Stalnaker (1972, [1974] 1991) was concerned with how presuppositions are understood in context. His work is the first to elaborate a full pragmatic account of presuppositions (see also Gazdar 1979). His definition of a presupposition is as follows: "To presuppose a proposition in the pragmatic sense is to take its truth for granted, and to presume that others involved in the context do the same" (Stalnaker 1972: 387–388). He explains the difference between assertion and presupposition:

> The distinction between presupposition and assertion should be drawn, not in terms of the content of the propositions expressed, but in terms of the situations in which the statement is made – the attitudes and intentions of the speaker and his audience. Presuppositions, on this account, are something like the background beliefs of the speaker – propositions whose truth he takes for granted, or seems to take for granted, in making his statement. (Stalnaker 1991: 472)

Note two things: (1) presuppositions are not simply the properties of sentences but involve the beliefs of speakers; and (2) presuppositions are part of the presumed common background beliefs of participants. Regarding (1), it is this fact that means a pragmatic account is required. This is not to say that semantics has no role to play, but rather that the interpretation of the semantics is constrained by the pragmatic context, as in fact we were suggesting in the previous paragraph. This is neatly illustrated by Stalnaker (1991: 475):

> For example, D.T. Langendoen points out in a paper on presupposition and assertion that normally, if one said "my cousin isn't a boy anymore" he would be asserting that his cousin had grown up, presupposing that he is male. But one might, in a less common context, use the same sentence to assert that one's cousin had changed sexes, presupposing that she is young. If a semantic account of presupposition is given of this case, then one would say that the sentence is therefore ambiguous. On the pragmatic account, one just points to two different kinds of situations in which a univocal sentence could be used.

Regarding (2), it is obviously more economic not to have to spell out all one's assumptions, and presuppositions are one way of achieving that. However, whether presuppositions involve *common* ground is more controversial (see, for example, Abbott 2000). Stalnaker was aware of some of the difficulties, pointing out that defining presupposition in terms of common ground works "in normal, straightforward serious conversational contexts where the overriding purpose of the conversation is to exchange information", but that "difficulties" "come with contexts in which other interests besides communication are being served by the conversation" (1991: 474).

Reflection: Exploiting presuppositions in discourses of power and persuasion

Presuppositions can be used to trick people into apparently accepting background assumptions which they do not have and/or would not have. Courtroom discourse is a case in point. For example, Izola Curry, on trial for the attempted murder of Dr. Martin Luther King in a restaurant in 1958, was asked:

[3.11]   Q: When did you find out that Dr. King was going to be at Bloomstein's this afternoon?
A: Well, I didn't find out I didn't find out. I'll answer that I didn't find out...

Clearly, Curry worked out the presupposition embedded in the WH-structure (i.e. that she had found out), despite the fact that it was not common ground. Blocking this kind of presupposition is difficult, as one has pointedly to avoid answering the question; to do so would mean accepting what is presupposed. Cross-examination discourse from prosecutors is often designed to get a defendant or witness to accept, inadvertently or otherwise, assumptions that point towards their guilt. And presuppositions are powerful. Loftus and Palmer (1974) tested the sentence with which we began this chapter: *About how fast were the cars going when they smashed into each other?* This is one of the questions they put to subjects about a film they had been shown. The WH-structures presuppose that the cars were going "fast" and, moreover, "smashed" into each other, something which seems to explain the fact that informants were more likely to subsequently recall the presence of broken glass (though none was actually to be seen in the film) than if, instead of "smashed", the question contained "hit" or "bumped" (see also Loftus 1975).

Another kind of discourse that regularly manipulates common ground is that of advertising. Consider these advertising slogans:

[3.12]   Heineken refreshes the parts other beers cannot reach. (Heineken) [Definite noun phrase; presupposes that there are parts which other beers cannot reach]
You'll wonder where the yellow went when you brush your teeth with Pepsodent. (Pepsodent) [Definite noun phrase (plus embedded WH-questions); presupposes that there was yellow]

One way of packing in information into the short space available in the slogan, and also of creating a dramatic and memorable slogan, is to deploy presuppositions. In addition, part of the sales pitch can be through the presupposition. In the Heineken advertisement, it is presupposed that there are other beers that cannot reach the relevant parts. Such presuppositions create the ground against which the product shines. In some cases, the presuppositions seem designed to create surreptitiously a problem or need for which the product is the solution. In the Pepsodent toothpaste advertisement, the existence of yellow on your teeth is presupposed (*the yellow*). In all these cases, presuppositions are part of the advertiser's "soft sell" strategy. For more on the persuasive use of presuppositions, see Sbisà (1999).

Reflection: Presuppositions, fictional worlds and stage directions in plays

When we comprehend language we create a model of what it is about in our heads, and this model includes our beliefs about the world. More accurately, we should say world*s*: not just the physical world in which we live, but fantasy worlds (e.g. the world of Harry Potter), wish worlds (e.g. the world in which I win the lottery), future worlds (e.g. the world in which I cope with being old). These are all **possible worlds** (Ryan 1991). Play stage directions, particularly at the beginning of plays, are usually dense with presuppositions, deployed to create fictional worlds. Consider an early stage direction from the script of Bernard Shaw's play *Candida* (1898):

[3.13]   *The chair for visitors has been replaced at the table. Marchbanks, alone and idle, is trying to find out how the typewriter works. Hearing someone at the door, he steals guiltily away to the window and pretends to be absorbed in the view. Miss Garnett, carrying the notebook in which she takes down Morell's letters in short-hand from his dictation, sits down at the typewriter and sets to work transcribing them, much too busy to notice Eugene. When she begins the second line she stops and stares at the machine.*

The existence of a chair for visitors is hardly common knowledge, but it is presupposed in the definite noun phrase *the chair for visitors*, and in the light of this trigger we fill in one element of this fictional world created within our model. One could make similar remarks for the other definite noun phrases, *the table, the typewriter, the door, the window* and so on. Note the proper nouns presupposing the existence of certain characters. We also have a number of change-of-state verbs. *Replaced* presupposes that something was there in the first place; *steals ... away to* presupposes that he was not there in the first place; *takes down* presupposes that they were not already taken down; and so on. *Trying* presupposes that he has not succeeded in getting the typewriter to work, but the WH-structure *how the typewriter works* presupposes that it does work. In the final sentence, the

> WH-structure at the beginning presupposes that she had begun the second line; the change-of-state verb *begins* presupposes that she had not started, whereas *stops* presupposes (by that point!) she had at least started.

3.4   Informational foreground

3.4.1   Foregrounding

In informational pragmatics, scholars have not fully explained what it is that pushes information into the foreground and makes it salient. Some work done on the pragmatic-grammar interface has addressed more formal aspects of foregrounding, and we will consider some of this work in the next section. Nevertheless, too many studies simply refer to, for example, something having been recently mentioned as evidence that it is in the foreground. There is much more to it than this. A key theory to turn to here is the **theory of foregrounding**. This theory does not restrict its focus to the sentence, but can work at various linguistic levels. It is concerned with how language can be made cognitively salient, with – recalling our distinction between semantic givenness/newness and cognitive givenness/newness (section 3.2) – **cognitive focus**. Though rooted in Russian Formalism and the work of the Prague School, its main development came about in the 1960s and after in literary studies, discourse analysis and cognitive psychology. Foregrounding theory has been shown to guide the interpretation of literary texts (van Peer 1986), though there is no reason for limiting it to literary texts since it encapsulates general principles.

Foregrounded elements achieve salience through deviation from a linguistic norm (Mukařovský 1970). This idea is analogous to that of figure and ground, as discussed in section 3.2. The characteristics of such foregrounded elements include "unexpectedness, unusualness, and uniqueness" (ibid.: 53–54). Unexpectedness is a notion that is not remote from cognitive newness as opposed to givenness (discussed in section 3.2). Consider an example of foregrounding. In Shakespeare's *Anthony and Cleopatra*, when Anthony says, *Let Rome in Tiber melt* (I.i.33), **deviation** occurs at a semantic level, since, quite obviously, a city cannot melt. Our attention is captured and we can work to construct an interpretation. Leech (1985) drew attention to the two sides of foregrounding: just as you can have deviation through irregularity, so you can also have deviation through regularity. The **parallelism** of the same kinds of elements where you would normally expect different ones is a type of deviation. In the above example, one can perceive a high degree of regularity in the metrical pattern:

[3.14]   x   /   x   /   x   /
          Let Rome in Tiber melt

The strict alternation between stressed and unstressed syllables picks this utterance out. It is foregrounded not only against the natural rhythms of spoken English, but also against the immediately preceding lines which contain no such regularity of patterning. This regularity helps foreground the serious nature of what Anthony has to say, his first statement of treason. There is also some degree of syntactic foregrounding. Syntactic norms are violated in that no definite article precedes *Tiber*. Furthermore, the ordering of this particular clause, the adverbial falling between subject and verb, seems odd. Perhaps the syntactic construction here was motivated by a desire to form a regular metrical pattern.

One of the main reasons for the success of the notion of foregrounding lies in its relevance to the study of the process of linguistic interpretation. Leech (1985: 47) points out that more interpretive effort is focused on foregrounded elements in an attempt to rationalise their abnormality, than on backgrounded elements. Leech writes:

> In addition to the normal processes of interpretation which apply to texts, whether literary or not, foregrounding invites an act of IMAGINATIVE INTERPRETATION by the reader. When an abnormality comes to our attention, we try to make sense of it. We use our imaginations, consciously or unconsciously, in order to work out why this abnormality exists.
>
> (Leech 1985: 47)

Furthermore, van Peer (1986) has provided empirical evidence to substantiate the claim that foregrounded elements are not only cognitively more striking but are also regarded as more important in relation to the overall interpretation of the text.

Foregrounding theory is generally focused on implicit foregrounding, achieved by making certain elements cognitively salient and thus likely to attract more attention. Sometimes, language deploys explicit foregrounding. An example of this is when we write in this chapter "note that ...". Here, we are explicitly directing you towards parts of the text which we think are important and so should be in the foreground of your attention (you can always ignore the instruction of course!). There are, needless to say, other structures that involve that kind of explicit direction and we will attend to some of them, amongst other things, in the following section.[2]

3.4.2 Focus

In this section, we will mainly discuss the notion of focus, especially as it is articulated in work on the pragmatics-grammar border. As outlined in

---

[2] The implicit/explicit distinction discussed in this paragraph is partly inspired by Jucker and Smith (1996).

section 3.2, focus can relate to what is being said about the topic of the sentence. Recalling our distinction between semantic givenness/newness and cognitive givenness/newness, we can label this **semantic focus**. However, as we pointed out in section 3.2, this notion overlaps with cognitive givenness/newness – what is in the mind's eye – and, indeed, there are some features that are better discussed in these terms. We can label this **cognitive focus**, encompassing the issues of salience discussed in the previous section. It is worth bearing in mind that here we are also dealing with how people package information into chunks. For example, a speaker can introduce new information about an entity in one chunk and provide further new information about that entity in another chunk. Below we touch on some key areas.

End-focus

A feature of English simple declarative sentences is that the topic tends to occur in the beginning while the focus – and here is meant cognitive focus – tends to occur at the end. Leech's (1983) **processibility principle** is relevant here: "This principle recommends that the text should be presented in a manner which makes it easy for the hearer to decode in time" (1983: 64). It includes two maxims: the maxim of **end-focus**, which "recommends that if the rules of the language allow it, the part of a clause which contains new information should be placed at the end"; and the maxim of **end-weight**, which concerns syntactic ordering in English (and other subject-verb-object languages) and recommends that " 'light' constituents proceed 'heavy' ones" (1983: 65). Consider example [3.15], which is the first sentence of a newspaper article about a famous fashion model:

[3.15]   Rosie Huntington-Whiteley has the kind of gentle beauty one might
have sketched on the back of a book during double maths in 1991.
(*The Observer Magazine* 6 October 13)

Here, semantic and cognitive focus overlap. The topic of the sentence, what it is about, is obviously "Rosie Huntington-Whiteley"; the focus is the rest of the sentence. It has end-focus, as this final part of the clause contains new information. It is also the heaviest constituent (the one with most syllables) and so also has end-weight. Both maxims, as Leech notes (Leech 1983: 66), are probably motivated by restrictions on human memory (usually said to be up to seven random items). Older information is easier for the mind to cope with than newer and, if shorter constituents appear first, there is less to remember before one gets to the final constituents of the sentence, so the cognitive load in interpreting utterances is reduced.

Focus and prosodic prominence

Sentences are almost always spoken with a particular part being more prominent than the rest. That part carries a **focal accent**, a word or syllable that is made prosodically prominent through marked pitch, amplitude and duration. The important point for us is that the focal accent generally indicates what the speaker is presenting as new information, it indicates cognitive focus (a case where this would not be so, for example, is marking a shift in discourse topic). Consider the following sentences (capitals are used to mark the focal accent):

[3.16]   JOnathan gave his students chocolate
Jonathan GAVE his students chocolate
Jonathan gave HIS students chocolate
Jonathan gave his STUdents chocolate
Jonathan gave his students CHOcolate

Let us add possible contexts to our examples and spell out possible implications for information:

JOnathan gave his students chocolate [Jonathan does not have a reputation for generosity, though others do, so it is quite a surprise that *he* gave something]

Jonathan GAVE his students chocolate [Jonathan rarely gives people things, though others do, so it is quite a surprise that he *gave* something]

Jonathan gave HIS students chocolate [Jonathan is peculiarly mean to his own students, though he is very generous to other students, so it is quite a surprise that he gave *his* students something]

Jonathan gave his STUdents chocolate [Jonathan doesn't usually give his students things, though he is very generous to other people, so it is quite a surprise that he gave his *students* something]

Jonathan gave his students CHOcolate [For years, Jonathan has given his students fruit, so it is quite a surprise that he gave his students *chocolate*]

Incidentally, in the square brackets we have used italics to do in writing the job of the focal accent in speech and, of course, there are other techniques (e.g. capitals, emboldening, underlining). Also, note that the clause beginning "it is quite a surprise ..." is actually capturing an inference that is made.

It is worth observing that the focal accent can overrule the normal ordering of topic and focus, both semantically and cognitively. This happens in the first case listed above, *JOnathan gave his students chocolate*. Without the focal accent here, *Jonathan* is clearly the topic and the rest of the sentence has end-focus. But with the focal accent it seems to be the other way round. One can think of plausible contexts. Imagine that this sentence follows a discourse on staff giving their students chocolates. In this case, giving students chocolate seems to be what the sentence is about and is old information, that is, it is the topic. The fact that Jonathan actually did it is what is being said about the topic and is new information, that is, it is the focus.

Let us briefly consider a real example. Anne Robinson, the host of the confrontational TV quiz show *The Weakest Link*, is famed for being dismissive and rude. After a round of questions the person who (at least theoretically) got the most answers wrong is voted off and Anne announces the verdict with the words *you are the weakest link*. Figure 3.2 offers a visualisation of her prosody (it is produced with *Praat*, www.praat.org). The first tier represents amplitude, the second the pitch and the third the words she spoke.

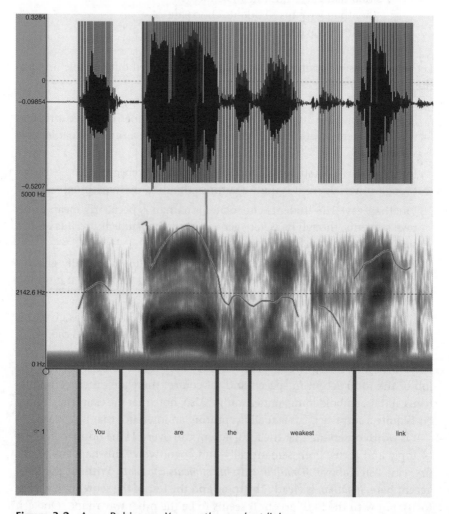

Figure 3.2 Anne Robinson: *You are the weakest link*

It is clear from the peaking of amplitude and pitch that the word *are* carries the focal accent. Its presence here seems to convey the meaning: "despite any indications or protestations you might have given to the contrary, the news is that you most certainly are the weakest link."

Focus and syntactic structures

Deviations from canonical word order can be pragmatic strategies to lend focus, whether cognitive or semantic, to particular elements or to de-focus or topicalise others. Such constructions do not represent a breakdown in the syntax. They are typical of spoken discourse, where they can serve additional functions such as holding the conversational floor and giving the speaker thinking time in which to plan ahead. Here, we will briefly note some constructions (for more detail, see Birner and Ward 1998 and Lambrecht 1994).

Preposed or fronted structures involve constituents you would expect to appear after the verb being placed before, as in the following example:

[3.17] [*Interviewer*] After playing characters in "The Hurt Locker" and "The Town" that are both sort of unpredictable, do you have to be careful to choose different kinds of roles to avoid being type-cast?

[*The actor Jeremy Renner*] I think that's where real life and cinema kind of blend for me. I like to play unpredictable characters, and I like to be unpredictable in what movie I'll do. I want to be – I want to skip to work. I don't want to repeat anything. So yeah, <u>what the future holds, I don't know</u>.

(*The Playlist*, 15 December 11)

The preposed item is the semantic topic, as it is what the clause is about. Usually, the preposed item contains information that is to some degree given (often discourse-old, but at least familiar), leaving the rest of the clause for end-focus. Indeed, *what the future holds* clearly picks up on the interviewer's question – it is old information; the new information is that he does not know what it holds. What is less usual is that the first constitutent is also the longest constituent, thus breeching the maxim of end-weight and fore-grounding the structure against canonical word order norms. What is made salient, then, is the topic. The structure is used to revitalise the earlier topic broached by the interviewer (an expanded version might be: "so yeah, in answer to your question about the kinds of roles I'd be taking on in the future, I don't know").

In **dislocated** structures, the noun phrase immediately to the left or right of the main clause of the sentence co-refers with a pronoun in that clause. The following is an example of **left dislocation** taken from a mountain climbing blog describing a jolly doctor:

[3.18] He [the doctor] shuffles past a Nepalese porter who is lugging nearly 200 pounds on his back up the mountain. The weight looks impossible to bear for more than a few seconds. Yet the young man pauses to observe the doctor. He smiles as if the weight has been lifted off his shoulders.

"That dancing man, he makes me happy," he says.

(http://www.theworldtri.com/archives/5272)

Here, the referent of *dancing man* (i.e. the doctor) has been introduced earlier, as has, before this quotation, the fact that he dances on the way up the mountain. *That dancing man* involves old information and is the topic. *He* co-refers to the same dancing doctor and is thus obviously old information. The remainder contains new information and is the semantic focus. However, in this foregrounded structure, it is the topic that seems to be more salient. The implication seems to be that this topic in particular is worthy of comment. We should also remember that in conversation flagging the topic in this way enables one to hold the conversational floor while formulating the comment one wants to make. Left-dislocated phrases can in fact contain new information, although this is not typical of semantic topics. Consider the first line of this English nursery rhyme: "The three little kittens, they lost their mittens." The notion of the three little kittens is entirely new (of course, the presence of this structure here may be partly to facilitate the rhythm and the rhyme scheme).

With **right dislocation** there is a much stronger requirement that what is referred to in the right-dislocated phrase refers to something that is not only participant-old but also discourse-old. This tallies with the fact that such structures tend to function to clarify the reference of a pronoun in the main clause, as in the following examples (both taken from Biber et al. 1999):

[3.19] That'll be a bit crispy, that bit.
       Oh I reckon they're lovely. I really do whippets.

The right-dislocated phrases do not usually carry the focal accent.

We briefly met cleft sentences in section 3.3.2 (Table 3.1), our example being an it-cleft: *It wasn't me that drove fast*. **Cleft sentences** are complex sentences, where what could have been represented as a simple sentence (e.g. *I didn't drive fast*) is cleft (split) into two clauses. In our it-cleft example the main clause is *It wasn't me* and the subordinate clause is *that drove fast*. It-clefts tend to foreground the new information they carry in the clefted constituent, after the verb "to be". Thus, *me* carries the focus. Conversely, the subordinate clause, *that* *drove fast*, is presupposed, old information and the topic. Compare our it-cleft example with *I didn't drive fast*. Here, *I* is the topic and the rest the focus.

Other functions are possible with cleft sentences. In the following example, the information in both the main clause and the subordinate clause is new; the focus seems to be on the entire sentence:

[3.20]   [The first sentence of a magazine article]
It was about two years ago that Michael Irvin first talked to me about a secret he's carried with him for 30 years.

(*Out* 12 July 2011)

As illustrated by this example, it-clefts often play a role in propelling the narrative.

Focus as contrastive or additive

Contrast is considered an important feature of focus (see especially Chafe 1976), whether semantic or cognitive. In the example above discussed in relation to prosody, the fact that Jonathan gave his students chocolate implicitly involves a contrast both with his usual lack of generosity and with the usual behaviours of others. Of course, such a contrast can be couched in terms of deviation, as articulated in foregrounded theory. There is a contrast with the known regularity of other behaviours. This is more of a cognitive contrast. In the literature on information structure, contrast involving semantic focus is usually taken to involve the contrast of an item with a restricted set of alternatives (see, for example, the special issue on contrast, Repp 2010; also Rooth 1992). Miller (2006: 512) provides a useful list of various types of focus, each with an example:

[3.21]   **Parallel focus**
John and Bill came to see me. John was nice but Bill was boring.
Replacing focus
John brought rice?
No, he brought coffee.
Restricting focus
John brought coffee and rice.
No, he only brought coffee.
Expanding focus
John brought coffee.
Yes, but he also brought rice.
Selecting focus
Would you like coffee or tea?
Coffee, please.

In each case, particular items are highlighted in specific contrastive ways with alternatives in a restricted set made explicit by the previous discourse.

As these examples also illustrate, contrast need not involve diametric opposites. Lambrecht (1994) argues that contrastiveness is a scalar notion, citing in support Bolinger (1961:87):

> In a broad sense, every semantic peak is contrastive. Clearly in *Let's have a picnic*, coming as a suggestion out of the blue, there is no specific contrast with *dinner party*, but there is a contrast with picnicking and anything else the group might do. As the alternatives are narrowed down, we get closer to what we think of as a contrast accent.

The notion of contrastiveness as scalar links to the notion of scalar implicatures, something we will discuss in section 4.3.1.

Focus formulae

The function of some pragmatic/discourse formulae, markers or particles is primarily to direct the hearer's or reader's particular attention to some information, that is, to foreground some information relative to other (we will further discuss how these might work in section 8.3.1). Following Tuggy (1996), here we refer to these generally as **focus formulae**. Sometimes that information may be new, but not necessarily so; the focus formula may be signalling merely that the interpreter should shift their attention. Besides directing attention, focus formulae can signal particular attitudes or help manage the discourse. Note that generally we are much more in the realm of cognitive issues than semantic ones.

There are a large number of formulae in English that communicators deploy to indicate how the reader or hearer should take the upcoming information. These include:

- Note (that) ...
- Consider (that) ...
- It is worth pointing out that ...
- The thing is that ...
- I'll tell you what ...
- I would have thought ...
- Regarding X, ...
- As for X, ...
- You know ...
- You see ...
- I mean ...
- ... not at all.
- ... isn't he/she/it/ etc.?
- Etc.

Reflection: Focus and foregrounding structures in other languages

The ordering of topic and focus structures, or given and new, is very much constrained by the workings of the languages in which they appear. Below we note some cases where other languages differ from English.

- The tendency for given information to precede new seems to apply to Subject-Verb (SV) languages like English. Some languages where the verb comes before the subject (e.g. Arabic, Hebrew, Welsh) have been said to put new before given (see Ward and Birner 2004: 173, footnote 1, for references).
- Prosodic prominence marking focus, as in English, is near universal, but there are a few exceptions. Gundel and Fretheim (2004: 183–184) report that no particular pitch contour encodes topic or focus in Norwegian and give the following example:

[3.22]   FRED spite BØNNENE
          Fred ate the beans
                              (Gundel and Fretheim 2004: 183)

With prosodic prominence (indicated by small capitals) on both the subject and object, one does not know whether the newsworthy statement concerns the fact that Fred did it or that beans were eaten. Instead, one must rely on contextual inferences to work out which.
- Different languages mark topics in different ways. Distinct intonation and word order, as in English, are common. Japanese and Korean topics, however, are morphologically marked (Gundel and Fretheim 2004: 187). In Japanese, for example, topic is often marked with a particle such as (は, -wa).
- Left dislocation plays a more important role in topic-prominent languages, like Chinese or Japanese, where topicalised constituents are placed sentence-initially (Li and Thompson 1976).
- Some languages use special highlighting positions. In Finnish any item at the beginning of the clause other than the subject is highlighted (Miller 2006).

3.5 Informational pragmatics: an interactional perspective

Much as we did in section 2.5, the point of this section is to show how informational packaging is not built on static given information, but is a dynamic, two-way phenomenon shaped in interaction. We will approach this from two perspectives: (1) presuppositions and backgrounding; and (2) informational common grounding.

3.5.1   Presuppositions and backgrounding

The everyday sense of presupposition encourages the view that presuppositions relate to something in the background. Indeed, this seems to be flagged by the etymological elements of the word: *pre-* meaning before, previous or earlier; and *supposition* meaning a hypothesis taken for granted. Lambrecht (1994: 52) emphasises that presuppositions contain old information, while new information is what is asserted by the sentence. Stalnaker (e.g. [1974] 1991), as we saw, not only links presuppositions to background knowledge, but background common knowledge. However, while it is often the case that presuppositions background information in some way, and quite often that background information is common to participants, it is not the case that presuppositions are always restricted in this way. They can be used to foreground information, and new information at that. Although some earlier scholars (e.g. Karttunen 1973; Atlas 1975) recognised the possibility of, what one might call, unpresupposed presuppositions, it has been necessary for later scholars, notably Abbott (2000), to reinforce the message.

As Abbott elaborates, some presuppositional triggers seem geared towards presupposing new information, not old. It-clefts are a case in point. Let's take our example in Table 3.1, *It wasn't me that drove fast*, which presupposes that there is somebody who drove fast. Note that the presupposition appears last in the sentence, it has end-focus, and appears to be part of what is asserted – a feature which we said in section 3.3.2 is not characteristic of presuppositions. Then there are definite NPs. Readers may recollect that in section 2.5.1 we showed how definite NPs, such as those in the Auden poem, were used to fill in a context; their referents were neither old information nor common information. We also demonstrated this in relation to stage directions in plays in the reflection box at the end of section 3.3.2. A more specific case, as noted by Abbott (2000), concerns announcements involving presuppositions triggered by factive verbs such as *regret*, as in: *British rail regrets that the ten o'clock train to Manchester has been cancelled* (see also Lambrecht 1994: 61ff.). What is presupposed is the complement of the factive verb, yet it is clearly unlikely to be old information. Generally, it is not difficult to find examples of factive verbs introducing new information, such as "I realised that he was the cause of the problem." One may wonder whether all these are in fact just exceptional cases. But they are rather more frequent than one might think. Abbott (2000: 1428) reports that Fraurud (1990) found that about 60% of definite NPs in a corpus of Swedish introduced new referents, while only about a third were used anaphorically. She also reports that these findings were confirmed by Poesio and Vieira (1998) investigating English, and that more than half of the definite NPs in that study introducing new referents into the discourse also seemed to involve new information for the hearer. Similarly, Spenader (2002, reported in Andersson 2009: 735), encompassing a wider spectrum of presuppositions, found that 58% of presuppositions in conversation are used to introduce new information, and even to highlight it. The extent to which presuppositions do this, however, is context sensitive.

Let us glance at therapeutic discourse through the work of Andersson. Andersson (2009: 735) found that only 10.6% of presuppositions in therapeutic discourse introduce hearer-new information, but this is not surprising in this context, given that such discourse revolves around limited and familiar issues. Andersson (2009: 724) suggests that in therapeutic discourse presuppositions:

> may serve (from both the patient's and the therapist's perspective) as technical tools whose objective is to maintain the overall continuity of the topic and enhance the discourse flow, but also as rhetorical devices used in order to influence the interlocutor, provide him/her with additional clues, enhance the claim, or, possibly, serve as avoidance or defence strategy.

Consider this example (T is the therapist, P is first initial of the client's name):

[3.23]   T: But what will <u>your life without him</u> look like, I mean ... after divorce?
         P: well ... I haven't told you that we'll get divorced ...

                                                                (Andersson 2009: 732)

In Example [3.23], the definite NP *your life without him* (underlined above) in the therapist's question presupposes that the patient has a life without his/her partner. This is reinforced by the temporal element *after*, presupposing that the divorce has happened. In response, P delivers a dispreferred second, challenging the presupposed information. Clearly, it is controversial. The therapist's strategy here is to use presuppositions to force P to reflect on a particular aspect of a future world. The important general point here is that presuppositions allow the speaker to shape the context – the common ground – that is shared with their interlocutor. It is not simply a matter of presuppositions relying on a context already being shared.

Stalnaker (1991: 474) was aware of the issue: "[a] speaker may act as if certain propositions are part of the common background when he knows that they are not." But Stalnaker downplays it, and his solution, namely that a speaker pretends that the hearer already knows the information, opens up all sorts of knotty problems. As noted by both Abbott (2000: 1425) and Atlas (2004: 45), Paul Grice (1981: 190) alludes to a solution:

> It is quite natural to say to somebody, when we are discussing some concert, *My aunt's cousin went to that concert*, when one knows perfectly well that the person one is talking to is very likely not even to know that one had an aunt, let alone know that one's aunt had a cousin. So the supposition must be not that it is common knowledge but rather that it is noncontroversial, in the sense that it is something that you would expect the hearer to take from you (if he does not already know).

So, rather than whether it is old information or common information, or asserted or not, the issue is whether it is controversial information. Presuppositions could be said to be about noncontroversial information, "a speaker's expectation that an addressee will charitably take the speaker's word" about what is presupposed, rather than "expectations that they have in common the thought" of what is presupposed (Atlas 2004: 46–47). None of the above researchers do much to define the notion of **(non)controversiality**. It has the benefit of being wider than common ground. Information that is part of common ground is not likely to be controversial, but much general background information would be noncontroversial too. Perhaps one way of looking at this is to take noncontroversial information as expectable information, that is, it is consistent with your background knowledge (schemata) and inferences derived therefrom. Further, the above researchers do not suggest how this notion could be operationalised in naturally occurring interactions.

Nevertheless, we would argue that such a notion lends itself well to an interactional perspective. Here, presuppositions are pragmatic tactics with particular interactional and social functions. Our reflection box in section 3.3.2 discussing the exploitation of presuppositions in discourses of power and persuasion is relevant here. In the courtroom discourse example given there, the defendant's interactional response made it clear that she took the information presupposed in the question as highly controversial; she produced a dispreferred second-pair part following a question (i.e. it was not an answer). Importantly, note that in this case, but even more clearly in the case of the advertisements, the strategy on the part of the person producing the presupposition is to dupe the target into accepting the presupposition in some way without noticing – in other words, that they take it as noncontroversial, even though in other circumstances (e.g. after more careful thought) they might take it as highly controversial.

3.5.2   Common grounding

In section 2.5.3, we pointed out that discourse is potentially part of participants' common knowledge. Indeed, it has the potential to be an important part.

All discourse is social in some way. Social actions, whether involving speech or not, do not happen randomly, but are co-ordinated to enable people to achieve their goals (even if the goal is simply to understand the other person). In many languages and cultures greetings may be achieved by reciprocal hand-shakes or "hellos", or information gained by asking questions and receiving answers; both rely on common ground for their success. When you stick out your hand, say *hello* or ask a question, you do so with expectations about how the other person will themselves act (e.g. you expect a reciprocal hand to be proffered, a hello or answer to follow shortly). Of course, there are reflexive assumptions about these expectations: your expectations about what the other expects that you will do, and so on. Moreover, it is not just a matter of co-ordinating actions but co-ordinating understandings. Your understanding of what you meant by an action needs to be co-ordinated with the addressee's understanding of what you meant by that action (and again there are reflexive assumptions about these understandings). Your agenda (a successful greeting, a successful elicitation of information) relies on common ground from which you can derive mutual expectations about the sequencing of actions, the meanings of utterances in certain contexts, and so on. Clark (1996), following Lewis (1969), notes a specific way in which this can be achieved. Behavioural conventions are part of common ground. Conventions such as a handshake, saying *hello* or using a questioning formula are likely to be recognised by the participants in a particular interaction (especially if they belong to the same cultures) and help co-ordinate actions and understandings.

However, as already mentioned in section 2.5.3, discourse does more than rely on common ground for its success, it can itself construct that common ground. Discourse offers the possibility of *sharing* knowledge, as opposed to relying on guesses about knowledge that is likely to be common (perhaps because, for example, certain socio-cultural experiences are assumed to be common). As pointed out by Brown (1995) and Lee (2001), by looking at discourse we gain some insight into how many levels of assumptions people make about common ground *in practice*. Somebody can present new informa-tion, as we might do with an assertion, for example, and, when it receives an acknowledgement, that somebody might reasonably believe that the target knows that information (i.e. it is old information). Moreover, the target might reasonably believe that the speaker now believes that she knows that information – the information has been assimilated into common ground – and the conversation moves on.

Jucker and Smith (1996) make a case for much of language use involving the negotiation of common ground. They point to the array of linguistic features that depend on assessments of (presumed) common ground. For example, all of the following depend on assessments of whether the speaker assumes that the target can provide or access relevant information: making an assertion as opposed to asking a question; tag questions with falling or rising intonation; definite or indefinite forms, the use of proper names or pronouns and the amount of elaboration in a noun phrase (as we noted in Chapter 2); and discourse markers such as *well* or *in fact* (Jucker and Smith 1996: 4–5). Such items are the bread and butter of common grounding. Jucker and Smith make a distinction between the implicit and explicit enhancing of common ground. When asking a question the speaker implicitly assumes that the target may be able to answer it; when using a definite noun phrase or pronoun the speaker implicitly assumes that the target will be able to identify the specific referent; when using the discourse marker *in fact*, the speaker implicitly assumes that what follows is inconsistent with what the target is assumed to know. But there are times when there may be much more explicit negotiation in order to, for example, establish correct reference, negotiate the meanings of key lexical items, negotiate story details or assess assumptions (ibid.: 10–15).

In the remainder of this section, we will examine one particular kind of discourse, emergency telephone calls, which is distinguished by the fact that establishing common ground through discourse is crucial. Shared understandings of what is going on enable the operator to issue accurate advice. But there are real challenges. With telephone calls, participants are visually separated; there is only co-presence of voices. Furthermore, the operator is almost always a complete stranger to the person ringing for help. Intimates, in contrast, have a catalogue of shared experiences on which they can base assumptions. In addition, the person ringing for help is in an extreme situation and, in their distress, are sometimes not thinking through the dynamics of the communication.

Below is a transcript of a phone call made by Rachel Barton[3], in an extremely agitated state, to the emergency telephone operator, when she discovered her house was on fire (audio was available, which enabled intonation to be checked). The transcript begins shortly after her address details have been established.

[3.24]   **Op**   ... Whereabouts are you, upstairs?
         RB   I'm at the front window.
         Op   You're at the front window, right.
         RB   I can't breathe.
         Op   Have you shut the door? Shut the door. Have you shut the door? Shut the door to your room.
         RB   Yeah, I've shut it.

---

[3] Available on *The Guardian* newspaper website (http://www.guardian.co.uk/society/2008/nov/29/unpublished-999-call-transcripts). The data dates from 2008.

Op Have you shut the door to your room, right? Is there smoke coming up the stairs?

RB Yeah, I can't breathe. [Coughing a lot]

Op All right, just stop a minute, calm down. [Sound of sirens in background] Can you put something under the door? Block the door with a pillow or a sheet or something. Across the bottom of the door.

(http://www.guardian.co.uk/society/2008/nov/29/
unpublished-999-call-transcripts)

Note how *the front window* presupposes the existence of a front window. This is discourse-new information, but it is participant-old information. Schematic knowledge of typical housing in the UK can provide relevant elements. Houses usually have front windows. Similarly, the operator can readily assume the existence of a door for the front room (*the door*) and a bottom for the door (*the bottom*). Interestingly, she suggests the use of *a pillow or a sheet*, yet there has been no mention of the fact that this is a bedroom, which would typically have such items. But here again, it can be strongly assumed, on the basis of schematic knowledge about the design of UK houses, that if she is in the upstairs front room, she is in the bedroom, a room that typically contains such items. Much of the operator's discourse seems to be designed to establish common ground with a high degree of certainty. RB's location is crucial, so that the firefighters are directed to the right place. Hence, she repeats the discourse-old information *at the front window*, adding the tag *right* with rising intonation in order to elicit confirmation. Similarly, it is crucial to shut the door to impede the progress of the fire, hence the repetitions and confirmatory tag.

The discourse continues directly thus:

[3.25] **RB** [In background to child] Daniel!

   Op Hello? Hello?

   RB Daniel!

   Op Hello?

   RB Hello.

   Op Listen to me, will you listen to me, I'm still ... Have you got your little boy?

   RB Yeah, I've got him now.

(http://www.guardian.co.uk/society/2008/nov/29/
unpublished-999-call-transcripts)

In the first turn, RB uses the proper noun *Daniel*. Hitherto, there has been no mention of this person nor any reason to suppose that the operator knows of his existence, this is both discourse-new and participant-new for the operator.

Yet the information appears in the guise of an existential presupposition. Of course, we should stress the fact that the addressee is Daniel, for whom the information is clearly not new. Nevertheless, the operator can infer the existence in this context of a person called Daniel. Interestingly, the operator also infers that Daniel is a *little boy* and specifically RB's *little boy* (*your little boy*). We do not hear Daniel at all. It is possible that the assumption is made on the basis of schematic assumptions about family groupings, along with, possibly, gender-based schematic assumptions – Daniel denotes a male person; if there was an adult male in the room, such as a husband, they might be assumed to be participating in the emergency call.

After a few more turns, the discourse continues:

[3.26]   **Op**   Right, right, you're all right. Just stay where you are by the window.

         RB   [Hysterical] It's coming in the window now!

         Op   No, just stop, you're all right. They're on their way to you. We'll be with you any second. Just stop where you are. All right. You're all right. You're all right.

         RB   Yeah.

         Op   You're all right. And your little boy's with you?

         RB   I can't breathe, I'm an asthmatic.

                             (http://www.guardian.co.uk/society/2008/nov/29/
unpublished-999-call-transcripts)

RB's first turn here begins *it*, but the referent of this pronoun is not obvious. Presumably it is the smoke (it is not clear whether the window is yet open), though it could be fire. Whichever, the lack of planning regarding what is common ground with the operator can be explained by her highly distressed state. We might compare this with the operator's *they're on their way to you*, in which the referent of *they*, the Fire Brigade, has been established repeatedly in the discourse and is also inferable on the basis of our schematic knowledge about fires and emergencies in the UK, not to mention the sound of sirens, which can be heard by RB and the operator. Although we see something of the operator's previous strategy of confirming common ground (e.g. *and your little boy's with you*, with rising intonation), these turns are dominated by a different strategy. *You're all right* is repeated five times (and also partially with *all right*), all with falling intonation. The point of the parallelism is to make salient the new and certainly controversial information, namely, that she is really all right. Similarly, we see repetition in *just stop*. *Stop* is a change-of-state verb which presupposes that RB has started to move away from the window, something that would obviously make her less accessible to the rescue efforts of the firefighters. The operator does not in fact know that this is the case, but it can be assumed on the basis of schematic knowledge about people's reactions to danger (they move away from it) and where RB is assumed to be (i.e. close to the window) in the current context which the operator has presumably constructed in her head. RB also uses the foregrounding strategy of parallelism. The two parallel syntactic structures (two juxtaposed clauses, each with the same number of words and beginning with "I" followed by a verbal element) invite interpretation: the reason she cannot breathe is because she is asthmatic.

This analysis, then, illustrates how common ground is far from given. It is built up incrementally, partly through utterance design, but also partly through assumed background information from which various inferences can be made.

3.6   Conclusion

This chapter has been focused on informational pragmatics, how we package and organise information, largely within the scope of the sentence. We introduced the concepts of figure and ground as a springboard into the various notions introduced in this chapter – the distinction between cognitive givenness/newness and semantic givenness/newness, for example – that involve some elements being in the background and others in the foreground. We approached the notion of backgrounded information through schema theory and related this to associative inferencing in particular. Amongst other things, we briefly noted how schemata can account for culturally varied understandings. We then examined presuppositions, broadly speaking, background assumptions conventionally associated with linguistic expressions. In particular, we looked at presupposition triggers, noting how these varied across languages (e.g. some languages have far richer aspectual systems than English, which can have implications for change-of-state presuppositions). We also dwelt on some of the functions and contexts of naturally occurring presuppositions. We approached the notion of foregrounded information through foregrounding theory, a theory that articulates general principles about how some elements are made more cognitively salient compared with others. We then went on to consider focus, a notion discussed on the pragmatics-grammar border and which can be considered in terms of either semantic newness, cognitive newness or salience. More specifically, we discussed the placing of focus (cf. end-focus), prosodic prominence, semantic contrasts, non-canonical syntactic structures and focus formulae. We noted how focus is achieved differently in different languages.

In our final section, we cast some aspects of the previous discussion in a different light. In the first subsection, we noted how presuppositions could be used to assert new information. Something that seems to run counter to how they have sometimes been defined. We suggested that one way of conceiving how presuppositions relate to information is in terms of that information's (non)controversiality. We also returned to the notion of common ground, a subset of background assumptions. Rather than looking at how discourse might rely on common ground for generating its full meaning, we considered how discourse can actively shape common ground itself. As in the previous chapter, in this final section we observed meanings in interaction, dynamic and emergent, and both shaping and being shaped by language.

It is worth contemplating that pragmatics books, especially textbooks, have largely overlooked the kinds of things we have discussed in this chapter. Thomas (1995) contains none of them; Leech (1983) merely the mention of some broad principles; Levinson (1983) an exclusive focus on presuppositions. Perhaps part of the problem is that they are not viewed as truly pragmatic. We hope to have demonstrated that these phenomena, like those of Chapter 2, have a full role to play in pragmatics and, notably, integrative pragmatics.

4 Pragmatic Meaning I

4.1 Meaning beyond what is said

In the previous chapter we mainly focused on information and how it is packaged as more or less prominent within sentences. In this chapter and the one that follows we move on to consider another key area of interest in pragmatics, namely, how we can mean much more than we say or express. We also start to move beyond a focus on sentence-level to a consideration of meaning as it arises in talk exchanges.

Consider example [4.1] from the comic strip *Peanuts*.

[4.1]

(*Peanuts* © 1965 Peanuts Worldwide LLC. Distributed by UNIVERSAL
UCLICK. Reprinted with permission. All rights reserved.)

While Lucy responds with just one word here, it is clear that she means something else in addition to what she has said. More specifically, she implies that she doesn't want Charlie Brown to shovel her walk (evident from the fact that she closes the door and so does not take up his offer), and perhaps also that Charlie Brown is somehow unsuitable for the task. The latter implication is in part indeterminate in that we do not know for what reason Lucy thinks Charlie Brown is unsuitable for shovelling snow (e.g. he is too weak, too incompetent, unlikely to finish and so on) and, moreover, just how certain she is about this evaluation. But it seems fair to say that Lucy has indeed meant something beyond what she has said here, namely, some kind of negative evaluation of Charlie Brown's suitability for the task, and a refusal of his offer. We know this intuitively because her answer invites an inference in order to count as an adequate answer to Charlie Brown's question, and also because we know (if we read *Peanuts* comics) that Lucy is always putting Charlie Brown down, and her behaviour here is consistent with that. The former involves some form of pragmatic inferencing in order to figure out what counts as an adequate answer, while the latter arises through the kind of knowledge-based associative inferencing we briefly discussed in the previous chapter in section 3.3.1. Pragmatic meaning thus involves content that is not straightforwardly expressed by the words someone utters but rather arises through some kind of inferencing, and so can be broadly characterised as meaning beyond what is said.[1]

In pragmatics, just as in semantics, we generally conceptualise such meanings in terms of cognitive **representations**. A representation is essentially a generalised meaning form or interpretation that we find displayed in or through natural language constructions. Meaning representations are important because they are usually held to have considerable theoretical significance. An important foundational claim in pragmatics made by H. P. Grice (1967, 1989), a British-educated philosopher of language, is that meanings like the ones above, which go beyond what is said, can be broadly classified as speaker-intended **implicatures**, that is, meanings that are *implied* or *suggested* rather than *said*. He further proposed that **what is implicated**, either by a speaker or an utterance, can be contrasted with **what is said**. This distinction between what is implicated (cf. *implying*) and what is said (cf. *saying*) lies at the core of almost all of the subsequent attempts at theorising about meaning representations in pragmatics, even those which have moved radically beyond it. We will thus start here by outlining Grice's claims in more detail, before turning, in the latter sections, to the more fine-grained distinctions of pragmatic meaning that have since been proposed.

4.2   What is said versus what is implicated

Grice proposed a formal framework by which speakers make implicatures available to hearers. Underpinning this distinction and framework were Grice's claims about meaning as speaker-intended. We will thus start in section 4.2.1 by outlining how Grice theorised meaning as tied to a particular

---

[1] The same applies to written discourse. For the sake of exposition we will use the terms speaker/hearer in this chapter. While speaker/hearer may appear to be largely interchangeable with writer/reader, additional complications arise when one considers the various kinds of user perspectives on pragmatic meaning, as we shall see later in Chapter 5.

kind of intention on the part of the speaker. We then move to introduce, in section 4.2.2, Grice's account of implicature in more detail.

4.2.1   Grice on speaker meaning

Grice was interested in a particular kind of meaning, namely, meaning that was neither "natural" nor purely "conventional" in nature, as one of his primary goals was to better understand how it is that speakers can mean something. He first clarified that the sense of *meaning* he was interested in differed from **natural meaning**, which is defined as instances where a certain sign is causally related to an event or concept (e.g. "Those clouds *mean* rain"). He then proposed that **non-natural meaning** (meaning$_{nn}$) includes, but is not exhausted by, linguistic (or word) meaning, where the latter is defined as signs that are conventionally related to a concept (e.g. "dog" in English *means* an animal which normally has four legs, a tail, barks and so on). Instead, he proposed that **meaning$_{nn}$** arises through the speaker having a specific kind of meaning intention. He defined this kind of complex intention in the following way (where "A" refers to the speaker and *x* refers to the utterance):

'A meant$_{nn}$ something by *x*' is (roughly) equivalent to 'Auttered *x* with the intention to produce some effect in an audience by means of the recognition of this intention.' (Grice [1957] 1989: 220)

This definition of intention, while complex, is critical for us to understand as it underpins much, if not most, of the theorising of pragmatic meaning representations to date. The essential idea is that a speaker means something by intending that the hearer recognise what is meant as intended by the speaker. What is meant is generally that the speaker has a particular belief, thought, desire, attitude, intention and so on. In other words, meaning$_{nn}$ necessarily involves the speaker thinking about what hearers will think he or she is thinking. This complex intention was further broken down into three levels by Grice (where "U" refers to the utterer, *x* refers to the utterance, and "A" refers to the audience):

"U meant something by uttering x" is true iff [if and only if], for some audience A, U uttered *x* intending:
(1) A to produce a particular response *r*
(2) A to think (recognize) that U intends (1)
(3) A to fulfil (1) on the basis of his fulfilment of (2). (Grice [1969]1989: 92)

Intention (1) is a first-order intention to produce a particular response in the hearer, which is embedded in a second-order intention (2) that the hearer recognise this first-order intention, which is further embedded in a third-order intention (3) that the hearer have this response on the basis of recognising the speaker's second-order intention.

As all this is somewhat hard to follow in the abstract, we will apply it here to a concrete instance of language use. Let us return to example [4.1] from *Peanuts* (the dialogue is extracted here as [4.2]):

[4.2]   Charlie Brown: Shovel your walk?
        Lucy: You?
        Charlie Brown: I never know how to answer those one-word
                     questions...

                     (*Peanuts* © 1965 Peanuts Worldwide LLC.)

Here Lucy could be said to be (speaker) meaning$_{nn}$ through uttering *You?* that she thinks Charlie Brown is somehow unsuitable for shovelling the snow outside her house by intending:

(1) Charlie Brown to think that Lucy has a certain belief, namely, she thinks he is somehow unsuitable for shovelling her walk;
(2) Charlie Brown to recognise that Lucy intends him to think that she has this belief;
(3) Charlie Brown to think that Lucy has this belief because he recognises that she intended him to think that (she has this belief).

A number of scholars have claimed that the above third-order intention is unnecessary for defining speaker meaning (Bara 2010; Searle 2007). Indeed, one might argue that the last kind of intention raises the question of whether Grice's notion of meaning$_{nn}$ is an abstract, theoretical notion of speaker meaning, or is something that is taken to actually arise in communication. At this point, however, the take-home message is that, following Grice, pragmatic meaning representations are generally understood as the speaker's reflexively intended mental state. In other words, a speaker's belief, thought, desire, attitude, intention and so on, which is intended by the speaker to be recognised by the hearer as intended.

Grice divided his notion of meaning$_{nn}$ or speaker meaning into two broad types of representation: what is said and what is implicated. He proposed that what is said can be traced to a certain understanding of *saying* involving meaning that is "closely related to the conventional meaning of the words (the sentence) [the speaker] has uttered" (Grice [1975]1989: 25). He elaborated this further in claiming that what is said is closely related to "the particular meanings of the elements of S [sentence], their order, and their syntactical character" (ibid.: 87). In other words, for Grice, what is said is **compositional**, as it arises through a combinatorial understanding of word meaning, syntax, and processes of reference assignment, indexical resolution and disambiguation (the latter referring to both different senses of words and different possible syntactic structures).

To illustrate what Grice meant by what said, let us recall Charlie Brown's offer to Lucy to clean up the snow on the path leading to her house.

[4.3]   Charlie Brown: Shovel your walk?

(*Peanuts* © 1965 Peanuts Worldwide LLC.)

In order to understand what is said by Charlie Brown, we need to work out the underlying syntactic structure of his utterance (i.e. *shovel* is a verb referring to a particular type of action, and *your walk* is a noun phrase, namely, the object of that action), the referent of *your* (i.e. the second person pronoun refers to Lucy), and disambiguate what sense of *walk* is meant here (i.e. it refers to a path not the action of walking) amongst other things. However, if you recall we have already largely discussed such processes in Chapter 2 (especially section 2.5), and so will not consider them further here.

Grice's account of what is said was arguably not very well developed, as he left it as primarily a matter for semantics to deal with. Instead, his primary focus was the second main type of meaning representation that he had proposed, namely, what is implicated. We will be returning to the issue of whether what is said really is just a semantic notion, as assumed by Grice, in section 4.3. However, before doing so we move to consider Grice's notion of what is implicated in more detail.

Reflection: On *saying*

One key question facing the Gricean notion of what is said is just how literal Grice envisaged it to be. Consider the following excerpt from the movie *Chicken Little*:

[4.4]   Mob leader: Chicken Little, you better have a good explanation for this.

Chicken Little: There's, there's, it's a, you have to, d'oh, doo wah.

Mob leader: What did he say?

Mayor: There's, it's a, you have to, d'oh, doo wah.

(*Chicken Little*, 2005, director: Mark Dindal, writers: Steve Bencich, Ron J. Friedman & Ron Anderson)

Here Chicken Little is responding to an accusation about the chaos he has caused by (falsely) raising an alarm that the sky is falling. His response is nonsensical, but that doesn't stop the mayor repeating back verbatim what Chicken Little has *said* when asked by the mob leader. A number of scholars have noted that *saying* in English encompasses at least two different senses (Bach 2001, 2012; Burton-Roberts 2010):

saying$_1$: act of *uttering* something
saying$_2$: act of *meaning* something

In the example above, the mayor interprets *say* as the act of uttering (say$_1$). We might have expected, however, that the mayor would interpret this as asking about what Chicken Little had meant (say$_2$) through his prior utterance.

Both the first and second senses of *say* are important for the analysis of pragmatic meaning from the perspective of users of English (see Bach 2012, for further discussion). A question that is not often considered, however, is whether such distinctions, which are commonly made in English, are as equally useful for examining pragmatic meaning in other languages (at least in the sense of being intuitively accessible to speakers of that language).

4.2.2   Implicated meaning

Grice proposed that meaning$_{nn}$ that goes beyond what is said comes under the scope of what is implied by the speaker. He coined the terms **implicate** and **implicature** to distinguish them from the way in which *imply* and *implication* can be used in logic and semantics. The word *imply* has two key senses:

[a] To involve or comprise as a necessary logical consequence.
[b] To express indirectly; to insinuate, hint at.

(Oxford English Dictionary Online 2011)

An implicature (which arises from implicating) is meant to exclude the first sense of *imply*, and to be limited to the second sense of "expressing indirectly", "insinuating" or "hinting at". The verb *implicate* was used as a cover term for various meaning-actions, including *implying, suggesting, meaning* (Grice [1975] 1989: 24), to which we might add *hinting, insinuating, intimating, indicating, alluding (to), inferring* and so on. In other words, what is implicated can arise through a variety of different meaning-actions, not all of which are necessarily equivalent. In this sense, Grice's notion of implicature is derived very much from natural language concepts, more specifically, the concepts of *implying* and *suggesting* in English. While the notion of implicature is not generally well-defined for that reason, it is generally agreed that it broadly encompasses something that is meant *in addition* to what is said (Haugh 2002), or meaning one thing *by* meaning (i.e. saying$_2$) another (Davis 1998). Implicated meanings can thus be distinguished from idiomatic or formulaic meanings as the latter are meant *instead* of what is literally said (Bach 2012; Haugh 2002).

Consider the following two examples from *The Simpsons*.

[4.5]   (Homer is in hospital waiting for an operation)
    Moe: Homer, I snuck you in a beer for old times sake.
           (Homer skulls the beer)
    Moe: You know, Homer, that beer ain't free.
           ("Homer's triple bypass", *The Simpsons*, Season 4, Episode 11,
           17 December 1992, director: David Silverman, writers:
           Gary Apple & Michael Carrington)
[4.6]   (Barney is giving Homer a tip on a winning bet at the dog races)
    Homer: Hey Barney, which one is Whirlwind?
    Barney: Number six. That's our lucky dog right over there. He won
           the last five races.
    Homer: What, that scrawny little bag of bones?
    Bart: Come on Dad, they're all scrawny little bags of bones.
           ("Simpsons roasting on an open fire", *The Simpsons*,
           Season 1, Episode 8, 17 December 1989, director:
           David Silverman, writer: Mimi Pond)

In example [4.5], Moe implies that Homer is going to have to pay for the beer by saying *That beer ain't free*, despite his prior offer of the beer being for *old times sake*. What is implied here, or implicated, in Grice's terms, is meant in addition to what Moe has said. In other words, Moe means both that the beer isn't free (what is said) and that Homer is going to have to pay for it (what is implicated). The fact that Homer rapidly drinks the beer (i.e. *skulls* it) is perhaps what alerts Moe to the possibility that Homer has assumed the beer was a gift from Moe (and thus free). In example [4.6], on the other hand, Homer describes the dog on which Barney is advising him to place a bet as a *bag of bones*. Clearly, Homer does not literally mean that the dog is a bag of bones, but rather that it is an extremely skinny animal with its bones showing. The latter is thus meant instead of what is said by Homer (and Bart) here. It counts as an instance of idiomatic or formulaic meaning rather than an implicature.

Reflection: On understandings of implication – implicature versus entailment

One sense of implication in English is something that necessarily follows as a logical consequence of some event or matter. Natural language representations can thus have **logical properties**, that is, the ability to act as input into logical inference rules and to enter into entailment or contradiction relations. For example, one *logical implication* of the statement that *John drinks whisky* (*p*) is that *John drinks alcohol* (*q*). This is termed an **entailment**, which is defined as a semantic relation between two propositions (*p* and *q*) where *p* entails *q* if and only if the truth of *p* guarantees the truth of *q* (Levinson 1983). In other words, if it is true that John drinks whisky then it must be true that he drinks alcohol. A second sense of *implication* in English is something that is expressed indirectly rather than said. For example, if someone asks me *Does John drink whisky?*, and I respond *He doesn't drink any alcohol*, I implicate (but do not say₁) that *John doesn't drink whisky*. However, while these two senses are formally separated into the notions of entailment (in logic and semantics) and implicature (in pragmatics) they are not always easy to keep apart in practice. In the example above, what is implicated is also entailed (i.e. *John doesn't drink whisky* is a necessary, logical consequence of the claim that *John doesn't drink any alcohol*). However, such entailments can be "removed" through the addition of further contextual information. For example, if I add *except for the odd tot of whisky* to my prior statement, *He doesn't drink any alcohol*, the *implication* (and thus implicature) that *John doesn't drink whisky* does not arise, and the entailment is thus removed (Haugh 2013b). Thus, while implicatures may have logical properties, it is important to distinguish between folk or pseudo-logical analyses of meaning (in pragmatics), and formal logical analyses of meaning (in semantics). The latter are constrained by a strictly defined and fixed set of assumptions, while the former are not.

What is implicated was further divided into those that are conventionally implicated and those are that are non-conventionally implicated, with conversational implicatures constituting a subset of the latter (Grice [1975]1989: 25–26). This resulted in three main representations within the category of what is implicated:

1. conventional implicature
2. conversational implicature
3. non-conventional, non-conversational implicature

Grice had little to say about non-conventional non-conversational implicatures, although he suggested in passing that these might encompass other dimensions of pragmatic meaning, such as politeness (ibid.: 28) or irony (ibid.: 53). This line of thought was developed in much more detail by Leech (1983), as we discuss further in Chapter 7 (section 7.2.2). In the remainder of this section we therefore first focus briefly on the first two types of implicature.

Conventional implicatures

Grice actually spent little time discussing **conventional implicatures**, which he characterised as being implicated by particular words or expressions such as *but* or *even*, rather than being part of their **truth-conditional content** (Grice [1975]1989: 25). What Grice meant in claiming conventional implicatures are not part of the truth-conditional content arising from an utterance was that such expressions are not straightforwardly truth-evaluable, that is, they cannot be evaluated against real-world conditions, and so the meaning representation in question properly belongs to the speaker. For example, if someone claims *the weather today is sunny but cold*, then he or she is committed to two distinct claims that can be evaluated against real-world conditions, that is, (1) it is sunny as opposed to cloudy or raining, and (2) the temperature is (relatively) cold as opposed to warm or hot. The additional claim that these two conditions (i.e. the weather today being sunny and cold) somehow contrast with each other, however, is not truth-evaluable against real-world conditions, but rather constitutes a stance taken by the speaker. For this reason, Grice treated this sense of contrast indicated through *but* as a conventional implicature rather than part of what is said.

The notion of conventional implicature has been relatively neglected in pragmatics (although see Levinson 1979b; Potts 2005), and has even been criticised as theoretically superfluous or unnecessary (Bach 1999; Wilson and Sperber 1993). However, an examination of examples of conventional implicatures in discourse points to the pivotal role they can play in interaction. Consider the following example from the novel *High Fidelity* (which is here reformatted like a film script):

[4.7] (Rob is desperate to find out whether his ex-girlfriend, Laura, has slept with Ian)
Rob: Is it better?
Laura: Is what better?
Rob: Well. Sex, I guess. Is sex with him better?
Laura: Jesus Christ, Rob. Is that really what's bothering you?
Rob: Of course it is.
Laura: You really think it would make a difference either way?
Rob: I don't know.
Laura: Well, the answer is that I don't know either. We haven't done it yet.
(Nick Hornby, *High Fidelity*, 1995: 95)

It is the word *yet* here that turns out to be critical in Rob's view. He takes it as *meaning* that Laura is planning to sleep with Ian, as we can see from the following excerpt.

[4.8] This business about not sleeping with Ian ... she only said she hasn't slept with him *yet*, and that was on Saturday, five days ago. Five days! She could have slept five times since then! (She could have slept with him twenty times since then, but you know what I mean). And even if she hasn't, she was definitely threatening to. What does "yet" mean, after all? "I haven't seen *Reservoir Dogs* yet." What does that mean? It means you're going to go, doesn't it?

(Nick Hornby, *High Fidelity*, 1995: 95)

Rob's gloss on *yet* is that it means some action which has not occurred is nevertheless likely to occur at some point in the future. While Rob is evidently rather paranoid about the sexual activities of his ex-girlfriend, it is also clear that *yet* here raises the distinct possibility that an event or activity which has not occurred is likely to occur in the future. Rob takes this further in interpreting this as a threat on the part of Laura that she expects she will sleep with Ian (sooner or later). Strictly speaking this possibility does not lie within the truth-conditional content of Laura's utterance (i.e. it does not affect the evaluation of this utterance as true against real-world conditions), yet without the occurrence of this word Rob could not have legitimately interpreted Laura's response as suggesting she has such plans or expectations. What is interesting here is that conventional implicatures often index particular mental states or stances on the part of the speaker vis-à-vis the hearer, a point which we noted earlier in relation to what we termed focus formulae (see section 3.4.2), and to which we will return to consider again in Chapter 8. However, for the moment, it is to conversational implicatures that we will turn, as it is these that have stimulated by far the most attention in accounts of pragmatic meaning.

Conversational implicatures

Grice introduced the notion of **conversational implicature** to refer to representations of what is implicated that arise in a principled way, namely, with reference to the **Cooperative Principle**, which was formulated as follows:

Make your conversational contribution such as is required, at the stage at which it occurs, by the accepted purpose or direction of the talk exchange in which you are engaged (Grice [1975]1989: 26).

The notion of cooperation proposed by Grice was a technical one that attempted to encompass the expectations we normally have when engaging in talk about the kinds of things people will say, how they will say things, how specific we need to be, the order in which things are said, and so on. These expectations change depending on the kind of talk involved. Consequently, the notion of cooperation has to be fleshed out with reference to the activity type of the "talk exchange" in question (Mooney 2004). An activity type is essentially a culturally recognised activity such as intimate talk, family dinner-table conversation, problem sharing, small talk, joke telling and so on (see section 6.6.3 for further discussion). The Cooperative Principle should not be confused with *cooperative* in the folk sense of jointly engaging in an activity with a particular common purpose in mind, although it often has been, as Davies (2007) points out.

The Cooperative Principle was further elaborated through the four **conversational maxims**:

Maxim of **quality**
Try to make your contribution one that is true, and specifically:
- Do not say what you believe to be false.
- Do not say that for which you lack adequate evidence.

Maxim of **quantity**
- Make your contribution as informative as is required for the current purposes of the exchange.
- Do not make your contribution more informative than is required.

Maxim of **relevance**
Make your contribution relevant.

Maxim of **manner**
Be perspicuous, and specifically:
- Avoid obscurity.
- Avoid ambiguity.
- Be brief.
- Be orderly.

(Grice [1975]1989: 26–27)

The idea is that the speaker makes available a conversational implicature through the expectation that he or she is observing the Cooperative Principle at a deeper level, and so not observing a specific conversational maxim in relation to the surface meaning of that utterance gives rise to a conversational implicature in maintaining that assumption. In other words, a conversational implicature arises because the speaker believes that such a meaning representation is required to make his or her utterance consistent with the Cooperative Principle.

A few examples will suffice here to illustrate the general mechanism by which speakers can implicate conversational implicatures by means of exploiting (or what Grice termed "flouting") the various conversational maxims. In [4.9], Grampa implicates that he doesn't want to talk to Homer and that he doesn't accept Homer's apology by flouting the Quality$_1$ maxim ("do not say what you believe to be false").

[4.9]   (Homer and his father are talking at Bea's funeral after Grampa missed saying goodbye to Bea because of Homer)
Homer: I can't tell you how sorry I am, Dad.
Grampa: Is someone talking to me? I didn't hear anything.
Homer: Oh no! Dad's lost his hearing!

("Old Money", *The Simpsons*, Season 2,
Episode 17, 28 March 1991, director: David Silverman,
writers: Jay Cogen & Wallace Wolodarsky)

It is quite evident that Grampa can hear what Homer is saying (although Homer apparently thinks otherwise). In order to maintain the supposition that Grampa is observing the Cooperative Principle, then, something must be implicated, a point that is strengthened by Grampa pointedly saying something he obviously doesn't believe to be true. In flouting the Quality$_1$ maxim by pretending he can't hear Homer's apology, he thereby implicates that he doesn't want to listen to Homer.

In the course of this next conversation, example [4.10], the two characters reach a consensus that it is not worth going for their appointment for marriage counselling with Dr Wexler:

[4.10]   (Jane and John are getting marriage counselling from Dr. Wexler)
Jane: So what d'you think of Dr. Wexler?
John: He seems very nice.
Jane: Very nice. Nice manner.
John: Very nice manner. Are his questions a tad wishy washy?
Jane: His office is clean across town.
John: The 4pm appointment means we hit rush-hour...
Jane: Good. That's settled then.

(*Mr and Mrs Smith*, 2005,
director: Doug Liman, writer: Simon Kinberg)

This decision is reached through a series of conversational implicatures. John and Jane both implicate that Dr. Wexler is boring or unhelpful (and thus sessions with him are boring and unhelpful) by flouting the Quantity$_1$ maxim ("make your contribution as informative as required"), since saying a professional counsellor is "nice" and has a "nice manner" is clearly not very informative. In order to maintain the supposition that John and Jane are observing the Cooperative

Principle, then, something else must be implicated here. What isn't said here is that Dr. Wexler is interesting or helpful (i.e. characteristics of a "good" counsellor), which leads us to what is implicated, namely, that Dr. Wexler is uninteresting and unhelpful, and thus so are their sessions with him. They then invoke the Relevance maxim ("make your contribution relevant") to implicate that there are other reasons for not going to the appointment, including the fact that it is a long way to his office from their home, and that they would have to drive through very busy traffic to make it in time for the appointment. While it is never said (cf. "Good. That's settled then"), it is clear by the end of the conversation that they have decided to miss their appointment.

Reflection: Cooperation and "not-jokes" in American English

We noted earlier that what counts as cooperation in applying the Cooperative Principle depends on the type of activity or talk the participants are engaging in. To engage in joke telling, for instance, requires the contextualisation of conversation maxims relative to the genre of joke telling. This genre involves a set of normative expectations that flesh out the Cooperative Principle and maxims in the form of a particular activity type (see section 6.3.3). Take the much maligned subcategory of "not-jokes", for instance, which originated amongst speakers of American English. This involves the speaker first violating the quality maxim by asserting something which he or she is seemingly committed to, and then explicitly signalling he or she has violated it by uttering "not". In this way, the speaker makes explicit that he or she is being sarcastic and also implicates that the hearer (or possibly a third party) is someone who is gullible or easily misled.

There are particular expectations, however, about the timing and intonation with which *not* is delivered for an utterance to count as a not-joke. Consider the following exchange between Borat (a satirical character allegedly from Kazakhstan) and a humour coach in the US.

[4.11]　Borat:　what is a <u>no</u>:t jokes?
　　　　 Pat:　　a not joke is when we're trying to make fun of something, and what we do is we make a statement, that we pretend is true but at the end, we say <u>NO::t</u>, which means it's not true.
　　　　 Borat:　so teach me how to make one.
　　　　 Pat:　　okay, so a not joke is- I would say, that suit is black (0.2) <u>NO::t</u>!
　　　　 Borat:　this a suit is <u>NO::t</u> <u>BLA::ck</u>.
　　　　 Pat:　　No no, not has to be at the end.
　　　　 Borat:　o::kay.

Pat: okay.

Borat: this suit is black not.

Pat: this suit is black. (0.3) <u>Pa</u>:use. You know what a pause is?

Borat: ye:s.

Pat: this suit is black. (0.2) <u>NO</u>::t.

Borat: this suit is black, pause, <u>not</u>.

Pat: .hhhh No y- y- you don't say pause. This suit is black (1.5) That's a pause. <u>NO</u>::t.

Borat: this suit is black.
        (2.5)

Pat: okayhhh .hhhh U::m I- I don't I don't I'm [(not quite-)

Borat: [<u>NO</u>::t.

> (*Borat: Cultural Learnings of America for Make Benefit Glorious Nation of Kazakhstan*, 2006, director: Larry Charles, writers: Sacha Baron Cohen, Anthony Hines, Peter Baynham & Dan Mazer)

In order to make the assertion *This suit is black* to subsequently count as initiating a not-joke rather than being simply a lie or mistaken observation on the part of the speaker, the speaker needs to indicate or signal that the "accepted purpose or direction of the talk exchange" here is to engage in a specific kind of joke telling. This is achieved through delivering the subsequent *not* with a particular intonation (i.e. with a markedly louder volume and elongation of the vowel sound) and after a "beat" of the conversation has passed (i.e. a pause of approximately 0.2 of a second). In the context of a not-joke, this is what it means to "make your conversational contribution such as is required, at the stage at which it occurs".

When a speaker **flouts** a conversational maxim, as in the above examples, it is done in a way that makes the non-observance of the maxim recognisable to others in normal circumstances by blatantly failing to fulfil it (Grice [1975]1989: 49). However, Grice proposed that conversational implicatures can be made available through other ways of not observing the conversational maxims. A number of different frameworks for categorising different types of non-observance of maxims have been proposed (see, for example, Greenall 2009; Mooney 2004; Thomas 1995), but we will concentrate here on just two of the most important types, namely, **violating** and **infringing** the conversational maxims.

Violating a maxim involves deliberate non-observance by the speaker of a maxim in a way that would not be recognisable to others in normal circumstances. In the following example, Rich implicates through his response that he graduated with a degree in maths from Edinburgh University.

[4.12]   (Rich is applying for a job teaching English in a Chinese school. The main qualification for the job is being a native speaker of English, but the Principal also asks about Rich's higher education.)
Principal: What did you study at university?
Rich: I studied maths at Edinburgh University in Scotland.
(Personal communication from a
British undergraduate)

This follows from the Quantity$_2$ maxim ("do not make your contribution more informative than is required") through standard inferences that follow from what is simply described here by Rich in order to maintain the supposition that he is observing the Cooperative Principle. However, Rich does not mention that he left Edinburgh after his first year of study, and so this constitutes a (deliberate) violation of the Quality$_1$ maxim. Violations of maxims thus always involve the speaker intending to mislead others or even lying (Mooney 2004: 914). This intention is a covert one, however, and so differs from the Gricean or communicative intention that we discussed in the previous section (4.2.1).

Infringing a maxim involves unintentional or non-deliberate non-observance of a maxim, which may or may not be recognisable to others. This type of non-observance seems to have been coined in Thomas (1995). In example [4.13], taken from the film *"Four Weddings and a Funeral"*, Charles assumes, incorrectly as it turns out, that John has broken up with his girlfriend.

[4.13]   (Charles is making conversation with a friend at a wedding reception)
Charles: How's that gorgeous girlfriend of yours?
John: She's no longer my girlfriend.
Charles: Oh, dear. I wouldn't get too gloomy about it. Rumour has it she never stopped bonking old Toby de Lisle in case you didn't work it out.
John: She is now my wife.
(pause)
Charles: Excellent, well ah…excellent, congratulations.
(*Four Weddings and a Funeral*, 1994,
director: Mike Newell, writer: Richard Curtis)

His attempt at comforting John by telling him that his girlfriend was sleeping with someone else, thereby implicating that she's not "worth" getting depressed about backfires spectacularly when John announces that he actually got married to the girl. Charles's assumption is based on an implicature that arises due to John (perhaps unintentionally) infringing the Manner$_1$

maxim ("avoid obscurity"). Charles takes John to be implicating through his ambiguous response that he doesn't want to talk about the girl, leading to the unfounded assumption that they have broken up. Thomas (1995: 74) notes that speakers who have an imperfect command of the language (e.g. children), impaired performance (e.g. they are drunk) or some cognitive impairment may be predisposed towards infringements.

Differentiating between these different types of non-observance can be difficult in practice, however, since they rely in part on recognising the *intentions* of the speaker, which are not necessarily always clear to others (or even to the speakers themselves). Distinguishing between flouting, violating and infringing maxims thus leads us beyond Grice's primary focus on what the speaker intended to a consideration of the recognition or reconstruction of the speaker's intentions by the hearer (see section 5.3.1).[2]

Generalised versus particularised conversational implicatures

Another key claim made by Grice was that conversational implicatures may be made available through one-off reasoning in a particular context by the speaker, which gives rise to **particularised conversational implicature**, or through regularised or conventionalised reasoning, which gives rise to **generalised conversational implicature**. To put it more straightforwardly, particularised conversational implicatures (PCI) require some specific contextual knowledge in order to be inferred by the hearer, whereas generalised conversational implicatures (GCI) do not.

The difference between particularised and generalised conversational implicatures can be illustrated by considering the following situation. Say, for instance, Michael is in a café with a friend who is eating some cake with her coffee, and he comments that the cake looks really nice. In saying that he thinks that his friend's cake looks nice, a particularised conversational implicature potentially arises (i.e. that Michael would like to try his friend's cake). Of course, whether this request is implicated on this particular occasion depends on the relationship between Michael and his friend (including whether they are close enough for such an offer to seem appropriate), whether Michael himself already has some cake at that time, and so on. It also depends, in part, on the response of Michael's friend; if she responds with something like "Would you like some?" then not only does she show that she has drawn this particularised conversational implicature, but also gives rise to a generalised

---

[2] There are, of course, other ways in which speakers may fail to observe conversational maxims, including opting out of (or suspending) maxims in certain situations, clashes between maxims, or even flagrant non-observance (Greenall 2009; Mooney 2004). However, these do not make available conversational implicatures per se, but rather lead us into issues of interpersonal implications, an area which we will discuss in further detail in Chapter 7.

conversational implicature by her saying "some cake", which through conventionalised reasoning implicates "[but] not all of it". Grice's claim was that the latter is implicated in all contexts unless somehow blocked or suspended in some manner by other information in the context (e.g. going on to say something like "in fact why don't you have it all?"). Generalised conversational implicatures were only treated in passing by Grice himself, but they have become a key focus of analysis in subsequent neo-Gricean accounts of implicatures, a point to which we will return in the following section (4.3.1).

We have discussed thus far a number of different types of implicature proposed by Grice. These different representations of what is implicated are summarised in Figure 4.1.

However, as we have seen, while various types of implicature were proposed, Grice himself focused primarily on conversational implicatures, as it is to these that the Cooperative Principle and conversational maxims were intended to apply.

Conversational implicatures as meant or communicated?

At this point it is important to reiterate that in introducing the notion of conversational implicature, Grice was proposing a normative apparatus, that is, a set of principled expectations, by which speakers could make what is implicated available to hearers (and in that sense speaker-meant or intended), rather than outlining how what is implicated is communicated per se (Saul 2002a). The Cooperative Principle and conversational maxims do not, therefore, refer to a set of rules for how speakers should speak, as they have sometimes been mistakenly interpreted. Instead, Grice was implicitly advancing a distinction between what a speaker is *meaning* versus what he or she is *communicating*, given that to mean$_{nn}$ something is for the speaker to have a particular set of intentions, while to communicate something depends in large part on the hearer's interpretation (including interpretations of putative intentions on the part of the speaker). Some scholars have argued that the Cooperative Principle and conversational maxims can be used by hearers to figure out what has been implicated by the speaker. However, Grice specifically formulated the Cooperative Principle and conversational maxims from the speaker's perspective, as we saw above, and so

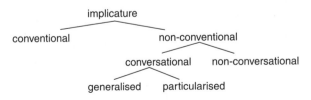

Figure 4.1 Types of Gricean implicature (adapted from Levinson 1983: 131)

they were evidently aimed at accounting for how speakers can make *available* meanings_nn that are not said but rather implicated, rather than explaining the cognitive processes by which hearers infer such meanings_nn.

This is also evident from the distinction Grice made between **implicature** (cf. implying) and **implicatum** (cf. what is implied) (Grice [1975]1989: 24). The term implicature was initially coined to refer to the process of intentionally meaning_nn something in addition to what is said, and so concerned only the speaker's meaning representation (i.e. what the speaker thinks he or she is implicating). The term implicatum, on the other hand, was used to refer to the "product" of this process, and thus involved the meaning representations of both speakers and hearers (i.e. what the hearer thinks the speaker has implicated, and what the speaker thinks he or she has implicated to the hearer). A conversational implicature (as opposed to a conversational implicatum), therefore, refers only to what the speaker intends to implicate, and in that sense involves making a particular meaning representation beyond what is said available to the hearer. It doesn't encompass what is actually implicated to the hearer, or what the speaker thinks has been implicated to the hearer.

Consider the following example, which we already have discussed above in relation to infringing conversational maxims:

> [4.14a] (Charles is making conversation with a friend at a wedding reception)
>   1 Charles: How's that gorgeous girlfriend of yours?
>   2 John: She's no longer my girlfriend.
>
> (*Four Weddings and a Funeral*, 1994, director: Mike Newell, writer: Richard Curtis)

At this point, what John evidently intended to conversationally implicate in turn 2 through his response to Charles's inquiry in turn 1 is that his relationship with the person in question has changed from being a girlfriend to something else (to being his partner as it turns out). The conversational implicature is thus strictly speaking only that John's relationship with the person being referred to has changed. For John, the conversational implicatum at this point, what he thinks Charles thinks he has implicated, is likely to be just that. However, for Charles the conversational implicatum that arises at this point from John's response to his inquiry is that John has broken up with his girlfriend. This becomes clear from his subsequent response below:

> [4.14b]   3 Charles: Oh, dear. I wouldn't get too gloomy about it.
>   Rumour has it she never stopped bonking old Toby de Lisle in case you didn't work it out.
>   4 John: She is now my wife.
>
> (*Four Weddings and a Funeral*, 1994, director: Mike Newell, writer: Richard Curtis)

Following Charles's response in turn 3, then, the conversational implicatum for John that arises from what he said in turn 2 changes. He now realises that Charles thinks he was implicating that he had broken up with his girlfriend. This leads to John's correction in the subsequent turn 4, which thus provides evidence of what he originally intended by his response in turn 2. Such cases illustrate why a distinction between implicature and implicatum was originally made by Grice. However, this important point has also been largely glossed over in subsequent work in pragmatics, as the term implicature has since gradually taken over both functions.

In sum, Grice arguably only focused on how a speaker makes available conversational implicatures (a kind of pragmatic meaning representation), but not on how they might be specifically understood (i.e. what is implied, namely, the conversational implicatum in question).[3] In this way Grice accounted for the way in which speakers can be sure about what they intend to mean, but what they are taken to implicate by others is not necessarily consistent with those intentions. We will return to discuss the question of how hearers (and indeed speakers) reach an understanding of what has been implicated (i.e. conversational implicatum) in actual communicative interaction in the following chapter (section 5.3). However, at this point we now move to consider how Grice's classic distinction between what is said and what is implicated has been fleshed out and altered in various ways. Most importantly, we will see that Grice's assumption that what is said is primarily a semantic notion that only requires minimal pragmatic input is a highly questionable one.

Reflection: On indeterminacy

Grice confined his analysis of meaning to the speaker's thoughts, beliefs, desires, attitudes, intentions and so on through his definition of meaning$_{nn}$, namely, the speaker's intention that the hearer recognise what thought, belief and so on is intended by the speaker to be recognised by the hearer, thereby allowing precision in modelling speaker meaning. However, defining pragmatic meaning representations in terms of the mental states of speakers is what makes it so difficult to precisely pin down meanings that go beyond what is said. As we saw from the example of Charlie Brown it is difficult to determine exactly what Lucy meant in two ways: (1) we do not know in what way Lucy thinks Charlie Brown is unsuitable for shovelling snow, and (2) we do not know how certain she is about her belief. This reflects, more generally, the two types of indeterminacy that are an inevitable feature of many pragmatic meaning representations:

- Type 1 indeterminacy in terms of the conceptual or informational **content** of meaning representations.

---

[3] Although cf. Grice ([1987]1989: 370).

> - Type 2 indeterminacy in terms of the **degree** of speaker commitment to that meaning representation.
>
> Grice's definition of meaning$_{nn}$ thus creates a natural source of indeterminacy as it is being pinned to the mental states of speakers. Grice, perhaps wisely, avoided the issue of the indeterminacy of many pragmatic meaning representations by shifting such problems to the hearer, and to understandings of what is meant that arise in communicative interaction and discourse more generally.

4.3   Between what is said and what is implicated

While a speaker can mean both what is said and what is implicated, Grice's main focus in theorising meaning$_{nn}$, as we have seen, was on what is implicated. He thus left what is said as something for those working in semantics to deal with. However, the assumption that speaker meaning is exhausted by Grice's notion of what is said and what is implicated has been challenged by subsequent work where it has been argued that pragmatics is, in fact, required in order to account for what is taken to be said. In other words, a complex layer of pragmatic meaning representation has been found to lie between Grice's minimalist notion of what is said and particularised conversational implicatures. At the risk of gross oversimplification, the various developments of pragmatic meaning representations can be roughly grouped into two schools. On the one hand, we have the so-called **neo-Griceans** who have expanded upon and further developed Grice's original distinction between what is said and what is implicated. They have emphasised the role of general expectations in relation to implicatures, focusing, in particular, on developing a more detailed account of generalised conversational implicatures. Neo-Gricean work has also tended towards a defence of a **literalist** notion of what is said, thereby maintaining a firmer boundary with semantics. On the other hand, **post-Griceans**, in particular Relevance theorists, have argued that we need a pragmatically enriched or **contextualist** notion of what is said, thereby abandoning Grice's essentially syntactically-constrained conceptualisation. They have focused on offering a detailed account of these pragmatic enrichments of what is said, leading to a much more looser boundary between the treatment of meaning representations in semantics and pragmatics. Another notable feature of post-Gricean approaches to pragmatic meaning is the shift away from a (neo-)Gricean focus on what a speaker intends to mean to a focus on how hearers figure out what speakers are meaning.

4.3.1 Literalist approaches: the neo-Griceans

Neo-Gricean work on pragmatic meaning has been concentrated on two key meaning representations: what is said and generalised conversational implicatures. This has resulted in two key lines of work amongst neo-Griceans. The first line of work has focused on the generally accepted problem of **linguistic under-determinacy**, namely, that Grice's notion of what is said does not in fact match with what we intuitively understand as said$_2$ (i.e. what is taken to be said; or what is taken to be meant by what someone has said). The second line of work in neo-Gricean pragmatics has focused on the claim that there is an intermediate layer of meaning that relies on the general expectations of speakers of a language about what particular expressions are taken to mean. Within this intermediate layer of **presumptive meaning**, it is the notion of generalised conversational implicature that has received the most attention from neo-Griceans, although the role of formulaic language more generally, in relation to speaker meaning, has been considered in passing.

Linguistic under-determinacy and what is literally said

One of the key challenges facing neo-Gricean accounts of speaker meaning concerns Grice's stipulation that what is said should be constrained by the particular elements of a sentence, including their order and syntactic character. These accounts argue that this is too strict, because what speakers are taken to say$_2$ is under-determined by linguistic forms. In other words, "filling in the boxes" provided by the words and syntactic structure through disambiguating sense, assigning reference, and resolving indexicals of the utterance via inference does not match with what we would generally understand a speaker to be saying$_2$. Linguistic under-determinacy is thus a critical problem because we normally understand what is said$_2$ to have both logical properties (i.e. it can enter into entailment or contradiction relations) and truth-conditional properties (i.e. it can be evaluated against real world relations). And yet, without such logical and truth-conditional properties it is difficult to maintain a distinction between what is said and what is implicated.

While this issue is still being debated amongst neo-Griceans, most have opted to defend a strictly *literal* notion of what is said, which is then supplemented with further levels of pragmatic meaning representations.[4] It is argued that a strictly literal notion of what is said is necessary in order to maintain the intuition of ordinary users that a literal meaning representation that is tightly aligned with what is said$_1$ is potentially available, even though we might not access it in normal circumstances (Bach 2001; Terkourafi 2010). Bach (2001: 17), for instance, proposes the Syntactic Correlation constraint,

---

[4] Although see Levinson (2000) for an alternative view of an enriched notion of what is said.

namely, "that every element of what is said correspond to *some* element of the uttered sentence". Notably, a literal notion of what is said is even more restricted than the definition of *saying* originally proposed by Grice, as it does not include reference assignment, unless it can be worked out from readily contextual information independent of the speaker's intentions. This pared down notion of what is said might be termed "what is literally said" in order to contrast it with the more or less enriched notion of Grice (and Levinson 2000).

Work on courtroom interactions (Mosegaard-Hansen 2008), as well as observations about political doublespeak and lying (Horn 2009), suggest that speakers can indeed retreat to the literal meaning of their utterances if challenged. Consider the following example from the television series *House* (adapted from Horn 2009: 27):

[4.15] (Kama is grilling Dr. Foreman about her brother Jack's serious but as yet undiagnosed illness)
Kama:　　　Is he gonna die?
Dr. Foreman: No, no one's gonna die.
Kama:　　　In the whole world? Ever? That's so great!
Dr. Foreman: I meant...
Kama:　　　I know what you meant.
　　("Whac-a-mole", *House*, Season 3, Episode 8, 21 November 2006, director: Daniel Sackheim, writer: Pamela Davis)

Here Kama deliberately takes Dr. Foreman's utterance *No one's gonna die* literally in order to express irony, and perhaps also to express her worry and frustration about not knowing what is wrong with her brother.

Whether this retreat to a literal notion of what is said is regarded as legitimate or plausible in each case it occurs is a separate matter. What concerns us here is this shows us that such meaning representations are potentially available to users, and so it constitutes another layer of meaning representation that any theory must account for.

Reflection: What is said in courts

A number of scholars have pointed out that in courtroom discourse participants may retreat to a notion of what is literally said (see, for example, Mosegaard-Hansen 2008). Questions and answers in the courtroom may therefore be formulated very carefully in some instances to ensure that what is said$_1$ matches what is normatively made available as meant or said$_2$. A retreat to literal meaning in courtroom discourse was made particularly infamous by former US President Bill Clinton in his deposition in August 1998 to a grand jury about whether he had lied, and so committed perjury, in a prior deposition in January that year in statements about his relationship with Monica Lewinsky. He was asked about reports that he had said to aides in reference to Monica Lewinsky *there's nothing going on between us*. He explained why this wasn't lying, even though it subsequently emerged that he had had an affair with her, through a retreat to what is literally meant by his claim, as we can see from the following excerpt from his deposition:

> [4.16] It depends on what the meaning of the word "is" is. If the- if he- if "is" means is and never has been, that is not- that is one thing. If it means there is none, that was a completely true statement ... Now, if someone had asked me on that day, are you having any kind of sexual relations with Ms. Lewinsky, that is, asked me a question in the present tense, I would have said no. And it would have been completely true.
>
> (Starr Report, 1998, footnote 1128)

While Clinton performed some fairly impressive – or disingenuous depending on one's perspective – verbal gymnastics in re-contextualising his prior statement, strictly speaking Clinton was quite right in what he asserted here. He never said there was never at any point anything going on between himself and Lewinsky. By saying$_1$ *there's nothing going on between us* he might have (reasonably) been understood as saying$_2$ "there has never been anything going on between us", but that's not what he said$_1$. Instead, he argued he had simply said$_2$, "there's nothing going on between us at the moment". The literal notion of what is said has thus saved a presidency, amongst other things.

Utterance-type meaning

A second key line of work amongst neo-Griceans relates to Levinson's (1995, 2000) claim that we need to recognise a third layer of pragmatic meaning, namely, **utterance-type meaning**, which lies between what is said and **utterance-token meaning** (where the latter encompasses speaker-intended particularised conversational implicatures). Levinson argues that utterance-type meaning involves representations that are not based on "direct compu-tations about speaker-intentions but rather on general expectations about how language is normally used" (2000: 22). Many of the examples he lists are relevant to the analysis of pragmatic acts and social action (e.g. speech acts, felicity conditions, conversational pre-sequences, preference organisation), and so do not constitute meaning representations per se because they do not involve the *content* of reflexively intended mental states (and for that reason will be discussed further in Chapter 6). He does, however, list three examples of utterance-type meaning which do involve some kind of meaning representation, namely, presuppositions (see section 3.3.2), conventional implicatures (see section 4.2.2), and generalised conversational implicatures. To this we would add formulaic expressions in general.

The main focus of work on presumptive or utterance-type meaning amongst neo-Griceans has been on generalised conversational implicatures (GCI). Such work has usually involved explaining a specific set of quantity implicatures termed **scalar implicatures** (Horn 1984, 2009; Levinson 2000), as well as revisiting Grice's conversational maxims in various ways. Scalar implicatures are claimed to arise through our assumed knowledge of underlying scales of degree, a point we touched upon in discussing contrastive focus in section 3.4.2. The most well-known example is the <*all, most, many, some*> scale, where *some* (and *many* and *most*) are treated as involving a relatively weaker epistemic claim than *all*. By uttering a relatively weaker value on a scale (e.g. *some*) a speaker can implicate by default, unless indicating otherwise, that he or she was not in a position to assert any stronger value (e.g. "not all") (Horn 2009). For example, if someone asks me *Who ate all the cake?*, and I respond *Well, I had some*, then I have scalar implicated "[but] not all of it". There are many other scales which are claimed to also work in similar ways, such as those based on <*and, or*>, <*the, a*>, <*always, usually, often, sometimes*>, <*certainly, probably, possibly*>, or <*hot, warm, cold*>. For instance, if someone were to ask me whether the weather will be fine tomorrow for a planned picnic, and I respond *probably*, then, I have thereby scalar implicated that "I am *not certain* (it will be fine tomorrow)".

We have already briefly touched on how the Givenness Hierarchy forms a scale that is the basis for implicatures arising from referents (see section 2.5.1), but there are other types of GCIs that do not necessarily draw from such underlying scales. Levinson (2000), for instance, has developed a tripartite distinction between the principles of Quantity ("what isn't said, isn't"), Informativeness ("what is expressed simply is stereotypically exemplified"), and Manner ("what's said in an abnormal way isn't normal") in accounting for generalised conversational implicatures. We can observe, for instance, two cases of GCIs arising through the Q[uantity]-principle in the following quote from (Senator and subsequently US President) Barack Obama.

[4.17]   Obama: "Look, when I was a kid, I inhaled frequently. That was the point."

(Meeting of the American Society of Magazine Editors, 24 October 2006)

Here, through Q-GCI, Obama not only admits that, when trying drugs as a kid, he inhaled frequently, thereby scalar implicating "not always", but also, and perhaps more crucially, implicates "not as an adult". The second implicature arises through the general principle of opposition in natural language, namely, that two attributes or positions can either be in "contrariety" (e.g. an adult versus a child) or in "contradiction" (e.g. an adult versus not an adult) (Horn 1989). In this case, mentioning something done "as a kid" implicates negation of the contrary (i.e. "not as an adult"). Or as Levinson (2000), puts it, "what isn't said, isn't".

As we briefly noted previously, however, utterance-type meaning involves not just GCIs but other kinds of formulaic meanings. The ubiquity of formulaicity in language use was recognised early on by neo-Griceans who proposed the notion of "short-circuited implicature" (SCI), to account for meaning representations that are implicated through "relevant usage conventions" (Horn and Bayer 1984: 404; see also Morgan 1978). Consider the following example transcribed from a recording of a telephone conversation between two American speakers of English, which is a typical opening to such conversations:

[4.18] Allen: Hello?
        John: Yeah, is Judy there?
        Allen: Yeah, just a second.
               (pause)
        Judy: Hello.

                                    (Schegloff 2007: 30)

John asks whether Judy is present to which Allen responds by confirming she is and then going off to fetch her. It is evident that both John and Allen have understood John's question to mean more than what is said here, specifically, John has implicated that he would like to speak to Judy. Opening a telephone call with "Is X there?" is a recurrent way of implicating in English that we would like to talk to someone other than the person who has answered the phone (the activity type of making telephone calls is what constrains the range of plausible interpretations here). Yet it is not a given that by uttering "Is X there?" one will implicate this, even in the more narrowly circumscribed context of making telephone calls. If it were the case, for example, that Allen knows that John doesn't like Judy, John might be understood as implicating (by flouting the relevance maxim) that he wants to talk to Allen without Judy overhearing. But this is a rather special case, and in most situations, "Is X there?" will indeed implicate something like "I want to speak to X".

Such usage conventions abound, including routine expressions that require some kind of minimal context for the pragmatic meaning to arise. Routine expressions, or what Kecskes (2002, 2008) terms "situation-bound utterances", include such expressions as *tell me about it* (which is standardly taken to mean an emphatic expression of agreement), *come again?* (standardly taken to mean the speaker is asking the hearer to repeat what has just been said, which may thereby also implicate scepticism or doubt about what has just been said), *I was held up* (standardly taken to mean the speaker was delayed due to circumstances outside of his or her control), *help yourself* (standardly taken to mean the hearer should feel free to choose and take what he or she wants), or *no worries* (standardly taken to mean the speaker does not have any negative feelings about a possible imposition or offence on the part of the hearer). Yet, while routine expressions standardly implicate something, they can, of course, be used in the literal sense as well. Routine expressions thus form another part of the layer of utterance-type meaning representations that Levinson (1995, 2000) describes, and to which we will return in section 7.4.3 when we outline the frame-based approach to politeness, and particularly politeness formulae.

Reflection: Formulaic expressions across varieties of English

There can be differences in the frequency of occurrence of at least some routine expressions across different varieties of English, and in some cases these arise through generalised conversational implicatures that have become somewhat fossilised. The routine expressions *tell me about it* and *you bet*, for instance, occur more frequently in American English compared to British or Australian English.

Another instance is the use of rhetorical questions in response to polar (i.e. yes/no) questions. Schaffer offers a long-list of such rhetorical questions that are commonly used as retorts in American English, from which we quote just a few examples:

[4.19] Is the Pope Catholic?
        Does a bear shit in the woods?

[4.20] Do chickens have lips?
        Can a white man dance?

(Schaffer 2005: 455–456)

Speakers can implicate through such responses not only "yes", as in the two examples in listed in [4.19], but also "no", as in the two examples listed in [4.20]. However, in being implicated via a tautology, that is, as (supposedly) having an "obvious" answer, the speaker also implicates that the original question was inapposite or inappropriate in some way. Given that the basic form of these utterances follows a recognisable and recurrent pattern, they are, as Schaffer (2005) argues, a strong candidate for treatment as a kind of utterance-type meaning. Interestingly, it was the "Pope question" that Bouton (1988) found L2 learners had difficulty interpreting – they clearly lacked the relevant utterance-type meaning. The fact that there are many such routine expressions, or preferred ways of saying things, is often relatively opaque to native speakers of English. However, it is all too familiar to those learning English as a second language, or even to those coming across routine expressions that are particular to a certain variety of English.

In sum, the neo-Gricean contribution to our understanding of pragmatic meaning representations, as we have discussed in this section, has been two-fold. On the one hand, emphasis has been placed on the importance of a literal notion of what is said as a meaning representation that is potentially accessible but not necessarily accessed by users. On the other hand, the importance of a layer of presumptive or utterance-type meaning representation has been highlighted. While some scholars, particularly Relevance theorists as we shall see in the following section, have argued that these two levels of meaning representation are unnecessary (Carston 2002), such a conclusion, we would suggest, is premature given the way in which speakers can retreat to what is literally said in particular circumstances, on the one hand, and given the extent to which formulaicity abounds in discourse and interaction, on the other.

However, it is worth noting that Levinson's (2000) move to shift the theorisation of generalised conversational implicatures out of a strictly neo-Gricean account of speaker-intended meaning into a broader account of what is communicated through the proposal of hearer corollaries for the maxims has been the source of considerable subsequent debate (see Carston 2002). Indeed, there is a growing body of experimental work that attempts to examine the cognitive processes and mechanisms which underpin pragmatic meaning, including the question of whether default inferences are involved. As this is primarily a matter of how users understand meaning, however, we will return to discussing this line of experimental work in the following chapter (section 5.3).

4.3.2 Contextualist approaches: relevance theory

Contextualist approaches are committed to the view that the underlying syntax of what is said should not determine pragmatic meaning representations. In other words, what a speaker is taken to be saying should not be limited to the compositional meaning that arises from what is said$_1$. This move away from a notion of what is said that is constrained by syntactic structure amounts to an emphatic rejection of Grice's stance that what is said should be treated as primarily a semantic concern, it is for this reason contextualist approaches are generally characterised as post-Gricean. Instead, it is argued by contextualists that we need pragmatics to properly account for what is said. In relevance theory, which is one of the most prominent of the contextualist approaches, this pragmatically enriched notion of what is said is termed an **explicature**, thereby contrasting it with the notion of implicature (Carston 2002; Sperber and Wilson [1986]1995). The distinction between explicature and implicature rests, in turn, on the (intuitive) distinction between explicitly and implicitly communicated meaning, that is, between explicitness and implicitness. Explicatures arise, just like implicatures, through inference. However, the former are tied to what is explicitly communicated because they are always "a development of (a) a linguistically encoded logical form of the utterance, or of (b) a sentential subpart of a logical form" (Carston 2002: 124); where **logical form** refers to a skeleton that can be derived from word meanings and syntactic structure of an utterance. Implicatures, on the other hand, arise solely through inference without any direct contribution from the logical form of the utterance. Notably, Relevance theorists prefer the term logical form over the Gricean notion of what is said, in order to avoid committing themselves to the claim that there is any psychologically plausible layer of pragmatic meaning representation below that of explicatures.

The issue of cognitive plausibility is one that Relevance theorists take very seriously. We will introduce in more detail the key claims made in relevance theory about how pragmatic meaning is understood or processed by hearers in the following chapter (section 5.3.1). At this point, however, it will suffice to note that Relevance theorists claim that what is explicated (explicature) and what is implicated (implicature) are both figured out by hearers with reference to the **Communicative Principle of Relevance**, namely, the assumption that "Every act of ostensive communication conveys a presumption of its own optimal relevance" (Sperber and Wilson 1995: 260). **Relevance** itself is defined in terms of a balance between the cognitive value of particular information, and the processing effort required to gain that information. In other words, something is more relevant when it involves more useful information that takes relatively little effort for the hearer to figure out, and is less relevant when it involves less useful information or takes relatively more effort to figure out for that hearer. In relevance theory, then, the neo-Gricean Cooperative Principle and attendant conversational maxims, which involve normative expectations by which what is implicated and what is said are made available by the speaker, are all replaced by a single cognitively-grounded notion of relevance. This means that for Relevance theorists what is implicated (i.e. implicature) and what is explicated (i.e. explicature) depends on a general tendency in cognitive processing for individuals to maximise the extraction of information at the same time as minimising their efforts in doing so.

The Relevance theoretic notion of explicature, as we have noted above, builds on the claim that we need pragmatics to properly account for what is said$_2$. In deriving these explicitly communicated meanings, or explicatures, Relevance theorists argue there are various different kinds of inferential processes involved. In that sense, relevance theory goes significantly beyond the neo-Gricean account of what is said, which is much more tightly aligned with what a speaker is literally saying$_1$, in arguing for the pragmatically enriched notion of explicature. In order to see the difference between the two positions, let us consider the following quote from the witness, Kato, at the trial of O. J. Simpson about the latter's state of mind leading up to the murder of his wife:

[4.21]   Kato: He was upset but he wasn't upset.

(Carston 2002: 324)

While seemingly contradictory at the level of what is said$_1$, here Kato is evidently saying$_2$ that while Simpson was emotionally disturbed (i.e. *was upset*) he wasn't disturbed to the point of reaching a murderous state of mind (i.e. *wasn't upset*). It is also evident that Kato is talking about not just any point in time prior to making this claim (what is strictly speaking said$_1$), but is specifically referring to the time leading up to the murder. The explicature that arises here is that Simpson was, at the time leading up the murder, upset$_x$ but not upset$_y$ (where *x* refers to emotionally disturbed, while *y* refers to a murderous state of mind). Grice's notion of what is said is arguably not well equipped to deal with inferences of this nature.

Relevance theory also advances a number of important theoretical claims about implicatures. The first is the observation that not only "conclusions" but also "premises" can be implicated (Sperber and Wilson [1986]1995). In order to see the difference, let us consider the following excerpt from the television series, *Everybody Hates Chris*. At the point the excerpt begins, Chris and his mother, Rochelle, have just entered a clothing store to buy some new clothes for Chris to wear for taking his picture at school.

[4.22]   Shop assistant: Welcome to Erwins.
         Rochelle: We're looking for an outfit.
         Shop assistant: With the right outfit you can beat any charge.
         Chris: I'm not charged with anything.

> Rochelle: We're just looking for an outfit for his school pictures.
>
> Shop assistant: Oh, oh, okay, good. Stay in school kid, it'll keep you out of jail.
>
> Rochelle: Yeah that and not breaking the law.
>
> ("Everybody hates picture day", *Everybody Hates Chris*,
> Season 1, Episode 13, 2 February 2006,
> director: Linda Mendoza, writer: Kevin A. Garnett)

We can see here that when the shop assistant responds to Rochelle's request, he also supposes that Chris is facing, or likely to face, criminal charges and will have to appear in court. This assumption is treated as an implicature, which arises through his response to Rochelle's request in her first turn, on a Relevance theoretic account. However, this implicature does not logically follow from what he says, but rather is presumed by it, a point we earlier addressed in passing in relation to unpresupposed presuppositions (see section 3.5.1). In other words, it is an **implicated premise** because it is supplied by others (i.e. Rochelle and Chris) figuring out what assumptions are required for the utterance to be sufficiently relevant on this occasion. That is, for the shop assistant's response to count as relevant in relation to Rochelle's request, she and Chris must infer that he is assuming Chris needs the outfit to appear in court. An **implicated conclusion** subsequently arises through Chris's response, where he implies that he doesn't need the outfit for appearing in court, something which naturally follows from his explicitly communicated claim that he is not facing any criminal charges. Carston (2002: 142) argues that the Relevance theoretic distinction between implicated premises and implicated conclusions points to the different "inferential roles that implicatures may play in the derivation process". However, it is arguably more than just this. The distinction between implicated premises and implicated conclusions in fact refers to two distinct ways in which implicatures can arise, that is, through speakers *implying, indicating, suggesting* and the like (what Grice termed "implicating"), versus them *supposing* or *assuming* and so on (which does not appear to fall under implicating), a point to which we will return in section 5.4 in the following chapter.

The second theoretical development of Grice's original characterisation of implicature is the claim that implicatures can vary in their degree of (in)determinacy. In other words, implicatures vary from being "strongly implicated" through to "weakly implicated" (Sperber and Wilson [1986]1995). Consider, for instance, the following interaction between Mark and his girlfriend, Erica, in the film, *The Social Network*. Mark has been talking quite a lot up until this point about wanting to get into a good "final club" (an undergraduate social club) at Harvard University.

[4.23] Erica: You're obsessed with finals clubs. You have finals club OCD and you need to see someone about it who'll prescribe some sort of medication. You don't care if the side effects may include blindness.

Mark: Final clubs. Not finals clubs and there's a difference between being obsessed and being motivated.

Erica: Yes (pause) there is.

Mark: Well you do, that was cryptic, so you do speak in code.

(*The Social Network*, 2010, director: David Fincher, writer: Aaron Sorkin)

Here Erica is suggesting that Mark is taking the issue of getting into a good final club far too seriously, to which Mark responds by implying that he is motivated rather than obsessed through claiming there is a difference between the two. However, it is Erica's response, which Mark subsequently casts as "cryptic" and "speaking in code", that is of particular interest here. While Erica ostensibly agrees with Mark's claim that there is a difference between being obsessed and being motivated, it appears that she is implying something else as well. However, what exactly she might be implying is left up to Mark. It could be taken as implying that Mark is indeed simply highly motivated, thereby agreeing with what he has both explicated and implicated. However, it is equally plausible that she is implying Mark is in fact obsessive, thereby agreeing with what he has explicated, but disagreeing with what he has implicated. Given what she has implied here is (deliberately) left up to him to decide, it constitutes an instance of a **weak implicature**, and for this reason it is difficult for Mark to hold Erica responsible for it. Moeschler (2012) claims that the continuum from strong through to weak implicatures represents one of the most important post-Gricean developments in theorising implicature, as it is through it that a distinction can be made between implicatures for which the speaker is held primarily responsible (strong implicatures) and those for which are left to the responsibility of the hearer (i.e. weak implicatures). We will also be returning to this point in section 5.4 in the following chapter when we consider how pragmatic meanings arise in interactional contexts.

Finally, Relevance theorists also propose that meaning representations can be further embedded within other meaning representations. For example, in the following excerpt from the film, *Four Weddings and a Funeral*, the shop assistant's suggestions for a wedding gift are, at first, taken by Charles to be helpful. It subsequently turns out, however, that the suggestions were, in fact, meant sarcastically.

[4.24] Charles: Do you have the wedding list for Banks?

Shop assistant: Certainly, sir. Lots of beautiful things for around about the £1,000 mark.

Charles: What about things around the sort of £50 mark? Is there much?

Shop assistant: Well, you could get that pygmy warrior over there.

Charles: This? Excellent!

Shop assistant: If you could find someone to chip in the other 950 pounds. Or our carrier bags are £1.50 each. Why don't you just get 33 of them?

Charles: Well, I think I'll probably leave it. Thanks very much. You've been very ...

(*Four Weddings and a Funeral*, 1994, director: Mike Newell, writer: Richard Curtis)

In order for Charles to understand that the shop assistant is being sarcastic, he must reconcile the ostensibly helpful suggestion that he buy a pygmy warrior or carrier bags, with the dismissive and evidently unhelpful stance on the part of the shop assistant about Charles's attempt to buy something in that shop. In other words, a meaning representation involving a thought (i.e. a proposal about what Charles could buy) is here embedded within an attitudinal stance involving the shop assistant's beliefs (i.e. about Charles's financial capacity, or lack thereof, to buy something in that shop). Instances where a representation of a thought, belief and the like is embedded within another layer of thought, belief and so on are termed **metarepresentations**. In the case of pragmatic meaning this involves cases where a meaning representation is embedded within a further, high-order meaning representation. These are sometimes termed **higher-order** explicatures or implicatures in relevance theory. Metarepresentations appear to be most useful when examining irony and other echoic phenomena, that is, when speakers attribute thoughts to others or when utterances are about the thoughts or utterances of others. Relevance theorists argue these are critical for developing a more nuanced understanding of pragmatic meaning (Wilson 2000). Our view, however, is that such phenomena are better understood from a metapragmatic perspective, as we discuss further in Chapter 8, given that they often involve attitudinal stances and other indicators of interpersonal meaning that go beyond an account of pragmatic meaning proper.

4.4 An interim conclusion: on pragmatic meaning representations

While Grice started with an initial distinction between what is said and what is implicated, both neo-Gricean and contextualist approaches to pragmatic meaning have proposed more nuanced and layered understandings of meaning representations, as summarised in Figure 4.2.

In Figure 4.2, the different layers of pragmatic meaning are represented vertically within distinct approaches, while the different ways of conceptualising these different layers are represented horizontally across approaches. Solid lines indicate representations that have been treated as key meaning representations in those approaches, while dotted lines indicate representations that are either the subject of ongoing debate (e.g. Gricean what is said), or are not recognised as meaning representations proper (e.g. logical forms). However, since the various types of meaning representations are theorised in different ways, Figure 4.2 represents only analogous, not equivalent, concepts of pragmatic meaning. But putting terminological and theoretical battles aside for the moment, it is apparent that there have been a number of key developments of Grice's initial approach to conceptualising pragmatic or speaker meaning representations.

One key development is that representations of what is said may be approached both at the level of what is literally said and at the level of a pragmatically enriched notion of what is said (i.e. explicature), which mirrors, to some extent at least, the folk distinction between saying$_1$ and saying$_2$. What contextualist approaches have added is a deeper understanding of the different types of representations that such pragmatic enrichments involve. A second key development is the claim that there is an important layer of utterance-type pragmatic meaning that has only received passing attention thus far, including routine expressions and short-circuited implicatures (SCI) (less controversially), and generalised conversational implicatures (GCI),

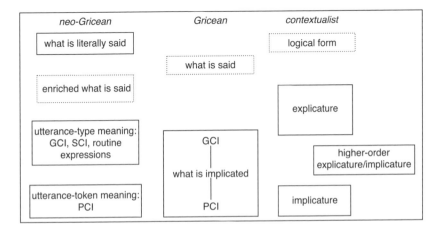

Figure 4.2 Types of pragmatic meaning representations

including scalar implicatures (more controversially). A third key develop-ment is that meaning representations may be further embedded within other meaning representations, a point we take up further in Chapter 8.

It is interesting to note that, throughout this discussion, natural language concepts from English have frequently been used to conceptualise and even define pragmatic meaning representations. The question we have already raised in relation to what is said (cf. *saying*) and what is implicated (cf. *implying*), and to which we might add the distinction between saying$_1$ and saying$_2$, is whether such distinctions, which can be made in English, are equally as useful for examining pragmatic meaning representations in other languages. If we take a purely analytical perspective then many would argue it does not matter. However, if we engage with the understandings of participants then such issues evidently require much more serious attention, a point to which we return in section 5.4 when discussing the ways in which pragmatic mean-ings can be created by speakers in interaction.

5 Pragmatic Meaning II

5.1 Analysing pragmatic meaning

In the previous chapter we focused on how we can mean much more than we say$_1$ or utter. We discussed how various types of pragmatic meaning representations have grown out of the classic Gricean distinction between what is said (cf. *saying$_2$*) and what is implicated (cf. *implying*). In the course of this discussion, we pointed out that some approaches to pragmatic meaning, for example (neo-)Gricean accounts, are essentially speaker-centred, that is, they focus on the meaning representations the speaker intends or makes available through what he or she says$_1$ (as well as doesn't say$_1$). Yet other approaches, for instance relevance theory, are largely hearer-centred approaches, that is, they seek to explain meaning representations attributed to the speaker by the hearer.

In this chapter, we consider in more detail this latter issue, namely, the question of *whose* meaning we are talking about, and suggest that this is in fact critical to pragmatics. Consider the following excerpt from an episode of *Seinfeld* where two characters are arguing over what is meant by Elaine's question. The conversation begins when Elaine tells Jerry that her colleague (Dick), who is a former alcoholic, picked up Jerry's drink by mistake at a party they recently attended, and has since started drinking again, leading to his dismissal.

[5.1]   Elaine: Dick was fired.
        Jerry: You mean to tell me if I had put that drink six inches over to the right, none of this would have happened.
        Elaine: You knew he was an alcoholic. Why'd you put the drink down at all?
        Jerry: What are you saying?
        Elaine: I'm not saying anything.
        Jerry: You're saying something.

Elaine: What could I be saying?

Jerry: Well you're not saying nothing, you must be saying something.

Elaine: If I was saying something I would have said it.

Jerry: Well why don't you say it?

Elaine: I said it.

Jerry: What did you say?

Elaine: Nothing. (sighs) It's exhausting being with you.

("The red dot", *Seinfeld*, Season 3, Episode 12, 11 December 1991, director: Tom Cherones, writer: Larry David)

Here, Jerry and Elaine argue about whether Elaine has meant something in addition to what she has expressed here, as they are using the word *saying* here, for the most part, in the sense of *meaning* rather than *uttering* something. The question then is, did Elaine mean something more than a simple question seeking information from Jerry? Did she mean, perhaps, to imply that it is Jerry's fault that Dick was fired? These are interesting questions in that these two characters clearly do not agree. Jerry appears to appeal to what would normally be understood by Elaine's question (e.g. *Well you're not saying nothing, you must be saying something*), while Elaine appears to appeal to her intention in denying that she has implied anything (e.g. *If I was saying something I would have said it*). The two characters eventually reach an understanding that they have diverging interpretations of what is meant by Elaine's question, and so leave unresolved the question of whether Elaine is *implying* something or simply *not saying* something here. The former entails a higher degree of commitment on her part to that unsaid content than the latter.

This example raises a number of interesting questions in regard to how we analyse meaning in pragmatics:

- What kind of content or information are we talking about?
- Whose meaning are we talking about?
- How do we understand these meanings?
- How do these meanings arise?

We have already largely dealt with the first question in the previous chapter, so in this chapter we will consider the latter three questions in turn. In doing so, we will sketch out a framework for analysing pragmatic meaning in context.

We start by tackling the question of pragmatic meaning from the perspective of users, showing how these different perspectives can add an additional layer of complexity to our understanding of pragmatic meaning. We then move to a consideration of how meanings are understood by users, not only at the utterance level but also across sequences of utterances, or what is normally called **discourse** (although this broader concern with discourse should not to be confused with discourse pragmatics, another term for informational pragmatics, as introduced in section 3.1). This involves a move away from the traditional focus on the meaning of single utterances to a consideration of how pragmatic meanings arise in interactions. Our chapter concludes with a consideration of pragmatic meaning in various contexts, and how these various dimensions of pragmatic meaning might intersect. In this way, we aim to show that pragmatic meaning is much more complex and multi-faceted than is often appreciated in approaches that focus primarily on accounts of pragmatic meaning representations.

5.2 Whose meaning?

The primary focus of many scholars in analysing pragmatic meaning has been on representations of *speaker* meaning. In this section, we point out that speaker meaning is much more complex than might appear at first. Indeed, it constitutes just one of a number of threads we need to consider in any analysis of pragmatic meaning, since what has been relatively neglected in many accounts of pragmatic meaning thus far is just whose meaning representation is at issue, in other words, the perspective of the user.

It is generally assumed that it is speakers who mean things, while hearers are the ones who figure out what speakers are meaning in or through what they say. However, a focus on speaker meaning can inadvertently mask two quite different perspectives: that of the speaker and that of the hearer. According to Grice, the notion of conversational implicature, for instance, is simply what the speaker makes available to hearers through maintaining the assumption that Cooperative Principle is being observed. The conversational implicatum (or implicata in the plural) that speakers and recipients actually entertain are thus regarded as a distinct matter, as we discussed in the previous chapter (in section 4.2.2). There was subsequently, however, a general move in pragmatics towards analysing the hearer's representation of the speaker's intended meaning representation, particularly amongst Relevance theorists (and other contextualists), who analyse speaker meaning from the perspective of the hearer's reconstruction of it via their inferences about speaker's intended meaning. There is thus an underlying assumption that in "successful communication" the speaker's intended meaning (e.g. an implicature) and the hearer's inference about it (e.g. an implicatum) can be treated as if they are virtually synonymous (Carston 2002; Sperber and Wilson [1986]1995; see also Levinson 2000).

Reflection: What are you inferring?

Consider the following conversation from an episode of *The Simpsons*.

[5.2] Bart: Dad, Mom's spending more time at Moe's than you are.
　　　 Lisa: They seem awfully chummy.
　　　 Homer: Just what are you inferring?
　　　 Lisa: I'm not inferring anything. You infer, I imply.
　　　 Homer: Well that's a relief.
　　　　　　　　　("Mommie beerest", *The Simpsons*, Season 16, Episode 7,
　　　　　　 30 January 2005, director: Mark Kirkland, writer: Michael Price)

In this example, Bart and Lisa can be understood to be implying that Marge (Homer's wife) might be having an affair with Moe. This latter proposition counts as an implicature, and it is drawn through a process of inference. Homer, being Homer, next commits the classic mistake of conflating implicature with inference, to which Lisa responds with the well-worn dictum that speakers imply, while hearers infer. Disputes about the distinction between implicature and inference, however, are not restricted to popular discourse. Horn (2004) and Bach (2006), for instance, contend that treating implicature and inference as synonymous constitutes a conceptual and analytical error.

However, there is reason to suspect that Homer may not be entirely wrong in inadvertently mixing up what is implied with what is inferred. First, *infer* has been used for almost five centuries in the sense of *"imply"* or *"convey"* (Horn 2012). Consider the following examples taken from the *Oxford English Dictionary Online* (2013):

[5.3] "This doth *infer* the zeal I had to see him" (Henry IV, Shakespeare)

"Consider first that Great or Bright *infers* not Excellence" (Milton, 1667)

"I should think you did miss my letters. I know it! but...you missed them in another way than you *infer*, you little minx!" (Ellen Terry letter, 1896)

"I can't stand fellers who *infer* things about good clean-living Australian sheilahs" (*Daily Telegraph*, 1973)

In all of the examples above, *infer* is used in the sense of "to involve as a consequence" or "to imply". Second, his claim that Lisa (and Bart) are inferring something here is actually quite correct. They have both inferred from their mother's recent behaviour (e.g. spending a lot of time with Moe, getting on very well with Moe, and so on), along with real-world knowledge about how affairs involving married partners normally arise, that she might be having an affair with Moe. Moreover, they have also presumably inferred that, if they raise this behaviour with their father, Homer might come to the same conclusion about the possible implications of Marge's behaviour. Everyone makes inferences, not just hearers. The distinction between *imply* (cf. implicature) and *infer* (cf. inference) therefore does not in itself help us distinguish between the speaker's and hearer's perspectives on speaker meaning.

Kecskes (2010) argues, however, that a hearer-centred account of pragmatic meaning neglects the speaker's own perspective, which is perhaps somewhat ironic considering the Gricean roots from which such accounts have sprung. Following Saul's (2002a) distinction between utterer and audience implicature, one solution to this might be that we must necessarily talk about **utterer** and **recipient** representations of speaker meaning. An utterer representation of speaker meaning is what the speaker understands he or she has meant through his or her own utterance. A recipient representation of speaker meaning is what the hearer(s) or other kinds of participants understand the speaker to have meant through his or her utterance. In this way, we can properly recognise, rather than confound, distinct perspectives on speaker meaning.

5.2.1 Participant footings

The move towards appreciating that there are multiple perspectives on speaker meaning was foreshadowed in Goffman's (1981: 129) seminal claim that we need to deconstruct the "folk categories" of speaker and hearer into "smaller, analytically coherent elements". He proposed the notion of **footing**, which refers to the alignment or interactional positioning of an individual in relation to a particular utterance. He further suggested that the footing of a speaker involves a **production format**, while the footing of a hearer involves a **participation status**. The idea is, essentially, that the particular footing of an individual encompasses different roles and responsibilities in interaction or discourse. A **participation framework** encompasses the different footings of all individuals involved in an interaction (i.e. both production format and participation status). The notion of footing thus allows us to develop a more nuanced understanding of speakers and hearers. One important upshot of this, as we shall see, is that pragmatic meaning representations can be understood differently depending on the footing of the individual concerned.

The production format of utterances concerns what might be called **production roles** in relation to pragmatic meaning (Levinson 1988).

According to Goffman there are four different speaker footings: animator, author, principal and figure. An **animator** (or utterer) is the one producing an utterance (or the talk), an **author** is the entity that creates or designs an utterance, a **principal** is the party responsible for an utterance, and a **figure** is the character portrayed within an utterance. Take, for instance, the statement made by then President of the United States, George W. Bush, soon after the September 11 attacks, *Either you are with us, or you are with the terrorists*. In this case, while Bush was the animator, it is an open question whether he was actually the author (this being the eternal question of whether politicians ever write their own speeches). He most certainly was not the only principal here, as the United States Government, and indeed in some circles the people of the United States, were held responsible for this utterance, along with Bush himself. There is also some degree of ambiguity in relation to the figures portrayed in this assertion. The first person plural pronoun (*us*), for instance, can be understood as either exclusive (referring to the US government) or inclusive (referring to all Americans) (see section 2.3, for this distinction). And the referent of the second person pronoun (*you*), and the implications, clearly varies according to who was listening to or reading this statement.

Speakers can mean things on behalf of others in more mundane situations as well. In the following interaction, reported by Kiesling and Johnson (2010), two mothers are talking after taking their children to a music class. Paula here initiates an invitation from her son to Julie's daughter Emma.

[5.4] 1 Paula: (to her son) Maybe Emma can come over to our house and play sometime this week.
  2 Paula: (to Emma) Would that be OK? Would you like that Emma?
  3 Paula: (to Julie) Would you like to do that? Drop Emma off for a while and you can have a rest?
  4 Julie: Oh, yeah, that would be great.

(Kiesling and Johnson 2010: 292–293)

In turn 1, Paula makes a suggestion to her son that he invite Emma over to their house to play. In turn 2, however, she goes on to make that invitation on behalf of her son as, while Paula is clearly the animator and author of turn 2, the principal is evidently meant to be her son, that is, the utterance is designed as if her son has already made the invitation. We can see this in the formulation of the invitation itself, which builds on Paula's prior suggestion to her son through the use of referring expression *that* (see also section 2.3). This is then followed up by an attempt to confirm acceptance through an invitation from Paula to Emma's mother in turn 3, which is once again tied back to the invitation that was ostensibly made by Paula's son to Emma.

It is also interesting to note that, given the figure of the suggestion in turn 1, namely Emma, is co-present, it also counts as an *indirect* invitation to her, a point to which we shall return in the following chapter on pragmatic acts.

Reflection: Production footing beyond the speaker

The different production roles are not limited, however, to speakers per se. In some instances, talk may depict someone who is co-present or involve attributing utterances to others (including others who are co-present). Let us consider the following example taken from a recording of conversation amongst some (African-American) children in the United States, where Chopper has just been asked what Tony said when confronted by a group of boys on the street.

[5.5] 40 Chopper: Lemme tell ya, An h(h)e sai(h)d,
       41 Tokay: WH:en!=
       42 Chopper: I ain't got no(h) mo(h)ney.
                               (Goodwin and Goodwin 2004: 224;
                                      see also Goodwin 1990: 249)

In lines 40 and 42, Chopper is attributing an utterance to Tony, namely, *I ain't got no money*. This means that although Chopper is the animator (or utterer) here, the figure is Tony. Thus, *me* in line 40 refers to Chopper, while *I* in line 42 refers to Tony, even though they're part of one and the same utterance. It also means Tony is the author and principal of the utterance quoted (at least so Chopper alleges). However, there are also laughter particles interspersed through this quotation of what was said by Tony. These laughter particles are attributable to Chopper, who is therefore the author and principal for what is implicated by attributing this statement to Tony, namely, that Tony is a coward. Through this laughter, Chopper also implicates that this is a laughable matter, both in the sense of laughing at what was said by Tony, as well as at Tony himself. Since Tony (the figure) is also present during this telling, he also becomes a **target** of the derision that arises through what is implicated here. In analysing the speaker meaning that arises in this case, then, we have two distinct footings: that of Chopper as the animator as well as the author and principal of what is implicated, and Tony as the author and principal of what is said.

A consideration of production roles opens up many interesting questions about the nature of speaker meaning, and a more nuanced understanding of whose meaning representation we are analysing, as earlier noted by Bertuccelli-Papi (1999). There is also, however, the issue of participation status to be considered, or what might be termed **reception roles** (Levinson 1988). Goffman (1981) made a distinction between recipients who are ratified and those who are not. This was based on the intuitive distinction we can draw in English between *hearing* and *listening*, where the latter entails some responsibility to respond to or participate in the talk, even if that only means showing one is paying attention to the talk and not something else. A **ratified recipient** (or participant) is an individual who is expected to not only hear but also listen to the talk. An **unratified recipient** (or non-participant) is an individual who can hear the talk but is not expected to listen. These two types of recipients, or participants, were further subdivided by Goffman into different footings. A participant may either be an **addressee** or an unaddressed **side participant**. An addressee is a person (or persons) to whom the utterance is (ostensibly) directed, but both addressees and side participants have recognised entitlements to respond to the utterance, although their degree of responsibility to do so varies (at least ostensibly). Unratified recipients, or non-participants, on the other hand can be divided, following Verschueren (1999: 82–86) into **bystanders** and **overhearers**. The former encompasses a person (or persons) that can be expected to be able to hear at least some parts of the talk, but is not ratified as a participant. A waiter who is standing next to a table while guests talk in a restaurant can be considered a bystander, for instance. An overhearer, on the other hand, refers to a person (or persons) that might be able to hear some parts of the talk. Overhearers include **listener-ins**, that is, persons who are in view, such as guests at an adjoining table in the restaurant, and **eavesdroppers**, that is, persons who are secretly following the talk.

There is experimental work that has demonstrated that the understandings of participants and non-participants cannot be assumed to be synonymous, even in situations where the non-participants can hear everything that is said by the participants (Schober and Clark 1989). In their experiments, Schober and Clark (1989) examined the understandings of addressees (the participants) of conversations between strangers about an unfamiliar topic versus the understandings of eavesdroppers (the non-participants) of those conversations. They found that the eavesdroppers' understanding of the conversation was significantly less than that of the addressees, despite the former having full access to all the same utterances, and sharing the same common ground as that existing between the participants, since they were all strangers in both cases (see section 3.2 for discussion of common ground). This shows that we cannot assume different recipients will all reach the same understandings of meanings arising in a particular conversation. In other words, depending on one's reception footing, a person's understanding of pragmatic meaning may vary.

Reflection: Irony in the eye of the beholder

In a recent study, LaMarre, Landreville and Beam (2009) examined how irony used by American political satirist Steven Colbert (from *"The Colbert Report"*, which plays on the "Comedy Channel") is interpreted by people with different political leanings. Colbert's irony is ambiguous in that he uses deadpan satire, leaving it somewhat open to the viewer to decide who he is mocking (a point to which shall return in Chapter 8). In one episode of the show in question, which played in 2006, Colbert was interviewing a radio talkshow host, Amy Goodman, who is a well-known liberal associated with the *Democracy Now!* movement. In the show Colbert introduced Goodman as a "super liberal lefty", and then went on to claim the Iraq war is "breaking down conservative and liberal lines" and that "the conservatives are 'right' and the liberals are 'wrong'" and so on (LaMarre et al. 2009: 220). Participants who identified themselves as ranging from "very liberal" through to "very conservative" were invited to watch the three-minute interview clip. It was found that while viewers of all political leanings agreed that Colbert was funny, "conservatives were more likely to report that Colbert only pretends to be joking and genuinely meant what he said, while liberals were more likely to report that Colbert used satire and was not serious when offering political statements" (2009: 212). In other words, we have a case here of multiple recipient understandings of speaker meaning. It is evident, then, that no matter what intent Colbert might have, "people will potentially see what they want to see" (2009: 229). Gibbs (2012) suggests that Colbert does not intend his irony to be necessarily understood by all, which further supports our view that in many cases we need to examine speaker meaning from multiple recipient positions.

An **audience** is a particular kind of reception role that combines characteristics of ratified and unratified participants (cf. Goffman 1981). On the one hand, an audience is expected to be able to hear clearly (and so is ratified), but on the other hand, an audience may not be in the sight of the speaker in the case of television or radio audiences, or may not receive any overt signal of recognition from speakers in the case of theatre audiences (and so are unratified) (Dynel 2011). This is because an audience is not always co-present despite being a ratified participant. The participation framework for recipients is thus also much more complex than the term *"hearer"* allows for, a point we will return to in section 5.4.

The layering of pragmatic meanings, which we can see in example [5.5], alludes to one point that was somewhat neglected by Goffman in his account of footing. As Goodwin and Goodwin (2004) argue, there remains a marked asymmetry between the rich cognitive and linguistic capabilities attributed to the speaker in the guise of production roles, and the cognitively and linguistically simple role attributed to recipients, whose participation status is determined primarily by the speaker. We propose here that reception roles should be attributed an equivalent degree of cognitive complexity to production roles (see also Haugh 2013c). The production role of animator (or utterer), who articulates talk, needs to be complemented by the different footings of the **recipient** (or recipients) who hear, and in most cases listen, to the talk. The role of the author who constructs the talk has a counterpart in the **interpreter** (or interpreters) who develop (multiple) representations of the meaning of this talk. The role of the principal who is socially responsible for those meanings is necessarily matched by the **accounter** (or accounters) who (explicitly or tacitly) hold the principal responsible. And finally, the production role of figure, namely the character who is depicted in the talk, is also a potential **target** when the character depicted is co-present or when an utterance is attributed to someone other than the speaker.

We can observe the importance of taking into account these different recipient footings when we examine cases of teasing, which can be seen as joking in some instances, but as annoying, goading or even bullying the target in other cases. Interactants can thus invoke these different recipient footings in such instances. Consider the following excerpt from a recording of a conversation taken from the Australian component of the International Corpus of English. In the conversation so far, Eddie has been talking about his new girlfriend over dinner with his sister, Shelley, his mother, Beryl, and his grandparents, Patty and Roger. This excerpt begins with Eddie's grandmother Patty teasing Eddie about his new girlfriend by singing lyrics from the song, "Getting to know you" (which is from the Rogers and Hammerstein musical, *"The King and I"*).

> [5.6] ICE-AUS: S1A-004: 9:15
> 295 P: ge- getting to <u>kno</u>::w <u>yo</u>:u, getting to <u>kno</u>:w
> 296   a:ll about °<u>yo</u>:u°. ((in singing voice))
> 297   (0.2)
> 298 P: getting to °↑<u>li</u>:<u>ke</u> you°= ((in singing voice))
> 299 R: =<u>oka</u>:y Na:n
> 300 E: =hhhe hhe
> 301 P: gettin' to hope you <u>like</u> >yheh heh heh heh< heh

While Eddie is clearly the target of the jocular mockery, and possibly the addressee, the other four participants, apart from Eddie, take recipient roles as side participants. And, although all five participants take interpreter footings, it is notable that it is in fact Roger, a side participant, who explicitly takes the footing of accounter when he implicates that Patty might be taking the mockery too far through a recognisable sequence-closing device, namely, *okay* (Beach 1995), rather than the target and likely addressee, Eddie. We will return to consider the interpersonal implications of teasing in Chapter 7 (see section 7.5).

The complex array of footings we have discussed thus far are summarised in Figure 5.1. The assumption that speaker meaning is simply a matter of what a particular speaker intended and/or what the hearer thinks the speaker intended can only be maintained by focusing exclusively on two-party conversations, where the complex array of participant footings (illustrated above) tends to coalesce into what we intuitively think of as speakers and hearers (although not always). While multi-party conversations are an obvious place where numerous participant footings may arise, and thus where multiple understandings of speaker meaning are even more likely to arise, computer-mediated communications between multiple parties, and online social networking sites and the like, are also where an analysis of speaker meaning can benefit from a consideration of participation footings.

The use of the copy field in email messages sent in the workplace can be used to demonstrate this point. Skovholt and Svennevig (2006), for instance, show how "copying in" superordinates when making a request via email can be used to increase pressure on the recipients to get something done. In

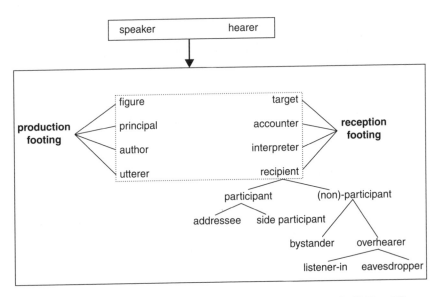

Figure 5.1 Types of participation footings (adapted from Haugh 2013c: 62)

the following excerpt, a systems operator (Geir Johnsen) is following up on getting the information that his superordinate (Line Myhre) had indirectly requested that another superordinate (Arvid Lervik) provide.

[5.7]   From: Johnsen Geir (Networks))
        Sent: August 26, 2004 10:30
        To: Lervik Arvid (Telecom)
        Copy: Myhre Line (Telecom)
        Subject: RE: Signatures

        I wonder if you could find the official titles that I'm going to publish together with the signatures.

        Regards Geir Johnsen

        - - - - - Original message - - - - -

        [.] (original thread deleted)

                                    (Skovholt and Svennevig 2006: 57)

Geir reminds Arvid of the original request from Line by appending the prior messages to the email. By copying Line into the email sent to Arvid, Geir implicates that the delay in getting the information to Line is due to the lack of response from Arvid, and thus the responsibility for this delay does not lie with him. Geir could also be implicating that he would like Line to take responsibility for the situation (i.e. Arvid's lack of response), especially given that Arvid is also Geir's superordinate. In this case, while Arvid is the addressee and Line is positioned as a side participant, much of what is implicated here is in fact directed at Line, which serves to increase the pressure on Arvid to comply with the request. In other words, the witnessing of this email by another participant alters the pragmatic meanings that can be attributed to it. Through the various examples we have discussed in this section we can see how the footings summarised in Figure 5.1 are themselves created through talk. Footings can shift during interaction and, in some cases, speakers may even exploit the porous boundaries between different footings (see, for example, Goodwin 2007).

5.2.2   Recipient meanings

Thus far we have focused on the intersection of perspectives on speaker meaning, and suggested that a distinction between utterer and recipient representations of speaker meaning is necessary in order for us to fully explore the question of whose meaning we are (and in some cases should be) analysing. Another question that has started to emerge in considering utterer and recipient representations of speaker meaning is whether we also need to consider other participant loci of pragmatic meaning. As we noted in the previous chapter, near the end of section 4.3.2, Relevance theorists have quite rightly pointed out that implicatures lie on a kind of continuum ranging from strongly implicated to weakly implicated (Sperber and Wilson [1986]1995). Some implicatures are fairly determinate and speakers appear at least ostensibly committed to them, while other implicatures, namely, weak implicatures, are quite indeterminate both in regard to their content and the degree to which the speaker appears committed to that content. At a certain point, then, it can be argued that weak implicatures no longer lie within the provenance of the speaker's intentions, and so can no longer be regarded as a form of speaker meaning. In such cases, we must necessarily invoke a different kind of meaning representation, namely, **recipient meaning**.

Recipient meanings are not well understood and have not yet been adequately theorised in pragmatics. They can be roughly characterised as encompassing meaning representations of recipients that arise independently of the speaker's intentions. In literary texts such as poetry, for instance, the writer may leave the choice of possible implicatures open to the reader (Haugh and Jaszczolt 2012). The understanding of the themes of short stories has also been shown to be constructed by readers rather than residing in the text (Kurtz and Schober 2001), which means a key meaning representation occasioned by reading a story is not as much a construct of the writer so much as it is that of the readers. This is not to suggest that writers do not have intentions to mean particular things, but rather that the meanings occasioned by texts are not exhausted by these intentions. In other words, readers can form all sorts of interpretations of texts that were not necessarily intended by the writer.

Recipient meanings are not restricted to non-co-present participants (i.e. those reading literature, watching television and so on), however. They are also to be found in spoken interactions. Clark (1997) divides them into two types: misconstruals and elective construals. Misconstruals may involve situations where the speaker accepts another understanding by the recipient, which was not necessarily intended by him or her. Consider the following example reported by Clark:

[5.8] (Clark has sat down to order a drink)
Waitress: And what would you like to drink?
Clark: Hot tea, please. Uh, English Breakfast.
Waitress: That was Earl Grey?
Clark: Right.

(Clark 1997: 589)

Here we can see that Clark is taken to be ordering Earl Grey tea by the waitress, and thus what he has said$_2$ is that he would like Earl Grey contrary to what he has just said₁. He notes that "I initially intended to be taken as meaning one thing, but I changed my mind" (ibid.). Here it is the recipient's understanding of the meaning representation of what is said, rather than that of the speaker, which has taken precedence.

Misconstruals may also involve situations where the speaker is not able to block another understanding by the recipient. While the speaker might claim a particular implicature was unintended, this may not be accepted by the recipient (Haugh 2008). In such a situation, the recipient's meaning may overshadow that of the speaker. Take the following excerpt from *The Sopranos*, for instance:

[5.9]   (Little Carmine Lupertazzi is hosting a meeting between mob families in New York and New Jersey. Little Carmine has just proposed a truce to which Tony Soprano and Phil Leotardo have both agreed)

Little Carmine: Your brother Billy, whatever happened there ...

Tony Soprano: All right then ...

Phil Leotardo: "Whatever happened there?"

Little Carmine: The shooting ...

Phil Leotardo: "Whatever happened there?"

Little Carmine: God rest his soul, huh?

Phil Leotardo: I'll tell you what fuckin' happened. This piece of shit's cousin

Tony Soprano: Calm down Phil.

Phil Leotardo: Put six bullets in the kid without any provocation whatsoever!

Tony Soprano: My cousin's dead.

Phil Leotardo: Fuck you!

Little Carmine: Phil, hey we were makin' headway here. I didn't mean to say ...

Phil Leotardo: Fuck what you meant, cocksucka! Come on!
(Phil and his gang leave)

Tony Soprano: Jesus Christ, Carmine. What the fuck? Why would you possibly bring that up?

("Kaisha", Season 6, Episode 12, *The Sopranos*, 4 June 2006, director: Alan Taylor, writers: Terence Winter, David Chase & Matthew Weiner)

The excerpt begins with Little Carmine bringing up the death of Phil Leotardo's brother, Billy. Phil becomes incensed by the fact that Little Carmine has brought this topic up, and insults Tony Soprano when Tony tries to calm him down. Little Carmine then attempts to correct Phil's "misconstrual" of what he meant by his question *whatever happened there*, but he is interrupted by Phil, who emphatically rejects such a claim. Tony's subsequent utterance after

Phil and his gang leave lays the blame not on Phil for misunderstanding what Little Carmine meant by his question, but rather on Little Carmine himself. What takes precedence here, then, is the recipient's meaning in spite of what the speaker claims to have intended.

Elective construals involve instances where speakers offer recipients a choice of interpretations. In making a choice, the recipients thereby help determine what is meant by the speaker's utterance (Clark 1997). In a study of responses to indirect speech acts, Clark (1979) examined how 200 managers of restaurants would respond to the utterance "Do you accept credit cards?" 44% of managers treated it as a polar question by responding with something like "Yes, we do." 16% treated it as a request for information, that is, the names of credit cards they accept, by responding with something like "We accept Visa and Mastercard", while 38% treated it as both a polar question and a request for information, by responding with something like "Yes, we accept Visa and Mastercard." Clark (1997) argues that what the speaker is taken to mean by the managers is not determinate. Instead, the study shows that it is established through the managers choosing amongst the options that are presented to them (i.e. as a question, request or both), because the speaker has "put herself in the position of being taken to mean whichever of the options the manager chose" (Clark 1997: 589).

In some cases the line between speaker and recipient meanings becomes somewhat blurred. Consider, for instance, an excerpt from *Everybody Hates Chris*, an American comedy. Just prior to the excerpt Chris (a semi-fictional younger version of Chris Rock, the actor/comedian) has helped Tasha, a girl he likes, who lives next door, get rid of a mouse. She gives him a kiss on the cheek to thank him, a kiss which is witnessed by an older boy, Jerome, who then goes up to Chris.

[5.10] Jerome: Now I know why they can't get nowhere. Little dude from across the street is on the case. Now why you ain't telling nobody?

Chris: Well, hey, you know.

Voiceover: That's what you said when you didn't wanna lie, but you didn't wanna tell the truth.

Jerome: I underestimated you little dude. I didn't think you had it in you. Tasha.

("Everybody hates a liar", *Everybody Hates Chris*, Season 2, Episode 4, 30 October 2006, director: Jerry Levine, writer: Adrienne Carter)

Chris responds to Jerome's assumption that he is going out with Tasha with a fairly formulaic non-committal response, "well, hey, you know". He thus allows Jerome to continue to maintain this assumption, although he hasn't actually said that he and Tasha are going out. He just has not said that they are not going out. This constitutes an interesting case of pragmatic meaning, as Chris is believed by Jerome to be going out with Tasha (a recipient meaning). Yet when given the chance to correct this assumption Chris does not do so, although he doesn't strictly endorse it either. The formulaic response *well, you know* seems to imply here that something does not need to be said as it is already mutually known (i.e. common ground). The question, then, is whether Chris can be understood to have *implied* he is going out with Tasha. In other words, does it count as a speaker meaning as well?

Chris continues to respond in this way whenever Tasha is mentioned, until finally he is overheard by Tasha herself.

[5.11]   Girl: You know I heard about you and Tasha.
　　　 Chris: Hey, well, you know.
　　　 Doc: Ahem.
　　　 Tasha: Hey, well, you know what?
　　　 Chris: Hi Tasha.
　　　 Tasha: Don't "hi Tasha" me. Hey, well, you know what? What were
　　　　　　　　 you going to say about me, Chris? You have something to
　　　　　　　　 say, say it to my face.
　　　　　　　　　　　　　　　 ("Everybody hates a liar", *Everybody Hates Chris*,
　　　　　　　　　　　　　　　　　 Season 2, Episode 4, 30 October 2006,
　　　　　　　　　　　　　　 director: Jerry Levine, writer: Adrienne Carter)

Here Chris is held to account for a response that Tasha seems to interpret as suggesting that something has been left unsaid. This is evident from her demand that Chris complete the utterance.

It becomes clear, then, that one can be taken as saying$_2$ something by not saying$_1$ something when the opportunity arises. This kind of "not saying" is a type of pragmatic meaning which does not fall under the received definition of implicature as a thought, or in this case a belief of the speaker that is intended by the speaker to be recognised by the recipient as intended (Haugh 2013d). Yet the characters, or at least Tasha and Jerome, nevertheless treat it as a kind of speaker meaning. This illustrates how raising questions about *whose* meaning we are talking about can pose challenges for the way in which we define speaker meaning in pragmatics. The way in which some utterances can offer a set of possible interpretations amongst which a recipient can choose is also a feature of many pragmatic acts, a point that will be discussed in further detail in the following chapter.

We have suggested through the examples above that pragmatic meaning is not exhausted by speaker meaning, proposing that it needs to be complemented by the notion of recipient meaning. Here, we go even further in suggesting that there are likely to be yet other kinds of pragmatic meaning, which have not yet been fully explored. One example is the normative kind of pragmatic meaning that Grice was proposing to tap through his notion of conversational implicature, and the attendant Cooperative Principle and conversational maxims. A normative notion of pragmatic meaning is rooted neither in the speaker nor the recipients, but across groups of users. The conversational maxims provide plausible accounts of what we might expect to be implicated in certain situations, or at least they arguably do so in English. However, in being inherently normative, it remains an open question, and a relatively under-explored one at that, just how applicable they are across languages.

5.3 Understanding meaning

Pragmatic meanings can arise through what people say, but ultimately always go beyond what is said. The question, then, is: how do users understand such meanings? Approaches to this issue have often been framed in terms of the **processing** of meaning. This generally refers to the cognitive operations that underpin or give rise to pragmatic meaning representations. The focus in pragmatics has traditionally been on how we understand or process meanings that arise from utterances. This reflects the folk view in English that an *understanding* is something we *reach* or *come to*. There is, however, an interesting distinction that can be made (in German) between "understanding" (*Verstehen*) and "coming to an understanding" (*Verständigung*) (Weigand 2009: 30). The former refers to a punctuated perspective on understanding as something which a participant reaches, subsequent to hearing an utterance. It generally comes under the rubric of **utterance processing**. The latter refers to a more dynamic perspective on understanding as something that emerges through the intertwining of actions and reactions in discourse. It is generally assumed in this approach that a two-party interaction is the most basic unit of analysis. This perspective generally falls within the scope of **discourse processing**. In this section, we assume that treating understanding as a particular point we reach in time (*Verstehen*), or as spread across a span of time – and thus across participants – (*Verständigung*) both represent valid, albeit quite different, viewpoints on pragmatic meaning. In order to better appreciate how pragmatic meanings are understood by users, we thus approach this question from the perspectives of both utterance and discourse processing.

5.3.1 Utterance processing

Work on how users understand meaning in pragmatics has traditionally focused on the inferences through which hearers attribute an intention to mean something on the part of the speaker. As we have already noted in the previous chapter, Grice himself was fairly ambivalent about the status of speaker meaning (i.e. meaning intended by the speaker to be recognised by the hearer as intended) in communication. It was only in subsequent work on how users understand or process meaning that speaker meaning was assumed to be synonymous with communicated meaning. This is part of the general move away from a philosophical, analytical framework to a cognitive, explanatory framework in approaching the issue of how users understand pragmatic meanings. An explanatory framework for instance, aims to ground the processing of pragmatic meaning in a more general model of cognitive processes. It thus approaches utterance processing primarily from the perspective of cognitive representations and how various cognitive processes give rise to them.

Relevance theory, which we briefly introduced in the previous chapter (see section 4.3.2), is the most widely utilised explanatory framework to have emerged to date, as it focuses for the most part on how hearers reconstruct speaker meanings. It is generally assumed in this approach that the utterance is the basic unit of analysis. The cognitive and communicative aspects of utterance processing are linked through the notion of relevance, which is defined in terms of information (Sperber and Wilson 1995). Information itself is more specifically represented through particular beliefs, thoughts, desires, attitudes, intentions and so on. As we previously indicated in Chapter 3, information has greater value for users when it is new as opposed to given, which in turn depends on, amongst other things, the common ground between the users in question. Furthermore, it is generally assumed that users will prefer, other things considered equal, information that is more easily processed, which in turn relates to issues of clarity, economy and processability. Relevance theory formalises these as two forces that jointly determine the relevance of information from a cognitive perspective. This new distinction is defined in terms of **contextual effects**, while clarity, economy and processability all come under the scope of **processing effort**. Contextual effects are divided into three types in relevance theory: (a) those that produce new information, (b) those that confirm or strengthen an existing assumption, and (c) those that contradict or weaken an existing assumption. When discussing contextual effects that arise in an individual user's mind, they are termed **positive cognitive effects**, which are contrasted with cognitive effects that do not provide any new information or do not strengthen/weaken existing assumptions for that user.

For example, if I take my car into a garage because it has developed a steering problem, a variety of positive cognitive effects might arise depending on what is said by the mechanic:

[a] The garage said the problem was serious. Thus, I realised that I'd be taking the bus home.

[b] I had assumed that the problem was with the steering rack. The garage said the problem was with the steering rack.

[c] I had assumed that the problem was with the steering rack. The garage said the problem was with the tyres.

The cognitive effect described in [a] involves new information for the user, namely, the thought that I will be taking the bus home (as well as contradicting the prior assumption that I would be driving home in my car). The cognitive effect in [b], on the other hand, represents the strengthening of my prior belief that the steering problem is due to a problem with the steering rack. Finally, the cognitive effect outlined in [c] involves contradicting my prior belief that the steering problem is due to a problem with the steering rack, and new information, namely, the assumption that the problem with the steering is due to the tyres. These are thus all instances of positive cognitive effects.

In relevance theory it is claimed that relevance is critical for both communication and cognitive processing more generally. The interplay of cognitive effects and processing effort is what determines relevance of information for an individual, which Wilson and Sperber (2004: 609) define in the following way:

a. Other things being equal, the greater the positive cognitive effects achieved by processing an input, the greater the relevance of the input to the individual at that time.

b. Other things being equal, the greater the processing effort expended, the lower the relevance of the input to the individual at that time.

The general idea is that the greater the cognitive effects, and the smaller the processing effort, the greater the relevance of information. In the case of cognitive processing, it is claimed that "Human cognition tends to be geared to the maximisation of relevance", or what is termed the Cognitive Principle of Relevance (Sperber and Wilson [1986]1995: 260). This amounts to the claim that users will pay attention to information that has greater relevance for them. In the case of communication, it is claimed that "Every act of ostensive communication conveys a presumption of its own optimal relevance", or what is termed the Communicative Principle of Relevance (ibid.). **Ostensive** refers to the assumption on the part of users that an utterance (or behaviour more generally) is intended by the speaker to mean something, while **optimal relevance** refers to the assumption that the utterance is "relevant enough for it to be worth the audience's effort to process it" and is "the most relevant one compatible with communicator's abilities and preferences" (ibid.: 270). This amounts to the claim that when speakers make it clear to the hearer they are communicating something through an utterance (or other kind of behaviour), what they are communicating can be assumed by the hearer to be relevant to them. These assumptions underpin the mechanisms by which pragmatic meanings are processed by users.

Let us consider the following example where B's response makes available a (particularised) implicature.

> [5.12]   (A is working at a computer in one of the Linguistic department's labs at Lancaster University when she experiences a problem)
> A: Can you help me?
> B: Graeme's office hour is in five minutes
>
> (Reconstructed from field notes)

The question is, how does A work out what B means by his response here? From a Relevance theoretic perspective, A proceeds on the assumption that B's utterance is optimally relevant to her. In this situation, B's utterance provides ready access to both an explicit and implicit premise. The explicit premise arises from a pragmatically enriched understanding of B's response (what is termed an explicature, as we discussed in section 4.3.2), namely, that the person they mutually know as Graeme has allocated a specified time to do things in that mutually known workplace in five minutes from the time of the speaker's utterance. The implicit premise made available is the contextual assumption that "Graeme helps with computing problems" (which is triggered in part by the existential presupposition that Graeme has an office hour, as discussed in section 3.3.2). By combining this explicit premise with this implicit premise, A can arrive at the implicit conclusion that B thinks Graeme can help A with her computing problem, and furthermore that he thinks A should ask Graeme for help rather than him (i.e. two related implicatures). This overall interpretation presumably satisfies A's expectations of relevance.

Reflection: Types of inference in utterance processing

One of the key measures of processing effort in relevance theory is the amount of inferential work that is required in order to derive explicatures and implicatures. These inferences are generally characterised as "pragmatic" as opposed to "logical". Logical inference involves a chain of reasoning in which the truth of the premises guarantees the truth of the conclusions (leading to entailments, for instance, as we discussed in section 4.2.2). **Pragmatic inference**, on the other hand, results in conclusions that may seem necessary, permissible or reasonable to draw, but their truth is not guaranteed (leading to implicatures, for instance) (Wood 2010). However, the pragmatic inferences that are said to underlie utterance processing by Relevance theorists (as well as neo-Griceans such as Levinson) are nevertheless pseudo-logical, in the sense that they still involve moving from premises (or assumptions) to conclusions. This kind of "logical" inferencing contrasts with the "associative" inferencing we briefly introduced in Chapter 3 (see section 3.3.1).

Recently, Relevance theorists have proposed a rather useful distinction between **intuitive** and **reflective** inference (Mercier and Sperber 2009). An inference is intuitive when a user accepts conclusions without attending to reasons, and so it is a representational process. An inference is reflective when a user derives conclusions from premises through reasoning. The latter thus requires reflection, that is, thinking about one's thoughts, which is a metarepresentational process, albeit not necessarily a consciously experienced one (see section 8.3.2 for further discussion of metarepresentations). This distinction is useful as it sidesteps the problem of calling the kinds of inferential work we normally assume to underlie pragmatic meaning as "pseudo-logical" or even "pragmatic". One question that remains somewhat open, however, is whether associative inference falls under the broader category of intuitive inference.

It is important to note that in a relevance theory account of utterance processing, it is not assumed that an explicature is always derived first, and then followed by inferences leading to implicatures. It is claimed instead that "explicatures and implicatures (i.e. implicit premises and conclusions) are arrived at by a process of mutual parallel adjustment, with hypotheses about both being considered in order of accessibility" (Wilson and Sperber 2004: 617). In this account of utterance processing, then, "Grice's circle", where "what is said seems both to determine and to be determined by implicature" (Levinson 2000: 186), is no longer a problem, because multiple representations of pragmatic meaning can be derived in a parallel rather than in a serial manner. In other words, users can process more than one pragmatic meaning representation at the same time. This is important because pragmatic meaning inevitably involves multiple layers of representations, as we discussed in the previous chapter (see section 4.3). There has thus been a shift away from the "traditional" Gricean view in pragmatics that what is said is always processed before what is implicated, to the view that in some cases the latter can be "directly" accessed in utterance processing (Gibbs 2002; Holtgraves 1999).

Reflection: Experimental pragmatics and defaults in utterance processing

Levinson (2000) has argued that relevance theory takes speaker meaning to be only a "matter of nonce inference" (2000: 25), that is, inferences which arise on a particular occasion, and that it ignores "default inferences" arising from "general expectations about how language is normally used" (2000: 23), including generalised conversational implicatures (GCIs) (see sections 4.2.2 and 4.3.1). However, Levinson's treatment of defaults as arising from the *localised* computation of GCIs, that is, at the time at which a particular scalar-inducing lexical item, such as *some, or, sometimes* and so on, occurs in an utterance, has not received strong support to date from psycholinguistic experiments. There is now significant experimental evidence mounting against the claim that scalar implicatures arising from *some* (i.e. "not all") and the disjunctive particle *or* (i.e. "not and"), for instance, are computed locally by default (Katsos 2012). Brehney, Katsos and Williams (2006), for instance, tested whether *some of the F's* implicated "not all the F's" and "X or Y" implicated "either X or Y but not both" across a range of different contexts. What they found was that such implicatures were only generated when explicitly warranted by the context, that is, when something in the context or co-text made the scalar implicature relevant to the interpretation of the utterance in question. Such experimental work has sometimes been interpreted by Relevance theorists as vindicating their view that scalar implicatures do not arise by default, but rather are only generated when the weaker term on a scale fails to meet the hearer's expectation of relevance. Others, however, regard such results as only falsifying the local default view and not necessarily supporting the relevance theoretic account (Garrett and Harnish 2009; Horn 2009). There has thus been an increasing focus on defaults for contexts, where default meaning representations are analysed as being contextually tied to the level of utterances and beyond (Jaszczolt 2005). One difficulty facing such experimental work, however, is that the same basic experimental methods can sometimes give rise to quite different results, depending on the details of the experimental protocol or conditions (Krifka 2009). Thus, while experimental pragmatics offers considerable promise in addressing our understanding of utterance processing, there still remains considerable work to be done in order to better understand what intuitions or processes we are actually testing through such methods.

5.3.2   Discourse processing

The question of how users understand pragmatic meaning can also be approached from the perspective of the emergent notion of *Verständigung* ("coming to an understanding"). Consider, for instance, how in the following recording of a conversation between two friends, they reach a converging understanding over a number of turns that Charlie won't be able to give a ride to Ilene, despite having previously promised to do so:

[5.13] Trip to Syracuse: 2
    1 Charlie: I spoke to the gi:r- I spoke tih Karen. (0.4) And u:m:: (.)
    2   it wz rea:lly ba:d because she decided of a:ll weekends
    3   for this one tih go awa:y
    4   (0.6)
    5 Ilene: Wha:t?
    6   (0.4)
    7 Charlie: She decidih tih go away this weekend.
    8 Ilene: Yea:h,
    9 Charlie: .hhhh=
   10 Ilene: =.kh[h
   11 Charlie: [So tha::t yihknow I really don't have a place tuh sta:y.
   12 Ilene: .hh Oh:::::.hh
   13 Ilene: .hhh So yih not g'nna go up this weeken'?
   14 Charlie: Nu::h I don't think so.

                                                        (Drew 1984: 130)

Charlie outlines potential trouble for their forthcoming trip to Syracuse when he reports that Karen is going away (lines 1–7), and so he doesn't have anywhere to stay (line 11). This is taken by Ilene as indicating that Charlie won't be able to go up to Syracuse, an understanding that is evident from her formulation of the upshot of his reporting (line 13), and subsequently confirmed by Charlie (line 14). Note, however, that Charlie has managed to indicate to Karen that he won't be able to give her a ride without having said as such, and, more importantly, that this joint understanding only emerges over a number of turns of talk.

In the above example we can see that the interpretation of utterances and turns by the two participants proceeds in an incremental fashion, and is dependent on what precedes and follows in sequence. Work on understanding pragmatic meaning from a discourse perspective thus focuses on the **incremental** and **sequential** intertwining of two or more participation footings. Incrementality refers to the processing of elements or components of pragmatic meaning within the same utterance or turn, while sequentiality refers to the processing of meaning across different speaker turns. Utterer and recipient representations of speaker meaning (as well as recipient meaning) become intertwined through participants incrementally interpreting utterances and displaying those understandings in sequences. The question of whose meaning is at issue, which we discussed in section 5.2, thus proves critical to any discourse-based account of how users understand pragmatic meaning.

The importance of incrementality in understanding meaning can be seen from the way in which users can use emerging syntax to project future talk, for instance. Consider the following excerpt from a recording of a conversation between Dianne and Claica, who are talking about a pie Jeff made.

[5.14]   G:50:03:45
        1   D: J̲e̲f̲f̲ made an asparagus pie.
        2   it was s̲:̲:̲s̲o̲:̲ [g̲o̲o̲:d
                              ((nod with eyebrow flash))
        3   C: [I love   it.   °Yeah I love that.
                              ((nod)) ((nod))
                                        (adapted from Goodwin and Goodwin
                                                        1987: 29, 2004: 226)

Dianne and Claica manage to accomplish simultaneously a positive assessment of Jeff's pie, namely, that they both think it was delicious. In order for Claica to chime in at the right time she must have been able to anticipate what Dianne was meaning here. One resource Claica likely drew from here, alongside the non-verbal cues, is the emerging syntax, where the intensifier "s::so:" occurs in a construction through which Dianne is obviously about to attribute something to the pie (by means of the referring expression "it"). The occurrence of an intensifier in an attribution syntactic construction primes an understanding of Dianne's utterance not only as an assessment (what Dianne does with her utterance), but also that this assessment is going to be a positive one (what Dianne means by her utterance).

The incremental and sequential nature of discourse processing is also clearly illustrated through the phenomenon of **co-construction**, where more than one participant contributes to the uttering of a single syntactic unit (either what is said or what is implicated). Take, for instance, the following excerpt from a conversation in the British National Corpus between an older married couple talking about fuchsias:

[5.15]   BNC: KBP 2506
        1   Nina: No, they die down (   )
        2   Clarence: Mm. Mm.
        3   Nina: Most of the ones that we brought seem to have erm
        4   Clarence: Survived.
        5   Nina: Survived. Which I'm glad.
        6   Clarence: Mm. Mm.
                                                (Rühlemann 2007: 100)

Here, in response to Nina indicating through the hesitation token *erm* that she is struggling to find the right word (line 3), Clarence completes the clause begun by Nina in the next turn (line 4). Nina then further expands upon the previously co-constructed utterance with the addition of *which I'm glad* (line 5). In this way, these two speakers can be seen to be co-constructing a single, complex syntactic unit through both completion and expansion of the prior speaker's utterance.

It can be argued from a discourse-processing perspective, then, that

> [m]eaning lies not with the speaker nor the addressee nor the utterance alone as many philosophical arguments have considered, but rather with the interactional past, current, and projected next moment (Schegloff et al. 1996: 40).

Such a perspective should not be taken to entail, however, that speakers are not generally held accountable for what they are taken to mean (a point to which we will return in the final section). Even in situations where utterances are co-constructed, the speaker who initiated the utterance (first speaker) nevertheless generally displays "ownership" of such meanings after the second speaker has "completed" the utterance, either through expressing agreement or disagreement with that utterance, or by repairing the co-constructed utterance (Haugh 2010; Lerner 2004). What a speaker is taken to have meant by participants, as opposed to how participants come to such understandings, are two distinct questions.

Reflection: Defeasibility of inference versus cancellability of pragmatic meaning

Pragmatic inference differs from logical inference in that it is **defeasible**, which means such inferences allow for the possibility of error. In practice, this has been taken to mean that implicatures and other pragmatic meaning representations which derive from such inferences are **cancellable** (as we briefly discussed in the case of presuppositions in section 3.3.2). It is important to note that defeasibility is a characteristic of a cognitive *process* (e.g. pragmatic inference), while cancellability is a characteristic of the *product* of that process (e.g. an implicature). In practice, this means that while inferences can be blocked or suspended, implicatures can only be corrected/repaired (Haugh 2013b).

Blocking inferences involves cases where a potential inference (which could conceivably follow from what is said) is not allowed through by the speaker (an anticipatory orientation). For example, we can see in the utterance *Some, in fact all, the people said they liked the food*, that by adding *in fact all* after *some*, the putative "not all" scalar implicature (see section 4.3.1) is blocked from arising (Jaszczolt 2009: 261). **Suspending** inferences, on the other hand, involves cases where the speaker removes his/her commitment to an inference that has more than likely already been drawn (a retroactive orientation). For instance, in the following interaction on the phone between friends, what starts out as looking like Cameron will invite Steve to go out somewhere, ends up with Cameron hinting that he would like Steve to invite him out.

[5.16]   (Cameron has called Steve on the phone)
         18 C: Whadaya doing tonight?
         19 S: I dunno, what are you gonna do?
         20 C: Oh I've been invited to a party that I don't wanna really want to go to.
         21   Hope to find an excuse.
         22 S: Oh right. I see. Um, haveya seen Lethal Weapon?

                              (adapted from Haugh 2009: 105)

We can observe here how a (potential) default inference, which arises from Cameron's utterance in line 18, namely that Cameron is very likely going to invite Steve somewhere if given a "go-ahead" response, is subsequently suspended by a nonce inference arising from Cameron's subsequent utterances in lines 20–21, where it becomes apparent that he is hinting that he would like Steve to invite him somewhere. Steve obliges with an invitation in line 22. In this sense, then, we can see that pragmatic inferences are always contingent on what precedes and follows the utterance in question, and this is what makes them defeasible. We will return to consider this issue further in Chapter 6 (section 6.6.2).

To **correct** or **repair** an implicature, in contrast, involves denying, retracting or clarifying what was meant (normally by the speaker), or at least attempting to do so. We saw an example of this at the beginning of this chapter (see example [5.1]). Defeasibility thus arises from cognitive operations on the part of individual users, while cancellability arises through social actions that are jointly achieved by participants.

5.3.3   Two types of pragmatic meaning?

We have presented two radically different accounts of how users understand pragmatic meaning in the prior two subsections on understanding pragmatic meaning vis-à-vis utterance and discourse processing. On the one hand, there has been an attempt to systematise the analysis of pragmatic meaning through theoretically motivated abstraction from the discourse context. This leads us to a logico-analytical focus on putative or potential speaker-intended meaning at the utterance level. Meaning according to this view is grounded in the subjective processing domain of speakers and/or hearers; in other words, understandings of meaning which a speaker and hearer each individually reach, but which are assumed to be shared. Those who view pragmatics as a component of linguistics, on a par with semantics, syntax and phonology, tend to subscribe to this view. On the other hand, there has been an attempt to treat pragmatic meaning in its full context, as both individuated and historically situated meaning. This leads us to a focus on emergent or joint meaning at the discourse level. Pragmatic meaning according to this view is grounded in the intersubjective processing domain of participants: in other words, how users come to interactionally share understandings of meanings over time (although it is not assumed those meanings will necessarily be the same, since there are often multiple participation footings involved in interactions). As we shall also see in the following section, an examination of meaning at the discourse level tends to lead to a focus on discursive responsibility (i.e. who is taken to be committed to or accountable for what is meant) and (in)determinacy (i.e. the inevitable difficulties faced in attempting to definitively fix pragmatic meaning).

Each approach represents a different perspective on understanding. In the utterance-processing view, the understanding of meaning is assumed to be relatively stable at punctuated points in time (cf. *Verstehen*). In the discourse-processing view, understandings of meaning are assumed to be dynamic and emergent over spans of time (cf. *Verständigung*). To illustrate this difference consider the following conversation:

[5.17] (Michael is staying at Sirl's house on holiday in London. Sirl and Michael have just met outside the bathroom in the morning)
1 S: What time are you leaving this morning?
2 M: Oh, in about an hour I suppose. Are you in a hurry to leave?
3 S: No, no. Just asking.

(cf. Haugh 2007a: 94)

Sirl's initial utterance in turn 1 appears to have at least two layers of meaning. On the level of what is said, he is inquiring about what time Michael plans to leave that day, while at the level of what is implicated, he is opening up the possibility that he would like to use the bathroom first. Michael orients first to the level of what is said in estimating what time he expects to leave, and then to the possible implicature by offering a possible candidate account for why Sirl might want to use the bathroom first. What remains left unsaid here is thus whether or not they are really talking about using the bathroom. However, Sirl denies that he is in a hurry in turn 3, thereby treating his first utterance as simply seeking information about Michael's movements. While it appeared from Sirl's initial turn that he was raising the issue of the bathroom, it appears from his subsequent response in turn 3 that he was not meaning to implicate that he would like to use the bathroom first. In other words, Sirl's utterance in turn 3 treats his prior turn as meaning something only at the level of what is said.

However, consider what subsequently followed in the same exchange:

[5.18] 3 S: No, no. Just asking.
        4   ((long pause))
        5 M: Would you like to use the bathroom first?
        6 S: Yeh, sure, if you don't mind.

(cf. Haugh 2007a: 94)

There is a long pause in turn 4 after Sirl's claim that he is not in a hurry. Indeed, the pause is so long it appears to indicate that something has been left unsaid. Michael's subsequent offer for Sirl to use the bathroom thus opens up again the possibility that what is left unsaid is that Sirl wants to use the bathroom first. This offer is subsequently accepted by Sirl, the upshot of which is that Sirl was indeed opening up the possibility of using the bathroom first through his initial utterance in turn 1 and was not just seeking information. However, what is left unsaid is ultimately realised through an offer on the part of Michael rather than a request from Sirl, which has consequences for the degree to which Michael can hold Sirl accountable for this implicature.

An utterance-processing account of this excerpt would focus on how Michael interprets Sirl's utterances, and vice versa, at the time at which they arise. A discourse-processing account of it would focus on how Michael's understandings of Sirl's utterances depends on the understandings he subsequently displays, and vice versa. One can argue that Sirl and Michael are doing both here. We can display this schematically as illustrated in Figure 5.2.

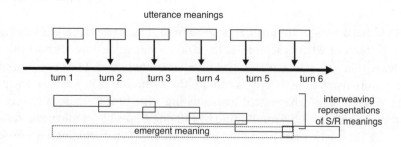

Source: Adapted from Kádár, Dániel Z. and Michael Haugh (2013) *Understanding Politeness*. Cambridge: Cambridge University Press: 118.

Figure 5.2 Utterance versus interactional meaning

The arrow pointing from left to right in this figure represents the temporal constraint on processing meanings in interaction. The individuated boxes pointing to the ends of each turn above the main time arrow represent representations of utterance meanings. The interwoven boxes under the main time arrow represent the interweaving of speaker and recipient representations of speaker (and recipient) meanings. The dotted box underneath the interwoven boxes represents an instance of emergent meaning. The difference between the representations above the time arrow (representing those derived via utterance processing) and those representations below the time arrow (representing those derived via discourse processing) is that the former are formally independent of each other while the latter are formally interdependent.

The point of this figure is not to argue for one approach over the other. Clearly we can view time in both ways: as either punctuated points on a continuum or as interleaving spans across a continuum. It might be suggested that there are thus two important levels of understanding when it comes to pragmatic meaning: utterance meaning and discourse or interactional meaning. How these two levels of pragmatic meaning might interrelate must remain a question for future research.

5.4   Meaning in interactional contexts

We conclude this chapter with a brief consideration of broader contextual influences on the ways in which pragmatic meanings arise in interaction. We have alluded to two key themes in relation to the way in which pragmatic meanings arise in context in our discussion thus far. First, speakers (and indeed recipients in some cases) can be held accountable or responsible for such meanings. Second, pragmatic meanings can be analysed as arising through various meaning-actions, such as *saying* and *implying*. In this section, we expand upon both of these claims in order to deepen our understanding of how pragmatic meanings arise in context.

5.4.1   Pragmatic meaning and accountability

One key issue that came up repeatedly in our discussion in section 5.2 of whose meaning we are talking about was that of **accountability**. We are held to (normatively) mean what we say. We are also held to be meaning what we don't say in many situations. As Cavell (1958) noted very early on in the development of pragmatics, "the 'pragmatic implications' of our utterances are meant...and what we mean to say, like what we mean to do, is something we are responsible for" (1958: 197). When pragmatic meanings arise in actual interactional contexts, then someone is always held responsible or accountable for those meanings, a point which was made in the early work of both ordinary language philosophers (Austin [1962]1975; Cavell 1958) and sociologists (Garfinkel 1967; Goffman 1967). To be held accountable means that the person concerned is taken to be committed to that belief, thought, desire, attitude, intention and so on (Carassa and Colombetti 2009), and/or responsible for the interpersonal and real-world consequences of making this belief, et cetera, a part of the conversational interaction (Garfinkel 1967). The question, however, is *why* a speaker can be held committed to or accountable for a particular pragmatic meaning, even though it has not been expressed. The answer lies, we would suggest, in the assumed **intentionality** of linguistic acts and the presumed **agency** of speakers (Haugh 2013d). Linguistic acts are held to be directed, to be *about* something, and we are presumed to be exercising our agency in producing them. This is why we are held accountable for producing them. How addressees figure out what these linguistic acts are *about* is a separate question (which we have already addressed in the previous section). Accountability thus arises as a consequence of presumptions about intentionality and agency, not exclusively speaker intentions, as has often been assumed.

In examining instances where accounts about pragmatic meaning do surface in interaction, it is evident that participants not only appeal to their own intentions, but also appeal to situational factors, automatic or formulaic actions (i.e. speaking without thinking), emotional stress, lapses in cognitive abilities and their own intentions (Arundale 2008). Speakers may also retreat to what is literally said in attempting to evade being held accountable for pragmatic meanings that have arisen in interactions. Consider example [5.19] from the film *Rush Hour*. When they first met, Chan, a detective from Hong Kong, did not immediately respond when Carter, a detective from LA, asked him *Do you speak any English?*, nor when he next asked in a loud voice, *Do you understand the words that are coming out of my mouth?* From that point onwards Carter assumed that Chan did not speak English. However, this assumption was subsequently proved wrong when Chan intervened at a later point as Carter was being accosted by another policeman. Chan, however, retreated to a literal notion of what is said when challenged by Carter about this.

[5.19] Carter: All of a sudden you speaking English?
Chan: A little.
Carter: My ass. You lied to me
Chan: I didn't say I didn't. You assumed so.
Carter: Assume I kick your little Beijing ass right now. I know you know that tricky shit.

Chan: I'm not responsible for your assumptions.

Carter: You full of shit, you understand that?

Chan: Not being able to speak is not the same as not speaking. You seem as if you like to talk. I let people talk who like to talk. It makes it easier to find out how full of shit they are.

Carter: What the hell did you just say?

> (*Rush Hour*, 1998, director: Brett Ratner,
> writers: Jim Kouf & Ross LaManna)

In the above excerpt, we have an instance of a speaker (Chan) treating a supposition, or possibly an implicated premise on the part of Carter (see section 4.3.2), as not part of what he can be held accountable for meaning (*I'm not responsible for your assumptions*). This is despite the fact that he did not say anything when Carter first greeted him, which could reasonably or normally be assumed to indicate that one does not speak English. Carter does not initially agree with Chan's denial of responsibility (*You full of shit*), but later ends up confused as Chan makes the (admittedly fair) point that *not being able to speak* [English] *is not the same as not speaking* [English].

Reflection: *No means no*

Routine expressions, which we discussed in section 4.3.1, may, in some instances, echo broader societal discourses. In such cases, the question of whether the user of the expression is held accountable for endorsing that broader societal discourse comes into question. Take the expression *no means no*. In the lead up to the 2010 election campaign in Australia, the leader of the opposition, Tony Abbott, was asked about the decision by Julia Gillard, who was Prime Minister at that time, to participate in a live televised debate with him despite earlier saying she would not. He responded as follows:

[5.20]   Are you suggesting to me that when it comes from Julia, "no" doesn't mean no? She said "no" repeatedly. And when she said "no", I thought she meant "no".

> ("Abbott trips on play with female voters", *Lateline*,
> Australian Broadcasting Corporation,
> 3 August 2010, reporter: Dana Robertson)

The use of the phrase *no means no* by a man (Abbott) in reference to a woman (Gillard) accepting or not accepting an invitation (in this case to a televised debate) generated considerable controversy. The then Minister for the Status of Women, Tanya Plibersek, for instance, was quoted as saying:

[5.21] I think he's obviously upset a lot of people, and he really needs to explain what he meant by that. He said it four times, so he obviously thinks it's a pretty clever line.

> ("Abbott trips on play with female voters", *Lateline*,
> Australian Broadcasting Corporation,
> 3 August 2010, reporter: Dana Robertson)

Here Plibersek holds Abbott to account for the meaning routinely associated with the phrase *no means no*, namely, issues of non-consensual sex. Karen Willis, representing the NSW Rape Crisis Centre, defined this meaning more explicitly in claiming that:

[5.22] It's a really clear statement about people's right to say "no" to sexual advances and sexual activity when that's what they choose.

> ("Abbott trips on play with female voters", *Lateline*,
> Australian Broadcasting Corporation,
> 3 August 2010, reporter: Dana Robertson)

In other words, the phrase *no means no* inevitably invokes the issue of non-consensual sexual activity. Abbott attempted to distance himself from this routine meaning and the broader societal discourse it invokes by claiming he could not have meant anything offensive towards women since he himself has daughters:

[5.23] I'm not going to cop this kind of vicious smear from the Labor Party. I'm the father of three daughters and no one respects women more than I do.

> ("Abbott trips on play with female voters", *Lateline*,
> Australian Broadcasting Corporation,
> 3 August 2010, reporter: Dana Robertson)

Gillard herself maintained that Abbott was responsible for his own words in responding, "Mr Abbott's words are a matter for Mr Abbott". In other words, speakers are accountable for what they are taken to mean.

5.4.2 Pragmatic meaning and meaning-actions

A second key issue in relation to pragmatic meaning in context, which came up in our discussion of meaning representations in the previous chapter, is that it can be analysed as arising through various "meaning-actions", including *meaning, saying, implying, suggesting, hinting, insinuating, indicating, alluding, inferring* and so on. This was a point that Grice himself acknowledged in coining the technical notions of *implicate/implicature/implicatum* (Grice [1975]1989: 24), which conflated rather than distinguished between these different types of meaning-actions. There has only been limited work on possible similarities and differences between these (Bertuccelli-Papi 1996; Parret 1994; Weizman 1985). Wierzbicka (1987), for instance, makes the following distinctions between *imply, hint* and *insinuate*:

> *hint*: "one is thinking something that one would quite like to say aloud, but that one refrains from doing so – presumably because one thinks that one shouldn't say it"
>
> (Wierzbicka 1987: 271)

> *imply*: "the speaker wants to cause the addressee to think something... [but] he refrains from saying the thing that he wants to cause them to think. Instead, he says something else... the speaker seems to *assume* that the addressee will be able to 'uncover' the hidden meaning as if it were somehow provided in the utterance itself – being hidden, but present"
>
> (ibid.: 272, original emphasis)

> *insinuate*: the speaker "wants to cause his addressee to think something bad about someone... [but] the speaker doesn't want his information to be too obvious... the attitude is 'I don't want people to be sure that I want to cause them to think this'"
>
> (ibid.: 273)

What is common across all three glosses is that the speaker wants others to think one thing by saying something else. What differentiates *hinting* and *implying* is that the speaker expects others <u>will</u> understand what is *implied*, while others <u>may</u> only understand what is *hinted* at (cf. Parrett 1994: 232). This is a function of the recipient's degree of certainty about the content of the hint, as well as the degree to which the speaker is committed to that meaning. The speaker may also think he or she should not say what is being *hinted at*, while there is no such necessary constraint on what is *implied*. *Insinuating*, on the other hand, involves the speaker wanting others to think something bad about the figure or target, as well as wanting to ensure he or she cannot be held accountable for meaning such a thing (cf. Austin 1962[1975]: 105). However, since the three meaning-actions are only distinguished from the speaker's perspective by Wierzbicka in the above glosses, there is still more work to be done to better understand how such nuances impact on pragmatic meanings in situational contexts.

One example of this is the work by Bertuccelli-Papi (1996) on *insinuating*. She suggests that the act of insinuating "occurs when *A* wants *B* to know *p* but does not want *B* to judge that *A* wanted to tell him *p*" (where *A* is the speaker, *B* is the addressee, and *p* is what is insinuated) (Bertuccelli-Papi 1996: 197). She then examines the machinations of Iago in Shakespeare's play, *Othello*, as an example par excellence of this kind of pragmatic meaning. Iago works on planting doubt in Othello's mind about his relationship with Desdemona: in particular, the idea that she may be having an affair with Cassio. Take the following excerpt from Act III:

[5.24] *Iago.* My Noble Lord.
   Oth. What dost thou say, *Iago*?
   Iago. Did *Michael Cassio*
        When he woo'd my Lady, know of your loue?
   Oth. He did, from first to last:
        Why dost thou aske?
   Iago. But for a satisfaction of my Thought,
        No further harme.
   Oth. Why of thy thought, *Iago*?
   Iago. I did not thinke he had bin acquainted with hir.
   Oth. O yes, and went betweene vs very oft.
   Iago. Indeed?
   Oth. Indeed? I indeed. Discern'st thou ought in that?
        Is he not honest?
   Iago. Honest, my Lord?
   Oth. Honest? I, Honest.
   Iago. My Lord, for ought I know.

(*Othello*, Act III, scene iii; First Folio, 1623)

Here, Iago brings up the issue of Cassio's relationship with Desdemona, and then subtly steers the conversation to the question of Cassio's "honesty". While Iago subsequently declares *Why then I thinke Cassio's an honest man*, his initial expression of uncertainty (*My lord, for ought* [all] *I know*), is enough to plant a seed of doubt' about Cassio in Othello's mind. This ultimately leads Othello to doubt Desdemona's faithfulness to him, which results in disastrous consequences for all.

There is, however, still much to be done in this area, as investigations of meaning-actions have been remarkably limited thus far. The characterisation of meaning-actions in English – and indeed across other languages – thus remains an important area for future investigation in our pursuit of a better understanding of how pragmatic meaning arises in situated contexts.

Reflection: Signifying in African-American Vernacular English (AAVE)

The term **signifying** is used by speakers of African American Vernacular English to refer to instances where the recognition of unsaid meaning is obscured by the ostensible content or function of what is said. Morgan (1996) focuses on two related practices of signifying:

Pointed indirectness: "when a speaker ostensibly says something to someone (mock receiver) that is intended for – and to be heard by – someone else and is so recognised"

Baited indirectness: "when a speaker attributes a feature to someone which may or may not be true or which the speaker knows the interlocutor does not consider to be a true feature"

(Morgan 1996: 406)

While these two ways of signifying are not necessarily unique to speakers of AAVE, the ways in which they are accomplished as *signifying* involves resources particular to this variety of English. These include what is termed **reading dialect**, where lexical or grammatical features of AAVE are mixed in with mainstream American English in an obvious way: certain prosodic features, such as loud talking, high pitch and so on; and interactional features, such as gaze or parallelism in grammatical structures and word order. In the following excerpt from a conversation between African-American family members, including the researcher (Marcyliena) and three others (Judy, Ruby and Baby Ruby), we can observe some of these resources deployed in framing their talk as signifying on one of the participants, Judy. Marcyliena is Judy's daughter, Ruby is Judy's sister, while "Baby Ruby" (her nickname) is Judy and Ruby's niece.

[5.25] Teenage days
```
 1  M:  What- what- what- I MEAN- what was teena- being a
 2          teenager like I mean what was::
 3  J:   O:h I was: gor[geous
 4  BR:              [OH well by that time HO:NEY? her hea:d
 5          was SO: big
 6  R:               [O:H my GO:D O:H my GO:D
 7          (.)
 8  M:   This is the Coca Cola pha:se?
 9  BR:  O:H BABY The whole works (.) She was the only one (.)
10          She ran in the Miss black WHAT↑EV?:ER thing
11          they was RUNNING in those da:ys=
12  R:  =Sure di:d
```
(Morgan 1996: 418)

This signifying episode is triggered by Judy's response in line 3 to the researcher's question about what it was like being a teenager at that time. Baby Ruby employs pointed indirectness, in line 4–5, by addressing the researcher, who is also Judy's daughter, rather than Judy herself in the subsequent turn, and baited indirectness through a negative assessment that is directed at Judy, namely, being conceited (despite the fact that Judy probably had good reason to think she was beautiful). What makes this signifying on Judy rather than just simply teasing or mocking is indexed through a number of features of Baby Ruby's, and subsequently Ruby's, talk. These include AAVE lexical items and prosody that signal a negative assessment amongst African-American women, such as *honey* (line 4), which is "often used among women to introduce a gossip episode or an unflattering assessment", and *baby* (line 9), which "can imply a negative assessment as well as address those present" (ibid. 420). The concessive noun phrase "whatever" also functions as a negative quantifier of "thing" (line 10), which in this case in AAVE refers to an "attitude, belief or life". In other words, it means something like "whatever fit her ego" (ibid. 420). Finally, Judy's silence also confirms that signifying has occurred here, since any response would only confirm Baby Ruby's negative assessment, thereby treating the baited indirectness as true. We will revisit the issue of mocking in other varieties of English in our discussion of impoliteness in section 7.5.

5.5 Conclusion

The analysis of pragmatic meaning, or meaning beyond what is said, as opposed to compositional or semantic meaning, has been one of the primary foci of research in pragmatics to date. The traditional Gricean view is that speaker meaning arises from inferences made by recipients about the speaker's intentions. This amounts to the claim that speaker meaning arises from recipients figuring out what speakers intend to mean. Since it arises through pseudo-logical inferences, pragmatic meaning is generally assumed to be cancellable as opposed to what is said$_1$, which is not as straightforwardly cancellable (see also section 3.3.2). Such a view raises questions about the interface between the two types of meaning, that is, between pragmatic and semantic accounts of meaning, an issue which remains the subject of considerable debate, as we have seen.

We have also suggested in this chapter and the preceding one that pragmatic meaning is much more complex and multi-faceted than the received view allows for. One key question that we have asked is: what kind of content or information are we talking about? In pragmatics we focus on meaning representations that encompass content or information beyond what is said or expressed. These include unsaid content such as presuppositions, which were discussed in Chapter 3, and implicatures, which were discussed in more detail in Chapter 4. But it also includes, as we saw in section 4.3, various representations that lie between what is (literally) said and what is implicated.

A second important question to ask is: whose meaning are we talking about? In pragmatics we are interested in users of language. The focus in pragmatics has traditionally been on so-called speaker meaning, which is generally conceptualised as either what the speaker intends to mean, or what the recipient thinks the speaker intends to mean. However, as we have seen, the received view underestimates the importance of other perspectives on pragmatic meaning, including those of various kinds of recipients, which arise independently of inferences about the speaker's intentions. We have introduced the notions of footing and participation framework to allow for a more fine-grained analysis of different user perspectives on pragmatic meaning.

A third key question to ask is: how do pragmatic meanings arise in discourse and interaction? There are two ways in which we have approached this question. One way has been by focusing on the processes by which we understand meaning. In pragmatics the focus has traditionally been on understanding meaning at the level of utterances, with a particular emphasis on the cognitive processes by which participants figure out the meaning of utterances (as opposed to sentences), and what guides those processes. However, as we have seen, we can also approach the understanding of pragmatic meaning from the perspective of discourse processing, both within and across utterances. According to this view, the processes underlying pragmatic meaning involve the incremental and sequential intertwining of the cognitive processes and pragmatic meaning representations of different users. We can approach the analysis of pragmatic meaning in both ways. This is not to suggest that these two approaches to analysing pragmatic meaning in context are complementary or even compatible, but simply to acknowledge there is always more than one way of looking at the world.

The flipside of understanding meaning is the way in which users can create meaning. Speakers may say something independently, or may jointly say something with another speaker. They may also imply or not say things in various ways. This has implications for the degree to which speakers (and/or recipients) are held to be committed to or accountable for particular instances of pragmatic meaning. This has generally been glossed over in many accounts of pragmatic meaning, although it was arguably central to Grice's original program on the normative ways in which speaker meanings are made available to participants.

Notably, much of the theorisation of pragmatic meaning rests on (intuitive) distinctions that are made in English between *saying, implying, hinting* and so on. There even appears to be some differences across varieties of English in the range of practices by which pragmatic meanings arise. The phenomenon of signifying in AAVE is a case in point. It thus remains a significant question for pragmatics whether such distinctions can always be straightforwardly applied across other languages. One thing is clear though: pragmatic meaning is complex. It can be understood and analysed from multiple perspectives. While this sometimes makes it difficult to pin down analytically, it is also what makes it such a rich area of study in pragmatics.

6 Pragmatic Acts

6.1 Introduction

Traditionally, philosophers of language such as Bertrand Russell, Gottlob Frege and Rudolph Carnap, have focused on the **truth value** of sentences, that is whether a sentence is a true or false representation of real-world facts or conditions. They have been particularly interested in linguistic manipulations of the truth value of sentences. Compare:

[6.1] a) Jonathan and Michael wrote this pragmatics book.
       b) Jonathan and Michael did not write this pragmatics book.

If (a) is true, then (b) is false; if (b) is true, then (a) is false. In his later works, Wittgenstein, however, took an entirely different tack, arguing that language was a social activity and that "the meaning of a word is its use in the language" (1953: §43, 20, cited in Bach 2004: 463). Use in language is very much what pragmatics is about. But if we are studying usage, then in fact we are not simply studying sentences, or words, or any other traditional linguistic unit. Many pragmatics scholars deploy the notion of the **utterance**. Utterances are not abstract like sentences. Sentences can, for example, be realised as many different utterances (think, for example, of the different prosodies with which the sentence *I'm sorry* could be uttered). Some utterances do have an aspect that can be analysed in terms of their truth value, but some do not. As exemplified by (a) and (b) above, utterances that have the form of declarative sentences are the main focus of many academic studies, because they express **propositions** or states of affairs which are **truth conditional**, that is, the state of affairs represented through the proposition can be evaluated against real-world conditions. This is not the case (or at least not straightforwardly the case) with interrogative or imperative sentences. Moreover, utterances do not even require traditional words in order to be pragmatically meaningful. Asking whether, say, the expressions *ah* or *oh* are true or not is simply an irrelevant question. Instead, the utterances are geared towards doing things – towards expressing surprise, confirming, acknowledging and so on. One drawback with the notion of utterance, which we should briefly mention, is that it suggests meanings are simply generated by speech. Of course, writing does this too, as the examples in this book illustrate. More particularly, the term utterance does not capture non-verbal meanings. For example, nodding one's head is a way of expressing the affirmative in a number of English-speaking cultures. More accurately then, we are dealing with pragmatic behaviours generally, though we shall focus on utterances in particular.

This chapter elaborates on actions constituting interaction. We start from traditional speech act theory, then discuss the ways in which it has been applied, along with some of its deficiencies, and then in the final sections we suggest some modified or alternative approaches.

6.2 Traditional speech act theory

6.2.1 Doing thing with words: J. L. Austin

The language philosopher J. L. Austin ([1962]1975: 5) observed, at the beginning of his published lectures, that some utterances "do not 'describe' or 'report'" something that is " true or false", that is to say, they are not truth conditional. In fact, they are not a matter of "'just' saying something" but of "doing an action" (ibid.). This essential observation, expounded in his works, gave raise to **speech act theory**, a theory that underpins much of pragmatics.

Austin initially focused on a special class of verbs, **performative verbs**, whose purpose is not to "describe" things but, "in the appropriate circumstances", to "do" them (ibid.: 6). Some examples are:

[6.2] I **pronounce** you man and wife.
       I **sentence** you to six months' imprisonment.
       I **apologise** for the noise.
       I **promise** to cook you a meal.

A cautionary note is in order here. The performativity of performative verbs does not rest entirely in their semantics but is sensitive to both linguistic and non-linguistic context. For example, if I said I *apologise all the time*, that usage of *apologise* does not seem to be performing an act of apology but describing what I do all the time. Performative verbs name the action they perform (e.g. *apologise* names the apology which the utterance performs); they have a metapragmatic aspect (see Chapter 8). If this is the case, there is a sense – contrary to Austin – in which such verbs are not simply engaged in performance (see Bach and Harnish 1992). At one level they name or describe the act being performed (e.g. whether somebody is pronouncing, sentencing, etc.), and at this level are truth conditional (e.g. whether someone is truly doing it). At another more indirect level they actually perform the action in the context of a wedding, and so on.

The utterances in which performative verbs occur are called **performative utterances** or simply performatives (Austin 1975: 6). Subsequent researchers (e.g. Thomas 1995) have pointed to different types of performative utterances, including:

> Ritual performatives e.g. *I baptise you, I name this ship* [These are associated with highly institutionalised contexts.]
> Self-referential performatives e.g. *I apologise, I plead not guilty* [These are somewhat ritualistic too, or at least formal, but note that because they refer to what the speaker is doing, they are difficult to falsify (literally speaking, one could not accuse someone of not apologising, pleading guilt, etc., when they have just labelled what they have done).]
> Collaborative performatives e.g. *I bet you, I challenge you* [These require the collaboration of another participant, e.g. if you propose a bet, it only works if the other participant accepts the bet.]

A test of whether one's utterance contains a performative verb, thus making it a performative utterance, is the *hereby* **test** (Austin 1975: 57–61; other tests are elaborated in Austin 1975: 79–80). If you can insert the word *hereby* between the subject and the verb, and it sounds acceptable, you probably have a performative verb on your hands. All of the above examples could accept the word *hereby* before the performative verb. In these contexts, *hereby* has the sense of "by these words or behaviours" I perform the action named by the verb. This is why examples such as *I hereby am tired* sound very odd. However, the test is not perfect. One problem is that the formality of the word *hereby* makes it sound odd for "everyday" apologies, promises, etc.. This formality, and specifically its association with institutional contexts, can be seen in the words with which it collocates most frequently. The top 25 most frequent collocates of *hereby* in the two-billion word Oxford English Corpus (OEC) are as follows:

> declare, agree, give, grant, order, find, sentence, acknowledge, consent, authorise, certify, undertake, invite, confirm, present, dismiss, call, announce, proclaim, request, covenant, appoint, offer, release, pledge

The actions of granting, sentencing, consenting, authorising and so on are all clearly associated with power in institutional contexts, and indeed scrutiny of the contexts of these collocates reveals governmental, legislative, bureaucratic and so on contexts. This association is also true of some of the other more innocuous items. For example, *find* is associated with the expression "find you (not) guilty" issued in the courtroom. A further problem is that *hereby* can sound fine in an utterance, yet need not have anything to do with performative verbs. In the following example, it refers to the means, spelt out in the first sentence, by which a film reappeared:

[6.3] The fetish value of films like Human Lanterns is proportional to the inflated wistfulness with which we desire them, and surpluses of pristine DVDs make us wistful no longer, deflating our infantile fantasies of cult-film deviance and transgression into a hesitant sigh of belated self-examination. Two such "deflationary films" by Shaw Brothers workhorse Ho Meng-hua have <u>hereby</u> resurfaced. (OEC)

However, we should also note that performative utterances often have other formal characteristics, including the following grammatical features (Austin 1975: 55–66) (the asterisk means that the utterance is infelicitous as far as being a performative promise is concerned):

- past tense (**I promised to cook you a meal*);
- simple or progressive aspect (*I am promising to cook you a meal. *I am promised to cook you a meal*);
- declarative and non-hypothetical (**Shall I promise to cook you a meal? *Promise that you will cook me a meal. *I might promise to cook you a meal*); and
- subject is usually a first person pronoun, but second or third person is possible if the speaker is acting as a "mouthpiece" (*You are hereby promised [...]. Lancaster University hereby promises you [...]*).

To these we could add other features, such as prosody (e.g. a rising intonation indicating an enquiry or question), or non-verbal actions (e.g. gestures) (cf. Austin 1975: 73ff.).

Beyond formal characteristics, performative utterances are crucially dependent not on truth conditions but on a set of contextual factors, the "appropriate circumstances" mentioned earlier. When something "goes wrong" with the act of the performative utterance, including its performance in inappropriate circumstances, it is not "false but in general *unhappy*" (ibid.: 14). Things that can be or go wrong are termed "infelicities", and are listed as a set of "necessary conditions" (ibid.) for a performative to function happily – hence **felicity conditions**. Austin (1975: 12ff.) devoted some space to these felicity conditions, because they are important. For example, if a judge sentenced somebody in a courtroom according to "an accepted conventional procedure having a certain conventional effect" (1975: 14) (e.g. using the conventional expression *I sentence you to X*), one could not dismiss the sentencing as false (untrue), as the judge would have acted in this respect felicitously in performing the *act* of sentencing. Compare this with a judge saying, for example, *you're going down for a long time*. If it turned out that the judge was in fact the courtroom cleaner, the act would be infelicitous with respect to "the particular persons or circumstances" being "appropriate for the invocation of the particular procedure invoked" (1975: 15). If the judge had sentenced the defendant before the verdict was reached, as the Queen of Cards tries to do in Lewis Carroll's fictional story *Alice in Wonderland*, or had fainted after saying just *I sentence you*, the act would be infelicitous with respect to the procedure being "executed by all participants both correctly and completely" (ibid.). Some performatives require participants to have certain "thoughts, feelings and intentions" (ibid.). Apologies are a case in point. Here, the apologiser must (appear to) be contrite about what they have done. Not only this, but with such acts Austin adds that the participant "must actually so conduct themselves subsequently" (1975: 15). Somebody who apologises for tripping somebody up and then does it again and again, would be acting infelicitously.

Reflections: Explicit performatives in early modern English

Explicit performatives were much more frequent in early modern English, especially as part of the grammatical frame FIRST PERSON PRONOUN + PERFORMATIVE VERB + SECOND PERSON PRONOUN (occasional optional elements include auxiliary *do* or adverbial elements). Thus we find *I thank you, I warrant you, I assure you, I beseech you, I entreat you, I pray you* and so on in abundance. With perhaps the exception of *I assure you*, all these are distinctly archaic today. *I pray you* is in fact the most frequent three-word collocational bundle in Shakespeare (and one that he uses more frequently than his contemporaries) (see Culpeper 2007). Consider the following excerpt from Shakespeare's play *Hamlet*.

[6.4]   *Ham.*   I do not well vnderstand that. Will you play vpon this
                Pipe?
        Guild.   My Lord, I cannot.
        Ham.   I pray you.
        Guild.   Beleeue me, I cannot.
        Ham.   I do beseech you.
        Guild.   I know no touch of it, my Lord.
                          (Hamlet, Act 3, Scene 2; First Folio)

In this scene, Hamlet tries to persuade Guildenstern to play the pipe. Guildenstern's reluctance can partly be explained by the fact that it is insulting for people of his standing to do so. *I do beseech you* is clearly an act of entreating. *I pray you* is a little trickier. Originally, it was an act of semi-religious supplication. However, as it came to be used frequently in conjunction with requests, its meaning bleached, so that it took on the sense of a politeness marker to facilitate requests. In fact, glossing *I pray you* with today's *please* would not be wide of the mark.

In his lectures, Austin first introduces the audience to performatives, and then moves on to a broader perspective. One step in this direction was the observation that utterances do not need a performative verb to perform an act (Austin 1975: 32ff.). Compare:

[6.5] (a) I promise to give you the money back tomorrow
       (b) I'll give you the money tomorrow

Both involve an act of promising; (a) is usually referred to as an **explicit performative**, and (b) an **implicit performative** (Austin 1975: 32). Another step was the observation that utterances could be viewed in terms of three different aspects, which we can simplify thus (for more detailed definitions, see Austin 1975: 94–132):

Locutionary act: "the act *of* saying something" (Austin 1975: 94; our emphasis); essentially, the production of an expression with sense and reference.

Illocutionary act: "the performance of an act *in* saying something" (ibid.: 99); essentially, the act the produced expression performs, such as informing, ordering, undertaking and sentencing (sometimes referred to as the **illocutionary force** of the utterance).

Perlocutionary act: "what we bring about or achieve *by* saying something" (ibid.: 109); essentially, the effects on the feelings, thoughts and actions of the participants brought about by the produced expression.

It is important to note here that Austin is separating meaning, traditionally defined in terms of sense and reference, from performing a function. For example, in a hot classroom a teacher might articulate to the student sitting next to the window the words *It's hot in here* (locutionary act), and in saying this they perform an act of request (illocutionary act), with the effect that the student opens the window (perlocutionary act). Although speech act theory encompasses all three aspects, in subsequent work the notion of a **speech act** is virtually synonymous with illocutionary act (or illocutionary force). Speech acts include, for example, assertions, requests, commands, apologies, threats, compliments, warnings and advice.

Initially, Austin (1975: 3ff.) had distinguished performatives from what he called "constatives", which are defined not in terms of "doing" but "saying", statements being a paradigm case. However, crucially, towards the end of his lecture series, he revisited this distinction in a broader perspective (1975: 133ff.). Even statements in the form of declarative sentences, such as *We are writing this chapter*, perform an act: they *state* or *assert* that a particular state of affairs applies. These too, then, perform an illocutionary act and, following on from that, an act that is subject to appropriate circumstances or felicity conditions. For example, stating something which you knew to be untrue would not meet the felicity condition of having the requisite thoughts. In the light of a general theory of speech acts, the distinction between performatives and constatives dissolves. Constatives have a performative aspect which we can refer to as their illocutionary aspect, just as the performatives discussed above do. What performative utterances have is a particular formal characteristic such that their verbs make explicit their particular illocutionary force.

Reflection: English verbs – English speech act theory?

There is no doubt that theorists such as Austin were influenced by performative verbs as they formulated speech act theory. Performative or speech act verbs offer tangible signs of conventional illocutionary acts. However, the danger here is that the theory is being shaped by the performative verbs of *English*, yet assumed to be appropriate for other languages and cultures. Rosaldo (1982: 228) points out that John R. Searle, a pupil of Austin's, "uses English performative verbs as guides to something like a universal law". But her study of the performative verbs used by the Ilongots illustrates that such verbs are not at all universal. Two quotations from her work elaborate the point:

> To Westerners, taught to think of social life as constituted by so many individuated cells, prosocial impulses and drives may seem a necessary prerequisite to social bonds, and so the notion of a world where no one "promises," "apologizes," "congratulates," "establishes commitments," or "gives thanks," may seem either untenable or anomic. Certainly, when in the field, I was consistently distressed to find that Ilongots did not appear to share in my responses to such things as disappointment or success, and that they lacked expressive forms with which to signal feelings of appreciation, obligation, salutation, and regret, like our "I'm sorry" or "good morning". (Rosaldo 1982: 217–218)

> The closest Ilongot equivalent to our "promise" is called *sigem*, a formulaic oath by salt, wherein participants declare that if their words prove false, their lives, like salt, will be "dissolved." But Ilongot oaths are different from our "promises" in the central fact that *sigem* speaks not

to commitments personally assumed (and for which subsequent viola-
tors might, as individuals, be held in fault) but to constraints based on
external, "supernatural" sorts of law. (ibid.: 219)

The problem described in this box spurred Anna Wierzbicka, Cliff
Goddard and colleagues to develop a **Natural Semantic Metalanguage**,
as elaborated in section 6.4. The point of this metalanguage was to enable
descriptions, including descriptions of speech acts, without the bias caused
by the particular descriptive language (see especially Wierzbicka's 1987
description of English speech act verbs).

6.2.2 Developing speech act theory: Searle

John R. Searle did much to develop Austin's work, especially the notion of illocutionary act, and also to bring it to the attention of a wider range of scholars.
We will focus on two of his contributions in this section – his formalisation of
felicity conditions and his development of a taxonomy of speech act types –
and one contribution in the following section – namely, indirect speech acts.

Austin's notion of felicity conditions was developed and formalised by Searle
(e.g. 1969). Searle tried to devise **constitutive rules** for speech acts; that is, rules
that create the activity itself, just as is the case with a game of football or chess (such
rules contrast with **regulative rules**, such as the rules to regulate car traffic). This
is rather different from Austin's tack whereby felicity conditions were conceived
of as necessary for the "happy" performance of a speech act, rather than actually
constituting them. Consider Searle's felicity conditions for the speech act of promising (the rightmost column is based on information in Searle 1969: 57–60):

Table 6.1 Felicity conditions for promising

Felicity condition	Clarification	Exemplification: promising
Propositional content	What the utterance is about (what the utterance predicates)	Future A (act) of S (the speaker)
Preparatory	Real-world prerequisites (the interlocutors' beliefs about ability to perform the act, the act's costs or benefits, its norms of occurrence, etc.)	1. H (the hearer) wants S to perform A 2. It is not obvious that S will do A in the normal course of events
Sincerity	The beliefs, feelings and intentions of the speaker	S intends to do A
Essential	What is needed for the act to be performed (i.e. the mutual recognition that the speaker intends an utterance to count as a certain act)	Counts as an undertaking by S of an obligation to do A

This scheme seems to have the potential to distinguish one speech act from another, and thereby to offer a robust and comprehensive description of speech acts. For example, in order to achieve a description of the speech act of threat, we simply need to tweak one felicity condition of promising: changing the first preparatory condition to "H does not want S to perform A". In practice, however, such descriptions are of limited use, notably because speech acts do not lend themselves to neat categorisation. For example, suggestions, advice, warnings and threats have a habit of blurring into each other. We will address the issue of indeterminacy further in section 6.5. One particular point to note about Searle's framework for speech acts, and also one that departs somewhat from Austin's, is its closer alignment with the internal properties of the speaker, their beliefs, feelings and especially intentions (see Sbisà 2002). For Searle (e.g. 2007: 28), speech acts express intentional states. Therein lies a problem, the effects of illocutionary acts depend upon the recognition of the speaker's intentions by the hearer, and this, as we noted in sections 5.3.2 and 5.3.3, is far from straightforward (but see Sadock 2004: 59). In contrast, Austin (e.g. 1975: 109) associated illocutionary forces more strongly with convention.

Reflection: Emoticons as indicators of illocutionary force

Emoticons in text-based forms of computer-mediated communication, such as email, SMS texting, Messenger, discussion boards and so on, are generally assumed to constitute iconic indicators of emotion, for example, the use of ☺ to indicate the producer is happy or pleased and the use of ☹ to indicate that he or she is somehow unhappy. While the use of emoticons to index such emotions is a complex topic in itself, Dresner and Herring (2010) have recently argued that emoticons can also be used to indicate the illocutionary force of the text they accompany. In other words, they can be used to help the recipient figure out the speech act(s) being performed by the text message. In the following example from a help chatroom, the guide's response to a query from a user is accompanied by a smile emoticon.

[6.6]   JKingsbury: GUIDE > have you ever made a homepage on aol?
        Guide ASH: JK, yes and I can't get rid of the stupid thing! :)
                                          (Dresner and Herring 2010: 258)

JK's query elicits a response from the guide that appears to be a strong complaint. This could be regarded as unhelpful considering he/she is supposed to be offering advice and information to users in the chatroom.

> However, the emoticon here functions to index this as "a mild, humorous complaint", as well as expressing a friendly attitude towards the user. In other words, the illocutionary force of the text message here is modified from a strong to a mild complaint through the deployment of an emoticon.

Searle (1979) was not the first to suggest that speech acts could be grouped into more general types. Austin (1975: 150ff.) had, in fact, proposed his own groupings, based on his understandings of a number of performative verbs. The result was not ideal, for a number of reasons, including the fact that some of the categories were less than watertight. Searle (1979) based his taxonomy on a number of pragmatic dimensions. These include the **illocutionary point** of an act, that is, its purpose (e.g. for a promise it is to create an obligation that the speaker undertakes); the **expressed psychological state** (e.g. for an apology it is the expression of regret); its degree of **strength** (e.g. a suggestion is less strong than an insistence); and, importantly, its **direction of fit** (the relationship between the words and the world). Table 6.2 displays the five speech act categories that constitute Searle's taxonomy, plus the additional category of rogative, proposed by Leech (1983). Inspired by Peccei (1999: 53), it also displays how those categories vary according to direction of fit, along with who is responsible for making that relationship happen.

Table 6.2 Searle's (1979) classification of speech acts (incorporating Leech's 1983 "rogatives")

Speech act type	Direction of fit	Responsibility
DECLARATIONS (e.g. naming, baptising, sentencing)	The words change the world	Speaker
REPRESENTATIVES (e.g. stating, affirming, describing)	The words fit the "outside" world	Speaker
EXPRESSIVES (apologising, thanking, congratulating)	The words fit the "psychological"	Speaker
ROGATIVES (questioning, asking, querying)	The words fit the world	Hearer
COMMISSIVES (promising, threatening, offering)	The world will fit the words	Speaker
DIRECTIVES (commanding, requesting, suggesting)	The world will fit the words	Hearer

By way of illustration, each of examples [6.7] to [6.12] contain a speech act belonging to each of these types (they are presented in the order of Table 6.2) (key elements in examples are underlined):

[6.7]   **Plead (type of declaration):**

Judge: How does your client plead to charges of providing material support for terrorism?

Lawyer: <u>Guilty</u>.

[David Hicks pleaded guilty on 27 March 2007. He was subsequently sentenced to nine months in jail.]

> ("Australian pleads guilty to terrorism charge", Associated Press, 27 May 2007, http://www.nbcnews.com/id/17801019/)

[6.8]   **Assertion (type of representative):**

George W. Bush: <u>Third, this bill meets our commitment to America's Armed Forces by preparing them to meet the threats of tomorrow. Our enemies are innovative and resourceful, and so are we. They never stop thinking about new ways to harm our country and our people, and neither do we. We must never stop thinking about how best to defend our country when we all must always be forward-thinking.</u>

(5 August 2004, http://georgewbush-whitehouse.archives.gov/news/releases/2004/08/20040805-3.html)

[6.9]   **Insult (type of expressive):**

Simon: Oh Scott, <u>it was dreadful</u>.

(quizzical look from Scott) No, no <u>really dreadful</u>. And uhm, I'm saying that to be kind because<u> you will never ever, ever, ever have a career in singing</u>.

Scott: I don't believe you.

> (*American Idol*, Season 1, Episode 1, 11 June 2002, director: Andrew Scheer)

[6.10] **Questioning (type of rogative):**

Julius: Hey man, <u>whatcha' doin'</u>?

Chris: I'm takin' canned goods to school for the needy.

Julius: That's $2.89 worth of food. <u>What're ya tryin' to do?</u> <u>Feed the needy or be the needy</u>?

> ("Everybody hates Christmas", *Everybody Hates Chris*, Season 1, Episode 11, 15 December 2005, director: Dennie Gordon, writers: Alyson Fouse & Ali LeRoi)

[6.11] **Promise (type of commissive):**

Farquad: Congratulations, ogre. You've won the honour of embarking on a great and noble quest.

Shrek: Quest? I'm already on a quest, a quest to get my swamp back.

Farquad: Your swamp?

Shrek: Yeah, my swamp! Where you dumped those fairy tale creatures.

Farquad: Indeed. Alright ogre. I'll make you a deal. <u>Go on this quest for me, and I'll give you</u> your swamp back.

          (*Shrek*, 2001, director: Andrew Adamson & Vicky Jenson,
          writers: Ted Elliot, Terry Rossio,
          Joe Stillman & Roger Schulman)

[6.12] **Request (type of directive)**

(*Lisa calls the "Corey hotline"*)

Corey: Hi, you've reached the Corey hotline. $4.95 a minute. Here are some words that rhyme with Corey: Gory. Story. Allegory. Montessori.

(*later*)

Marge: Why didn't you ask our permission, Lisa?

Lisa: I did!

(*flashback*)

Lisa: Dad, <u>can I...</u>

Homer: Yeah, yeah, yeah.

          ("Brother from the same planet", *The Simpsons*,
          Season 4, Episode 12, 3 February 1993,
          director: Jeffrey Lynch, writer: Jon Vitti)

Reflection: Speech act types and Irish English

How are speech act types distributed in English? A robust and detailed answer to this question has been provided by John Kirk and Jeffrey Kallen with respect to Irish English. They pragmatically annotated the Irish component of the International Corpus of English (626,597 words in total), thereby creating SPICE-Ireland (Systems of Pragmatic annotation for the spoken component of ICE-Ireland). With over 54,612 speech act annotations, the result is a remarkably rich resource. Regarding speech act types, they revealed representatives and directives to be outstandingly frequent; other speech act types have much lower frequencies. Further, speech act types vary according to text type. For example, representatives are especially frequent in face-to-face conversation, spontaneous commentary and telephone conversation; directives are outstandingly frequent in demonstrations, but also frequent in business transactions, classroom discussion, face-to-face conversation, telephone conversation and legal cross-examination. For more detail, see Kallen and Kirk (2012).

Reflection: Changing speech act type over time – the example of *cursing*

Speech acts can change speech act type over time. Consider the speech act of cursing, as elaborated in Culpeper and Semino (2000). The example below reports an act of cursing in early modern England.

[6.13]   And she this Examinate further saith, That about sixe or seuen yeares agoe, the said *Chattox* did fall out with one *Hugh Moore* of Pendle, as aforesaid, about certaine cattell of the said *Moores*, which the said *Moore* did charge the said *Chattox* to haue bewitched: for which the said *Chattox* did curse and worry the said *Moore*, and said she would be reuenged of the said *Moore*: whereupon the said *Moore* presently fell sicke, and languished about halfe a yeare, and then died. Which *Moore* vpon his death-bed said, that the said *Chattox* had bewitched him to death.

(*Pendle witches*, 1612: 47)

At this time, the belief system supported the idea that witches' words had the power to change the world (e.g. cause sickness and death). Being bewitched was a perlocutionary effect of cursing. Curses were a type of declaration. Now consider an example of recent use:

[6.14]   I looked out of the wind-shaken carriage, where people were moaning and cursing and making vows to start going by bus

(*BNC* G0A 1364, imaginative prose fiction, *The Crow Road*)

Here, note that the verb collocates with *moaning*. Today, cursing is more about expressing ill feelings, being bad-tempered and using taboo language; it now fits the expressive group. This particular shift in speech act type represents a shift towards the expression of the speaker's feelings, a shift that is in tune with Traugott's (e.g. 1982) hypothesis of a general process of semantic change towards increasing subjectivisation (i.e. the expression of the speaker's attitude).

There have been numerous other attempts to classify speech acts, of which we should mention Bach and Harnish (1979), Ballmer and Brennenstuhl (1981) and Wierzbicka (1987). The fact that no definitive taxonomy has emerged is evidence of the fact that classifying language functions of any type is very difficult. Having said that, taxonomies have emerged that have sufficed for some analytical purposes (see, for example, the above reflection box involving the analysis of historical change).

6.3   Directness/indirectness; explicitness/implicitness

Searle (1969: 30) coined the term **illocutionary force indicating devices (IFIDs)** for the formal devices of an utterance used to signal its illocutionary force. We have already met a highly explicit IFID, namely, performative verbs. IFIDs need not be lexical or grammatical, a rising intonation contour is thought to have some kind of conventional association with speech acts that question or inquire. It is crucial, however, to remember that even with IFIDs there is no guarantee of a particular illocutionary force; that depends on the rest of the discourse and the context (e.g. *I promise I'll withhold your pocket money* is a threat, not a promise, despite the IFID). The issue of form, and whether it matches a particular illocutionary force, is pertinent to the apparent correspondence between grammatical sentence type (or form) and speech act (or illocutionary force). In English there are three major sentence types which are associated with three speech acts, as displayed in Table 6.3.

The problem is that in present-day English there is frequently a mismatch between sentence type and speech act. Consider Table 6.4. Despite the mismatches between requests and the interrogative and declarative sentence types, it is not difficult to imagine contexts where these would count as requests. Note that they differ in terms of how directly the speech act is performed. *Give me a hand* is direct; *Can you give me a hand?* is indirect (in direct terms, it is a question about whether the addressee has the ability to give a hand); and *I can't do this on my own* is off-record (i.e. a hint). The second example here fits Searle's classic definition of **indirect speech acts**: "cases in which

Table 6.3   Sentence type and speech act correspondences

Sentence type	Example	Speech act
Imperative	Finish your homework!	Command
Interrogative	Have you finished your homework?	Question/inquiry
Declarative	My homework is finished.	Assertion

Table 6.4   Sentence type and speech act mismatches

Sentence type	Example	Speech act
Imperative	Pass me the salt.	Request
Interrogative	Can you give me the salt?	Request
Declarative	This could do with a little salt.	Request

one illocutionary act is performed indirectly by way of performing another" (1975: 60). However, there is little agreement on the status of direct/indirect speech acts or how indirect speech acts work (see Aijmer 1996: 126–128, for a brief overview), and some have even proposed that a scale of directness be dispensed with altogether (Wierzbicka 1991[2003]: 88–89).

Perhaps the single most important application of speech act theory, and specifically the application of notions of indirectness to requests, is the work undertaken by Shoshana Blum-Kulka and colleagues (e.g. Blum-Kulka et al. 1989b) as part of the *Cross-cultural Speech Act Realisation Project* (CCSARP's). What is of particular interest to us here is how they systematised indirectness, because the approach affords insights into how indirectness works in requests. Blum-Kulka and her colleagues identified nine (in)directness strategy types. We give them in brief below (details can be found in Blum-Kulka et al. (1989b: 18), and the CCSARP coding manual in Blum-Kulka et al. (1989a: 278–281)):

Direct (impositives)

1. Mood derivable (e.g. Give me a hand)
2. Performatives (e.g. I ask you to give me a hand)
3. Hedged performatives (e.g. Might I ask you to give me a hand?)
4. Obligation statements (e.g. You must give me a hand)
5. Want statements (e.g. I want you to give me a hand)

Conventionally indirect

6. Suggestory formulae (e.g. Why don't you give me a hand?)
7. Query preparatory (e.g. Can you give me a hand?)

Non-conventionally indirect (hints)

8. Strong hints (e.g. This would be easier if somebody gave me a hand)
9. Mild hints (e.g. This is going to take me ages to do)

It is worth noting, at this point, that requestive strategy taxonomies vary widely in the number of strategies they propose. Aijmer (1996: 132–133), for example, identifies 18. We cannot assume, therefore, that any set of strategies "fit" any data. In addition, the term "direct" in Blum-Kulka's work does not have the sense that Searle intended for it. If that were so, "obligation *statements*" (e.g. *you must go now*) and "want *statements*" (e.g. *I want you to go now*) would be considered indirect, as they are statements or assertions doing the job of requests. Instead, "directness" seems to refer to the explicitness with which the illocutionary point is signalled by the utterance, and complex processes of conventionalisation or standardisation feed that explicitness. Indeed,

Blum-Kulka and House (1989: 133) refer to indirectness as "a measure of illocutionary transparency".

In our view Searle's (1975) notion of directness, essentially concerning (mis) matchings of syntax and speech act, only captures one aspect, though an important one, of what is going on with indirectness. Generally, we prefer the notion of **pragmatic explicitness**, which is based on the transparency of three things: the illocutionary point, the target and the semantic content. The transparency of the illocutionary point is roughly what Searle was talking about. This is essentially where a speech act is not achieved through its base sentence type or, more broadly, where one act is achieved through performing another; for example, saying one is busy (an assertion) to imply one cannot go to a party (a refusal). The transparency of the target can also increase directness. Compare *Be quiet!* with *You be quiet!* The latter example is more explicit in picking out the target through the use of *you*. And the transparency of the semantic content can also increase directness. Compare *Be quiet!* with *Be noiseless!* In this case, *quiet* has a closer match with the desired state than the circumlocution *noiseless*.

One particular contribution made by Blum-Kulka and colleagues was to widen the scope of their consideration of indirectness to include linguistic material working in conjunction with the central speech act utterance. They analysed requests in terms of three major structural categories: the **head act**, **alerter** and **support move** (Blum-Kulka et al. 1989b). The second turn in example [6.15] provides an illustration (square brackets distinguish the categories):

[6.15] **Tony**   <-|-> At the moment <-|-> at the moment I don't know because er I had er one or two problems with organising that. But I will leave that with me and I'll come back to you.

        Unknown speaker [Sir] [could you do something] <unclear> [because ages ago you promised to do a chip-pan fire for us].
                             (*BNC* FLX 466–468. Classroom in UK secondary school. 11th year science lesson on chemistry. Tony is a teacher, the other speaker is a pupil)

The head act here is *could you do something*. This is the "minimal unit which can realise a request" (Blum-Kulka et al. 1989b: CCSARP coding manual: 275); if the other elements of the request were removed, it would still have the potential to be understood as a request. *Sir* functions as the alerter, "whose function it is to alert the hearer's attention to the ensuing speech act" (Blum-Kulka et al. 1989b: CCSARP coding manual: 277), and also as a term of address expressing deference. *Because ages ago you promised to do a chip-pan fire for us* is the support move and, more specifically, a grounder, giving grounds as to why the target should perform the action. Support moves can occur before or after the head act and their function is to mitigate or aggravate the request (Blum-Kulka et al. 1989b: CCSARP coding manual: 287).

It is worth noting that in some contexts the mere presence of a support move (without a head act) can be enough to trigger the inference that a request is being performed (the support move alone in the above example could have been interpreted as a request). This is not reflected in Blum-Kulka-inspired research, which has been overly preoccupied with head acts. In naturally occurring conversation things are rather more complex. For instance, requests are frequently elliptical. A parent commanding a child not to touch something may well say *no*, an expression which would not fit any of Blum-Kulka's categories.

Reflection: Cross-cultural variation in directness

The idea that speech acts vary in their degree of directness has had a huge impact on scholarship. British English culture is usually assumed to favour greater indirectness. Is this just a stereotype? Blum-Kulka and House (1989: 134) report the distribution of the major categories of directness across the languages of the CCSARP project. British English speakers use the most direct category least, so the stereotype seems partly true. But all speakers tend to avoid hints. This might not seem surprising, as conducting conversations in hints raises the risk of misunderstandings and creates a lot of work for hearers. However, it is worth remembering that hints have the advantage of leaving more room for negotiation of meaning across sequences of utterances by participants, a phenomenon which is not necessarily fully tapped into through the discourse completion tests utilised in the CCSARP project.

Other things being equal, one might expect some correlation between these directness strategies and politeness (cf. Leech 1983; see section 7.3.1). However, Blum-Kulka (1987) found that informants considered conventionally indirect strategies more polite, arguing that they represented a trade-off between the indirectness required to be polite and not overloading the target with inferential work. Indeed, as Blum-Kulka et al. (1989a: 24) point out, we need to test "the possibility that notions of politeness are culturally relativized, namely, that similar choices of directness levels, for example, carry culturally differentiated meanings for members of different cultures". This is an important point. For example, according to Wierzbicka ([1991]2003: 36), today in Polish the "flat imperative, which in English cultural tradition can be felt to be more offensive than swearing, in Polish constitutes one of the milder, softer options in issuing directives". Stronger options include the use of impersonal syntactic constructions with the infinitive. Imperatives, in contrast, assume a second person addressee (some take this to be part of the semantics of imperatives). The explanation,

Wierzbicka (2003: 37) suggests, is that "in Anglo-Saxon culture, distance is a positive cultural value, associated with respect for the autonomy of the individual. By contrast, in Polish culture it is associated with hostility and alienation". However, we would go further in suggesting that, even within Anglo-English cultures, levels of directness in making requests are not necessarily used or perceived in the same way by all members across different contexts.

As for how indirect speech acts work, Searle's account (1975) is focused on the inferencing required to bridge the gap between the direct speech act and the indirect speech act, and suggests the use of a framework such as Grice's conversational implicature (1975) (see section 4.2), coupled with shared background information (see section 3.2). Thus, the claim is that the utterance *can you pass the salt* would first be taken as a rogative speech act (a question), and this direct speech act would flout the conversational maxims. This, coupled with background knowledge (e.g. the bland food, the position of the salt relative to the speaker), would then lead to the computation of the indirect speech act of request. In this account, **conventional indirect speech acts** have a systematic relationship with the direct speech act's felicity conditions. Thus, *can you pass the salt* orientates to the preparatory condition of the speaker having the ability to perform the act denoted in the request. Searle (1979: 73–74) spells out in detail the supposed inferential steps that we are supposed to take when processing the request *can you pass the salt*. However, even to arrive at Step 1, "X has asked me the question as to whether I have the ability to pass the salt", the interpreter has already undertaken some inferencing, as s/he has inferred that the utterance counts as a "question" in this context and that they are the target of it. So, in fact, even the first step is not the literal step – the literal interpretation of form – it is supposed to be.

Given that Searle's account emphasises the interpretation of speech acts rather more than their linguistics, it makes sense to assess it in terms of psychological validity. Three particular and related questions can be addressed:

1. Are two speech acts entertained by the comprehender, first the direct one and then the indirect one?
2. In order to arrive at the indirect speech act, is the kind of Gricean inferencing outlined by Searle the only route?
3. Is it the case that orientation to felicity conditions is the basis for conventional indirect speech acts?

Answers to the first question are somewhat mixed. Clark and Lucy (1975), for example, seem to find evidence that the literal meaning is computed first and then the indirect meaning, but Gibbs (1983) found the contrary for certain types of indirect requests. Nevertheless, Holtgraves (1998: 80) states that in the psycholinguistic literature "there does seem to be an emerging consensus that the literal reading of potentially indirect remarks need not be activated to comprehend a speaker's intended meaning" (note that the wording here allows for occasions when they are activated). If the literal, direct meanings are not always activated, then already we have a challenge to the issue behind question 2 – that indirect speech acts involve two-stage Gricean inferencing, as there would be no deviation from the literal meaning of the utterance to account for. Some forms of indirect speech act, particularly requests, have developed conventional meanings which short-circuit, through associative inferencing, the two-stage processing model implied by the Gricean framework (see discussion of short-circuited implicatures in section 4.3.1). An indication of this is that, in cases like *can you pass the salt*, the word "please" is frequently added; pre-verbal "please" creates grammatical difficulties if the utterance is taken as a question. More specifically, Holtgraves (1994) provides experimental evidence to suggest that processing the literal meaning and then the implied, as Grice suggests, is not required for conventional indirect requests (e.g. *can you pass the salt*), but is sometimes required for non-conventional indirect requests (e.g. *this could do with a little salt*). As for the final question, Holtgraves (2005) conducted a production experiment in order to assess the ways in which people perform "implicit performatives", including indirect requests. He found good support for Searle's proposal that indirect speech acts are performed by referencing the relevant felicity condition.[1]

> ### Reflection: An alternative approach to indirect speech acts from cognitive science
>
> An attractive alternative approach to indirect speech acts, especially conventionally indirect speech acts, has been proposed by Thornburg and Panther (1997) and Panther and Thornburg (1998), and further developed by Pérez Hernández and Ruiz de Mendoza (2002). In their view, the identification of illocutionary force has its basis in conceptual metonymies, that is, concepts linked by association. Thus, by uttering a component of an **illocutionary scenario** a speaker enables the hearer to retrieve the illocutionary meaning for which the component stands (i.e. is metonymically linked, such as mentioning somebody's ability to do a job enables the hearer to retrieve the associated illocutionary meaning of request). This, they plausibly claim, accounts for how indirect illocutions can be rapidly and efficiently retrieved by hearers. An illocutionary scenario

---

[1] Additional evidence of this point can also be found in corpus-based studies. For example, the requestive strategies that Aijmer (1996: Chapter 4) reveals largely orientate to felicity conditions.

is taken to be a generic knowledge organisation structure, and hence has strong similarities with the schema-theoretic view of speech acts to be outlined in section 6.5. Importantly, Pérez Hernández and Ruiz de Mendoza (2002) broaden the basis of illocutionary scenarios beyond Searle's felicity conditions to include interpersonal features. Specifically, they include the powerrelationshipbetweenthespeakers,thecost/benefittothespeaker/hearer and the degree of optionality of the illocution, because of the role played by features such as in conceptualising and interpreting the illocutionary act.[2]

Reflections: An alternative approach to indirect speech acts from conversation analysis (CA)

Yet another promising approach to indirect speech acts is that proposed by Walker et al. (2011), where they analyse the sequential environments in which indirect speech acts arise in everyday conversation. In this approach, the focus is not on the psychological conditions for what counts as a felicitous speech act or how they are processed, but rather on what actions are interactionally achieved through indirect speech acts. In their study they analyse, in particular, indirect responses to polar interrogatives (i.e. yes-no questions). In their view, indirectness is treated as a property of the relationship between current and preceding turns, that is, between the design or form of responses to preceding inquiries. More specifically, indirect responses to polar questions are treated as indirect when they: (1) are non-type-conforming (i.e. they are not yes/no prefaced); (2) do not use ellipsis, repetition or pronominalisation to tie the response back to the preceding inquiry; (3) require some kind of inferencing to be understood as responses to the prior turn. These inferences draw from prior talk that is **non-contiguous** (i.e. not in the immediately preceding turn) (cf. co-text) and/or from shared knowledge (cf. common ground).

The key assumption underlying a CA approach to indirect speech acts is that users accomplish interactional business through them; indirect speech acts are not simply deployed as a way of being polite. Walker, Drew and Local (2011) propose that indirect responses to polar questions are used to manage two recurrent interactional issues: (1) uncovering the perceived purpose or agenda displayed in the prior turn; (2) treating the prior inquiry as inapposite, that is lacking or deficient in some way. In example [6.16], Roger's inquiry is treated as inapposite by Ken, because it involves "basic knowledge" that he would be expected to know as a "hotrodder" (teenage boys who make their reputations by driving their cars fast, or at least by talking about driving fast cars).

---

[2] The fact that these three features appear in Leech's (1983) model of politeness is not incidental.

[6.16] 1 Ken: bu-that convertible we went to Huntington Beach an'
he jumped. He jumped outta the convertible goin'
sixty miles an hour.
[big fat slob-
2 Rog: [six<u>teen</u> or sixty?
3 Ken: we-i-di-wu-we were on the f-on that Huntington Coast
Road?

(Walker, Drew and Local 2011: 2447)

Ken is narrating a story about "reckless behaviour" when he is interrupted by an inquiry from Roger in the form of a polar question (turn 2). Rather than responding with a type conforming "sixteen" or "sixty", however, Ken reiterates the fact that they were driving on *that Huntington Coast Road*. Through the demonstrative *that*, Ken appeals to shared knowledge, namely, "what speed they (as hotrodders) were likely to be going" on Huntington Road. This knowledge is treated as "basic", hence the inappositeness of Roger's inquiry.

6.4   Speech acts in socio-cultural contexts

One particular problem speech act theory has is its underestimation of the role of context, especially social context. Holdcroft (1994: 360–361), from his more philosophical perspective, highlights the issue through an example (VP = verb phrase):

> Suppose that S is in a position of authority and that he has made it clear that he is going to give us instructions. In that case it would be much simpler to try to corroborate the hypothesis that S is requesting us to VP directly without going through Searle's elaborate inference schema…In other words the inferential process tries to corroborate the most likely hypothesis given the background assumptions, including crucially the conversational goals of the participants.

This idea is in tune with Levinson's ([1979a] 1992) discussion of activity types; knowing the activity type of which an utterance is a part helps us to infer how that utterance should be taken (i.e. what the illocutionary point of the act is) (see section 6.6.3). More generally, the issue is that key interpersonal information is missing from Searle's account (it is more salient in Austin's account). This information alone can trigger a requestive interpretation, circumventing the Gricean inference process. Holtgraves (1994), for example, found that knowing that the speaker was of high status was enough to prime in one's head a directive interpretation in advance of any remark having been actually made (see also Ervin-Tripp et al. 1987 and Gibbs 1981, for the general importance of social context in speech act interpretation). In other words, knowing the speaker is of high status makes it more likely that you will take what they say as a request, because high status is associated with requestive activity. Also, when non-conventional requests were made by high status speakers, the processing of those requests was quite similar to that of conventional requests (such as *can you pass the salt?*) – both involve associative inferencing circumventing the Gricean inferencing process. This would suggest that speech act theory needs to bring social information on board if it is to account for the inferencing related to indirect speech acts. Indeed, given that indirect requests are largely motivated by interpersonal considerations and that even Searle (1975: 76) admits that politeness is a key motivating factor, it seems odd that such considerations have been so studiously ignored.

Another consideration that has been glossed over in accounts of speech acts is the influence of the broader cultural milieu in which they are performed. Speech acts are understood in different ways across languages and cultures. This point has been made most emphatically by researchers employing the **Natural Semantic Metalanguage (NSM)**, which employs a core set of basic words that are claimed to have equivalents in all languages to define concepts, including speech acts, across cultures (Goddard 2006; Wierzbicka 1985, [1991]2003). Let us consider apologies, first approaching them in terms of traditional speech act theory and then NSM. The felicity conditions for performing an apology given in Table 6.5 are based on Owen (1983), who in turn drew from Searle's (1969: 66–67) preliminary sketch of them.

The key felicity condition for apologies is generally regarded to be sincerity, namely, the speaker sincerely feeling bad about what s/he has done to the recipient (an apology is an expressive speech act, and the sincerity condition is key for all such acts).

Table 6.5   Felicity conditions for apologising

Felicity condition	Exemplification
Propositional content	Past A (act) of S (the speaker)
Preparatory	1. The act specified is an offence against H (the hearer)
	2. H would have preferred S not to have done A, and S believes H would have preferred S not to have done A
Sincerity	S regrets (is sorry for) having done A
Essential	Counts as an expression of regret by S for having done A

Turning to NSM, Goddard and Wierzbicka capture the meaning of the speech act verb *apologise* in English using **semantic primes**, semantic concepts that cannot be expressed in simpler terms and are claimed to be universal:

X apologized to Y (for doing A).
a. someone X said something to someone else Y at that time
b. this someone said something like this:
> "I feel something bad now because I think like this:
>> 'I did something (A) before, you can feel something bad because of it'"

c. this someone said it like someone can say something like this to someone else when this someone thinks like this:
> "I know that this someone can feel something bad towards me
> I don't want this"

(Goddard and Wierzbicka 2014: 171)

The emphasis here is on the speaker having done something that makes the recipient feel bad (an offence), and the speaker showing s/he feels bad about what has happened (sincerity). In other words, the speaker implies responsibility for doing something that (may have) made the recipient feel bad. Importantly, to *apologise* is something the speaker (nominally) chooses to do.

In Japanese, apology IFIDs, such as *sumimasen* (lit. to not finish or be satisfied) are used very frequently, including in situations in which an English speaker would generally expect "thanking" to occur. Wierzbicka (2010) suggests that one reason for this is that a different understanding of "apology" prevails in the form of the following cultural norm, which is characteristically (though not exclusively) Japanese:

> many people think like this:
> if at some time something bad happens somewhere because I did something
> it will be bad if I don't say something like this a short time after this:
>> "I feel something bad because of this"
>> "it will be bad if I don't do something because of this at the same time"
> if something bad happens to someone because of me, I have to say something like this to this person:
>> "I feel something bad because of this."

(Wierzbicka 2010: 69)

Wierzbicka suggests that the use of an apology IFID in Japanese does not presuppose that the speaker has done something bad to the recipient per se, but rather that something potentially bad (or at least "not good") from the perspective of the recipient has happened, which relates in some way to the speaker. This is why an "apology" IFID can be issued when thanking someone in Japanese, in order to highlight the inconvenience for the recipient of having proffered whatever has occasioned this thanking (Kumatoridani 1999). There is also a stronger expectation that the speaker will issue an apology in Japanese, as opposed to English (which explains the components "I have to say something like this" and "it will be bad if I don't say something" in the Japanese script versus their absence in the English script). This means that one is expected to express something like *sumimasen* even when the inconvenience for the recipient is only indirectly related to the speaker's actions.

One question that remains open, however, is whether such scripts are really able to capture all the pragmatic nuances of the use of such expressions. Subsequent work on "apologies" in Japanese has suggested they arise in the course of negotiating role-relations between participants (Long 2010). More specifically, they occur more frequently when "thanking" for something that lies outside of the participants' role-relationship (or what is termed *tachiba* in Japanese). Further work on interactional shifts in the use of "apology" expressions has found they are not only deployed to avoid or end interpersonal "conflict", but can also be used to index "attitudinal distance" (Sandu 2013). Thus, while the point is well taken that using English speech act verbs, such as *apologise* and its accompanying felicity conditions in analysing "apologies" in Japanese, can be misleading, as it imposes an understanding that does not accurately reflect that of those speakers (Wierzbicka 2010), the alternative scripts appear to be overly reductive from a pragmatic perspective. In that sense, they constitute a good starting point, but not an end point, for analyses of pragmatic acts.

Reflection: What counts as an apology?

The performance of public apologies, even within nation states, is often more complex than at first appearance, due to the different understandings and footings of recipients (see section 5.2.1). In early 2008, then Prime Minister Kevin Rudd delivered a formal apology in the Australian parliament to the "Stolen Generations", indigenous Aboriginal and Torres Straits Australians who were forcibly taken from their homes as children and forced to assimilate with white Australian families over a period of 100 years from 1869–1969. The core of the "sorry speech" was the issuing of apologies for three offences:

[6.17] For the pain, suffering and hurt of these Stolen Generations, their descendants and for their families left behind, we say sorry. To the mothers and the fathers, the brothers and the sisters, for the breaking up of families and communities, we say sorry. And for the indignity and degradation thus inflicted on a proud people and a proud culture, we say sorry.

(Prime Minister Kevin Rudd, 13 February 2008, *Department of Foreign Affairs and Trade website*, www.dfat.org.au)

This apology was received by many Australians as genuine and sincere as it conformed to both "everyday and formal understandings of the necessary linguistic features of a legitimate apology" (Augustinos et al. 2011: 527), at least in English, we might add. However, the reaction amongst indigenous Australians was more mixed. On the one hand, the address was treated as an appropriate and sufficient apology by some, as illustrated by the following reaction from a member of the Stolen Generations, Uncle Albert Holt:

[6.18]   I think the apology has changed things. I see a future now for my grandchildren and great-grandchildren. There's a lot more people intent on closing the gap. You have to remember this is not going to happen overnight.

("After the apology", Q-Weekend, *The Courier Mail*, 7–8 February 2009)

On the other hand, other (indigenous) Australians regarded it is as less than an apology. They focused on two points. The first is the way in which it has been (mis)perceived by white Australians.

[6.19]   The key point is that it's not in fact an apology to Aboriginal people at all and yet that's what most Australians have perceived it as being…Given the duplicitous wording of it all, it means nothing. It is completely without meaning. Some people have responded emotionally to what they perceived is the intent, but their perceptions of the intent and the actual wording of the apology are two completely different things.

(Ken Foley, indigenous activist, "After the apology", Q-Weekend, *The Courier Mail*, 7–8 February 2009)

The point argued here by Foley is that, while the apology was perceived by most Australians as an apology to all indigenous Australians, it was in fact only an apology for what happened to the Stolen Generations. Such activists contend that a real apology should address all injustices against all indigenous Australians. The second point of contention is that an apology must be accompanied by meaningful compensation or reparations to count as real or sufficient:

[6.20]   Those pains can't be addressed by nice words. They're addressed by what you actually do after the apology. I think we're all waiting for that final paragraph".

(Max Lenoy, academic, "After the apology", Q-Weekend, *The Courier Mail*, 7–8 February 2009)

The "sorry speech" was thus perceived, by some at least, as reflecting the "discourse of minimising responsibility" that Kampf (2009) argues is characteristic of public, political apologies.

Differences in the performance and understanding of speech acts can be divided into two main types following the **pragmalinguistic-sociopragmatic** distinction that was initially made by Thomas (1983; see also Leech 1983). The pragmalinguistic aspect of speech acts refers to the linguistic forms and strategies (more generally "resources") that are utilised in their performance. The sociopragmatic aspect of speech acts, in contrast, refers to the social values and perceptions that underlie their performance and interpretation. The cross-cultural differences in apologies in English and Japanese we have just discussed are largely sociopragmatic in nature. However, in comparing speech acts across cultures, we often find that differences are both pragmalinguistic and sociopragmatic in origin. For example, a review of the literature indicates that while Chinese and English speakers draw from a largely similar range of pragmalinguistic resources in performing apologies (e.g. explanations for the offence, acknowledgements of responsibility and offers of redress), one resource used much more commonly by Chinese compared to English speakers is the repetition of apology IFIDs (e.g. *duìbùqǐ* or *bùhǎoyìsu*) (Chang and Haugh 2011). This pragmalinguistic difference can be traced to a key sociopragmatic difference underlying apologies in English and Chinese, namely, the way in which "sincerity" (or what is termed *chéngyì* in Chinese) is conceptualised. In Chinese, *chéngyì* in relation to apologies is realised through repetition of an apology IFID several times to "show what s/he intends to do is genuine" while also giving the recipient the opportunity to confirm the speaker's "genuine intention" (Hua et al. 2000: 99). This pragmalinguistic resource, while available to English speakers, is not as commonly employed due to the different sociopragmatic value placed on repetition of speech acts (particularly IFIDs).

Reflection: Speech acts across varieties of English

There is a growing body of research in variational pragmatics (Barron and Schneider 2005; Schneider and Barron 2008) that is starting to tease out differences in the ways in which speech acts are performed across different varieties of English (both national and regional varieties). Barron (2005), for instance, has compared the form of offers amongst Irish versus British (specifically, English) speakers of English. In British English, speakers tend to reference the preparatory condition of "desire" (*Did you want a cup of tea?* or *You want a hand?*) or ask for permission (*Oh, let me help you with that*). In Irish English, on the other hand, speakers tend to make "direct offers" via imperatives more often (*come in and have a cuppa*) and predication-type interrogatives (*Will I take you to the hospital?*). There is also a higher level of external mitigation of offers through grounders (*Would you like me to help you with that, you seem weighed down*) and the expression *if you like*, which allows an explicit "out" for the recipient to refuse the offer.

Other work has focused on request forms, for instance, comparing their occurrence in American English versus British English (Breuer and Geluykens 2007) and British English versus Irish English (Barron 2005). The use of external mitigators to accompany standard conventional indirect requests that arise through referring to standard preparatory conditions, such as the ability to comply, was found to occur more frequently in Irish English compared to British English (ibid.) but, in turn, more often in British English than in American English (Breuer and Geluykens 2007). Syntactic downgrading through negation (*I couldn't get a drink could I?*), conditional (*Do you mind if I use your phone?*) or hypothetical forms (*I wonder if you'd be good enough to fax those details over to me?*) was found to occur more frequently in Irish English compared to British English (Barron 2005) but, once again, more frequently in British English compared to American English (Breuer and Geluykens 2007). While much of this work has examined pragmalinguistic differences in the performance of speech acts across varieties of English, there is a slowly growing body of work that also examines sociopragmatic differences, as we shall see in Chapter 7.

6.5 Pragmatic acts and schema theory

It will be clear by now that speech acts are not fixed by the words or behaviours with which they are performed. Furthermore, speech acts have fuzzy edges. An assertion can easily shade into advice, which can shade into a request or a warning. It is difficult to specify where one speech act ends and the next begins. Moreover, speakers may intend speech acts to be indeterminate (i.e. resistant to classification). As Leech (1983: 23–24) neatly puts it:

> The indeterminacy of conversational utterances...shows itself in the NEGOTIABILITY of pragmatic factors; that is, by leaving the force unclear, S may leave H the opportunity to choose between one force and another, and thus leaves part of the responsibility of the meaning to H. For instance,
>
> "If I were you I'd leave town straight away"
>
> can be interpreted according to the context as a piece of advice, a warning, or a threat. Here H, knowing something about S's likely intentions, may interpret it as a threat, and act on it as such; but S will always be able to claim that it was a piece of advice, given from the friendliest of motives. In this way, the "rhetoric of conversation" may show itself in S's ability to have his cake and eat it.

However, despite this, many speech act theorists fail to take proper account of indeterminacy in their theoretical and methodological models. Of course, we should not exaggerate indeterminacy, vagueness, ambiguity and so on, since communication is successful by and large – and we are not constantly lost in a fog of indeterminacy. This leads to a second issue: how is it that interlocutors (and analysts!) recognise examples like Leech's as either a piece of advice, a warning or a threat in the first place?

Mey (2001, 2010) argues that it is primarily through the context in his proposed **pragmatic act theory**. Note the term "pragmatic act". The term "speech act" is something of a misnomer. As noted in section 6.1, we can do communicative acts in writing or even non-verbally. Mey suggests that what makes a particular pragmatic act recognisable is a set of conditions or "affordances":

> for any activity to be successful, it has to be "expected", not just in the sense that somebody is waiting for the act to be performed, but rather in a general sense: this particular kind of act is apposite in this particular discursive interaction. (Mey 2010: 445)

In other words, social actions are dependent on the "situation being able to 'carry' them" (ibid.). Indeed, note that the Leech example above lacks a context to help determine, at least to a degree, the pragmatic act. The question is, then, what is it about a particular situation that generates these affordances? Mey himself proposes the notion of "pragmeme", a kind of "general situational prototype capable of being executed in a situation" (2001: 221). The notion of "meme" draws from the philosopher Daniel Dennett's (1991) proposal that we absorb memes from surrounding culture, including ideas, stories, songs, methods, theories and so on.[3] A **pragmeme** is said to consist of an activity part and a textual part, which, when instantiated in a particular situated context, constitutes an "individuated, individual pragmatic act", or what Mey terms a "pract" (2001: 221). While this goes some way to helping us better understand that speech acts are inherently situated, we are still left with the question of how to formalise these conditions or affordances.

Our approach echoes that of Mey, except that we attempt to specify more precisely what it means for a situation to be able to "carry" a pragmatic act. Following Jucker and Taavitsainen (2000), we propose that pragmatic acts be viewed as fuzzy, complex concepts that can vary both synchronically

---

[3] Dennett in turn draws this from the evolutionary biologist Richard Dawkins (1976), who proposed that genes are akin to memes whose basic function or purpose is replication in the broader process of evolution.

and diachronically across multiple dimensions in the **pragmatic space** that they share with neighbouring acts (Jucker and Taavitsainen 2000: 74, 92). Jucker and Taavitsainen (2000: 74) also suggest that a prototype approach is required. We would endorse this. Prototype theory (see Rosch 1975) constitutes an alternative approach to Aristotelian categories, one that is not based on necessary and sufficient conditions, as seems to be the case with Searle's felicity conditions, but on typical features as acquired through experience. For example, for the category "bird" the ability to fly might be taken as a necessary feature, but that would exclude an ostrich, which nevertheless has some birdlike features (e.g. feathers). Prototype theory offers proper theoretical status to such gradience, and takes account of the varied nature and complexity of criteria for category membership: of formal, functional and affective factors; of culturally specific and goal-derived criteria; and of appropriateness conditions (cf. Coleman and Kay 1981). However, a limitation of prototype theory is that it has been developed in relation to single categories or simple hierarchies of categories. Schema theory, as introduced in section 3.2.1, is compatible with prototype theory, but tends to consider clusters of categories organised in complex structures. It is thus better suited to accounting for pragmatic acts (note that the notion of illocutionary scenario, mentioned in a reflection box in section 6.3, is a very similar approach). In fact, in one variant, that of Schank and Abelson (1977), schema theory is designed to account for appropriate sequences of actions in a particular context, something that is consistent with the kind of view we develop in section 6.6.

Let us illustrate how this might work in relation to a request. Searle's (1969: 66) felicity conditions for a request provide a useful starting point for outlining the possible features that might contribute to the constitution of a request, and so we present them here:

Table 6.6 Felicity conditions for requesting

Felicity condition	Exemplification
Propositional content	Future act A of H
Preparatory	1. H is able to do A. S believes H is able to do A.
	2. It is not obvious to both S and H that H will do A in the normal course of events of his own accord
Sincerity	S wants H to do A
Essential	Counts as an attempt to get H to do A

However, the above conditions do not encompass all the possible formal, co-textual and contextual features that can be associated with requests. Indeed, pulling together relevant features mentioned in the literature reveals the following (references can be found in Culpeper and Archer 2008):

Formal features

- Particular conventionalised pragmalinguistic strategies (or IFIDs)
- A future action is specified in some proposition

Contextual beliefs

- It is not obvious that that future action will be performed by the target in the normal course of events
- It is not obvious that the target is obliged to perform the future action or the speaker is obliged to ask for the future action to be performed in the normal course of events
- The target is able to undertake the future action
- The target is willing to undertake the future action
- The source of the speech act wants the target to do the future act
- The target takes the source's desire for the future act as the reason to act

Interpersonal beliefs

- The future action represents benefit for the source but cost for the target
- The speaker is likely to be of relatively high status

Co-textual features

- Author: Pre-request
- Target: Unmarked compliance/marked non-compliance

Outcomes (i.e. perlocutionary effects)

- Target performs the action specified in the earlier speech act

The above describes the schema for the pragmatic act of request. Space precludes illustrating all these features. How the schema is constituted will be dependent on cultural context, a point we made in section 3.3.1. As we noted in section 6.4, for example, the repetition of apology IFIDs seems to be more central to the Chinese apology than the English one. Furthermore, the schema-theoretic approach helps us account for empirical findings. Also in section 6.4, we observed the findings of Holtgraves (1994) that knowing a speaker is of high status makes it more likely that you will take what they say as a request. This can be explained by the fact that high status is associated with requestive activity. Active schemata form expectations and such expectations help us interpret and predict the complexities of the world. Schema theory researchers have made the point that what you see is, in part, determined by what you *expect* to see (e.g. Neisser 1976: 20–21).

We will return to a schema-theoretic approach to pragmatic acts in section 6.6.3, where we show how it can be fused with more interactional notions in the guise of activity types.

6.6 Pragmatic acts in interaction

The form of pragmatic acts depends not only on whatever prior plan or agenda the speaker may have in mind, but, crucially, on the responses of the other participant(s) and the broader activity or event in which they occur. This has three important consequences. First, the development of pragmatic acts is inevitably incremental and thus fundamentally sequential in nature, a point we have previously made in relation to pragmatic meanings (see sections 5.3.2 and 5.3.3; see also Geis 1995, an attempt to bring together speech act theory and conversational analysis). Second, pragmatic acts are jointly constructed through the efforts of not just the speaker but also the recipient(s), sometimes termed **co-construction**. Third, the ways in which pragmatic acts arise is constrained by (but also in itself constitutive of) the broader **activity types** in which they are framed.

6.6.1 Pragmatic acts in sequence

We noted in the previous chapter that the processing of pragmatic meanings progresses incrementally (within utterances and turns) and sequentially (across utterances and turns). The very same principles apply to the way in which pragmatic acts are produced and interpreted in interaction. **Incrementality** with respect to pragmatic acts refers to the way in which speaker's adjust or modify their talk in light of how the progressive uttering of units of talk is received by other participants. **Sequentiality**, on the other hand, refers to the way in which current turns or utterances are always understood relative to prior and subsequent talk, particularly talk that is **contiguous** (immediately prior or subsequent to the current utterance or turn). The fundamentally sequential organisation of pragmatic acts means that "next turns provide evidence of the understandings of recipients of prior turns" (Heritage 1984b: 260). It follows from this that participants can use next turns as a resource in producing their own talk and in interpreting the talk of others (as well as in interpreting how others interpret their talk). It also means that we, as analysts, have access to a record of "publicly displayed and continuously up-dated intersubjective understandings" (ibid.: 259) when examining pragmatic acts in interaction. It is very important to remember, however, that this is an *indirect* record from which both participants and analysts can only make inferences. Our reliance on inferences in interpreting pragmatic acts is the source of their indeterminacy in many situations, just as is the case in the processing of pragmatic meaning in many instances.

Let us consider the case of invitations. In speech act theory, the key felicity conditions include that the proposed action encompassed by the invitation is of benefit to the addressee (preparatory), the addressee is (theoretically) able and willing to accept (preparatory), the speaker's psychological state is apposite (they sincerely wish to offer hospitality, etc.) (sincerity), and the utterance counts as an offer of hospitality (essential). The key components of an invitation are generally said to include some kind of availability checking (pre-invitation), the invitation head act (e.g. *would you like to...?*, *do you want to...?*), and supportive moves, including grounders and reconfirmations. However, if we consider invitations from the perspective of pragmatic act schema theory and examine them in their sequential environment, we find there is a much more nuanced and complex story to tell.

Consider the following interaction between two friends, where Oscar has called Martin to talk about his forthcoming visit to Canberra.

[6.21] (*Oscar and Martin are friends. Oscar lives in Sydney, while Martin lives in Canberra*)
 1 O: so- (.) ↑we'll be in Canberra this: (.) comin' weekend of cou::r[se,
 2 M: [ye:::s,
 3 (0.7)
 4 ?: .hh
 5 O: an:: (0.4) goin' t' th' <u>game</u> on Sat'rday ni:ght,
 6 M ri::ght¿
 7 (1.0)
 8 O: a- (.) an (0.5) and (.) <u>we</u> had sort of planned on seeing you (0.2) on our retu:rn¿ (0.3) [to <u>Sy</u>dney¿ (.) on <u>Sun</u>day.
 9 M: [.hh
 10 (0.4)
 11 M: o:ka:y¿
 12 O: is that (0.4) okay with you?=[or or:
 13 M: [.hh eh-eh-w-we-well look, uh uh (.)<u>pr</u>obably it's okay, .hh a- we- we've been d'invited for a bir-a fiftieth bi<u>r</u>th[da:y ah:, (0.2)]
 14 O: [*a:::h¿*   ]
 15 M: <<u>ce</u>lebra:tion:> at tw<u>e</u>lve th<u>i</u>rty on <u>Sun</u>da::[y?
 16 O: [aah::.

17   (0.5)
18 M: [right?
19 O: [(ook) it's::::: <u>not</u> gonna work¿ is it.

(Nevile and Rendle-Short 2009: 79)

Regarding Oscar's emerging proposal, one thing we can note initially is that Oscar frames his opening of the sequence as reiterating something that they both already know, namely, that Oscar and his family will be going to Canberra that coming weekend. In other words, the use of *of course* in turn 1 presents this as information that is not new to the participants (cf. section 2.5.1; see also section 8.3.1). Oscar goes on to outline his plan to go to watch a sports game, one which they are both aware of, which is evident from his use of the definite article here (see also section 2.5.1). This plan is prefaced with *and*, which indicates that this utterance (turn 5) is linked to his prior talk in turn 1 as "part of a bigger project" (Heritage and Sorjonen 1994), in this case, a proposal to visit Martin, which becomes evident in Oscar's subsequent utterance in turn 8. The self-invitation itself is formulated as a tentative or hedged plan in turn 8 (*sort of planned*). Oscar's projected expectations about whether this proposal will be accepted or not are further downgraded by the trailing-off disjunctive (*or or*) in turn 12, which opens up interactional space for a declination through implicature (i.e. implying either "or not" or "or [something else]"). What is important to note about the production of this proposal is that each increment of it (in turns 1, 5, 8 and 12) follows minimal responses from Martin (i.e. *yes*, *right*, *okay* in turns 2, 6 and 11), as well as relatively lengthy pauses (in turns 3, 7 and possibly 10). These responses prompt Oscar to continue his talk, but show no commitment to the under-lying agenda that Martin is likely to have realised right from the beginning, when Oscar brings up his forthcoming trip to Canberra. Oscar's formulation of the components of this proposal are thus influenced by the responses from Martin, being adjusted and perhaps re-ordered in light of what Martin says (and indeed does not say, namely, pre-emptively inviting Oscar and his family to come to visit).

Now let us consider Oscar's realisation that his proposal is being declined. A display of such an understanding emerges progressively over the course of this sequence. It is evident in part from the tentative nature of the proposal Oscar makes (turn 8), and the provision of an "out" for Martin through implicating that such a visit might not be okay (turn 12). It is also shaped by Martin's earlier minimal responses, as well as the way in which he frames his subse-quent response to the proposal in turns 13 and 15. Martin's response is framed with a number of markers, including an audible in-breath (that indicates a lengthy response is likely to follow), hesitation and restarts, and *well*-prefacing (a common marker of dispreferred responses), thereby framing his response as **dispreferred** (in the CA sense of responses that are marked as delayed or non-straightforward). While he offers qualified acceptance (*probably it's okay*), the preceding markers of a dispreferred response, together with the subsequent account for that qualification (i.e. that Martin has to attend another – important – event, i.e. a 50th birthday celebration), guide Oscar to infer that his proposed visit is not feasible. That Oscar makes this inference is evident from the occurrence of the pragmatic marker *ah* that receipts new information in turn 16 (Heritage 1984a) (a point we will discuss further in Chapter 8), as well as making explicit what he has inferred through his formulation in turn 19 (see also section 5.4.2). What is important to note is that Oscar's inference is not only influenced by what Martin says here in response, but also by the surrounding sequence where Martin does not offer a pre-emptive invitation despite having multiple opportunities to do so; Oscar thus does not end up 'soliciting' an invitation from Martin despite his tentatively framed proposal.

It is evident from our analysis of the way in which Oscar's proposal develops incrementally and the way in which Martin's responses shape the overall **trajectory** of the sequence (i.e. the overall structure and the individual components of the proposal) that this sequence emerges as a joint effort on the part of both Oscar and Martin.

Reflection: Exploiting the power of sequentiality

In 2001 in the British version of the TV series *Who Wants to be a Millionaire*, Major Charles Ingram won a million pounds. However, he was subsequently stripped of the prize in 2003 and charged, along with his wife, with tricking the gameshow host. The issue discussed in the court trial was did Ingram cheat and, if so, how? The answer lies in the way in which Ingram and his wife exploited the power of sequentiality to alert him to the "correct" answers. One of the most obvious cases of this – in hindsight at least – was in his winning response to the million pound question. The question itself was as follows:

A number one followed by 100 zeros is known by what name?
  A: googol   B: megatron
  C: gigabit   D: nanomole

Part of Ingram's response to the question is transcribed below. We can see that he articulates each of the possible answers in turn, starting with nanomole, then megatron, and then googol. It was what happened after he said googol that eventually caught the attention of the producers of the show (T = the host, Chris Tarrant; I = Ingram).

[6.22] 1 I: I <u>think</u> it's nanomole. (3.4) but it <u>could</u> be
        2   a gigabit. (0.4) .hhhh(he) (8.2) I'm not sure I
        3   can go- I just don't think I can do this one.

```
 4    (0.5) .hhhh Go(hh):d. (0.7) I do:n't think it's a
 5    megatron.(3.5) and I have to say I haven't-
 6    (0.4) I <don't think> I've heard of a googol.
 7    (2.6)
 8    [COUGH] COUGH [COUGH ]
 9  I: [googol  ]            [°googol.°]
10  T: google.
11    (1.0)
12  I: google. °googol >google<°
13    (1.6)
14  I: in- by the process of elimination I actually
15    think it's googol. but I don't know what a
16    google is? so. hhh.
```
(Who Wants to be a Millionaire UK, Season 10, 18 September 2001,
creators: David Briggs, Steve Knight & Mike Whitehill)

Following Ingram's articulation of googol as a possible although unlikely response (lines 5–6), there was noticeably marked coughing in the audience (line 8). Immediately following this Ingram started repeating googol (lines 9 and 12), eventually coming to the conclusion that the answer was googol (lines 14–15), which indeed it was. It turned out that the wife had agreed to signal an answer as correct through coughing after it was listed by Ingram. By doing so they had exploited the power of sequential placement of a seemingly meaningless cough to convey a particular meaning (i.e. that's the correct answer), thereby enabling Ingram to go on to win the million pounds. At the time it was not obvious what was going on as anyone who attends concerts or shows would not normally consider coughing from members of the audience to be interactionally meaningful.

6.6.2 The co-construction of pragmatic acts

In the preceding examples we have seen how not only the speaker but also other participants can influence the trajectory of a pragmatic act as it develops in interaction. This, we have suggested, is another key characteristic of pragmatic acts in interaction, namely, that they are co-constructed by two or more participants rather than simply being the "output" of the speaker or tied to individual utterances. In some cases, the pragmatic act, by definition, cannot be achieved by one participant on their own, as noted with respect to collaborative speech acts in section 6.2.1. Bribing others is a case in point. If the recipient does not accept the offer of money and so on in order to gain some particular favour (or reject the offer in such a way as to register it as asking for a favour), it does not count as a bribe. Bribing is thus an instance of a pragmatic act where co-construction of an act itself surfaces in interaction (cf. Mey 2001). An important consequence of the way in which pragmatic acts are co-constructed by two or more participants is that they can sometimes involve multiple possible understandings. This is precisely the point explored by Thomas (1995: 195–204). She notes: "The concept of ambivalence is particularly important in taking forward the view of pragmatics as 'meaning in interaction' in which both speaker and hearer have a part to play." Schegloff (2006: 147) argues that since participants pursue possible understandings of talk "along multiple lines... they are therefore prepared to recognise even ones arrived at by others that might have been thought elusive". In other words, pragmatic acts can initially be indeterminate and so mutual understanding of them is very often co-constructed (or interactionally achieved in CA parlance). The co-construction of pragmatic acts can be clearly seen in the case of utterances where speakers offer interpretive choices to recipients, or alternatively, recipients exercise their agency in such a way as to transform the upshot of the speaker's preceding talk.

We have already seen such phenomena in our discussion of recipient meanings in Chapter 5 (see section 5.2.2). Here we offer another brief example where unsaid pragmatic meanings (termed not-saying) arise in the course of the co-construction of a pragmatic act, namely, questioning, which, in turn, arises within the frame of a broader activity type, getting acquainted:

> [6.23] ERCH (Chris and Emma have been talking about Emma's acupuncture business)
> 1 C: how do you go generally with most of your
> 2   customers °are they happy or°
> 3   (0.8)
> 4 E: ↑YEAH
>
> (Haugh 2011: 207)

In [6.23], we find evidence of an utterance-type through which speakers can allow recipients to choose inclusive or exclusive interpretations of disjunctives, namely, utterances ending with a trailing-off *or* (Haugh 2011). It is evident that such utterances are (nominally) open to interpretation as either polar questions (*p* or *not p*) or alternative questions (*p* or *q*). The former necessarily presupposes an exclusive interpretation of *or*, while the latter presupposes an inclusive interpretation. Here, the speaker's utterance can be understood in two ways by the recipient. Emma could understand Chris's utterance as a polar question ("are they happy or not?") or as an alternative question ("are they happy or generally satisfied"?). It is left up to Emma to choose.

One further point to note is that it should now be evident from our discussion of examples of "soliciting" and "trailing-off questioning" that many pragmatic acts are not "named" in vernacular discourse. Speech act theory picks up on many of the important social actions we can observe in interaction, at least it does for those we find in English. However, there are many other pragmatic acts that are not necessarily salient in folk discourse (see Chapter 8 for further discussion). Our job in pragmatics is to further our understanding of not only what ordinary folk can readily recognise through speech acts they name, but also pragmatic acts that are not always immediately obvious to the casual observer.

6.6.3 Pragmatic acts and activity types

In section 6.5, we suggested that schema theory provides a flexible conceptual approach to pragmatic acts. But we have not seen how the kind of interactional issues we have been discussing in the two previous subsections of section 6.6 might be accommodated. In this section, we propose that activity types provide a more holistic approach to the analysis of interaction, and also one that is compatible with schema theory.

The notion of an **activity type** is usually credited to Stephen Levinson, though similar notions can be seen in earlier research (see Allwood 1976). An activity type, according to Levinson, refers to:

> any culturally recognized activity, whether or not that activity is coextensive with a period of speech or indeed whether any talk takes place in it at all ... In particular, I take the notion of an activity type to refer to a fuzzy category whose focal members are goal-defined, socially constituted, bounded events with *constraints* on participants, setting, and so on, but above all on the kinds of allowable contributions. Paradigm examples would be teaching, a job interview, a jural interrogation, a football game, a task in a workshop, a dinner party, and so on.
>
> (Levinson [1979a] 1992: 69)

He goes on to say that:

> Because of the strict constraints on contributions to any particular activity, there are corresponding strong expectations about the functions that any utterances at a certain point in the proceedings can be fulfilling. (ibid.: 79)

This has the important consequence that:

> to each and every clearly demarcated activity there is a corresponding set of *inferential schemata*. (ibid.: 72)
>
> [activity types] help to determine how what one says will be "taken" – that is, what kinds of inferences will be made from what is said. (ibid.: 97)

As can be seen from these quotations, activity types involve both what inter-actants do in constituting the activity and the corresponding knowledge – schemata – one has of that activity; they have an interactional side and a cognitive side.

Despite indicating that every activity type has a "corresponding set of *inferential schemata*", Levinson says nothing more about the cognitive side of activity types. Likewise, subsequent researchers have paid little attention to this dimension (as we saw in section 6.3, Searle just briefly mentions it in connec-tion with explaining how indirect speech acts work). But it is a crucial part of how meanings are generated and understood in interaction. Participants use schematic knowledge in interpreting and managing the particular activity they are engaged in. For example, *how are you?* is a typical phatic question in many circumstances, but this would be an unlikely interpretation in the context of a doctor-patient consultation. Levinson saw activity types as rescuing the more general inferential framework of the Cooperative Principle (Grice 1975), which could not account for the more particular knowledge-based inferences drawn in particular situations. Inferential schemata are a mechanism for such knowledge-based associative inferencing, as we elaborated in section 3.2.1.

An important aspect of activity types is that breaks away from traditional approaches to context, which take the view that context is external to the text and relatively stable – it is, in some sense, "out there". This might be described as the "outside in" approach to context and language; in other words, the analyst looks at how the context shapes the language. But the reverse is also possible. Gumperz's notion of **contextualisation cues** is based on this idea. He defines them as "those verbal signs that are indexically associated with specific classes of communicative activity types and thus signal the frame of context for the interpretation of constituent messages" (Gumperz 1992: 307; see also Gumperz 1982). This might be described as the "inside out" approach to context and language; in other words, the analyst looks at how language is used to shape the context. Of course, in reality meanings are generated through an interaction between both context and language. Current views in linguistics, of which activity types are a part, emphasise that context is dynamically constructed *in situ*; both approaches to context are involved.

Let us illustrate the points made in this section. Culpeper and McIntyre (2010) demonstrated how the notion of activity type can capture some of the ways in which script writers exploit dialogue for dramatic effect. We will briefly summarise their analysis of an extract from the BBC award-winning comedy series *One Foot in the Grave*, specifically the episode "The big sleep" (Series 1, 11/1/90). The plots of this series revolve around Victor Meldrew, a grumpy (though inadvertently humorous) man dealing with the trials and tribulations of being retired. At the beginning of the episode from which our extract is taken, the female window cleaner claims that she is going to report Victor to the police for indecent exposure while she was cleaning the bathroom window (Victor had accidentally exposed himself while grappling with a towel in the bath). Later, Victor has just come in from the garden to be told by his wife that there are two men in the living room waiting to speak to him. Victor goes to speak to them. (V = Victor; S1 = dark suited man; S2 = dark suited man.)

[6.24]   1. S1   Victor Meldrew?
         2. V   Yes.
         3. S1   Wondered if we might have a little word with you sir?
         4. V   Oh God.
         5. S2   On the subject of obscene behaviour.
         6. V   Look, it's all very simple really...
         7. S1   Rather a lot of it going on these days wouldn't you say?...acts of unbridled filth perpetrated by perverts and sexual deviants who should know better at their age
         8. V   Look . I...I just got out of the bath and I was just rubbing...I was rubbing...
         9. S1   How do you think God feels about all this?
        10. V   What?
        11. S1   How do you think the Lord feels about so much sin and wickedness in his holy kingdom on earth?
        12. S2   If we look at Proverbs 6 verse 12 I think we can find the answer. A naughty person a wicked man walketh with a...
        13. V   You're Jehovah's Witnesses! You're bloody Jehovah's Witnesses! I thought you were policemen.
        14. S1   Oh, we are policemen but on our days off we work for God.
        15. V   Get out!
        16. S1   Let me just read you something sir. In the beginning there was...
        17. V   Get out of my house!
        18. S1   Sir, we all of us need a moment of soul searching reflection in these iniquitous times...
        19. V   I know my rights, you can't search my soul without a warrant. Now go on get out of it. Bloody cheek.
                 ("The big sleep", *One Foot in the Grave*, Season 1, Episode 2, 11 January 1990, director: Susan Belbin, writer: David Renwick)

Given that shortly before this scene the audience learns of the threat that Victor will be reported to the police for indecency, it is quite likely that a police-related activity type schema is primed. Research suggests that schemata that have been recently activated are more likely to spring to mind (see the references in Fiske and Taylor 1991: 145–146). Indeed, the activity type constructed here appears to be a police interview. Apart from the fact that the two dark suited individuals readily fill the (plain-clothed) police participant slots of the activity type schema, the opening pragmatic acts (turns 1, 3 and 5) – checking the identity of the interviewee and requesting permission to commence the interview on a particular topic – are strongly associated with the police interview. As for how the pragmatic acts are realised, note that the pragmatic act in turn 3 is indirect, it is literally an assertion concerning the speaker's wonderings. Such indirectness might be considered, other things being equal, an indication of politeness, as might be the use of the apparently deferential vocative *sir*. However, politeness on the part of police officers in this activity type is a conventional part of the activity type and cannot be automatically taken to reflect a sincere wish to maintain or enhance social relations with the interactant – it is surface or superficial politeness. Indeed, according to Curl and Drew (2008), the use of "[I was] wondering if" may indicate an orientation to a relatively low entitlement to make the request in the first place rather than to issues of politeness per se. The police officers initiate the conversation, ask the questions and control the topic, all contextual cues of power within the interview activity type. Victor treats S1 and S2 in a manner that suggests that he has conceived of them as police officers. He answers their questions and complies with their requests. Moreover, he adopts a tentative style in accounting for his actions, a style which is apparent in his two instances of the minimiser *just*, hesitations and two false starts. Victor is playing the appropriate role of interviewee in the police interview activity type.

However, S1's question *How do you think God feels about all this* clashes with the police interview activity type. The fact that this clash also registers with Victor is clear from his response: *What?* While asking questions is perfectly consistent with the police interview activity type, the religious topic is not. This is reinforced by the question *How do you think the Lord feels about so much sin and wickedness in his holy kingdom on earth?*, and the quotations from the Bible. The idea that this is a police interview activity type can no longer be sustained. The activity type that emerges is one of religious proselytising, allowing the inference that these are Jehovah's Witnesses, a religious group that is well-known for making door-to-door visits. In fact, the setting is appropriate to proselytising, but not a police interview, as police interviews are usually conducted at the police station. This detail was inconsistent with the earlier police interview interpretation, but was probably drowned out by the weight of evidence in the earlier part of the extract pointing towards a police interview. Victor's linguistic behaviour also quickly changes in accord with the new activity type. He abandons the role forced upon him as a result of the power dynamics of the police interview activity type. He uses commands, makes statements about what the two Jehovah's Witnesses are and are not allowed to do, and evaluates the situation using semi-taboo language. Note that the activity types we see in this abstract, the police interview and the proselytising activity types, share some linguistic and contextual characteristics but differ in others. The focal point of *obscene behaviour* is common to both, as are speech acts of questioning and asserting. As for the differences, the religious aspects are only relevant to proselytising; the initial identity check and the superficial politeness are only relevant to the police interview; the power relationships are diametrically opposite in the two activity types; and so on.

Interestingly, the writer resolves the potential conflict in S1 and S2 being Jehovah's Witnesses and yet at the beginning of the extract sounding like police officers by providing the information that they are indeed police officers, but off duty. This, then, explains the "leakage" from the police interview activity type into the proselytising activity type. In the final turn of the extract, Victor demonstrates that he is now conscious of the cause of his confusion by blending linguistic elements of the two activity types. His assertion that *you can't search my soul without a warrant* would be an appropriate turn of phrase for police discourse were it not for the word *soul*, which is incongruous and seems more appropriate to religious proselytising. Victor appears to blend aspects of the two activity types together, a neat comedic finale to the scene.

6.7   Conclusion

Speech act theory is perhaps the most important theory in pragmatics. Those early pioneers, such as Austin, dissatisfied with limited semantic descriptions with their focus on propositions and truth conditionality, did much to galvanise the field of pragmatics. Austin is sometimes classified as an **ordinary language philosopher,** one of a group of scholars who thought that philosophy should not remain content with abstractions but consider those abstractions in the light of ordinary language usage. Attention to language usage is clearly evident in his work, both the use of formal features, such as performative verbs, and the social contexts within which they are used. However, one can immediately see a limitation, Austin considered the language around him and that language was English (and indeed limited to particular varieties of English). This fact was overlooked by subsequent researchers, who often assumed that Austin's ideas were universal. Searle's developments of Austin's ideas pushed them towards formalisation, but did not do so in the light of empirical study of speech acts across languages and cultures. We have repeatedly pointed out the cross-cultural variability in speech acts, both in terms of their pragmalinguistics and their sociopragmatics. This is not to say that those ideas are without value; indeed, they have enabled scholars to capture speech act aspects in various languages/cultures. Nevertheless, the traditional speech act theory that emerged was overly rigid, too narrowly focused, static and atomistic. In a nutshell, it is simply not up to the job of coping with speech acts, or rather pragmatic acts, in situated interactions.

Searle articulated the important notion of (in)directness with respect to speech acts, a notion that has been explored cross-culturally by later scholars. We have argued that (in)directness is a complex evaluation of speech activity, derived from a number of distinct bases, including the transparency of the illocutionary point, the target and the semantic content. Searle's account of how (in)directness works relies too much on Gricean inferencing. Experimental evidence casts some doubt on whether literal meaning is accessed as a first step. Moreover, the role of associative inferencing, taking on board knowledge about the socio-cultural context, is again underplayed.

We suggested that schema theory (blended with prototype theory) provides a way of capturing pragmatic acts that allows them to be complex and fuzzy-edged. We also briefly noted alternative approaches to indirectness, one oriented towards cognitive science and the other to conversation analysis. In our final section, 6.6, we elaborated on the fact that pragmatic acts depend not just on what one speaker has in mind but also on: (1) participant responses, with the consequence that they must be considered incremental, sequential and co-constructed; (2) the broader activity of which they are a part, with the consequence that they must be considered to be constrained by and constraining of that activity. In our final subsection, we introduced the notion of activity types, an especially useful notion for approaching pragmatic acts in a broader interactional perspective.

7 Interpersonal Pragmatics

7.1 Introduction

At the beginning of Chapter 3, we briefly mentioned Leech's (1983) usage of the term "interpersonal rhetoric", which in turn draws on Halliday's (e.g. 1973) use of "interpersonal" for one of his three semantic or functional components of language (the others being "ideational" and "textual"). Halliday ([1970] 2002: 175) writes that the interpersonal function "serves to establish and maintain social relations". Leech (1983: 56) interprets the interpersonal function as "language functioning as an expression of one's attitudes and an influence upon the attitudes and behaviour of the hearer". Together, these quotations capture the two important areas of concern for **interpersonal pragmatics**, namely, **interpersonal relations** (mutual social connections amongst people that are mediated by interaction, including power, intimacy, roles, rights and obligations) and **interpersonal attitudes** (perspectives, usually value-laden and emotionally charged, on others that are mediated by interaction, including generosity, sympathy, like/dislike, disgust, fear and anger). These areas are strongly linked. Love, for example, involves both. Consider that the expression *lovers* refers to two or more people intimately and/or sexually connected with each other, whereas the expression *in love* refers to a perspective on someone else. Both relations and attitudes shape, and in turn are shaped, by language in interaction. To give a simple example, being in love may give rise to loving talk, and in turn that loving talk may result in the target falling in love and reciprocating the loving talk, which may establish their connection as lovers, and so on. It is worth briefly noting that the area of interpersonal attitudes is linked to (1) **interpersonal emotions**, which encompass embodied feelings or states of mind often characterised by participants as "irrational and subjective, unconscious rather than deliberate [and] genuine rather than artificial" (Edwards 1999: 273), and (2) **interpersonal evaluations**, which involve "appraisals or assessment of persons, or our relationships with those persons, which influence the way we think and feel about those persons and relationships, and consequently sometimes what we do" (Kádár and Haugh 2013: 61) (for the nature of those links, see the work of Teun van Dijk, e.g. 1987: 188–193).

The main area which Leech (1983) discusses under the heading of inter-personal rhetoric is **politeness**, and we will do likewise in this chapter. Both politeness and **impoliteness** can be seen as interpersonal attitudes. We should note at this early stage Leech's (1983: 62) point that interpersonal pragmatics plays a greater role in strongly **situated** uses of language (e.g. face-to-face interaction with an assistant in a coffee shop) as opposed to "unsituated" uses (e.g. encyclopaedia articles). The notion of situated can be understood with reference to Goffman's ([1964] 1972: 63) definition of a social situation as "an environment of mutual monitoring possibilities, anywhere within which an individual will find himself accessible to the naked senses of all others who are 'present', and similarly find them accessible to him".[1]

What exactly is politeness? Need the question be asked? We all know what politeness is, don't we? Imagine you are ensconced at a dinner table in England: politeness might include remembering to use *please* when you want something passed, saying something nice about the food and defi-nitely not burping. Actually, all of these particular things are somewhat more complex – even problematic – than they first appear. The word *please* is the "magic word" that British parents impress upon their children to use with all requests, and it looms large in the British psyche. But how is it actually used? Aijmer (1996: 166–168) provides some evidence. It matters how the rest of the request is worded: *please* is most likely to be used in conjunction with an imperative (e.g. "please make me a cup of tea") or with *could you* (e.g. "could you please make me a cup of tea"), but much less likely to be used with *can you* or *will you*. You will note that we failed to specify whether you were ensconced at a family meal or had been invited to dinner. Differences in situa-tion would influence whether you use the word *please. Please* tends to be used in relatively formal situations, and in business letters and written notices. It is particularly frequent in service encounters, notably via the telephone (all too often we hear "can you hold the line please!"). So, if the dinner were a formal invitation, *please* would be more likely to be used. Complimenting the cook on the food may also seem a straightforwardly nice thing to do, but it is not straightforward: you place the recipient of the compliment in a rather tricky position. If they simply accept the compliment, they may sound rather

---

[1] Intriguingly, one might note that this definition seems to be echoed in Sperber and Wilson's (1986[1995]: 41–42) description of context from a Relevance theory perspective: "Any shared cognitive environment in which it is manifest which people share it is what we will call a *mutual cognitive environment*". This is in spite of the fact that the data discussed in their book is far from situated.

immodest, but if they simply reject it, they may offend the person who made it. Consequently, responses to compliments in Britain tend to weave a path between these two positions. A response such as "it's kind of you to say that" suggests that the compliment is (at least in part) a product of the complimenter's kindness and not necessarily a true reflection of the value of the food. Finally, even burping cannot always with certainty be seen as the antithesis of politeness. Cultural considerations come into play. In some cultures, burping may be acceptable, or even a sign of appreciation of the food – a compliment! Needless to say, culture keenly influences politeness. The use of the word *please* is more typical of British culture than North American, being used about twice as frequently (Biber et al. 1999: 1098). This is not to say that American culture is less polite. There are other ways of doing politeness, and those other ways might be evaluated as polite by North Americans, just as using *please* in certain contexts might be evaluated as polite by speakers of British English. Politeness, or impoliteness for that matter, is in the eyes and ears of the beholder. It is a particular attitude towards behaviour, and one that is especially sensitive to the relational aspects of context. The fact that politeness involves both the interpretation of a behaviour in context and working out its attitudinal implications (rather than the straightforward decoding of a sign of politeness) is what makes it a pragmatic and interpersonal matter.

Politeness, then, involves a polite attitude towards behaviours in a particular context. In fact, that attitude is often extended towards the people who do politeness: they are considered polite people. What those behaviours, linguistic and non-linguistic, consist of, how they vary in context, and why they are deemed polite are some of the key areas of politeness study. The first part of this chapter introduces two different approaches to politeness. The middle and largest part of this chapter focuses on the most popular politeness framework, namely, that of Brown and Levinson ([1978] 1987) (hereafter Brown and Levinson). The chapter then briefly considers a new, rapidly developing area, closely related to politeness, namely, impoliteness. Finally, the chapter concludes by looking at relatively recent work which argues that the notion of politeness and its place within interpersonal pragmatics be reconsidered from an interactional perspective.

7.2 Two general approaches to politeness

7.2.1 The socio-cultural view of politeness

A notion at the heart of much work on the socio-cultural view of politeness is that of social norms. Social norms are of two types. A **prescriptive social norm** is a rule of behaviour enforced by social sanctions. Thus, throwing litter on the floor breaks a social norm. Social norms are driven by social rules ("do not litter"), and breaking those rules incurs sanctions. Impolite language – that is, abusive, threatening, aggressive language – is often explicitly outlawed by signs displayed in public places (e.g. hospitals, airport check-in desks). Sanctions are underpinned by social institutions and structures (e.g. a legal system) and enforced by those in power. Moreover, if social norms become internalised by members of society, as they regularly do, sanctions can take on a moral dimension in the form of attitudes, such as disapproval from others or guilt emanating from oneself. Interestingly, the word *morals* is derived from the Latin *mores*, meaning customs. The obligations associated with social norms are what underlie their morality. Such obligations can be articulated in rules of conduct. Goffman (1967: 49) makes the link with morality clear:

> Rules of conduct impinge upon the individual in two general ways: directly, as obligations establishing how he is morally constrained to conduct himself; indirectly, as expectations, establishing how others are morally bound to act in regard to him.

Those expectations are attitudes about how things should be, and their violation leads to a sense of immorality.

What he refers to as the "social-norm view" of politeness is neatly summed up by Fraser (1990: 220):

> Briefly stated, [the social-norm view] assumes that each society has a particular set of social norms consisting of more or less explicit rules that prescribe a certain behavior, a state of affairs, or a way of thinking in context. A positive evaluation (politeness) arises when an action is in congruence with the norm, a negative evaluation (impoliteness = rudeness) when action is to the contrary.

Politeness, in this sense, subsumes everyday notions such as "good manners", "social etiquette", "social graces" and "minding your ps and qs". Parents teaching their children to say *please* typically proscribe requests that are not accompanied by that word. Social norms, of course, are sensitive to context: the social politeness norms that pertain to a family dinner are rather different from those pertaining to a formal dinner occasion. Actually, there are some situations where communicative behaviours are not subject to politeness prescriptions; in other words, situations in which behaviours which might be viewed as "impolite" are unrestricted and licensed. Often, such situations are characterised by a huge power imbalance, as might be the case in army recruit training, but not necessarily so. Harris (2001), for example, describes the sanctioned impoliteness that takes place in the UK's House of Commons, giving

Opposition MPs opportunities to attack the Government that they might not have had in other contexts.

There is another sense in which social norms underpin much research on politeness. **Experiential** or **descriptive social norms** have their basis in an individual's experience of social situations. Repeated experiences of social situations may lead one to expect certain kinds of interaction to happen, be able to hypothesise what others' expectations are, and know how to meet them. Opp (1982) argues that regular behaviours develop into expectations, those expectations give people a sense of certainty, and it is this certainty that has value – value which feeds politeness attitudes. People generally like to know what will happen next, a point made forcefully in social cognition in relation to schema theory (see, for example, Fiske and Taylor 1991: 97). Additionally, in the area of human relations, Kellerman and Reynolds (1990: 14), investigating the link between expectancy violations and attraction, state that deviations from expectations are "generally judged negatively". However, it is important to note context dependency. It is not the case that all thwarted expectations are judged negatively. Aesthetic pleasure and entertainment are often achieved through surprise (as in the surprise ending of a film).

Etiquette books and parental instruction are simply not detailed enough to help us through the mass of social occasions we will tackle in our lives. We acquire politeness routines from our regular experiences of social interactions. **Politeness routines** or **formulae** are expressions which have become conventionally associated with politeness attitudes in specific contexts. **Linguistic politeness** can be taken to mean the use of expressions that are both contextually appropriate and judged as socially positive by the target (some researchers, such as Watts 2003, take "socially positive" primarily to mean showing "consideration" to the target) (cf. Locher and Watts 2005). Remember the use of *please*? It is not just used by anybody to anybody, or in any context, and when it is used, it is generally considered socially positive. The point about politeness routines/markers is that knowledge of both their appropriate context and their positive social meaning has become conventionally associated with the linguistic expression. This is why we can pronounce on how polite or otherwise an expression sounds even when considering that expression out of its normal context (e.g. in a list of politeness expressions). Of course, this does not mean that simply using a politeness routine/marker will result in people viewing it as polite. Politeness always involves an overall **contextual judgement**. Thus, *Go to hell please*, said to get rid of somebody, might well be considered socially negative, despite the fact that a conventional politeness formula (*please*) has been used. In fact, this particular utterance achieves its power, because politeness is part of the conventional meaning of the expression *please*. The contexts of usage and socially positive meanings of that word clash with its actual usage on this

...a a note of **sarcasm** (which can be regarded as a form of

...prescriptive social norms and experiential social norms can –
...– coincide and interact. Thanking a host for dinner, for example,
...oth: it is something we are under social pressure to do and we often
...ne socio-cultural view of politeness has been given a new lease of life
in ...e last decade, notably in the guise of discursive politeness, and we shall
consider relevant work in section 7.4.1.

7.2.2 The pragmatic view of politeness

The classic, and most frequently cited, politeness studies lean heavily towards
a **pragmatic view**. From roughly the late 1970s to the early 2000s, politeness theories have concentrated on how we employ communicative strategies to maintain or promote social harmony (e.g. Leech 1983: 82; Brown
and Levinson 1987: 1). Thomas (1995: 179) neatly summarises the research
agenda of scholars engaged in the study of pragmatic politeness:

> All that is really being claimed is that people employ certain strategies
> (including the 50+ strategies described by Leech, Brown and Levinson,
> and others) for reasons of expediency – experience has taught us that
> particular strategies are likely to succeed in given circumstances, so we
> use them.

In our dinner table scenario, an example would be selecting a **pragmatic
strategy** in order to achieve the goals of both being passed something *and*
maintaining "social equilibrium" and "friendly relations" (Leech 1983: 82)
despite inconveniencing the target of our request. For example, *could you pass
the salt please* may be more expedient in this sense at a formal dinner event
than *pass the salt*. We take pragmatic strategy here to mean a conventional
means of achieving the goals of a participant.

Given the dominance of the pragmatic view in politeness research, we will
devote the next section to outlining classic theories positioned within it.

7.3 The two classic pragmatic politeness theories

7.3.1 The conversational-maxim view: Lakoff (1973) and Leech (1983)

The classic theories of politeness draw, as one might guess, on the classic
pragmatic theories, notably, Gricean conversational implicature and speech
act theory, as outlined in Chapters 4, 5 and 6. Given that pragmatic theory

has moved on, this is one of the weaknesses of those politeness theories. The bulk of the work in politeness studies has been based on or related to Brown and Levinson (1987), which we will outline in the following section. First, however, we will also note an alternative theory, mainly as a way of illustrating how politeness can interact with the Cooperative Principle (see section 4.2.2).

Robin Lakoff (1973) was the first to posit a **maxim-based view** of politeness. In brief, she proposes that there are two rules of pragmatic competence, one being "be clear", which is formalised in terms of Grice's (1975) Cooperative Principle, and the other being "be polite", which is formalised in terms of a Politeness Principle. The latter Politeness Principle consists of the following maxims: (1) don't impose, (2) give options, and (3) make your receiver feel good. Lakoff notes that sometimes the need for clarity would clash with the need for politeness. Leech (1983) also posits a Politeness Principle, one which is more elaborate than that of Lakoff. The central mechanism of his Politeness Principle is involved in "trade-offs" with the Cooperative Principle. As an illustration, consider this event. At the annual general meeting of an undergraduate university society at which the major business was to vote for the president for the coming year, an author of this book witnessed that a candidate for the presidency had gained only one vote from the forty people present in the room. The candidates had been waiting outside, and the first author of this book was asked to summon them inside to receive the results. Upon meeting the candidate who got one vote, the candidate immediately asked him how many votes she had gained. He could not reveal the truth, since that would upset her; on the other hand, he did not want to be seen to be lying. Cornered by her question, he decided to be vague and replied, *not many*. His response thus avoided both a prototypical lie and the upset to the hearer that would have accompanied a more cooperative – in Grice's sense (1975) – reply. By flouting Grice's maxim of Quantity (1975) (*not many* relative to what?), he hoped that she would draw the implicature that a more cooperative reply would have been more damaging to her, and that was why he had been uncooperative. In Leech's (1983) terms, the reason why he had expressed himself unco-operatively was to uphold the Politeness Principle, which Leech defines as: "Minimize (other things being equal) the expression of impolite beliefs ... (Maximize (other things being equal) the expression of polite beliefs)" (1983: 81). More specifically, he had abided by the Approbation maxim (minimise dispraise of other/maximise praise of other), by minimising "dispraise" of the candidate. The other maxims of the Politeness Principle are: Tact, Generosity, Modesty, Agreement and Sympathy (see Leech 1983: 131–139, for details). The key point is that the Cooperative Principle accounts for *how* people convey indirect meanings, the Politeness Principle accounts for *why* people convey indirect meanings.

Reflection: Indirectness, (im)politeness and cultural variation

Gricean implicature underpins the notion of directness (cf. Searle 1975). This is the main dimension for both of the classic politeness theories, Leech (1983) and Brown and Levinson (1987). Leech's (1983: 108) comments on the relationship between politeness and indirectness are frequently cited: indirect utterances, such as *Could you possibly answer the phone*, tend to be more polite because they increase optionality for the hearer, while decreasing illocutionary force (ibid.). However, we must be careful not to assume that implicitness or indirectness *always* conveys politeness, a point we discussed in section 6.3. It may be typical of British culture, but is not so for all cultures. More directness is not always interpreted as less politeness (particularly, it seems, in less individualistic cultures) (see also Field 1998 on directives in a native American culture).

We should briefly note that researchers typically mis-report Leech's work (see Leech 2007). As far as indirectness and politeness are concerned, they usually ignore the fact that he also points out that indirectness might *increase* impoliteness when expressing "impolite beliefs". He comments "because 'You have something to declare' is an impolite belief, the more indirect kinds of question [e.g. 'Haven't you something to declare'] are progressively more impolite, more threatening, than the ordinary yes–no question" (1983: 171). While intuitively there seems to be something in this, it has not as yet been fully empirically investigated.

Perhaps the biggest problem for all classic approaches to politeness, both those subscribing to the maxim view and those subscribing to the face-saving view (to be discussed below), is that they focus on politeness arising from deviations from the Cooperative Principle, and pay little attention to politeness that does not. Merely saying *good morning* to a colleague at the beginning of the working day may be considered "polite", but this does not involve a deviation from the Cooperative Principle triggering the recovery of the speaker's intention – it is more a case of performing a routine expected by the hearer, given the social norms. A number of researchers have accounted for the fact that politeness can be expected, normal, not noticed and thus not a deviation from the Cooperative Principle (e.g. Escandell-Vidal 1998; Jary 1998; Terkourafi 2001; Watts 2003). This kind of politeness is labelled **anticipated politeness** by Fraser (1999, cited in Terkourafi 2001). Anticipated politeness is based on associative inferencing, as described in section 3.2.1. The distinction between anticipated politeness and **inferred politeness** is elaborated by Haugh (2003) (see also Terkourafi 2001: 121–127). Inferred politeness is based on "logical" inferencing as mentioned in section 3.2.1 and elaborated in Chapters 4 and 5. It is this kind of politeness that is discussed by the classic theories. In a nutshell, "politeness is anticipated when the behaviour giving rise to politeness is expected, while it is inferred when the behaviour giving rise to politeness is not expected" (Haugh 2003: 400). The distinction between anticipated and inferred politeness is also echoed in the distinction between politic behaviour and politeness, which we will discuss in section 6.4.2.

7.3.2 The face-saving view: Brown and Levinson (1987)

The main proponent of the face-saving view is Brown and Levinson (1987). Their theory consists of the following inter-related components: face, face-work and face-threatening acts, parameters affecting face threat and pragmatic and linguistic output strategies. We shall deal with each in turn.

Face

What is **face**? Notions such as reputation, prestige and self-esteem, all involve an element of the folk notion of face. The term is perhaps most commonly used in English in the idiom *losing face*, meaning that one's public image suffers some damage, often resulting in humiliation or embarrassment. Such reactions are suggestive of the emotional investment in face. Much modern writing on face draws upon the work of Goffman (e.g. 1967). Goffman (1967: 5) defines it thus: "the positive social value a person effectively claims for himself by the line others assume he has taken during a particular contact. Face is an image of self delineated in terms of approved social attributes." Brown and Levinson's conception of face consists of two related components, which they assume are universal: "*every* member wants to claim for himself" (1987: 61) [our italics]. One component is labelled **positive face**, and appears to be close to Goffman's definition of face, as it is defined as "the want of every member that his wants be desirable to at least some others ... in particular, it includes the desire to be ratified, understood, approved of, liked or admired" (1987: 62). One may assume, for example, that you want your existence acknowledged (e.g. people to say *Hello*), approval of your opinions (e.g. *You're right about that student*), or the expression of admiration (e.g. *I thought you did a good job*). Note that positive face clearly involves particular attitudes. The other component, **negative face**, is defined as: "the want of every 'competent adult member' that his actions be unimpeded by others" (1987: 62). One may assume, for example, that you want people to let you attend to what you want, do what you want and say what you want (hence, requests that inconvenience you are tentatively worded). Incidentally, the words "positive" and "negative" in the labels for these two kinds of face carry no implications of good and bad; they are simply technical terms for different kinds of face.

Reflection: Face and cultural variation

In the introduction to this chapter, we noted cross-cultural variation in the linguistic formulae by which politeness is achieved. But what if the concepts with which we are analysing politeness are themselves culturally biased? In the last decade or so, discussion has focused on the precise definition of "face" (see, in particular, Bargiela-Chiappini 2003). Much of this has been a reaction to Brown and Levinson's (1987) idea that face can be described in terms of universal individualistic psychological "wants". Brown and Levinson (1987: 61) claim that their notion of face is "derived from that of Goffman and from the English folk term". Compare the definitions above. That of Brown and Levinson is a very reductive version of Goffman's. With Goffman, it is not just the positive values that you yourself want, but what you can claim about yourself from what *others* assume about you – much more complicated! The point is that how you feel about yourself is dependent on how others feel about you. Hence, when you lose face you feel bad about how you are seen in other people's eyes. This social interdependence has been stripped out of Brown and Levinson's definition. Recent approaches to politeness (e.g. Arundale 2006) have tended to shift back towards a **reflexive** notion of face (i.e. involving what you think others think of yourself), as originally advocated by Goffman (see Chapter 8 for further discussion of reflexivity in pragmatics).

Furthermore, some researchers have criticised the **individualism** reflected in Brown and Levinson's definitions, particularly in negative face. Positive face is about what you as an individual find positive; negative face is about not imposing upon you as an individual. But this seems to ignore cases where the positive attributes apply to a group of people (e.g. a winning team), or where an imposition on yourself is not the main concern, but rather it is how you stand in relation to a group (e.g. whether you are afforded the respect associated with your position in the team). From a cultural perspective, some researchers have argued that Brown and Levinson's emphasis on individualism is a reflection of Anglo-Saxon culture, and not a universal feature, despite the fact that their politeness theory is pitched as a universal framework (cf. the title of their book: *"Politeness: Some universals of language usage"*). Matsumoto (1988) and Gu (1990), for example, point out that Japanese and Chinese cultures stress the group more than the individual. These are cultures that lean more towards **collectivism**. However, we should briefly note that not everybody thinks that Brown and Levinson got it wrong. Chen (2010), for example, argues that differences of this kind are differences in surface phenomena, while the underlying motivations have a more general application. Furthermore, one should remember that Brown and Levinson's description is based on the analysis of three very different languages, only one of which is English.

Reflection: Do cultures in England orientate to negative politeness?

As just noted, Brown and Levinson's politeness model is said to reflect the characteristics of politeness in England, notably, an emphasis on individualism (e.g. Matsumoto 1988; Gu 1990; Nwoye 1992; Wierzbicka [1991]2003). Similarly, one might observe of Leech (1983) that it is the politeness maxim of Tact, encompassing indirectness, that receives most attention. The Tact maxim covers the "most important kind of politeness in English-speaking society" (1983: 107) (presumably Leech had in mind British English-speaking societies). More generally in research, the politeness cultures of England are often said to be characterised by off-record or negative politeness (e.g. Blum-Kulka et al. 1989b; Stewart 2005; Ogiermann 2009) (e.g. *Could you make me some tea* or simply *I'm thirsty* as requests to somebody to make tea). The emphasis on the individual, privacy and non-imposition fits work in social anthropology. Kate Fox, in her book, *Watching the English: The Hidden Rules of English Behaviour* (2004: 173), writes:

> The identification of England as a predominantly "negative-politeness" culture – concerned mainly with the avoidance of imposition and intrusion – seems to me quite helpful. The important point here is that politeness and courtesy, as practised by the English, have very little to do with friendliness or good nature.

For anybody familiar with the cultural practices of the people of England, there is something that rings true about the claim that they have a preference for negative politeness practices. However, it is a cultural generalisation, a stereotype (see Mills 2009, who elaborates on this point during her discussion of culture and impoliteness). For anybody familiar with the North of England, it is likely not to ring so true. Strangers are often met with terms of affection (e.g. *love, pet, darling*) in conjunction with relatively direct utterances, as well as banter – not the stuff of negative politeness. Unfortunately, empirical research on the intra-cultural politeness practices of England is lacking, so we cannot substantiate these intuitions. Incidentally, it is worth pointing out here that cultures continually experience diachronic change as well as synchronic, though this seems to have escaped the attention of most researchers in cross-cultural pragmatics. The evidence points quite strongly to early politeness practices in England being oriented towards positive politeness rather than negative, the shift from one to the other commencing in the early modern period (see Jucker 2008). Culpeper and Demmen (2011) provide evidence showing that the current most common negative politeness structures for achieving requests – namely, *could you X* and *can you X* – were not established as politeness formulae before the 19th century. They argue that Victorian values, with their emphasis on the self (e.g. self-respect, self-sufficiency), did much to drive the rise of negative politeness in the English cultures of Britain.

Face-Threatening Acts (FTAs)

Facework, according to Goffman, is made up of "the actions taken by a person to make whatever he is doing consistent with face" (1967: 12). Any action – though Brown and Levinson almost always discuss speech acts – that impinges to some degree upon a person's face (e.g. orders, insults, criticisms) is a **face-threatening act** (hereafter, FTA). Facework can be designed to maintain or support face by counteracting threats, or potential threats, to face. This kind of facework is often referred to as **redressive facework**, since it involves the redress of an FTA. Facework, in Brown and Levinson's (1987) model, can be distinguished according to the type of face redressed, positive or negative. One might say that positive facework provides the pill with a sugar coating in that one affirms that in general one wants to support the other's positive face (e.g. in saying *Make me a cup of tea, sweetie*, the term of endearment expresses in-group solidarity with and affection for the hearer, thereby counterbalancing the FTA). In contrast, negative facework softens the blow in that one specifically addresses the FTA (typically, in British culture, this is achieved by being less direct, as in *I wondered if I could trouble you to make me a cup of tea*).

Reflection: Beyond FTAs

It is important to note that Brown and Levinson's work is oriented to acts that threaten face, and facework that attempts to redress those threatening acts. What about acts that simply enhance face? An important merit of Leech's Politeness Principle is that it is not confined to the management of potentially "impolite" acts (i.e. FTAs), such as asking somebody to do something for you, but also involves potentially "polite" acts (Leech 1983: 83) (i.e. face-enhancing acts), such as a compliment out of the blue. Leech's Politeness Principle allows for the minimisation of impolite beliefs and the maximisation of polite beliefs. This helps account for why, for example, the direct command *Have a drink* at a social occasion, which would appear to be impolite in brusquely restricting the hearer's freedom of action, in fact maximises the polite belief that the hearer would like and would benefit from a drink but might be too polite to just take one. And what about acts that simply attack face – threats, insults, put-downs, sarcasm, mimicry and so on? Goffman (1967: 24–26) mentions "aggressive facework". Clearly, politeness is not the issue here but rather "impoliteness", an area we will attend to near the end of this chapter. Recent "relational" approaches (e.g. Locher and Watts 2005; Spencer-Oatey 2008; see also section 7.4.2) within politeness studies are based on the full range of facework, and locate potentially polite behaviours within that framework.

We should also note here that FTAs are acts, reflecting the fact that speech act theory underpins Brown and Levinson (1987). We already discussed the limitations of speech act theory in Chapter 6. Speech act theory is discussed in relation to single short utterances with single functions, single speakers and single addressees. This ignores the multi-functionality and complexity of discourse situations, and the fact that speech acts are often constructed over a number of turns (see section 6.6). Brown and Levinson (1987: 10) recognise that the adoption of speech act theory as a basis for their model has not been ideal: "speech act theory forces a sentence-based, speaker-oriented mode of analysis, requiring attribution of speech act categories where our own thesis requires that utterances are often equivocal in force". The sort of decontextualised speech acts they use do not reflect the indeterminacies of utterances and the face-threatening ramifications they may have for any of the participants in a particular speech event. Their work includes no extended examples.

Variables affecting face threat

Brown and Levinson argue that an assessment of the amount of face threat of a particular act involves three sociological variables, the first two of which are much-discussed social relations: (1) the **social distance** between participants, (2) the **relative power** of the hearer over the speaker, and (3) the **absolute ranking** of the imposition involved in the act (see, in particular, 1987: 74–78). For example, Brown and Levinson would predict that asking a new colleague for a cup of tea is more face-threatening than asking a long-standing colleague (the distance variable); asking one's employer for a cup of tea is more face-threatening than asking a colleague (the power variable); and asking for a glass of vintage port is more face-threatening than asking for a glass of water (the ranking variable). They claim that these three variables subsume all other factors that can influence an assessment of face threat, and also that numerical values could be attached to each variable, so that the degree of face threat can be summed according to a formula (ibid.: 76). The point of calculating face threat, according to Brown and Levinson, is that it will lead to "a determination of the level of politeness with which, other things being equal, an FTA will be communicated" (ibid.). They do not, however, attempt to apply this formula in a quantitative analysis of face threat.

Reflection: Beyond sociological variables

Note that Brown and Levinson's book was published in a sociolinguistics series. It is perhaps not surprising then that the methodological flavour of the dominant sociolinguistics paradigm, that of Labov, with its emphasis on quantification had affected subsequent politeness studies (and we should note the role of studies in social psychology, which traditionally emphasise quantification). Numerous researchers began administering questionnaires (a favourite though not the only methodology) to quantify the kind of politeness strategies used by people of different relative power, social distance and so on (see Spencer-Oatey 1996, for many references). In general, the studies confirmed Brown and Levinson's predictions for power and to a lesser extent social distance, but generally avoided testing ranking. However, the basis of these studies is now being questioned. Spencer-Oatey (1996) demonstrated that researchers varied widely in what is understood by power or social distance. In fact, these variables were subsuming other independent variables. Baxter (1984), for example, showed that the attitude **affect** (i.e. whether there is liking or disliking between participants) was getting muddled up with social distance, despite the fact that it is an independent variable. More fundamentally, research on social situations and context generally has moved on. Social values, it is argued, are not static but dynamic, and they are not given values (i.e. known by participants) but negotiated in interaction (e.g. I may start by assuming that somebody is more powerful than me but re-evaluate that in the course of an interaction). To be fair to Brown and Levinson, they did acknowledge this vision, stating that values on their variables "are not intended as *sociologists'* ratings of *actual* power, distance, etc., but only as *actors'* assumptions of such ratings, assumed to be mutually assumed, at least within certain limits" (1987: 74–76; original emphasis). But they did not back this vision up with a suitable methodology (one which is more qualitative in nature and thus able to handle the complexity), and certainly subsequent researchers chose to ignore it.

Pragmatic and linguistic politeness output strategies

Brown and Levinson (1987) suggest that there are five pragmatic super-strategies for doing politeness, the selection of which is determined by the degree of face threat. We summarise these below (the examples are ours). They are ordered from least to most face threat, and include examples of linguistic output strategies:

Bald on record: The speaker performs the FTA efficiently in a direct, concise and perspicuous manner, or, in other words, in accordance with Grice's maxims (1975). Typically used in emergency situations, or when the face threat is very small, or when the speaker has great power over the hearer.

Positive politeness: The speaker performs the FTA in such a way that attention is paid to the hearer's positive face wants. Includes such strategies as paying attention to the hearer (*Hello*), expressing interest, approval or sympathy (*That was so awful, my heart bled for you*), using in-group identity markers (*Liz, darling ...*), seeking agreement (*Nice weather today*), avoiding disagreement (*Yes, it's kind of nice*), assuming common ground (*I know how you feel*) and so on.

Negative politeness: The speaker performs the FTA in such a way that attention is paid to the hearer's negative face wants. Includes such strategies as mollifying the force of an utterance with questions and hedges (*Actually, I wondered if you could help?*), being pessimistic (*I don't suppose there would be any chance of a cup of tea?*), giving deference, that is, treating the addressee as a superior and thereby emphasising rights to immunity (*I've been a real fool, could you help me out?*), apologising (*I'm sorry, I don't want to trouble you but ...*), impersonalising the speaker and the hearer (*It would be appreciated, if this were done*) and so on.

Off-record: The speaker performs the FTA in such a way that he can avoid responsibility for performing it. The speaker's face-threatening intention can only be worked out by means of an inference triggered by the flouting of a maxim.

Don't do the FTA: The speaker simply refrains from performing the FTA because it is so serious.

Reflection: The role of prosody

Brown and Levinson (1987) devote considerable attention to detailing output strategies, their exposition extends to approximately 150 pages. However, hardly any attention is devoted to how what is said sounds, how the prosody can influence politeness (or impoliteness) interpretations. Yet, it is not an unusual occurrence that people take offence at *how* someone says something rather than at *what* was said. Consider this (reconstructed) exchange between two pre-teenage sisters:

[7.1] A: Do you know anything about yo-yos?
       B: That's mean.
       (field notes)

On the face of it, Speaker A's utterance is an innocent enquiry about Speaker B's state of knowledge. However, the prosody triggered a different interpretation. Speaker A heavily stressed and elongated the beginning of *anything*, coupled with marked falling intonation at that point (we might represent this as: "do you know \ANYthing about /yo-yos?"). It signals to B that A's question is not straightforward or innocent. It triggers the recovery of implicatures that Speaker A is not asking a question but expressing both a belief that Speaker B knows nothing about yo-yos (the prosodic prominence of *anything* implying a contrast with nothing), and an attitude towards that belief, namely, incredulity that this is the case – something which itself implies that Speaker B is deficient in some way. Without the prosody, there is no clear evidence of the interpersonal orientation of Speaker A, whether positive, negative or somewhere in between. Yet, despite the importance of prosody in communication, the vast bulk of research on politeness or impoliteness pays woefully little attention to the role of prosody. The single exception of note is the work of Arndt and Janney (e.g. 1987), whose notion of politeness involves emotional support conveyed multi-modally through verbal, vocal and kinesic cues (for prosody and impoliteness, see Culpeper 2011b).

Brown and Levinson's politeness theory has been applied, in full or part, to a wide variety of discourses, situations and social categories, including "everyday" conversation, workplace discourse, job interviews, healthcare discourse, political discourse, media discourse, literary texts, historical texts, gender and conflict, not to mention a huge literature examining intercultural or cross-cultural discourses. For the purposes of exemplifying the kind of analysis that can be done, we will examine an example of healthcare discourse. Our data is taken from Candlin and Lucas (1986), where politeness issues are in fact only very briefly touched on. The lineation has been slightly changed. The context is an interview at a family planning clinic in the USA. CR is a counsellor, who interviews clients before they see the doctor. CT is a client, who is pregnant.

[7.2] 1 CR: have you ever thought about discontinuing smoking?
2 CT: uh. I've thought about it (*laughs*)
3 CR: do you think you'd be able to do it?
4 CT: I don't know (*laughs*) I guess if I really wanted to .. I've been smoking for a long time.
5 CR: are you under more stress now?
6 CT: um. I guess you could say so. yeah, because it was last year that I started smoking more.
7 CR: do you think if you worked on those things you might be able to cut down?
8 CT: on the stress you mean?
9 CR: well. I don't know what the stress is and I don't know if you're open to talking about that but .. from your facial expressions .. it seems like you're really hesitant to make a decision to discontinuing smoke. I mean smoking, that gonna have to be something up to you .. do you think if the stress was eliminated that maybe ..
10 CT: I could cut down.
11 CR: or quit

[*A few more turns elapse, with minimal contributions from CT*]

12 CR: well. you know it's not easy. cause everybody. well I've got my bad habits too. so I know it's not easy ... I smoked for eight years too so I know it's not easy.

13 CT: Did you quit?
14 CR: yeah.

(adapted from Candlin and Lucas 1986: 32–33)

CR's goal is to get CT to stop smoking. She repeatedly uses the speech act of request. However, this request is realised indirectly. A very direct request might be "quit smoking". In contrast, in turn 1 her request is couched as a question about whether CT has *ever thought* about stopping, and in turn 3 it is a question about what CT thinks of her ability to stop. This does not meet with success, so in turn 5 CR tries another tack, engaging CT in talk about a possible cause of the smoking, rather than directly talking about stopping. Then in turn 7 CR links the cause to cutting down. Note how indirect this is: it is phrased as a question about whether she has thought about whether she would be able to *cut down*. CR's strategy thus far is largely off-record politeness: by flouting the maxim of Relation (it is improbable in this context that CR is only inquiring about CT's thoughts) and the maxim of Quantity (what is to be *cut down* is not specified), she leaves it to CT to infer that she is requesting her to stop smoking (i.e. CR's implicature).[2] Turn 7 is further modified by hedging the possibility that she has the ability to cut down (cf. *might*), and making it conditional (cf. *if you worked on those things*). These linguistic strategies – conditionals and hedges – are the stuff of negative politeness. Note that a downside of this kind of indirectness is the loss of pragmatic clarity. In turn 2 CT either chooses to ignore or possibly was not aware of CR's implicature requesting her to stop, and just replies to the literal question (*I've thought about it*). Similarly, after turn 7 CT either exploits or is simply confused by the lack of clarity regarding what she should *cut down* (*on the stress you mean*). In turn 9 CR probes what the reasons for not giving up might be. The frequent hesitations signal tentativeness, a reluctance to impose, and thus can be considered a negative politeness strategy. In the final part of that turn, she again uses a question, but notably she refrains from completing the question and spelling out the other half of the if-structure (i.e. if the stress is eliminated, the smoking will be). This could be considered an example of don't do the FTA. Thus far, CR does not seem to be making much progress with her goal, and in the following turns (not presented in the text above) she makes only minimal responses. In turn 12 CR tries a completely different tack. She not only self-discloses (*I've got my bad habits too...I've smoked for eight years too so I know it's not easy*), but reveals information that (a) is negative about herself, and (b) is something that she has in common with CT. The kind of strategy in (a) is not well covered in Brown and Levinson, but could be accounted for by Leech's Modesty maxim (minimise praise of self/maximise dispraise of self); the strategy in (b), claiming common ground, is an example of positive

---

[2] See Haugh (in press, 2014) for an alternative account of such phenomena through the lens of the notion of "politeness implicature".

politeness. Importantly, note the effect of this on CT. For the first time, CT has engaged CR in conversation: instead of simply responding in a fairly minimal way, she asks a question (*Did you quit?*).

7.4   Recent developments

While over the decades there has been a strong chorus of critical comment on the classic politeness theories, including the issues raised in the boxes above, no single replacement model has yet emerged. Instead, over the last decade three different, yet partly overlapping, approaches have emerged, approaches which we will label discursive, relational and frame-based. We will give the flavour of these approaches in the following subsections. These will be followed by (1) a section on what might be seen as the opposite to politeness, namely, impoliteness, an area of study that has grown rapidly in the last decade, and (2) a section on the interactional approach to politeness, an approach that has made an appearance in recent years and is in tune with the interactional thread running through this book.

7.4.1   Discursive

Generally, recent work on politeness has usefully stressed that politeness is not inherent in linguistic forms but is a contextual judgement (see also comments at the end of section 7.2.1). More fundamentally, Eelen (2001) and Watts (e.g. 2003) argue vigorously that the classic pragmatic approaches articulate a pseudo-scientific theory of particular social behaviours and label it politeness (so-called politeness2), while ignoring the lay person's conception of politeness (so-called politeness1) as revealed, for example, through the use of the terms *polite* and *politeness* to refer to particular social behaviours. The key issue here is who decides that some piece of language counts as polite? Is it the analyst applying a politeness theory to a recording of language or is it the actual user of the language making comments about it?

Discursive politeness approaches lean towards politeness1, and indeed share some of its characteristics (see, for example, the discussion of politeness1 in Eelen 2001: 32–43). For example, they share a dislike of universalising generalisations. A key feature of discursive approaches is that they emphasise that the very definitions of politeness itself are subject to discursive struggle (what might be polite for one participant might be impolite for another). Discursive approaches typically have at least some of the following characteristics:

- the claim that there is no one meaning of the term "politeness" but that it is a point of discursive struggle;
- the centrality of the perspective of participants;

- an emphasis on situated and emergent meanings rather than pre-defined meanings;
- the claim that politeness is evaluative in character (that it is used in judgements of people's behaviours);
- an emphasis on context;
- the claim that politeness is intimately connected with social norms, which offer a grasp on the notion of appropriateness (note here the connection with the socio-cultural view of politeness discussed in section 7.2.1);
- the reduction of the role of intention in communication (it is rejected, or at least weakened or re-conceptualised);
- a focus on the micro, not the macro; and
- a preference for qualitative methods of analysis as opposed to quantitative.

Works that might claim to be discursive include: Eelen 2001; Locher and Watts 2005; Mills 2003; Watts 2003 (Locher 2006 is a very useful outline of the approach). In 2011 the volume *Discursive Approaches to Politeness*, edited by the *Linguistic Politeness Research Group (LPRG)*, appeared.[3] However, one problem for this approach is that the publications which cover it vary widely in what they take to be discursive, often mixing discursive elements with non-discursive elements (see Haugh 2007b). For example, work by Richard Watts and Miriam Locher incorporates the notion of "politic behaviour", which will be discussed in the following section. Politic behaviour is not a label that is at all familiar to the lay person. Further, discursive analyses of data sometimes seem suspiciously reminiscent of the kinds of analyses undertaken by scholars who are considered non-discursive (e.g. because they deploy intuitions and interpretations flowing from the analyst rather than the lay person).

The discursive approach is concerned with "developing a theory of *social* politeness" (Watts 2003: 9, *et passim*; our emphasis), though creating a "theory" of politeness seems not to be the objective for the discursive politeness approach (cf. Watts 2005: xlii). A consequence of focusing on the dynamic and situated characteristics of politeness is that politeness is declared not to be a predictive theory (Watts 2003: 25), or, apparently, even a post-hoc descriptive one (ibid.: 142). This is unlike classic politeness theories, especially Brown and Levinson (1987), which predict the choice of pragmatic strategies in the light of the degree of face threat as determined by sociological variables. A pragmatic approach has a different agenda:

The starting point of pragmatics is primarily in language: explaining communicative behaviour. By studying this we keep our feet firmly on the

---

[3] Whilst it is clear that this volume did much to set the agenda for the new discursive approach to politeness, it should be noted that not every paper within it could be described as discursive.

ground, and avoid getting lost too easily in abstractions such as "face" or "culture". The basic question is: what did *s* mean [to convey] by saying X? It is useful to postulate the Politeness Principle (PP), I claim, not because it explains what we mean by the word "politeness" (an English word which in any case doesn't quite match similar words in other languages), but because it explains certain pragmatic phenomena.

(Leech 2003: 104–105)

Bearing in mind section 7.2.1, one can see that the discursive approach is more sympathetic to the prescriptive social norm view (etiquette manuals, for example, provide insight into what the lay person would label *polite*). In contrast, the pragmatic approach is more sympathetic to the experiential social norm view, given that it often focuses on regular usages (cf. strategies) in context – usages which have usually become regular because they are expedient.

Reflection: The discursive approach and relevance theory

Watts (e.g. 2003) embraces relevance theory (Sperber and Wilson [1986]1995; see sections 4.3.2 and 5.3.1) as an explanatory framework. Mills (2003) also argues, though not uncritically, that relevance theory can make a contribution to the discursive approach (see also Christie 2007: 278–279). Given that relevance theory is a "grand" theory of universal application, this would seem a rather odd move. It has been used to account for politeness by a number of scholars (e.g. Escandell-Vidal 1996; Jary 1998; Christie 2007). In particular, relevance theory can account for the anticipated versus inferred distinction (see section 7.3.1). So few cognitive effects arise from anticipated politeness (behaviour following social norms) that it is not relevant enough to spend inferential effort on it; but when there are sufficiently large cognitive effects to reward processing effort, inferred politeness can take place. What makes it attractive to scholars pursuing the discursive approach is that it emphasises the hearer and does not have generalised norms of behaviour as a starting point, instead, it focuses on specific situated behaviours, "it provides an extremely powerful interpretive apparatus" (Watts 2003: 212). However, relevance theory has three problems for politeness-related studies. First, the relevance theory account of communication still involves the recognition of speakers' intentions. It does not suit politeness to place a relatively restricted notion of intention at its centre. Second, Haugh (2003: 406) points out that the notion of cognitive effects has not been sufficiently characterised:

> [T]here is no distinction made between cognitive effects which have "positive effect" (such as feelings of approval or warmth and so on), and those which have "negative effect" (such as antagonism

or alienation and so on). For example, there is no distinction made between showing that one thinks well of others (which can give rise to politeness), and showing that one thinks badly of others (which can give rise to impoliteness).

Third, no publication has shown how relevance theory can produce effective analyses of stretches of naturally occurring discourse, a limitation Watts (2003: 212) concedes: "[o]ne major problem with RT is that it rarely, if ever, concerns itself with stretches of natural verbal interaction".

7.4.2 Relational

Relational approaches have a central focus on interpersonal relations in common, rather than a central focus on the individual performing "politeness" which is then correlated with interpersonal relations as variables, as happens with Brown and Levinson (1987). This, in fact, has important implications. The term polite has been stretched, especially in the classic theories, to cover a range of different phenomena, not all of which would readily be recognised as polite by the lay person. In Britain, saying *please* or *thank you* would readily be recognised as polite, but would giving someone a compliment attract the same label? Perhaps the latter is just seen as an example of "nice", "kind" or "supportive" behaviour, or even "sneaky", "manipulative" or "arse-licking" behaviour. Of course, it is an empirical question as to what perceptions and labels particular behaviours attract, but there is no doubting that their discussions of politeness encompass such a breadth of phenomena that the label polite is unlikely to be the descriptor of choice for each individual phenomenon. Relational approaches avoid seeing everything through the prism of politeness. In point of fact, they also encompass impolite behaviour. We will briefly outline the two main relational approaches, the relational work approach of Locher and Watts' (e.g. Locher 2004, 2006; Locher and Watts 2005; Watts 2003) and the rapport management approach of Spencer-Oatey (e.g. 2008).

Locher and Watts state that "relational work can be understood as equivalent to Halliday's (1978) interpersonal level of communication" (2005: 11) and, further, that "[r]elational work is defined as the work people invest in negotiating their relationships in interaction" (2008: 78). Relational work is not switched off and on in communication but is always involved. The concept of face is central to relational work, though not as defined by Brown and Levinson (1987) but by Goffman (1967: 5). Face is treated as discursively constructed within situated interactions. Watts (2005: xliii, see also Locher and Watts 2005: 12; Locher 2004: 90) offers a diagram which usefully attempts to map the total spectrum of relational work, reproduced in Figure 7.1.

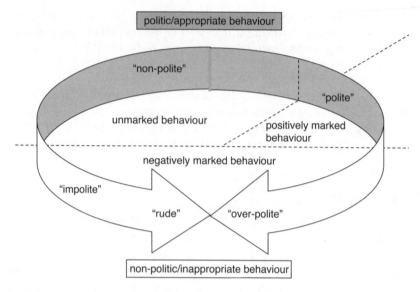

Figure 7.1   Relational work (Watts 2005: xliii)

Relational work in this perspective incorporates the issue of whether behaviour is marked or not. Markedness here relates to appropriateness; if the behaviour is inappropriate, it will be marked and more likely to be noticed. Note that the notion of appropriateness can be viewed in terms of acting in accordance or otherwise with social norms (see section 7.2.1). Unmarked behaviour is what Watts (e.g. 2003) refers to in his earlier work as "politic behaviour": "[l]inguistic behaviour which is perceived to be appropriate to the social constraints of the ongoing interaction, i.e. as non-salient, should be called *politic behaviour*" (Watts 2003: 19), and is illustrated by the following examples:

> [7.3]   A: Would you like some more coffee?
>   B: Yes, *please.*
>
>   M: *Hello*, Mr. Smith. *How are you?*
>   S: *Hello* David. Fine *thanks. How are you?*
>   (Watts 2003: 186, emphasis as original)

Politeness, on the other hand, is positively marked behaviour. Watts (2003: 19) writes that "[l]inguistic behaviour perceived to go beyond what is expectable, i.e. salient behaviour, should be called *polite* or *impolite* depending on whether the behaviour itself tends towards the negative or positive end of the spectrum of politeness". By way of illustration, we can re-work Watts's examples accordingly:

> [7.4]   A: Would you like some more coffee?
>   B: Yes, *please, that's very kind, coffee would be wonderful.*

M: *Hello*, Mr. Smith. *It's great to see you. We missed you. How are you?*
S: *Hello* David. *I'm fine thanks. It's great to see you too. How are you?*

Reflection: To be politic or not to be politic?

Watts's and Locher's view that politeness is associated with a marked surplus of relational work clearly rings true. One problem, however, is that Watts's definitions, as given in the previous paragraph, suggest a hard line between politic behaviour and politeness: if it is not one, it is the other. This seems unrealistic; surely there is a scale between politic behaviour and politeness that captures degrees of difference between relatively "normal" behaviours and situations, such as greetings and leave-takings in expected contexts, and those which are more creative (see Leech 2007: 203, for a similar comment). Indeed, contrary to the definitions, the dotted lines in Figure 7.1 suggest fuzziness.

Spencer-Oatey (e.g. 2002, 2005, 2008) proposes a model of **rapport management**, which concerns the management of harmony–disharmony amongst people. A particular concern was that "Brown and Levinson's (1987) conceptualisation of positive face has been underspecified, and that the concerns they identify as negative face issues are not necessarily face concerns at all" (2008: 13). Thus, her model not only consists of three types of face – "quality", "relational" and "social identity" – but also two types of "sociality rights". These are summarised in Table 7.1.

In addition to face and rights, Spencer-Oatey (2008: 17) argues for the importance of interactional goals:

People often (although not always) have specific goals when they interact with others. These can be relational as well as transactional (i.e. task-focused) in nature. These "wants" can significantly affect their perceptions of rapport because any failure to achieve them can cause frustration and annoyance.

Threats to positive rapport or harmony between people can be related to face, rights/obligations or interactional goals. However, rapport management is not confined, as in the case of Brown and Levinson (1987), to counterbalancing threats. Spencer-Oatey (2008: 32) suggests that there are four orientations:

1. Rapport enhancement orientation: a desire to strengthen or enhance harmonious relations between the interlocutors;
2. Rapport maintenance orientation: a desire to maintain or protect harmonious relations between the interlocutors;
3. Rapport neglect orientation: a lack of concern or interest in the quality of relations between the interlocutors (perhaps because of a focus on self);
4. Rapport challenge orientation: a desire to challenge or impair harmonious relations between the interlocutors.

Table 7.1 Categories in the rapport management framework

Face	**Quality face**
(defined with reference to Goffman (1967: 5): "the positive social *value* a person effectively claims for himself [*sic*] by the line others assume he has taken during a particular contact" (2008: 13).	(related to the self as an individual): "We have a fundamental desire for people to evaluate us positively in terms of our personal qualities, e.g. our confidence, abilities, appearance etc" (Spencer-Oatey 2002: 540).
	Relational face
	(related to the self in relationship with others): "[s]ometimes there can also be a relational application; for example, being a talented leader and/or a kind-hearted teacher entails a relational component that is intrinsic to the evaluation" (2008: 15).
	Social identity face
	(related to the self as a group member): "We have a fundamental desire for people to acknowledge and uphold our social identities or roles" (2002: 540); "[social identity face involves] any group that a person is a member of and is concerned about. This can include small groups like one's family, and larger groups like one's ethnic group, religious group or nationality group" (2005:106).
Sociality rights	**Equity rights**
defined as the "fundamental social *entitlements* that a person effectively claims for him/herself in his/her interactions with others" (2008: 13).	"We have a fundamental belief that we are entitled to personal consideration from others, so that we are treated fairly: that we are not unduly imposed upon, that we are not unfairly ordered about and that we are not taken advantage of or exploited" (2008: 16).
	Association rights
	"We have a fundamental belief that we are entitled to social involvement with others, in keeping with the type of relationship that we have with them" (2008: 16).

Rapport enhancement tallies with Leech's (1983) accommodation of acts that simply enhance politeness, for example, to strengthen friendship. Rapport maintenance could be simply a matter of performing polite behaviour, or a matter of restoring relations in the light of threatening behaviour. Rapport neglect accommodates Brown and Levinson's (1987) observation about the bald on record strategy that in emergency situations politeness is not an issue, along with the many other reasons why somebody may neglect relations (e.g. weighting their own concerns above those of others). Finally, rapport challenge accommodates impoliteness, to be discussed in the next section.

Spencer-Oatey (e.g. 2008) devotes considerable space to elaborating how these three components are linked to pragmatic, linguistic and contextual features. This elaboration goes well beyond simple lexically and grammatically defined output strategies or simple social variables. The important point for the model is that Spencer-Oatey provides a detailed analytical framework which we can apply to language data.

7.4.3 Frame-based

Terkourafi (e.g. 2001) is certainly not the first, or indeed only, scholar to have related politeness to the notion of a (cognitive) "frame" (Watts 2003; Locher 2004; and Locher and Watts 2005 do likewise). However, Terkourafi produces the most elaborate account of the frame-based approach to politeness, anchoring it in pragmatic theory. For this reason, we will focus on her work in this section.

Terkourafi argues that we should analyse the concrete linguistic realisations (i.e. formulae) and particular contexts of use which co-constitute "frames". This avoids problematic notions like directness (see section 7.3). Moreover, "[i]t is the regular co-occurrence of particular types of context and particular linguistic expressions as the *unchallenged* realisations of particular acts that create the perception of politeness" (2005a: 248; see also 2005b: 213; our emphasis). It is through this regularity of co-occurrence that we acquire "a knowledge of which expressions to use in which situations" (2002: 197), that is, "experientially acquired structures of anticipated 'default' behaviour" (ibid.). Note that we are tapping into experiential norms, and also that we are dealing with anticipated politeness. The fact that the expressions are not only regularly associated with a particular context but also go unchallenged is an important point. This feature seems to be similar to Haugh's point that evidence of politeness can be found in, amongst other things, "the reciprocation of concern evident in the adjacent placement of expressions of concern relevant to the norms in both in that particular interaction" (2007b: 312). That we are dealing with regularities means that we can deploy quantitative as well as qualitative methodologies (a simplistic quantitative methodology, such as counting up a particular form, is not possible, however, as we must count up forms in particular contexts that are unchallenged).

Of course, it is not the case that such conventionalised formulae – the stuff of anticipated politeness – constitute the only way politeness is conveyed and understood. Terkourafi (e.g. 2001, 2005b) develops neo-Gricean pragmatics (see section 4.3.1) to account for more implicational/inferential modes. Hitherto, standard, classical Gricean accounts of politeness (e.g. Leech 1983) have made no explicit connection with generalised implicatures, instead discussing politeness in terms of the recovery of the speaker's intentions in deviating from Gricean cooperativeness on a particular occasion (i.e. in terms of particularised implicatures). In the introduction to their second edition, Brown and Levinson (1987: 6–7) concede that they may have underplayed the role of generalised conversational implicatures. Terkourafi, in contrast, argues that, while politeness can involve full inferencing in a nonce context, what lies at its heart is a generalised implicature, that is, a level of meaning between particularised implicatures and fully conventionalised (non-defeasible) implicatures (cf. Levinson's utterance-type meaning; see section 4.3.1). More specifically, she argues that generalised implicatures arise from situations where the implicature is weakly context-dependent, requiring a minimal amount of contextual information relating to the social context of use in which the utterance was routinised and thus conventionalised to some degree. Her argument is neatly summarised here (Terkourafi 2005a: 251, original emphasis):

> Politeness is achieved on the basis of a generalised implicature when an expression *x* is uttered in a context with which – based on the addressee's previous experience of similar contexts – expression *x* regularly co-occurs. In this case, rather than engaging in full-blown inferencing about the speaker's intention, the addressee draws on that previous experience (represented holistically as a frame) to derive the proposition that "in offering expression *x* the speaker is being polite" as a generalised implicature of the speaker's utterance. On the basis of this generalised implicature, the addressee may then come to hold the further belief that the speaker *is* polite.

7.5 Impoliteness

Although the study of impoliteness has a fairly long history (usually in the guise of the study of swearing), and although early scientific attempts to address the topic (e.g. Lachenicht 1980) did not galvanise scholars, momentum has been increasing, with the arrival of Lakoff (1989), Culpeper (1996), Tracy and Tracy (1998), Mills (2003), Bousfield (2008), Bousfield and Locher (2008) and Culpeper (2011a), to mention but a few. A key question is: should a model of politeness account for impoliteness using the same concepts, perhaps with an opposite orientation, or is a completely different model required? Impoliteness phenomena are not unrelated to politeness phenomena. One way in which the degree of impoliteness varies is according to the degree of politeness expected: if somebody told their University Vice-Chancellor to be quiet, most likely considerably more offence would be taken than if they told one of their young children to do the same. Moreover, the fact that sarcasm trades off politeness is further evidence of this relationship. For example, *thank you* (with exaggerated prosody) uttered by somebody to whom a great disfavour has been done, reminds hearers of the distance betwee favours that normally receive polite thanks and the disfavour in this instance. There are, however, also some important differences between politeness and impoliteness. Recollect that both of the relational frameworks discussed in section 7.4.2 accommodate, explicitly or implicitly, both politeness and impoliteness. It is true that within a relational approach such as Locher and Watts (2005) there is a ready opposition: impoliteness can be associated with a negative evaluation as opposed to a positive evaluation, which can be aligned with politeness. However, the categories "positive" and "negative" are very broad. When we look at the specifics, the polite/impolite opposition runs into some difficulties.

One possible characteristic of politeness, as noted in section 7.2.1, is consideration. In a very broad sense any impoliteness involves being inconsiderate, but defining something in terms of a negative (i.e. what it is not) is not very informative about what it actually is. Moreover, Culpeper (2011a) reports a study of 100 impoliteness events narrated by British undergraduates. 133 of the total of 200 descriptive labels that informants supplied for those events fell into six groups (in order of predominance): *patronising, inconsiderate, rude, aggressive, inappropriate* and *hurtful* (see Culpeper 2011a: chapter 3). Clearly, being *inconsiderate* is a descriptive label that strikes a chord with participants. However, *patronising*, by far the most frequent label, does not have a ready opposite concept in politeness theory. Presumably, it relates to an abuse of power, a lack of deference, but neither power nor deference are well described in the classic politeness theories. Similarly, *aggressive*, with overtones of violence and power, has only a very general opposite in politeness theory, namely, harmonious. And there are yet other differences or cases where there do not appear to be easy diametric opposites between impoliteness and politeness. Anger is one of the most frequent emotional reactions associated with impoliteness, particularly when a social norm or right is perceived to have been infringed (see Culpeper 2011a: chapter 2). But anger lacks a similarly specific emotional opposite associated with politeness. Furthermore, taboo lexical items appear relatively frequently in impolite language. Lexical euphemisms, however, while they are associated with politeness, play a minor role.[4]

An important point is that relational frameworks are not models of politeness or impoliteness themselves; they are models of interpersonal relations which may accommodate at least some aspects of politeness, impoliteness, and so on. So, while they will provide insights, we cannot expect a complete apparatus for accommodating or explaining the rich array of communicative

---

[4] Leech (2009) argued that taboo language is one of two impoliteness areas which politeness theory, specifically his own, cannot adequately account for. The other concerns the negative acts, threats and curses.

to achieve and/or perceived by participants as achieving
͟r example, the descriptions in Culpeper 1996; Bousfield
ʟifference between politeness and impoliteness is that
ͳits own set of conventionalised impolite formulae. We under-
ͳventionalisation here in the same way as Terkourafi (e.g. 2003),
ͳnely, items conventionalised for a particular context of use. As we saw in
section 7.4.3, for such items to count as polite, they must go unchallenged
(e.g. Terkourafi 2005a; see also Haugh 2007b, for a related point). Conversely,
then, a characteristic of conventionally impolite formulae is that they are
challenged. In Culpeper's (2011a) data, by far the most frequent impolite
formulae type is insults. These fall into the following four groups (all examples are taken from naturally occurring data; square brackets give an indication of structural slots, which are optional to varying degrees, and slashes
separate examples):

1. Personalised negative vocatives:
    [you] [fucking/rotten/dirty/fat/little/etc.][moron/fuck/plonker/dickhead/
    berk/pig/shit/bastard/loser/liar/minx/brat/slut/squirt/sod/bugger/etc.] [you]
2. Personalised negative assertions:
    [you] [are] [so/such a] [shit/stink/thick/stupid/bitchy/bitch/hypocrite/
    disappointment/gay/nuts/nuttier than a fruit cake/hopeless/pathetic/fussy/
    terrible/fat/ugly/etc.]
    [you] [can't do] [anything right/basic arithmetic/etc.]
    [you] [disgust me/make me] [sick/etc.]
3. Personalised negative references:
    [your] [stinking/little] [mouth/act/arse/body/corpse/hands/guts/trap/
    breath/etc.]
4. Personalised third person negative references (in the hearing of the target):
    [the] [daft] [bimbo]
    [she] ['s] [nutzo]

Apart from insults, other important impoliteness formulae types are: pointed
criticisms/complaints; challenging or unpalatable questions and/or presuppositions; condescensions; message enforcers; dismissals; silencers; threats;
curses and ill-wishes; non-supportive intrusions (further detail and exemplifi-
cation can be found in Culpeper 2011a).

Reflection: Impoliteness and cultural variation

Culpeper et al. (2010) investigated the cross-cultural variation of impoliteness. Their data consisted of 500 impoliteness events reported by students
in England, China, Finland, Germany and Turkey. Of course, there is no

claim to be comparing all the cultural communities that live in England with all those in China, and so on, but rather groups of students of similar age who are geographically separated and likely to be influenced by different cultural practices. The main analytical framework adopted was Spencer-Oatey's (e.g. 2008) Rapport Management, as outlined in section 7.4.2 and specifically Table 7.1, covering various types of face as well as sociality rights. Their quantitative analysis reveals some distinct differences amongst the groups. For example, China-based data had the highest number of impoliteness events involving either relational face or equity rights (or sometimes both together). Here is an example from the Chinese-based data involving relational face:

[7.5] I saw her immediately after I went to the cafeteria. I told her ideas for some activities for our class. I intended to collect some suggestions from my classmates by telling them the activities ahead of the schedule. I was shocked at her answer. She rejected the ideas loudly with a tone of ordering in front of all the people in the cafeteria. Despite explaining to her softly and humbly, she rejected them more disrespectfully than before, paying no attention to my good manner. I was greatly annoyed because my classmates all respected me and I had never come across situations like that before.

This informant comments thus on this interaction: *My good intention was rejected coldly and rudely. That was a great threat and puzzle to a leader of a class* (our emphasis). What troubled this informant is that her relational value as a leader of her classmates had been threatened. Here is an example from another China-based informant involving equity rights:

[7.6] In a cafeteria I greeted my classmate. But he did not respond.

One key principle underlying equity rights is reciprocity, the principle that costs and benefits should be fairly balanced amongst participants. Here, one participant has made the effort to greet another, but this has not been reciprocated. Of course, none of this is to say that the same kind of event could not have caused offence to the England-based informants. The point is simply that the greater frequency with which this occurs in the China-based group may be evidence of greater cultural sensitivity to the relational and equity of social interactions in China. This tallies in fact with points made about face and cultural variation in section 7.3.2, specifically that Chinese cultures may be less focused on the individual. Certainly, this would tally with the long-standing influence of Confucianism, which advocates reciprocity, in Chinese cultures (cf. Pan and Kádár 2011 for another view on impoliteness in Mainland China).

Of course, whether or not impoliteness formulae result in impoliteness will depend on the hearer's assessment of its usage in context. Consider this example:

[7.7] [Lawrence Dallaglio, former England Rugby captain, describing the very close family in which he grew up]
As Francesca and John left the house, she came back to give Mum a kiss and they said goodbye in the way they often did. "Bye, you bitch," Francesca said. "Get out of here, go on, you bitch," replied Mum.
(*It's in the blood: My life* (2007), from an extract given in *The Week*, 10 November 2007)

Here, in the direct speech, we see a conventionalised insulting vocative, *you bitch*, and also a conventionalised dismissal, *get out of here*. McEnery (2006: 39, 236) provides corpus evidence that there is a strong tendency in British English for *bitch* to be used between women, as here. Nevertheless, these items project contexts that are dramatically at odds with the situation within which they are uttered. Rather than antagonistic relationships, hate, coercion and so on, we have a strong loving family unit (Francesca has just demonstrated her affection by giving her mother a kiss). The recontextualisation of impoliteness formulae in socially opposite contexts reinforces socially opposite effects, namely, affectionate, intimate bonds amongst individuals and the identity of that group. Here we have the opposite of genuine impoliteness, that is, mock impoliteness, which consists of impolite forms whose effects are (at least theoretically for the most part) cancelled by the context (the term "mock impoliteness" is used in Leech 1983). Banter is a key everyday label (at least in English), though most types of teasing and some jokes and types of insults also have in common the fact that they involve mock impoliteness. One of the lacunae in Brown and Levinson (1987) is that they do not treat banter at all; in contrast, Leech (1983: 144) describes mock impoliteness within his Banter Principle:

"In order to show solidarity with *h*, say something which is (i) obviously untrue, and (ii) obviously impolite to *h*" [and this will give rise to an interpretation such that] "What *s* says is impolite to *h* and is clearly untrue. Therefore what *s* really means is polite to *h* and true."

Banter, of course, also exists in a heavily ritualised form as a kind of language game – a specific activity type. In America some forms of this activity are known as "sounding", "playing the dozens" or "signifying", which takes place particularly amongst black adolescents (e.g. Labov 1972; for a nuanced account of banter in a community in France, see Tetreault 2009).

Reflections: Mock impoliteness in Britain and Australia

Haugh and Bousfield (2012) undertook a cross-cultural study of banter in interactions amongst British (specifically North England) and Australian speakers of English. They focused on two particular forms of banter, jocular mockery and jocular abuse, and analyse how these can give rise to understandings of mock impoliteness (as opposed to genuine impoliteness) amongst participants. Jocular mockery and abuse are pragmatic acts. The former is a specific form of *teasing* where the speaker diminishes something of relevance to the target within a non-serious or jocular frame. The latter refers to a specific form of *insulting*, where the speaker casts the target into an undesirable category or as having undesirable qualities, using conventionalised impoliteness formulae within a non-serious or jocular frame. Both jocular mockery and jocular abuse are interactionally achieved, that is, they emerge as a joint effort of two or more participants. It is suggested that when they arise in a non-serious or jocular frame these pragmatic acts can be evaluated as having particular relational and attitudinal implications. These include reinforcing solidarity, disguising repressive intent, or amusing (at least some of) the participants (Culpeper 2011a). The existence of multiple interpersonal implications allows for slippage between evaluations of these pragmatic acts as mock impolite or as genuinely impolite in some cases. Haugh and Bousfield found that jocular mockery and jocular abuse were recurrent practices in both the British and Australian datasets, with only limited variation arising in the target themes of such forms of banter. They traced this to a shared societal ethos that places value on "not taking yourself too seriously" (Fox 2004; Goddard 2009). This contrasts with banter being treated as a kind of competitive activity where individuals attempt to "outdo" each other, as found in at least some situational contexts in American English (Butler 2007). However, this latter type of more competitive banter can also be observed in British and Australian English. There thus remains considerable research to be done to better understand the relational and attitudinal implications of banter across varieties of English, and indeed across other languages more generally.

Needless to say, impoliteness is frequently achieved and understood without the use of formulae; in other words, through implicit means, as illustrated in the following example (a diary report from a British undergraduate):

[7.8]   As I walked over to the table to collect the glasses, Sarah said to Joe "come on Joe lets go outside", implying she didn't want me there. This was at the pub on Sunday night, and I just let the glasses go and walked away.

I didn't particularly feel bad, but angry at the way she had said that straight away when I got there. We aren't particularly friends but she was really rude in front of others.

The interpretation of Sarah's utterance partly rests on assumptions about for whom the message is intended. Clearly, the informant assumes that, while the addressee is Joe, the target is her, something which seems to be supported by the fact that it was said "straight away when I got there". It is possible, of course, that the offender also used non-verbal means to clarify the target, such as looking at her while she spoke. Taking the informant as the target, the utterance "come on Joe lets go outside" seems to have no relevance at all for her: it flouts the maxim of relation. The informant draws the implicature that going outside entails moving away from where she is, in other words, she is being excluded (see Haugh 2014 for further discussion of impoliteness implicatures).

In Culpeper's (2011a) data, the most frequent implicit strategy by which impoliteness is understood is sarcasm. Sarcasm can be evaluated as mock politeness, that is, politeness which is not understood to be genuine (cf. Culpeper 1996, who draws on Leech 1983). The message conveyed is partially mixed: some aspects, such as the use of politeness formulae, suggest politeness; other aspects, typically contextual or co-textual, suggest impoliteness. For example, a member of staff at Lancaster University, writing to complain about somebody backing into her car in the car park and then disappearing, concludes her complaint: *Thank you SO VERY MUCH*. Note the capitalisation here. The parallel in spoken language is the prosody. Mixed sarcastic messages often involve multi-modality; specifically, the verbal content conflicting with the prosody or visual aspects. In all such cases, the overall assessment must be weighted towards aspects suggesting impoliteness, leaving the aspects suggesting politeness (typically the formulaic polite words) as a superficial veneer, reminding the target of the distance between a polite context and the current impolite one.

7.6   The interactional approach to politeness

As an antidote to the classic politeness theories, discursive politeness work has been valuable. In particular, it has drawn attention to the fact that (im) politeness is not inherent in particular forms of language, in the sense that a judgement of politeness is solely determined by the usage of particular language. It argues instead that it is a matter of the participants' evaluations of particular forms as (im)polite in context. However, discursive approaches have generally emphasised social aspects at the expense of close consideration of pragmatic aspects of politeness. The interactional approach to politeness (and interpersonal attitudes more generally) has much in common with the discursive, relational and frame-based approaches we discussed in section 7.4, but it also advocates a number of theoretical and methodological moves that mark it as distinct from those approaches. One key claim is the idea that user (cf. politeness1) and observer (cf. politeness2) perspectives on politeness are both equally important, so we very often have to deal with multiple understandings of behaviour vis-à-vis im/politeness (see Kádár and Haugh [2013] for more detailed discussion).

To see what we mean by multiple understandings of politeness, consider the following apology that arose in an intercultural setting (Chang and Haugh 2011). The background to the apology is that Wayne (an Australian) and his wife had been invited by Joyce's mother (a Taiwanese) to go out with her family to a restaurant for dinner, as they had just met and found they shared a common interest in vegetarian food. Wayne and his wife did not, however, turn up, and did not respond to Joyce's call from the restaurant. It was only the next day that Wayne sent an SMS text to Joyce saying *Sorry I forgot I was busy with something.* Joyce decided to call Wayne and the entire call was recorded.[5] The excerpt below features the head act of Wayne's apology and the first part of the interaction that followed:

[7.9] (Joyce has just apologised for calling Wayne)
  13 W: it's just, a:h, I really apologise for not getting back
  14   to you the other day but we couldn't make it?
  15 J: oh, that's okay. yeah, yeah, yeah. I- I just
  16   thought oh probably you are busy with something
  17   so you ah probably were easy to- to (0.2)
  18   for(hhh)get it.
  19 W: yeah we were pretty busy actually?
  20 J: oh, okay, yeah, yeah that's fine. I just want to
  21   call you, that- that- that's oka:y.
                                        (Chang and Haugh 2011: 420)

The question is: is Wayne's apology polite (or not)? Asking such a question already presupposes a number of different perspectives. You, the reader, may form your opinion about this particular incident. Your perspective (as the analyst) is grounded as an observer (although sometimes the analyst can also be a participant), specifically, an overhearer. Your footing therefore differs from that of the speaker (Wayne) and the addressee (Joyce). You evaluate it without having direct access to the minds of either participant and so, inevitably, draw

5 The permission of the researchers to use this recording was gained from both participants.

more from generalised or shared perspectives on the kinds of apologies that arise when one does not turn up to a social occasion. The participants themselves, Wayne and Joyce, not only draw from their own cultural perspectives, but also draw from their shared interactional history with each other, and perhaps with other Australians and Taiwanese. The recipient footing of Joyce is also somewhat complex as, while she is the interpreter and accounter in this interaction, she is not the exclusive target (i.e. the apology is for Joyce's family as well, not just Joyce).

The first footing to consider is that of Joyce. Did she consider it polite or not? Clues to this can be observed in the interactional data. After Wayne issues the apology in lines 13–14, Joyce responds in line 15 with an absolution (*that's okay*) that is *oh*-prefaced, thereby increasing the level of absolution, at least in English (Robinson 2004). In framing it as a preferred response, it appears on the surface that Joyce displays acceptance of Wayne's apology. However, in the subsequent talk, a more complex picture emerges. Joyce offers a proposed account for why Wayne did not turn up (lines 15–18), and then subsequently repeats her absolution (*that's fine, that's okay*) in lines 20–21, in spite of the fact that Wayne hasn't actually apologised again. Joyce repeats this absolution two more times before the call ends (data not shown). We need to turn to studies of apologies in Chinese to consider what might be meant by the repetition of this absolution. What we find is that typically in Chinese, apologies are repeated in order to show sincerity (Hua et al. 2000). The repeated absolutions from Joyce therefore open up interactional space for Wayne to repeat his apology. He does not do this, which lends support for the inference that Joyce found Wayne's apology to be inadequate and thus impolite. This was independently verified by Joyce herself; she claimed she found it impolite in subsequent talk with the researchers.

The second footing to consider is that of Wayne. Did he consider his apology polite? From close examination of the interaction it appears that his understanding was that it was sufficiently polite. To begin with, the choice of the performative verb *apologise* is a marked IFID, as it appears only very infrequently in corpora of spoken discourse in English (Aijmer 1996; Deutschmann 2003). It is also preceded by an intensifier (*really*) which arguably increases the illocutionary force of this apology, as well as an account (*we couldn't make it*), the latter being a standard feature of apologies in English (see section 6.4). That Wayne does not perceive this apology to be inadequate is evident from the fact that he does not take up the interactional opportunities to repeat the apology created by Joyce. It is also evident from his attempts to "catch up" with Joyce despite her moving to close down the conversation at a number of points (data not shown), thereby displaying genuine (on the surface at least) interest in Joyce and her family (see Chang and Haugh 2011 for further discussion).

The third footing to consider is that of you, the reader. Here we would suggest, based on Chang and Haugh's (2011) study, that your understanding is likely to vary. Chang and Haugh elicited metapragmatic evaluations of the apology as (very) polite, neither polite nor impolite, or (very) impolite from a sample of Australian and Taiwanese respondents. While there was interesting intra-group variation found across these evaluations, particularly amongst the Australians, there was nevertheless a very clear inter-group difference. Overall, the Australians found it not impolite, while the Taiwanese found it impolite. This difference results from different cultural perspectives on the apology that these respondents brought to bear. The Australian respondents emphasised Wayne's attempts to show friendliness as increasing the level of sincerity (and thus acceptability) of his apology. The Taiwanese respondents, on the other hand, emphasised the lack of repetition as indicative of a lack of sincerity, which was one of their main reasons for evaluating the apology as impolite. Both the Australian and Taiwanese respondents shared the view that the account Wayne gave was somewhat inadequate, but ultimately judged the apology overall quite differently.

From this brief analysis a number of issues emerge. One key question that needs to be asked according to the interactional approach is *whose* understanding of politeness is it that we are analysing. In section 5.2.1, we outlined the multiple participation footings that underlie pragmatic meaning. This complex array of participation footings is also relevant to interpersonal attitudes such as politeness. Recipients may be addressees, side participants, overhearers or bystanders, for instance, and their evaluations of a particular pragmatic meaning or act may vary not only with those of the speaker but also amongst themselves (see Haugh 2013c for further discussion).

A second key question according to the interactional approach is *how* is it that participants (and so analysts as well) know something counts as polite, mock polite, mock impolite, impolite, over-polite, and so on. In other words, what are the moral grounds for making such an evaluation? To date a technical notion of "face" has generally been invoked in analysing politeness (see sections 7.3 and 7.4). In the interactional approach, however, we argue that there are other possible explanations of politeness from an **emic** perspective, namely, that of members of the (sub)cultural group in which the interaction is situated. The notion of face as a publicly endorsed social image of individuals is just one. There are others, including an orientation to one's sense of "place" relative to others or the heart/mind of others, for instance (see Haugh 2013a for further discussion).

A third question is how do we as analysts establish that evaluations of politeness, impoliteness and so on have indeed arisen. In the interactional approach we argue that the study of politeness (at least in interaction) necessarily involves very close analysis of the dynamics of interaction, including not only what is said, but also how it is said, that is, issues of prosodic and non-verbal delivery. The latter can provide important clues for the analyst in making inferences about attitudes on the part of participants. Such an approach also directs the analyst to examine responses to potentially polite (or impolite) meanings or acts to gather further evidence for making such inferences. However, as interpersonal attitudes often remain tacit rather than visibly surfacing in interaction, we also propose that the analyst needs to make recourse to metapragmatics in the study of politeness (see Kádár and Haugh 2013: chapter 9), and to interpersonal attitudes more generally. We will discuss metapragmatics in more detail in Chapter 8, but suffice to say at this point that it involves drawing from evidence that language users are aware of (potential) evaluations of politeness.

An interactional approach to politeness thus not only considers the understandings of participants in particular situated instances of interaction, but also draws from the understandings of users and observers over time. In this way, we can arguably build a much richer and more nuanced understanding of politeness and, more broadly, interpersonal attitudes.

7.7 Conclusion

This chapter has surveyed various approaches to politeness, and also briefly considered impoliteness. As we have identified the phenomena that pertain to (im)politeness, we have shown how they are culturally variable and, in particular, pointed to some distinctive aspects of British politeness. Readers may be wondering how exactly we conceive of politeness. So we will recap and clarify. We see politeness as an interpersonal attitude. Attitudes, of course, are well established in social psychology, and especially in language attitude research. An attitude involves a favourable or unfavourable reaction to stimuli, and has cognitive, affective and behavioural elements (see Bradac et al. 2001, and references therein). Note that conceiving of politeness as an attitude accommodates the frequently stated point that politeness is subjective and evaluative (e.g. Eelen 2001; Watts 2003; Spencer-Oatey 2005; Ruhi 2008). However, it should be noted that simply referring to "positive" evaluative beliefs is not sufficiently specific. It is unlikely that politeness involves *any* positive belief. For example, amusing somebody is an interpersonal activity that is generally viewed positively, but it is not at all clear that it would normally be considered a matter of politeness. A key objective for researchers is to understand the subset of positive evaluative beliefs that count as politeness on a particular occasion. The concept of face (Goffman 1967) is one mechanism for trying to doing this. However, we are not convinced that face easily accommodates all politeness-relevant positive beliefs. People also have such positive evaluative beliefs about social organisation and behaviours within social organisations – how people should be treated; what is fair and what is not; and so on. Some of these morality-related beliefs are associated with politeness. Spencer-Oatey's (e.g. 2008) Rapport Management framework does a good job of accommodating this array of evaluative beliefs, incorporating as it does the notion of sociality rights, although it will perhaps inevitably require further adjustments as our understanding of politeness continues to evolve in light of work that further teases out alternative emic perspectives on politeness.

Linguistic politeness refers to linguistic or behavioural forms that are (conventionally) associated with contexts in which politeness attitudes are activated (this view is consistent with, for example, Terkourafi e.g. 2001, outlined above). We acquire linguistic politeness from our experience of social interactions (e.g. Ervin-Tripp et al. 1990; Escandell-Vidal 1996; Snow et al. 1990). It involves the use of expressions that are both contextually appropriate and positively evaluated by the target (cf. Locher and Watts 2005). Remember the use of *please*, as discussed towards the beginning of this chapter. It is not used by anybody to anybody, or in any context, and when it is used it is generally considered interpersonally positive. The point about politeness routines/markers is that knowledge of both their appropriate context and their positive social meaning has become conventionally associated with the form. Of course, this does not mean that simply using a politeness routine/marker will result in politeness being achieved. Politeness always involves a contextual judgement; as is frequently pointed out, politeness is not solely determined by forms alone (e.g. Watts, 2003: 168; Locher and Watts, 2008: 78). Not only this, politeness is not some fixed value waiting to be retrieved. It emerges dynamically in interaction, and different participants may make different judgements. So, how do we tap into these judgements? It makes sense to examine the interaction in which they are mediated, as well as the broader societal milieu in which these interactions are situated, as, for example, happens in the interactional approach to politeness outlined in section 7.6.

Impoliteness has been accommodated by recent frameworks designed more with politeness in mind. In fact, it is also accommodated by Leech's (1983) Politeness Principle, which has a "negative" side to it. It clearly has some connections with politeness, as evidenced not least by the phenomena of mock politeness and mock impoliteness. But it is also obvious that it is not the same as politeness. The interesting issue is to specify in what ways. A key feature is that impoliteness involves emotion – especially emotions such as hurt and anger – in a much more intense way than politeness. Impoliteness obviously has its own set of conventionalised formulae and pragmatic strategies. It is also the case that the social contexts that give rise to impoliteness are not the same as those that give rise to politeness. As far as at least some British cultures are concerned, perceived abuses of power relations, resulting, for example, in patronising behaviours, are key to many instances of impoliteness.

8 Metapragmatics

8.1 Introduction

Language use involves choices. In the previous chapters we have examined the consequences of such choices for language users. One point that we have only alluded to so far is that language users are self-aware: we are aware not only of the choices we make when using language, but also the choices of others.

Consider the following extract from the column *You've got male* in an Australian newspaper, where the columnist is reporting on an interaction between a married couple that he recently witnessed. The columnist begins by describing relevant contextual details about the incident, which involves his friend, Jeff, who is hosting, along with his wife, a group of friends for a barbeque lunch. Jeff has just offered a piece of steak to the dog, but it has been rejected by the dog, so Jeff has picked it up and turned to walk back to the kitchen:

[8.1]   His wife then emasculated him in front of his guests. "Don't put that back with the steak. Put it in the bin." Jeff froze on the spot, his face a mask of incredulity. I instantly saw his dilemma.

He could meekly let the comment go through to the keeper and proceed silently to the bin in the interests of a harmonious lunch, thereby running the risk that his guests would go away thinking that he's someone who regularly scavenges for food the dog has slobbered over and his wife has to admonish him for it.

Or he could have pointed out to his wife how utterly absurd it was for her to suggest he would do such a thing, thereby running the risk of upsetting her in front of the guests, spoiling the mood of the lunch, or seen to be protesting too much to hide the fact that he is indeed an eater of rejected dog food.

> Jeff toughed it out with a bit of banter, but I could see in his eyes
> that a little piece of him died that day.
>
> ("How to have a long and happy marriage (part 4)",
> Rory Gibson, *U on Sunday*,
> 5 February 2012)

By now we hope you will be able to readily observe that the above passage interweaves allusions to numerous pragmatic phenomena, including particular referring expressions, pragmatic meanings and inferences that go beyond what is said, including not only what is implicated but also assumptions about presumed common ground, pragmatic acts such as admonishing and ordering, as well as indications of what others think of Jeff and his relationship with his wife (i.e. interpersonal relations and attitudes). The columnist is, of course, not an objective observer of events in making such comments, but rather is occupying a particular participation footing (namely, that of a side participant who is friends with one of the actors involved). Moreover, there are allusions to social discourses about what it means to be a (married) man in contemporary Australian life, which arise in part through the way in which the columnist makes reference to the other protagonist alongside Jeff as "his wife", thereby identifying her vis-à-vis a particular social category or role, rather than using her first name (in clear contrast to references to "Jeff"). Underpinning these social discourses are numerous assumptions about what constitutes an ideal relationship between married couples, as well as (stereotypical) assumptions about how such relationships are often assumed to play out in reality. Such assumptions might be widely accessible to users of English around the world, but inevitably you, our readers, will have your own "take" on this commentary. And this is only how it should be. Pragmatics matters for all of us, not just for the columnist and his mate, a point we have made repeatedly in this book.

An important phenomenon underpinning this anecdote is the way in which the columnist displays awareness of the ways in which participants at the party themselves would be aware of a whole raft of pragmatic meanings, pragmatic acts, interpersonal relations, attitudes and evaluations, as well as social discourses that go way beyond what the wife was reported to have said. In reporting on possible interpretations of these, the columnist thus makes a number of assumptions about what the others might have been thinking, including what the other guests might have been thinking Jeff's wife thinks of Jeff, as well as what Jeff might have been thinking the other guests were thinking about what Jeff's wife thinks of Jeff, and so on. It is often difficult to talk about this kind of reflexive thinking, yet it is something we easily accomplish in the course of using language. This kind of reflexivity, or recursive awareness (briefly touched on in section 2.5.3), lies at the heart of what is studied in metapragmatics.

In this chapter, we first introduce in more detail what is encompassed by metapragmatics, and the notion of reflexive awareness which lies at its core, before outlining the three main dimensions of reflexive awareness that underpin the pragmatic phenomena we have discussed in the preceding chapters. In our concluding section we discuss how such reflexivity is drawn upon in negotiating pragmatic meanings, pragmatic acts and interpersonal relations and attitudes, and so on, in interaction.

8.2   Metapragmatics and reflexivity

The prefix *meta*, which comes from the Greek μετά meaning "above", "beyond" or "among", is normally used in English to indicate a concept or term that is *about* another concept or term. For example, *metadata* is data about data, *metalanguage* is language about language, while *metapragmatics* refers to the use of language about the use of language. In order for participants to talk about their use of language they must, of course, have some degree of *awareness* about how we use language to interact and communicate with others. This type of awareness is of a very particular type, however, in that it is almost inevitably **reflexive**. What this means is that awareness of a particular interpretation on the part of one participant, for instance, is more often than not interdependently related to the awareness of interpretations (implicitly) demonstrated by other participants. In other words, in using language to interact or communicate with others, participants must inevitably think about what others are thinking, as well as very often thinking about what others think they are thinking, and so on. And not only do participants engage in such reflexive thinking in using language, they are also aware of this reflexivity in their thinking, albeit to varying degrees. We can thus observe various indicators of such reflexive awareness in ordinary language use.

Consider, for instance, the following excerpt from an episode of the HBO comedy, *Flight of the Conchords*. The two characters, Brett and Jermaine, have just met a lady in the park who was looking for her lost dog. They start singing a song about being in love with a girl, at the conclusion of which they realise they are singing about the very same lady they have just met (hence the title of the song, *We're both in love with a sexy lady*). Much of the song involves a back and forth between the two characters as they attempt to establish who they are referring to:

[8.2]   Brett: Maybe I'm crazy but when did you   **temporal deixis**
                      meet this lady?
        Jermaine: Just then.
        Brett: When?
        Jermaine: Then.
        Brett: Right then?
        Jermaine: Right then.

Brett: Where?   ⎤ **spatial deixis**
Jermaine: Here.   │
Brett: Over there?   │
Jermaine: Over there.   │
Brett: Over there, there?   │
Jermaine: Over there, there, there!   ⎦

[...]
Both: Oh, oh, oh, oh, no, oh no, no, no, oh no, no no
Jermaine: What?
Brett: Are you thinking what I'm thinking?   ⎤ **metapragmatic**
Jermaine: No, I'm thinking what I'm thinking.   │ **commentary**
Brett: So you're not thinking what I'm thinking?   │
Jermaine: No, cause you're thinking I'm thinking   │
                what you're thinking!   ⎦

("Love is a weapon of choice", *Flight of the Conchords*,
Season 2, Episode 6, 22 February 2009, director:
James Bobin, writer: Paul Simms)

In the course of this excerpt Brett and Jermaine attempt to establish the real world referent of "the lady" each is in love with. They begin by attempting to establish the time they met the girl (temporal deixis), then move to discussing where they met her (spatial deixis) (see section 2.5). Eventually, they start to realise they might be singing about the same girl. This metapragmatic discussion breaks down, however, when Brett's suggestion that they might be referring to the same girl (*Are you thinking what I am thinking?*) is treated literally by Jermaine. What happens here is that while Brett implies that they are talking about the same girl, Jermaine only responds to what is said by Brett (that Brett is thinking what Jermaine is thinking). In that sense, Jermaine's response to the reformulation of the question by Brett is strictly speaking correct (*No, cause you're thinking I'm thinking what you're thinking*). However, since it is a very complex utterance – about Jermaine's belief about Brett's belief about Jermaine's thought in relation to Brett's thought – it becomes almost impossible to follow in the context of the song. Nevertheless, while up until this point in the song they have not yet successfully established the referent in question, it is clear that they are reflexively aware of the other's use of language and, moreover, that this reflexive awareness enters into the language they use in the form of explicit metapragmatic commentary.

Such reflexive awareness does not, however, always surface so explicitly in language use. As Niedzielski and Preston (2009) point out, participants may not always be able to articulate their reflexive understandings of language use, despite such understandings being inherent in that very same usage. It is also apparent that such awareness may be more or less salient across different situated contexts. Thus, while metapragmatics often involves the study of instances where participants attend *to* communication, that is, where language is used to "evoke some kind of communicative disturbance" (Hübler and Bublitz 2007: 7) or "to intervene in ongoing discourse" (ibid.: 1), it is not restricted to instances that are explicitly recognised by participants, as we shall see in the remainder of this chapter.

Reflection: The metalanguage of explicit metapragmatic commentary

In the example above, a number of instances of explicit metapragmatic commentary have arisen. These explicit metapragmatic comments drew, in turn, on a folk **metalanguage**. The term metalanguage was introduced into academic discourse in the work of Alfred Tarski, a Polish logician. It refers to language that is used to talk about language, and in the case of "scientific" metalanguage, to theorise about it. In the instance above, clearly Brett and Jermaine do not use the term *think* in any scientific sense. In order to analyse these explicit metapragmatic comments, then, we must carefully examine this folk metalanguage. In the case of *thinking*, there are at least four (inter-related) senses in which it can be used in English, with the first sense arguably being basic to the other three:

think$_1$: cogitate (e.g. Brett is *thinking$_1$* about the girl he just met)
think$_2$: infer/presume (e.g. Brett *thinks$_2$* Jermaine is *thinking$_1$* about the same girl)
think$_3$: believe (e.g. Jermaine *thinks$_3$* Brett is *thinking$_1$* about a different girl)
think$_4$: evaluate/judge (e.g. Brett *thinks$_4$* highly of the girl he has just met)

Such metalanguage, in English at least, directs us towards an account of Brett and Jermaine's *thinking* as distinct and separate from what they might be *feeling*, but this is not a distinction that is necessarily as salient across all languages. It is apparent, then, that metapragmatics not only involves the study of reflexive awareness on the part of participants in relation to their use of language in interacting and communicating with others, but it also involves an analysis of the metalanguage those participants inevitably draw upon.

Thus, what we mean by metapragmatics in this chapter is that it concerns the use of language on the part of ordinary users or observers, which reflects awareness on their part about the various ways in which we can use language to interact and communicate with others. It is worth briefly noting that the term metapragmatics itself was initially coined by Michael Silverstein (1976, 1993), a linguistic anthropologist, who drew, in turn, from work by the linguist Roman Jakobson (1971) on the metalingual function of language, which refers to the ways in which we can use language to "explain, gloss, comment on, predicate about or refer to propositional meaning" (Hübler and Bublitz 2007: 2). However, while Jakobson was focused more narrowly on how language can be used to help participants to understand what the speaker is meaning in light of what has been said, Silverstein took a much broader view, as he defines metapragmatics as awareness that helps users to discern the relationship between linguistic forms and situated contexts (which is what allows the use of language in interaction to be an ordered, interpretable event). Metapragmatics in the broad sense advocated by Silverstein is essentially about anchoring linguistic (and non-linguistic) forms to contexts, a point we have largely covered in the preceding chapters.[1] Metapragmatics in the narrower, more focused sense of Jakobson, in contrast, is concerned with the use of language that reflects reflexive awareness on the part of users about their use of language. In other words, metapragmatics involves the study of "the language user's reflexive awareness of what is involved in a usage event" (Verschueren [1995] 2010: 1), including choices they have made in producing and interpreting talk or discourse. It thus generally encompasses the study of pragmatic indicators of this kind of reflexive awareness, and the communicative purposes to which these metapragmatic indicators are put. It is this latter, more focused sense of metapragmatics that we explore further in this chapter.

8.3   Forms of metapragmatic awareness

Metapragmatics, in our view, encompasses the study of language usages that indicate reflexive awareness on the part of participants about those interactive or communicative activities they are currently engaged in. A number of indicators of metapragmatic awareness have been identified in studies thus far. These range from those that are expressed explicitly when language use becomes the subject matter of speech, through to those that arise implicitly insofar as the production of talk "takes account of its own nature and functioning" (Lucy 2000: 213). The latter involves anchoring linguistic (and non-linguistic) forms to contexts, an area that we have already discussed in this book. We have therefore only focused on relatively explicit indicators of metapragmatic awareness in Table 8.1. The four key types listed are (1) pragmatic markers, (2) reported language use, (3) metapragmatic commentary, and

---

[1] This contrasts with the very broad definitions of metapragmatics as either metatheory or the analysis of constraining conditions on language use (such as the Cooperative Principle, conversational maxims, speech act theory, felicity conditions etc.) (Caffi 1998; Mey 2001). The former involves debate about what constitutes pragmatics and what the field should properly comprise (a stance on which is implicitly taken by the contents of this textbook, for instance). The latter is to some extent what the field of pragmatics itself is all about, namely, the analysis of the units that are constitutive of language use (and which has been the focus of the preceding chapters).

(4) social discourses. Underpinning all of these different forms of metapragmatic awareness is the folk metalanguage drawn upon by users, in this case, users of English.

Table 8.1 Explicit indicators of metapragmatic awareness

Type	Description	Examples
Pragmatic markers	Expressions that signal how something should be understood in relation to:	
	(a) surrounding talk	(a) *anyway, okay, even, also, but, however, so, on the contrary*
	(b) epistemic status of what is meant	(b) *you know, actually, frankly, undoubtedly, of course*
	(c) evidential status of what is meant	(c) *think, believe, suppose, guess, according to*
	(d) specificity or precision of what is said	(d) *sort of, kind of, in a sense, so far as I know*
Reported language use	(a) Quotative use of language	(a) *John <u>said</u> he can't go.* *He <u>thought</u> he sounded angry.*
	(b) Echoic instances of language use	(b) A: *I was a bit surprised.* B: <u>*A bit surprised?*</u>
Metapragmatic commentary	Situated comments about or evaluations of language use, which often involve the use of metalinguistic descriptors such as:	
	(a) linguistic action verbs	(a) *Am I <u>complaining</u>?* *What are you <u>saying</u>?*
	(b) attitudinal categorisers	(b) *That's not <u>very polite</u>.* *He's a very <u>courteous</u> young man.*
	(c) emotive-cognitive state-processes	(c) *What are you <u>thinking</u>?* *I <u>intend</u> to take a day off tomorrow.*
Social discourses	Elements of metapragmatic commentary which form persistent frames of interpretation (and are often treated as no longer open to doubt or questioning)	Value placed on *not taking oneself too seriously* amongst Australian and British speakers of English
		Value placed on *closure* amongst American speakers of English

It is important to note that we have collapsed finer distinctions in some cases for the sake of simplicity in our presentation of these indicators. Categories such as pragmatic markers, for instance, can be further sub-divided by making distinctions between discourse markers, sentence adverbs, hedges, self-referential expressions, explicit intertextual links and so on (see Verschueren 2000). Such classifications, and the theoretical debates around them, are indeed important, at least to a point, but they often neglect the fact that the same indicator can often be used for a range of quite distinct functions. Therefore we have chosen to focus instead on exemplifying how these different indicators can be used by participants to display different forms of reflexive awareness in language use. It is to these different kinds of reflexivity that we now turn.

We propose that there are three key types of reflexive awareness underpinning this ability to recognise or talk about pragmatic phenomena: metacognitive awareness, metarepresentational awareness and metacommunicative awareness (see also Lucy 2000). **Metacognitive awareness** refers to reflexive *presentations* of the cognitive status of information, such as whether it is known, new, expected (and so on) information for participants (see especially Chapter 3). **Metarepresentational awareness** involves reflexive *representations* of the intentional states of self and other (as in their beliefs, thoughts, desires, attitudes, intentions etc.), or what we have earlier termed pragmatic meaning representations (see Chapter 4). Finally, **metacommunicative awareness** refers to reflexive *interpretations* and *evaluations* of talk, which arise as a consequence of our awareness of self and other as social beings (see Chapters 5–7). There is, in addition, a specific form of metacommunicative awareness worth drawing attention to in passing, namely, **metadiscursive awareness**. The latter refers to a persistent frame of interpretation and evaluation that has become objectified, or reified, in ongoing metapragmatic commentary about a particular pragmatic phenomenon. Metadiscursive awareness underpins particular **ideologies** relating to language use, that is to say, ways of thinking about language and language use that intersect with ways in which language is actually used. Given the evident influence of such ideologies vis-à-vis language use, metadiscursive awareness is arguably deserving of analysis in its own right, separate and distinct from the metacommunicative awareness through which it is ultimately derived, although space does not permit us to do so here.

We shall now discuss each of these different forms of metapragmatic awareness in greater detail.

8.3.1 Metacognitive awareness

Metacognitive awareness refers to the reflexive *presentations* of the cognitive status of information and understandings of context and common ground amongst participants. It includes reflexive awareness about who knows what and how certain they are about it (i.e. its epistemic status), and what counts as new or given information for participants (i.e. its given/new status), as well as the expectations of participants about what can, may or should happen (i.e. its deontic status). In other words, it involves reflexive presentations amongst participants of cognitive-emotive states or processes, such as what is assumed to be known (or not known), their respective attitudes, expectations and so on.

This may involve speakers directing the attention of recipients to particular elements in the context, for instance. We have already discussed one of the key ways in which this occurs in Chapter 2, namely, through referring expressions. In section 2.5.1, we introduced the Accessibility Marking Scale and the Givenness Hierarchy. These both involve the speaker making assumptions about how accessible the referent is for the recipient. More generally, the use of referring expressions involves a consideration of the assumed cognitive status of the referents in question for the recipient. The cognitive status of a referent can range from being in focus, through being in memory but not currently active, to being completely unknown. The metapragmatic exchange between Brett and Jermaine that we discussed in the prior section is, in part, an example of metacognitive awareness surfacing in interaction. The confusion arises in this instance because while the referent should have been in focus for both of them (at least from the perspective of the viewing audience), they treat the referent as unknown to the other. In other words, the interaction is driven by both parties assuming the other participant does not know this contextual information.

Reflexive presentations of information may also involve attempts by speakers to direct the attention of the recipient to some particular information. We briefly discussed this in Chapter 3, when we introduced discourse markers, particles and formulae that speakers use to direct the attention of recipients to particular information, or more generally, to indicate how recipients should take or process upcoming information (section 3.3.2). We also briefly touched upon this issue in Chapter 4, when we discussed the particle *yet*, which is analysed by (neo-)Griceans as giving rise to a conventional implicature. For the sake of simplicity, we did not point out that Relevance theorists offer a somewhat different account of such phenomena, namely, their claim that there is another kind of meaning that contrasts with the conceptual or representational type of pragmatic meaning, which was the primary focus of Chapter 4. This second type of meaning is termed **procedural meaning** (Blakemore 1987, 2002; Wilson and Sperber 1993), and is assumed to encode "constraints on the inferential phase of comprehension" (Wilson and Sperber 1993: 102) rather than having any conceptual content. Conventional implicatures, for example, have thus been re-analysed by Relevance theorists as forms of procedural meaning, in part because it is well-known that the meanings of words such as *but, even,* and *yet* are notoriously difficult to be brought to consciousness. Relevance theorists argue that this difficulty indicates we are dealing with a fundamentally different kind of meaning. Here, we suggest that a metapragmatic account allows us to acknowledge that while certain linguistic units do not necessarily have any conceptual "content" that can be readily pinned down, they nevertheless do indicate a particular cognitive state or stance on the part of the speaker vis-à-vis the recipient.

Let us reconsider the example of the use of *yet* from the novel *High Fidelity*:

[8.3] (Rob is desperate to find out whether his ex-girlfriend, Laura, has slept with Ian)

Rob: Is it better?

Laura: Is what better?

Rob: Well. Sex, I guess. Is sex with him better?

Laura: Jesus Christ, Rob. Is that really what's bothering you?

Rob: Of course it is.

Laura: You really think it would make a difference either way?

Rob: I don't know.

Laura: Well, the answer is that I don't know either. We haven't done it yet.

(Nick Hornby, *High Fidelity*, 1995: 95)

The question for Rob is what is meant by *yet* here? It belongs to the general class of discourse markers used to indicate contrast. But this begs the question of just what is being contrasted here. From a metacognitive perspective, Laura is reflexively presenting her expectations vis-à-vis Rob. In other words, Laura indicates that what she expects might happen in her relationship with Ian (i.e. a possibility), contrasts with what Rob might expect should, or to be precise, should not happen (i.e. an obligation). The upshot is what we have here, a contrast in their respective expectations in regard to her relationship with Ian (and by implication, with Rob). This contrast involves a reflexive display of the cognitive status of particular expectations on the part of those participants.

Another well-known instance of a pragmatic marker that can be analysed as reflexively displaying awareness of the cognitive status of information for participants is the use of *oh*. Heritage (1984a) was the first to demonstrate that when *oh* is produced in response to information, it indicates (on the surface at least) a change of knowledge state on the part of a participant. In other words, it is used to register this information as new in some way for that user. Take the excerpt below, which is taken from a recording of a conversation between two friends:

[8.4] 1 J: When d'z Sus'n g[o back.=

2 M: [.hhhh

3 J: =[(   )
4 M: =[u-She: goes back on S̲atida:y=
5 J: =O̲[h̲:.
6 M: [A̲:n' S̲tev'n w'z here (.) all las' week...
(adapted from Heritage 1984a: 308)

After hearing the information offered by Mel that Jack sought (i.e. when Susan is going back), he responds with *oh* in line 5. Heritage argues that when *oh* occurs in this position, and is followed by a shift to a new action (in this particular example, an assertion of other information by Mel about Steven), the user reflexively displays the assumption that the information is somehow new to him or her. In other words, the use of *oh* in this way involves issues of epistemics, that is, how certain a participant is about information, and whether it is taken to be given or new. It thus indexes reflexive awareness of the cognitive status of information for the participants in a manner analogous to the example of *yet*, which we considered above. It is important to note, however, that the particular cognitive state that such pragmatic markers reflexively index depends on their sequential environment. *Oh* may also be used to register or mark a change of state in orientation or awareness, such as when noticing something, as well as to foreshadow possible forthcoming trouble in responding to a question (see Heritage 1998).

Actually is yet another example of a pragmatic marker where the metapragmatic function of the particle depends on its sequential environment. In early work it was characterised as marking an assumption as "true at one particular point in the past time (which the speaker does not further specify) but not necessarily at any other point in time" (Watts 1988: 254). In subsequent research, the work that *actually* does was broadened to include the negotiation of (often implicit) claims that contradict the recipient's expectations (Smith and Jucker 2000). These expectations relate specifically to either (1) a user's commitment to a particular claim, (2) an affective evaluation of a fact or set of facts, or (3) a judgement about the newsworthiness of information. Consider the following excerpt from a conversation between two undergraduate students:

[8.5] Ann: do you like psychology?
         Betty: er yeah, actually I think it's really interesting.
(adapted from Smith and Jucker 2000: 223)

Here, Betty marks the information in her response as unexpected in that she is making a stronger claim (i.e. she *really* likes it) than the candidate answer offered in the initial question (i.e. she likes it). Through the formulation of her question, then, Ann indicates, in the form of an implicated premise (see section 4.3.2), that Betty wouldn't be expected to "really like" psychology. It is towards this *expectation* that Betty orients through her use of *actually*.[2]

Pragmatic markers are very complex. As we have seen, they are not restricted to reflexive presentations or displays of the cognitive status of information or understandings of context/common ground amongst participants (i.e. markers of metacognitive awareness). They may also involve other kinds of reflexivity, both metarepresentational and metacognitive awareness (which we will discuss in further detail in the following subsections), and so they can evidently indicate various different types of metapragmatic awareness. It is for this reason that pragmatic markers are so difficult to define categorically. It is also for this reason that we propose that they are analysed more productively from the perspective of different types of reflexive awareness. In the case of metacognitive awareness, we are dealing with the reflexive presentation of the cognitive status of information.

This cognitive status can encompass a number of different dimensions, as summarised in Figure 8.1. There are arguably three key loci for the cognitive status of information. The first is the so-called epistemic gradient between participants (Heritage 2012; Heritage and Raymond 2012). This involves the degree to which participants are aware (or, more accurately, display awareness of) who knows what, and to what degree of certainty. This degree of certainty lies on a gradient from "definitively knowing" (K⁺) through to "not knowing" (K⁻). A second related dimension is that between given and new information. The former is treated as lying within the common ground of participants, while the latter is treated as lying outside of it. Third, we can also talk of reflexive awareness in relation to expectations. The expectations be may be deontic (i.e. what participants think *should* or *ought* to be the case), probabilistic (i.e. what participants think is *likely* to be the case), or volitional (i.e. what participants *want* to be the case) in nature.

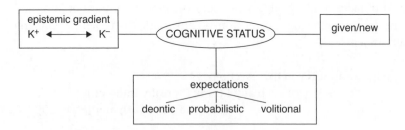

Figure 8.1 Loci of metacognitive awareness

---

[2] Note that in example (8.5), B's response can be divided into two distinct analytical units: "er yeah" and "I think it's really interesting". The pragmatic marker "actually" is thus in utterance-final position here on this analysis (although not in turn-final position).

Pragmatic markers can be used to index reflexive awareness of all these different forms of cognitive status amongst participants, as we have discussed. Most importantly, the same linguistic form, as we have seen, can be used to present different cognitive states depending on its sequential environment. Accounts that treat pragmatic markers as either encoding constraints on the inferential phase of comprehension (i.e. as forms of procedural meaning), or as conventionally implicating non-truth-conditional meaning (i.e. as instances of conventional implicature), are arguably not able to do sufficient justice to such interactional nuances, although, to be fair, such accounts were not originally designed to do so.

8.3.2 Metarepresentational awareness

Metarepresentational awareness, as we noted earlier, involves reflexive *representations* of the intentional states of self and other (as in their beliefs, thoughts, desires, attitudes, intentions etc.). It is thus most salient when we come to consider pragmatic meaning representations (see Chapter 4). This is because a particular meaning representation, for instance, what is (literally) said, can be embedded within another meaning representation, for instance, an attitude. Instances where there is a lower-order representation (e.g. what is literally said) embedded within a higher-order representation (e.g. an attitude) are termed **metarepresentations**, that is, a "representation of a representation" (Wilson 2000: 411). Irony, for example, arguably constitutes a case of metarepresentation where a meaning representation attributed to a particular speaker (or set of speakers) is further embedded within "a wry, or sceptical, or mocking attitude" towards that attributed meaning representation (Wilson 2000: 433).

Consider the following example from a segment broadcast throughout the US, where comedian Steven Colbert spoke at the 2006 White House Correspondents' Dinner for then US President George W. Bush:

[8.6] Mr. President, my name is Stephen Colbert, and tonight it is my privilege to celebrate this president, 'cause we're not so different, he and I. We both get it. Guys like us, we're not some brainiacs on the nerd patrol. We're not members of the factinista. We go straight from the gut. Right, sir? That's where the truth lies, right down here in the gut. Do you know you have more nerve endings in your gut than you have in your head? You can look it up. Now, I know some of you are going to say, "I did look it up, and that's not true." That's 'cause you looked it up in a book. Next time, look it up in your gut. I did. My gut tells me that's how our nervous system works.

("Colbert Bush Roast", White House Correspondent's' Dinner, Washington DC, 29 April 2006, C-SPAN Cable television; cf. Gibbs 2012: 110–111)

Colbert is alluding to the way former US President George W. Bush frequently made references in the media to "trusting his gut" when making decisions. Whether the ironic attitude (higher-order representation) Colbert expresses towards this kind of decision-making (lower-order representation) is wry, sceptical or even mocking is open to debate (LaMarre et al. 2009) (see reflection box in section 5.2.1 for further discussion). But the point stands that we are dealing here with a meaning representation being embedded within another meaning representation, and thus metarepresentational awareness on the part of users.

Relevance theorists have argued that irony, reporting talk (including quotations of others' talk), echoing questions and interrogatives can be productively analysed as involving higher-order representations within which lower-order representations are embedded. Quotations, for instance, involve a higher-order utterance that attributes a lower-order utterance to someone other than the speaker. Wilson (2000) suggests that metarepresentations inevitably involve resemblances, which are either **metalinguistic** (i.e. involve a resemblance in form) or **interpretive** (i.e. involve a resemblance in semantic or logical properties). Direct quotations – where the speaker claims the words being reported match exactly what the prior speaker literally said – involve metalinguistic resemblances, while indirect quotations – where the speaker claims the words being reported match what the prior speaker was taken to mean – involve interpretive resemblances. Irony, on the other hand, involves only interpretive resemblances, through which the speaker echoes a tacitly attributed thought or utterance with a tacitly dissociative attitude (Wilson and Sperber 1992). This thought or utterance may be attributed to someone specifically or may simply be attributed to the participants' common ground (e.g. cultural stereotypes), while the dissociative attitude may be wry, sceptical or mocking, as we noted in relation to the example from Colbert (see also the example of sarcasm [4.27] we discussed near the end of section 4.3.2).

Reflection: "He-Said-She-Said" in African-American Vernacular English (AAVE) and recursivity in reporting talk

While at their most basic level metarepresentations involve embedding a meaning representation relative to another meaning representation, these initial metarepresentations can be further embedded within other metarepresentations. This embedding is termed **recursivity**. The potential for recursive embedding of representations means that instances of reported talk, for example, can involve multiple levels of representations.

Consider, for instance, the practice termed "He-Said-She-Said" that is claimed to occur in AAVE (Goodwin 1990), particularly in disputes about gossip amongst pre-adolescent, working class African-American girls. The practice involves one participant accusing another participant of talking "behind her back". More specifically, the accuser uses "a series of embedded clauses to report a series of encounters in which two girls were talking about a third" (Goodwin and Goodwin 2004: 232). In the example below, taken from recordings of conversations between some African-American girls, Annette is accusing Benita of talking behind her back:

[8.7]   Annette (to Benita):   And Tanya said
                               that you said
                               that I was showin' off
                               just because I had that bl:ouse on.
                                         (Goodwin and Goodwin 2004: 233)

Annette implicates this accusation by reporting on what Tanya has said Benita had previously said. It involves a complex form of recursive quotation where Annette is speaking to Benita about what Tanya told Annette (*and Tanya said*) that Benita said to Tanya (*that you said*) about Annette (*that I was showing off just because I had that blouse on*). Hence the term "He-Said-She-Said" or, to be more precise in this case, "She$_{Tanya}$-Said-She$_{Benita}$-Said". This involves, from a metapragmatic perspective, a metarepresentation embedded within a higher-order metarepresentation. That is:

[a higher-order utterance]$_3$ about [an attributed higher-order utterance]$_2$ about [an attributed lower-order utterance]$_1$

The use of recursive quotation is not, of course, unique to pre-adolescent, working class African-American girls. But it is used here in a specific way, namely, as a response to situations where an "instigator" (here Tanya) tells someone (Annette) that another girl (Benita) has been talking about her behind her back. The He-Said-She-Said practice is thus not only a way for someone to hold another person to account for gossiping behind her back about her (or him), but also to implicate yet another person as the source of this accusation. It therefore becomes a way of establishing schisms and alliances within what is ostensibly a group of friends.

One challenge facing the Relevance theoretic account of irony as echoic, however, is the relationship between the examples of utterance-based verbal irony that they generally analyse, and instances of **situational irony**. The latter is generally understood to involve some kind of incongruity between what might be expected and what actually occurs. Littman and Mey (1991) and Clift (1999) have both argued that any account of irony should be able to deal with all kinds of irony, not just verbal irony à la relevance theory. Let us consider for a moment the rather savage situational irony that arises in the following news report that originated from an international news agency based in the US:

[8.8]   A man ended up in hospital after ordering a Triple Bypass burger at the Heart Attack Grill, a Las Vegas restaurant that jokingly warns customers "this establishment is bad for your health."
Laughing tourists were either cynical or confused about whether the man was really suffering a medical episode amid the "doctor," "nurses" and health warnings at the Heart Attack Grill, restaurant owner Jon Basso said yesterday.
"It was no joke," said Basso
[section omitted]
Giggles can be heard on the soundtrack of amateur video showing the man on a stretcher being wheeled out of the restaurant where patrons pass an antique ambulance at the door and a sign: "Caution! This establishment is bad for your health."
Eaters are given surgical gowns as they choose from a calorically extravagant [cf. calorie-extravagant] menu offering "Bypass" burgers, "Flatliner" fries, buttermilk shakes and free meals to folks over 350 pounds [cf. 159kg]. Another sign on the door reads, "Cash only because you might die before the check clears."
("Bypass burger lives up to its name", Associated Press,
17 February 2012)

Multiple layers of irony arise in the above excerpt from the news report. First of all, we have the ironic status of the place in question. The name of the restaurant (the *Heart Attack Grill*), its menu (*Triple Bypass burger, Flatliner fries,* etc.), the explicit warnings (*this establishment is bad for your health*), and the associated surroundings (e.g. having workers dressed as health care workers) all constitute potential instances of irony. They all echo in various ways general warnings that we have all heard about the negative impact that excessive consumption of fast food, such as the burgers and fries served at that restaurant, can have on our health. In echoing these warnings with exaggerated formulations, the restaurant management is echoing these warnings (which are attributable to the medical establishment and government bodies) with a dissociative attitude, more specifically, a kind of defiant scepticism or even mockery, and encouraging their customers to take a similar stance.

The second layer of irony arises from the primary focus of the news report, namely, that a customer at the restaurant fell ill and was taken to hospital after ordering a *Triple Bypass burger*. Notably, it is implicated through the formulation of the leading sentence that the man might have ended up in hospital because of ordering that burger (i.e. "A after B" implicates "A because of B"). It is, of course, moving into the realm of the ludicrous to even suggest this, but therein lies the situational irony: a man was taken ill in a place that ironically mocks health warnings about fast food. The incongruity arises from a man falling ill (what actually occurred) in a restaurant that appeared confident enough to take an ironic stance on such a possibility (i.e. what appeared to be expected is that no one would ever really fall ill from the food, at least not there in the actual restaurant). The headline of the report plays on this situational irony (*Bypass burger lives up to its name*), by wryly echoing the ironic stance of the restaurant.

The third, and perhaps most savage, layer of irony arises from the report about the response of other customers to the man falling ill, namely, that some of them treated it as a laughing matter. Once again we have an instance of situational irony as there is a clear incongruity between what might be expected in such a situation (i.e. that no one would treat someone falling ill as a joke) and what actually occurred (i.e. some customers treated it as a joke). As a reader of the news report, we are, of course, privy to all these multiple instantiations of irony. What is significant here is that echoic irony, of the kind described by Relevance theorists, is interwoven with situational irony, for which they do not offer an explicit account. However, it is worth noting that their general claim nevertheless stands, namely, that metarepresentations lie at the heart of irony, and that irony inevitably involves some kind of dissociative attitude.

In summary, then, metarepresentational awareness involves reflexive representations of the intentional states and utterances of participants, as illustrated in Figure 8.2. Reported talk involves, at minimum, a first-order metaprepresentation (e.g. an utterance about another attributed utterance), while irony involves, at minimum, a second-order metarepresentation (e.g. an attitude expressed about an utterance about an attributed intentional state). However, these metarepresentations can be further embedded in other metarepresentations as we saw in the case of He-Said-She-Said or in the report on the incident at the Heart Attack Grill. In the latter case, for instance, the name of the restaurant is assumed to echo general health warnings (first-order metarepresentation), about which customers are assumed to have a wry or dismissive

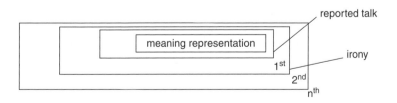

Figure 8.2 Orders of metarepresentational awareness

attitude (second-order metarepresentation), but which is then quoted in a news report in light of their confused response to a person who was reported as falling seriously ill in that restaurant (third-order metapresentation), and towards which the writer presumably has a mocking, or at least wry, attitude (fourth-order metarepresentation), which we the readers attribute to that publisher, and may or may not entertain ourselves (fifth-order metarepresentation). In other words, both instances of echoic and situational irony, as well as reported talk/conduct, arise in the course of we, the readers, *attributing* to the publisher or writer of the report an *attitude* towards the customer's *allegedly* confused response in light of their presumed *attitude* towards the warnings and name of the restaurant that (ironically) *echo* general health warnings. In theory, metarepresentations can be extended to the nth order. In practice, they normally become to become too complex for users to process, or at least to talk about, at around the fifth or sixth order of metarepresentation (cf. the research mentioned in section 2.5.3).

8.3.3 Metacommunicative awareness

At the beginning of Chapter 7 we noted the importance of the "environment of mutual monitoring possibilities" that underlies all social situations (Goffman [1964] 1972: 63). Critical to these "mutual monitoring possibilities" is our awareness of self and other as socially constituted persons. This means that not only do we interpret and evaluate what we ourselves say and do and what others say and do, but we also reflexively interpret and evaluate these pragmatic meanings, acts and the like through the eyes of others. In other words, we include the perspective of others in our interpretations and evaluations of pragmatic phenomena. This kind of perspective-taking is what underpins the two forms of metacommunicative awareness that are critical to social interaction: interactional awareness and interpersonal awareness.

A key manifestation of metacommunicative **interactional awareness** is what is commonly termed recipient design, that is, where meanings and actions are reflexively designed with particular recipients in mind (a point we briefly discussed in section 6.6.1). The fine-tuned specificity of recipient design becomes evident in the incremental production of utterances, that is, in cases where speakers add further segments to utterances in order to adapt to changes in the participation footing of recipients. Goodwin (1979), for instance, examines in very close detail an excerpt from a conversation where the speaker, John transforms his utterance in line 3 from a *discovery* or *noticing* of an anniversary (i.e. having given up smoking for one week), about which the direct addressee, Beth (whose recipiency is signalled through John's gaze), already knows, into a *report* about having given up smoking which is deemed to be *newsworthy* for another direct addressee, Ann (whose recipiency is signalled through a subsequent shift in gaze by John).

[8.9]　1　John:　I gave, I gave u[p smoking cigarettes::.=
　　　　　　　　　　　　　　[((gazes at Don))
　　　　　2　Don:　=Ye:ah,
　　　　　3　John:　I-uh: [one- one week ago t'da:[y acshilly
　　　　　　　　　　　　　[((gazes at Beth))　　　　　[((gazes at Ann))
　　　　　4　Ann:　Rilly? en y'quit fer good?
　　　　　　　　　　　　　　　　(adapted from Goodwin 1979: 111–112)

Notably, the utterance-final *actually* here marks this news as perhaps contrary to Ann's expectations (see section 8.3.1), and thus as reporting something that is likely previously unknown to her. In this way, he transforms the utterance from its previous design, when it was being constructed as a "noticing" directed at Beth of it already having been one week since he had given up smoking, into an utterance designed to function as reporting news to Ann. In interpreting talk or discourse, then, participants are inevitably aware of this finely-grained recipient design.

Metacommunicative **interpersonal awareness** involves reflexive evaluations of relations with and attitudes towards others, an area which was largely covered in Chapter 7. Here we focus on how manifestations of reflexive awareness of interpersonal relations (such as face, status and so on), attitudes (such as like/dislike, disgust and so on), and evaluations (such as politeness, impoliteness and so on) are critically dependent on a reflexive awareness of self vis-à-vis other. In the following example from the TV series, *Everybody Hates Chris*, we can see how Chris manipulates his mother's (over-)concern about how others evaluate their family. Prior to the excerpt below, Chris has been complaining to his mother about having to wear his younger brother's old clothes for picture day at school, but to no avail. He concludes (in the voice of the narrator) that the only way he can get his mother to buy him new clothes is through invoking the idea of what others might think of their family if he wears old clothes:

[8.10]　Chris:　　Mom, I'm the only black kid in the whole school. They already think I'm a crack baby. Wearing this sweater they'll probably think we're on welfare.
　　　　　Rochelle:　Who said we were on welfare? Be home from school on time tomorrow. We're gonna go shopping.
　　　　　Julius:　　I thought you said we didn't have the money?
　　　　　Rochelle:　Oh, I'll get it. Not havin' people think we on welfare.
　　　　　　　　　　("Everybody hates picture day", *Everybody Hates Chris*, Season 1, Episode 13, 2 February 2006, director: Linda Mendoza, writer: Kevin A. Garnett)

What Rochelle, Chris's mother, is most concerned about here is that other people might think they are *on welfare*, or in other words, poor. This motivates her to go out and buy new clothes for Chris, even though they can't really afford them. Once again irony arises here, as Rochelle seems much less concerned about people thinking they have a drug problem (*they already think I'm a crack baby*) than their being seen as poor. There is also epistemic slippage in this excerpt from others potentially "thinking" something (Chris's claim), to people actually "saying" these things (Rochelle's assumption).

Reflection: "Yeah-no" as an emergent pragmatic marker

According to Burridge and Florey (2002), the pragmatic marker *yeah-no* is increasingly used by speakers of Australian English, although it is clearly not restricted to Australian English, as it can also be found in talk amongst speakers of other varieties of English. The basic function of *yeah-no* is to indicate reflexive awareness that there is more than one line of interpretation of current talk at play in the interaction (i.e. it is reflective of metacommunicative awareness on the part of users).

In the following excerpt from a conversation, two Australian friends are discussing football (specifically, rugby league), and who they are tipping (i.e. putting their bet on) for the upcoming game:

[8.11] Clive: Yeah so who ya tipping this weekend? You got ah?
        Bruce: Yeah-no I, have a look here. I made some bold
                 statements actually¿
        Clive: Broncos definitely¿
        Bruce: Yeah Broncos I- did I pick the Broncos?
                 No. [No
        Clive: [gone against them¿
        Bruce: I've gone against them¿
        Clive You're kidding.

                                (Burridge and Florey 2002: 163)

In this example, *yeah-no* is used by Bruce to indicate reflexive awareness of two possible lines of interpretation here. The first involves a "yeah-no" response to Clive's trailing-off question (*You got ah?*) about whether Bruce has a team in mind to tip. Through responding *yeah*, Bruce indicates that he does have a tip in mind. At the same time Bruce also projects that his tip this time will not be in line with Clive's expectations, by subsequently uttering *no*. This latter interpretation becomes clear when Bruce says that he is not going to tip for the Broncos (the name of a rugby league team in Brisbane). That this is counter to Clive's expectations is apparent from his expression of surprise (*You're kidding*). In other words, *yeah-no* is used here by Bruce to introduce a "surprise departure from his usual tipping practices" (Burridge and Florey 2002: 163), and so constitutes an example of an orientation to the metacognitive status of particular information that is assumed to lie in the common ground of Bruce and Clive, namely, Bruce's usual tipping practices.

This pragmatic marker has been ironically adopted most infamously by Vicky Pollard, a satirical character on the British television series, *Little Britain*. She uses the catch phrase *yeah but no but yeah but*, and variants of it, to launch long rants where her breakneck speed of talk and the irrelevant information or gossip she offers is intended to confuse or annoy the recipient. *Yeah-no* is apparently being used by the comedian Matt Lucas, in the guise of Vicky, to invoke or comment on social discourses about "declining standards" of spoken English amongst younger generation speakers in Britain.

Such evaluations inevitably involve appeals to normative ways of thinking, speaking and doing things. Verschueren, for instance, argues that such normativity necessarily involves a "metalevel of awareness", and it is at this level that "the norms involved are constantly negotiated and manipulated" (2000: 445). Silverstein (2003) goes further in proposing that these norms form what he terms **orders of indexicality**. This refers to the idea that normative notions about "how language works, and what it is usually like, what certain ways of speaking connote and imply" are reflexively layered. At the first layer (or first-order) of norms we find probabilistic conventions for language use. These are formed for individuals through their own history of interactions with others, and so while they may be similar, they are never exactly the same across individuals. At the second layer (or *second-order*) we find localised ideologies and evaluations of language use. In other words, normative ideas about language use that are shared across particular social groups. Finally, at the third layer (or *third-order*) we find language conventions as they are represented in supra-local (i.e. societal) ideologies and evaluations of language use. In being ordered, it is not necessarily assumed that third-order norms will always take precedence over second-order ones and so on (although they often do), but rather that in invoking first-order norms we inevitably invoke second- and third-order ones as well. In pragmatics our specific concern is evaluative norms relating to language use, namely, assumptions "about what is 'correct', 'normal', 'appropriate', 'well-formed', 'worth saying', 'permissable', and so on" (Coupland and Jaworski 2004: 36), and how these cut across all three orders.

These ordered layers of normativity can be represented as in Figure 8.3. There it is suggested that the localised norms which develop for individuals or localised relationships are necessarily embedded (and thus interpreted) relative to communities of practice, organisational or other group-based norms, which are themselves necessarily embedded relative to broader societal or "cultural" norms. While all three layers of normativity can be studied, we would argue that they are most productively analysed at the second-order level, namely, localised ideologies shared across identifiable communities of practice, organisations or other recognisable groups (see also

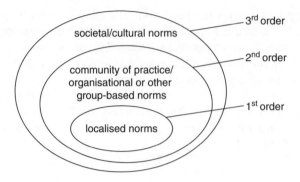

Sources: Kádár and Haugh 2013: 95; cf. Culpeper 2008: 29–31; Holmes et al. 2012: 1065.

Figure 8.3 Orders of normativity

Culpeper 2010, which argues for the middle, as in second-order, level with respect to historical sociopragmatics).

Consider, for instance, the following excerpt from a radio interview with the singer, Justin Bieber, which went horribly wrong when the interviewer, Mojo, made a joke about Harry Styles and Bieber's mother:

[8.12] Mojo: do you <u>wo</u>rry about Harry, uh, you know when he's
around your mom, since it seems he likes older women?
Bieber: do I wonder (.) <u>wha</u>t?
Mojo: do you worry Harry around your mum, since he (.) u:h (.)
he likes older women?
Bieber: I think you should worry about yo- your mom bro.
Mojo: .hhhHahhh I should worry about <u>my</u> mum?
Bieber: <u>ye</u>:a(hh)h
Mojo: Justin, my mum's d[ead so unfortunately (.) that wouldn't
work.
Bieber: [jeez
(10.0)
((line goes dead))

(*Mojo in the Morning*, Radio Channel 95.5, Detroit,
broadcast 28 June 2012)

Here the interactional trouble begins when the interviewer, Thomas " Mojo" Carballot, teases Bieber about Harry Styles, who was reported in the news at the time to be dating older women, having an interest in Bieber's mother. Bieber initially responds with a request for a repeat of the question, which is indicative of a possible challenge to the askability of that question, but when the question is essentially repeated by Mojo, Bieber then responds with a tease of his own about Mojo's mother. After Mojo deflates Bieber's tease in countering that his mother is already dead (and thus not someone with whom Harry Styles could be trying to date), there is a long ten-second silence, and then Bieber (apparently) hangs up. It was subsequently reported that when the technician tried to get Bieber back on the line to continue the interview that "He [Bieber] got a little upset with the question".

The following day Mojo discussed what went wrong in the interview with two other announcers, Rachael and Spike:

[8.13] Rachael: but even (.) even the <u>way</u> he said it back to you
                         ↓"you got watch out for yer m- uhm yer mum"
        Mojo: mm
        Rachael: like you could tell, at <u>that</u> point he was pissed already
        Mojo: ye:ah
        Spike: here's the thing I'm kinda getting bummed out because,
                  you know (0.2) I don't listen to his <u>music</u> but I always
                  thought Justin was pretty cool but
        Rachael: he i:s.
        Spike: he['s
        Rachael: [he usually [is
        Spike: [he- he's starting to take himself <u>way</u> too
                  seriously.

                         (*Mojo in the Morning*, Radio Channel 95.5, Detroit,
                                                   broadcast 29 June 2012)

Here it is claimed by Rachael that Bieber's initial tease (before hanging up) was indicative of him taking offence. The way Bieber dealt with the interview is then characterised by Spike as him taking himself *too seriously*, thereby casting the offence as not warranted.

We can analyse the metapragmatic comments by these two other observers in relation to the three different orders of normativity that we introduced above. At the first-order, or localised level, we can see in [8.12], about which they are commenting, how Mojo is evidently trying to establish a "joking" relationship with Bieber where this kind of "ribbing" or teasing is allowable. This reflects, in turn, second-order norms associated with the practices of radio "shock jocks", such as Mojo, where guests are subject to joking, teasing, mocking and the like, and how celebrities, in particular, are expected to deal with that by not taking themselves "too seriously". Finally, the negative assessment accomplished through casting Bieber as "starting to take himself way too seriously" in [8.13] invokes, in turn, third-order norms, namely, the social sanctions directed at those who take themselves "too seriously", and the positive value placed on not taking oneself too seriously amongst Anglo speakers of English (see Fox 2004; Goddard 2009).

However, just because particular participants invoke these kinds of third-order norms, this does not mean to say that what counts as offensive or sanctionable behaviour is not open to dispute by others. In the following post, after a report about the incident was published in the online version of the *Daily Mirror*, one user claimed that Mojo was being "rude":

[8.14] That was rude for him to say if he worries about Harry around his mom he is just a kid not an adult. Mojo was wrong with the question. U all r adults expecting kids to act like adults. Inappropriate question! Grow up Mojo.

(http://www.mirror.co.uk/3am/celebrity-news/justin-bieber-hangs-up-on-radio-946516)

Here a different set of third-order norms are invoked, namely, what counts as (in)appropriate around adults versus kids, thereby challenging the second-order normative practices of radio jocks such as Mojo.

Investigating localised, as well as second-order, ideologies is a useful way to better understanding the normative features of interaction that are so often treated as simply "commonsensical" and thus rarely questioned by users (Blommaert and Verschueren 1998). And it is this line of work that leads us into the analysis of metadiscursive awareness at the third-order level of normativity on the part of users (see Verschueren 2012 for a useful introduction to such work). This is not to say, however, that the pragmatic meanings and interpersonal relations and attitudes which arise in discourse through invoking such norms are not open to negotiation or dispute, as we saw above. Indeed, metapragmatic commentary can be strategically deployed for that very purpose, as we shall now discuss.

8.4 Metapragmatics in use

Metapragmatic awareness lies at the core of a number of important pragmatic phenomena. In many instances, this reflexive awareness is not always accessible or highly salient to participants. It may be inherent to their use of language, but it is not necessarily something they can articulate. There are, however, cases where metapragmatic awareness itself may become highly salient in discourse. The most obvious example of this is the use of metapragmatic commentary to "influence and negotiate how an utterance is or should have been heard, or [to] try to modify the values attributed to it" (Jaworskiñ et al. 2004: 4); in other words, the strategic deployment of comments about language use in order to (re-)negotiate interpretations of pragmatic meanings, pragmatic acts, and interpersonal relations, attitudes and evaluations. Hübler and Bublitz (2007) term such phenomena "metapragmatics in use". They list some of the functions of metapragmatic commentary, including:

- evaluating self and others
- doing conflict
- doing affiliation
- constructing identity
- reinforcing or challenging communicative norms
- negotiating meaning
- discourse organisation

(adapted from Hübler and Bublitz 2007: 18)

Given this list is not by any means exhaustive, it is clear that metapragmatic commentary (or, more broadly, acts) can be used to accomplish all sorts of different pragmatic work.

In a study of metapragmatic utterances that arise in computer-mediated interactions in a number of different mailing lists, for instance, Tanskanen (2007) illustrates how participants can use metapragmatic utterances to accomplish assessments of the degree of appropriateness of either their own or others' posts, or to clarify their own contributions where some misunderstanding is perceived. Such comments were thus found to be designed to (1) accomplish judgements of appropriateness (see example [8.15]), (2) control and plan subsequent interaction (example [8.16]), or (3) give feedback on ongoing interaction (example [8.17]):

[8.15] I am loathe to add yet another message to what has been an extremely long thread, but...
(WMST-L) (Tanskanen 2007: 92)

[8.16] Well, you've certainly ended this discussion effectively. All that's left to say is "I rest my case."
(YAHOO) (ibid.: 100)

[8.17] Such a wonderful discussion is being held here!!!
(DBB) (ibid.: 101)

Such metapragmatic comments thus illustrate how users display reflexive awareness in making posts to such lists, as through them we can see how they "adopt the perspective of their fellow communicators" in "anticipating potential problems" in such forums (Tanskanen 2007: 88). More generally, we can observe how metapragmatic comments are designed to *avoid* both misinterpretation and unwanted relational or attitudinal implications, by other participants.

In some cases, however, metapragmatic comments are deployed in order to negotiate or even dispute particular pragmatic meanings, pragmatic acts, interpersonal relations and attitudes, and so on. Consider the following extract from a documentary where four Indians have been touring to get a first-hand understanding of race relations. Preceding this particular excerpt, Gurmeet has suggested to an Aboriginal elder that indigenous Australians should have "specific educational institutions for Aboriginals", to which the elder responds that such institutions already exist. The excerpt itself begins when Gurmeet subsequently asks why the elder has "complaints" about the past and current situation of indigenous Australians:

[8.18]   14 Gurmeet: then what are the complaints.
         15 Elder: ((cocks her head)) uh uh, beg your pardon?
         16 Gurmeet: why are you complaining then.
         17 Elder: ((steps back)) am I ↑complaining?=   ←
         18 Radhika: =no::
         19 Gurmeet: ((smiles)) heh [heh]
         20 Elder: [I'm] answering questions that they ←
         21   asked. I'm not complain-
         22 Gurmeet: but but [you are   ] saying   ←
         23 Elder: [you don't]
         24   you don't live in my country, you don't- this is my ←
         25   country, ((points her finger at Gurmeet)) Kamilaroi is
         26   my country. I see what happens here, whatever
         27   happens in your country.

(*Dumb, Drunk and Racist*, Episode 4, 11 July 2012,
ABC2 and Cordell Jigsaw Productions)

While the elder's initial response in line 15 is indicative not only of possible forthcoming disagreement with what is supposed through Gurmeet's question (i.e. that the elder has been *complaining*), but also that there is some issue in regards to the propriety of Gurmeet's question. Gurmeet nevertheless repeats essentially the same question in line 16. This time the elder's offence at the terms of the question becomes more evident in her rising pitch, stepping backwards and formulation of a "rhetorical question" in line 17. She then attempts to reformulate her prior turns as simply *answering questions* rather than *complaining* (lines 20–21), and then finally makes explicit what appears to be the source of the offence she is taking at Gurmeet's line of questioning, namely, his implicit assumption that he has the right to judge the situation of "her" country (lines 24–27).[3]

---

[3] See Haugh (in press 2014) and Kádár and Haugh (2013: 119–122, 127–131) for further analysis of this particular example.

We can observe a number of metapragmatic comments in the above extract, which are indicated by the arrows, in relation to the construal of pragmatic acts (lines 17, 20–21), pragmatic meaning and accountability (line 22), and relational entitlements (lines 23–27). In lines 17 and 20–21, the elder disputes the way in which Gurmeet has framed her prior talk as *complaining*, and offers an alternative formulation of her actions as simply *answering questions*. In this case, it is the way in which her prior talk is being construed as a particular pragmatic act, namely "complaining", that is at issue (see Chapter 6). Studies of complaints in English have shown that complaining is regarded as an inherently moral act, and thus to characterise some talk as "complaining", involves the question of whether there are sufficient grounds for launching the complaint, and thus whether the person complaining has the right to make such a complaint (see Drew 1998). Such research has also shown that participants will often engage in considerable interactional work to avoid what they are meaning being construed as *complaining* (Edwards 2005).

In line 22, Gurmeet moves to hold the elder accountable for *complaining* rather than *answering questions* by invoking the sense of *saying$_2$* as meaning something (see sections 4.2.1 and 5.4.1). In other words, Gurmeet construes the elder as previously *implying* that the situation of indigenous Australians has not been very good because of the actions of others (in particular, the Australian government). He thus attempts to hold her accountable for this particular reflexively *intended* assumption.

Finally, in lines 23–27, we can see the elder disputing Gurmeet's right to evaluate and comment on the situation of indigenous Australians by construing herself as an "insider" and Gurmeet as an "outsider" to "Kamilaroi country" (where the Indians are currently visiting). In other words, she is explicitly referring to her entitlement to comment on the circumstances of "her people", as opposed to the lack of such an entitlement on Gurmeet's part, thereby alluding to issues of interpersonal relations and their respective "sociality rights" (see section 7.4.2). It is also evident throughout that the elder is treating Gurmeet's line of questioning as "inapposite", if not outright offensive, thereby indicating an implicit orientation to a particular interpersonal attitude on the part of Gurmeet, namely, that he is being "impolite" or "offensive" (see section 7.5).

In order to understand the above excerpt, however, it is evident that we also need to have a clear understanding of what these participants mean by such terms as *complaint/complaining*, *asking questions*, *saying*, and *impolite/offensive*, as well as what these words mean for English speakers more generally, given the interaction was broadcast on television to an "overhearing" audience. Thus, while "technical" meanings can be ascribed to such terms, it is important to remember that this metalanguage means something to ordinary participants too.

Reflection: Inter-ethnic metapragmatic discourse in New Zealand English

Metapragmatic commentary may, in some cases, be directed not only at pragmatic meanings or acts, but also at the norms that are assumed to underlie them. In an extensive program of research about discourse in New Zealand workplaces, the Language in the Workplace project has uncovered ethnic variation amongst speakers of New Zealand English. Holmes et al. (2012) report on the explicit negotiation of politeness norms between European (termed Pākehā) and Māori ethnolects of New Zealand English. The former has traditionally been considered dominant or mainstream, but in workplaces where Maori predominate, such assumptions can be challenged. In the following excerpt, we can observe a clash between Pākehā and Māori interactional norms that surfaces in the form of metapragmatic commentary. The exchange occurs in one of the regular meetings of Kiwi Consultations, where only three out of the sixteen participants are Pākehā:

[8.19] 1 Steve: we have capability development um
     2   the g m oversight here
     3   ((overlapped by a quiet conversation involving Frank
     4   and Daniel))
     5   is from Frank with Caleb
     6   the manager in charge budget of a hundred and
     7   eighty seven k ((pause)) obviously key area we
     8   want to ensure that um one of the important
     9   things in communication is not to talk when
    10   others are talking:
    11   ((loud laughter))
    12 Steve: I hope that the cameras picked up (that)
    13   ((loud laughter))
    14 Frank: Steve this indicates a need for you to be out in hui
    15   ((laughter))
    16 Frank: one of the things that you learn very quickly
    17   is that a sign of respect is that other people are talking
    18   about what [you're saying while you're saying it]
    19   [((laughter))   ]
    20   ((laughter))
    21 Steve: I see I see
              (adapted from Holmes et al. 2012: 1070–1071)

Holmes, Marra and Vine claim that while Steve asserts a (Pākehā New Zealand English) interactional norm, namely, that one should not speak while others are speaking (lines 8–10), this is treated as an inappropriate assertion by Frank, another Pākehā. Frank implies in line 14 that Steve is not sufficiently acquainted with Māori New Zealand English ways of speaking by suggesting that he needs to attend more *hui* (i.e. traditional Māori meetings). By doing so it is suggested that Steve would gain an appreciation of the Māori English interpretive norm that *a sign of respect is that other people are talking about what you're saying while you're saying it* (lines 17–18). By asserting a Māori interactional norm, Frank reframes Steve's metapragmatic comment as inappropriate for that workplace because it involves the assertion of a Pākehā interactional norm. Speaking English thus inevitably raises questions about just whose norms are assumed to be at play. Such issues can be approached at various orders of indexicality, including through the lens of ethnic varieties of English.

8.5 Conclusion

In this chapter, we have suggested that reflexive awareness underpins all language use. We have alluded to our preceding discussions of referring expressions (Chapter 2), informational pragmatics (Chapter 3), pragmatic meaning (Chapters 4 and 5), pragmatic acts (Chapter 6) and interpersonal pragmatics (Chapter 7), in describing how metarepresentational, metacognitive and metacommunicative awareness lie at the core of such pragmatic phenomena. We have also suggested that some pragmatic phenomena, such as irony, reported talk, pragmatic markers, metapragmatic descriptors and commentary, and social discourses cannot be explained without making recourse to these different forms of reflexive awareness. It is for this reason that we have intentionally concluded this volume with an explicitly metapragmatic perspective on pragmatic phenomena.

A metapragmatic perspective takes pragmatic phenomena to be consequential for people in the real world. What people are taken to be referring to or meaning, for instance, has real-world implications for those people involved. People talk about language use and such discussions matter. In analysing metapragmatics in use it is clear that an analysis of the metalanguage that is both explicitly and implicitly invoked by participants (and observers) is necessary. It is important to remember, however, that this metalanguage is unlikely to be completely synonymous across languages, or even across groups of users of that language. Metapragmatics is thus ultimately a language- and culture-specific enterprise, a point we have tried to emphasise through using examples that not only highlight the ways in which English speakers display reflexive awareness of their use of English, but also touch upon the variation in such awareness across speakers of English.

9 Conclusion

9.1 Pragmatics as language in use

Pragmatics is broadly understood as the study of language in use. It has traditionally focused on what the speaker means by an utterance and what the hearer understands by it. From its inception it has been widely recognised that in order for hearers to figure out what speakers mean, they need to draw not only from the utterance itself but from aspects of the context in which the utterance arises. This has led, in turn, to a focus on a range of topics that are now considered core in pragmatics, including deixis, presupposition, (conversational) implicature, speech acts and, at least in our view, politeness. This set of topics is generally associated with the micro view approach to pragmatics, sometimes termed Anglo-American or linguistic pragmatics, where the focus has been on the relationships between linguistic units, the things they designate and users. From this viewpoint , pragmatics is conceptualised as a sub-field within linguistics, and so complements work in phonetics, phonology, morphology, grammar/ syntax and semantics towards a general theory of language.

An alternative account of pragmatics is that it analyses linguistic phenomena as they are actually used, and in that sense focuses more solidly on what people do with language (including non-verbal aspects) in social contexts. This macro approach to pragmatics, which encompasses a much broader set of topics that touches upon issues of identity, ideology, culture, the place of discourse in society and so on, is sometimes termed Continental European pragmatics. The latter broad treatment of pragmatics positions it as a superordinate field, to which disciplines such as linguistics, sociology and psychology all contribute as sub-fields.

The approach we have implicitly advocated in this book has been carving out a middle path between these two broad conceptualisations of pragmatics. Lying at the heart of this book is, we think, an account of core topics of interest in the micro approach to pragmatics. However, we have approached these key pragmatic phenomena from a broader perspective that pays particular attention to the *interactional* and *socio-cultural* grounding of these phenomena. Indeed, the importance we place on the latter has led us to explicitly position this account of pragmatics in relation to the English language, rather than claiming, implicitly or otherwise, that what we are describing here applies universally across all languages. We have placed particular importance on how the understandings of *participants* are reliant on the concepts, distinctions and ways of thinking that the English language both affords and, at least to some extent, constrains (Goddard 2006; Wierzbicka 2003). The intuitive distinction in English between *saying* and *implying* is one such example, as is the distinction we make between $saying_1$ in the sense of *uttering*, and $saying_2$ in the sense of *meaning*, but there are numerous others that we have touched upon throughout this book. This is not to say that we are endorsing a strong version of cultural determinism, but simply to point out that the ways in which we analyse the use of a particular language are influenced, in turn, by the language we use to analyse that language in use. In other words, we need to consider more seriously the place of *observers*, and the linguistic (and cultural) resources they use, when forming understandings of what particular linguistic units mean for *users*, that is, those people who are engaged in those instances of language in use. This has also led us to emphasise the importance of taking into account the awareness of participants themselves in relation to the interactive or communicative activities they are engaged in, and, in particular, the use of language which reflects such reflexive awareness. This *metapragmatic* perspective once again underscores the need to take more seriously the influence of the metalanguage drawn upon by those observers as well as the users themselves, which is, in the case of this book, English for both users and observers. To put it another way, we have been interested in this volume in working towards a pragmatics *of* English, by showing how an account of pragmatics developed primarily, although not solely, with reference to the use of English, can be applied to explaining English language in use.

We might add, on a final note, that throughout this book we have been alluding to a dynamic tension between what might be broadly called first-order and second-order perspectives on pragmatics. A first-order perspective, as we mentioned in the introduction, is that of the participants themselves, the ones who are using language to mean and do things. A second-order perspective encompasses that of the analyst, including ourselves, the writers of this book, and you, the readers. Pragmatics was traditionally rooted primarily in a second-order perspective, but has more recently undergone a shift towards a first-order perspective. In this volume, we have advocated neither exclusively. Instead, we have proposed a middle way that grounds the second-order theorisation and analysis of pragmatic phenomena in the first-order perspective of participants as they arise in interaction. This is not to say that the aim of pragmatics should be to replicate such perspectives or to be constrained by them, but rather to suggest that any analysis should necessarily be informed by them. Our book has been structured accordingly. In each chapter, we have outlined various theoretical perspectives on key phenomena of interest in pragmatics, and then suggested how these might be approached from an interactional perspective that takes into account the understandings of participants. In being informed by the understandings of participants our discussion has necessarily been tied to a particular language and cultural milieu, namely, that of English.

In the following two sections, we briefly reflect upon some of the implications of the approach taken in this book, first, for the development of an integrative pragmatics, and second, for the study of the English language and pragmatics more broadly.

9.2   Integrative pragmatics

While we readily acknowledge the existence of a variety of different approaches to pragmatics, the approach we have developed in this book has attempted to bridge these through close attention to the role of interaction in shaping how participants both come to mean things through their use of language, and form understandings of what particular instances of language in use mean for them. This emphasis on the critical role that interaction plays in shaping pragmatic phenomena and the perspectives of both users and observers on these can be broadly described as an integrative pragmatics. The primary focus of integrative pragmatics is the study, by observer-analysts, of what particular form-function relationships are taken to mean by user-participants in particular situated, sequential contexts, and how this can vary across those participants. The above definition is, out of necessity, somewhat compressed, so in this section we first unpack the various elements of an integrative pragmatics before going on to briefly consider the implications of taking such an approach for the methodologies we, as analysts, employ.

9.2.1   First-order and second-order perspectives on pragmatics

A first-order perspective encompasses that of users, that is, those persons who are participating in the instance of language in use in question. A second-order perspective encompasses that of observers, that is, those persons who are analysing the instance of language use in question. The key elements that constitute such instances of language in use, which we briefly alluded to in the introduction and have subsequently discussed in more detail throughout this volume, are summarised in Figure 9.1:

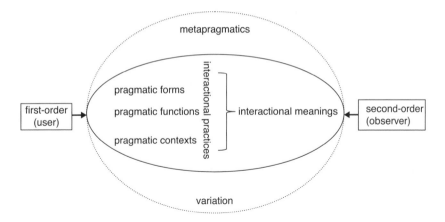

Figure 9.1 Overview of integrative pragmatics

At the heart of all pragmatic phenomena lies a relationship between pragmatic forms, pragmatic functions and pragmatic contexts, and the interactional meanings they give rise to. Interactional meaning, in our account, is a broad concept that refers to what is taken to be meaningful by participants in particular occasions of sequentially situated talk and conduct. These encompass:

(1) pragmatic meanings, that is, what participants are (taken to be) referring to, presuming, and saying, implicating and inferring;
(2) pragmatic acts, that is, what kinds of socially recognisable acts and activities those participants are (taken to be) doing; and
(3) the interpersonal relations, attitudes and evaluations they are (taken to be) instantiating.

These interactional meanings arise through interactional practices, that is, through regular and recurrent ways in which these pragmatic forms, functions, contexts co-occur in meaningful ways for participants. Pragmatic forms, in our account, constitute any linguistic (or indeed non-linguistic) unit that can be linked to a particular pragmatic function, where the latter refers to some purpose or activity for which the form is fitted or employed to accomplish. Given it is now well accepted that there is almost never a straightforward relationship between pragmatic forms and functions, we acknowledge, as does pragmatics more broadly, that this relationship is inevitably mediated through pragmatic contexts. Pragmatic contexts refers to broader discourse and social elements that together underpin the recognisability for participants (and observers) of those (non-)linguistic units as pragmatic forms, the recognisability of particular purposes or activities as pragmatic functions, and the recognisability of the (sometimes complex) relationships between those pragmatic forms and functions. It is, of course, important to remember that pragmatic contexts are the cornerstones by which we connect the use of language to the real world. Not only do we draw from contexts in understanding the interactional meanings arising through the use of language, but language itself is also shaped through the use of language, as sociolinguists and others have long noted (Hymes 1974; Gumperz 1982; Goodwin and Duranti 1992). Finally, the issue of recognisability leads us, in turn, to consider both the awareness of users (and observers) vis-à-vis those interactional meanings, and the interactional practices through they are constituted (i.e. what is termed metapragmatics), and the inevitable variation in awareness, understandings and instantiation of these pragmatic forms, functions and contexts, and thus interactional practices and meanings across participants (and observers).

Such an approach naturally has implications for the range of methods we might employ in studying pragmatic phenomena. Our view has been that there is a wide range of methods and disciplinary approaches that are relevant to the analysis of language in use, as we discuss in the following section.

9.2.2 Methods in pragmatics

While there are a multitude of different methodological and disciplinary approaches that are drawn upon in pragmatics, at the risk of gross oversimplification, we venture to divide them into three broad groups. The first involves **formal** analysis, where the analyst attempts to generate an ordered, theoretical account of pragmatic phenomena. Formal analysis has traditionally been carried out at the utterance level of instances of language use accessed through introspection, although more recently it has also involved analysis of naturally occurring language use. Much of the work in philosophical pragmatics comes under the guise of formal analysis. The second involves **observational** analysis, where analysts undertake systematic examination of instances of language in use vis-à-vis particular contextual variables. Observational analysis is often undertaken at the utterance level, and instances of language use are sometimes elicited rather than occurring naturally, especially in experimental pragmatics work. However, observational analysis can also involve large tracts of naturally occurring data, or what are more commonly termed corpora, in the emerging field of corpus pragmatics. Some approaches, such as cognitive pragmatics, on the other hand, draw from both formal and observational analyses. Finally, the third broad type involves **interpretive** analysis, where the analyst attempts to tease out what pragmatic phenomena arising in particular, situated occasions of language use mean for those participants. Interpretive analysis generally involves recourse to naturally occurring stretches of talk. Work in discursive and phenomenological pragmatics tends to come under the guise of interpretive analysis.

While integrative pragmatics might seem, on the surface, to favour the broad, interpretive grouping, our view is that all three broad methodological approaches, and associated disciplinary groundings, are valid. It all depends, in the end, on the questions being asked by the analyst, as Jucker (2009) rather nicely argues in relation to research on speech acts. To this end, we have made reference in the course of this book – at least as much as possible given the obvious constraints of this being a single volume – to various different types of studies that draw from formal, observational and interpretive approaches to pragmatics. Our coverage of these approaches and methods may not be quite as even as we might have hoped for, but omissions, where they are perceived, should not be taken as neglecting the import of such studies, but as simply reflecting the constraints of a book where the primary focus is on developing an account of pragmatic phenomena. The complex issues that are inevitably raised when attempting to discuss various methods and discipli-nary approaches in pragmatics is clearly deserving of a book in its own right (see Culpeper, Haugh and Terkourafi in preparation).

9.3   The pragmatics of Englishes

Studies of English language have, by and large, neglected pragmatics, as we pointed out in the introduction. One key aim in this book has thus been to illustrate how pragmatics can contribute more broadly to the study of the English language. In the course of discussing various pragmatic phenomena in English we have observed instances of inter-English variation (i.e. simi-larities or differences amongst Englishes), intra-English variation (i.e. simi-larities or differences amongst the sub-varieties of a particular English), and diachronic variation (i.e. similarities or differences over time in a particular English). We have, unfortunately, only been able to refer briefly to studies and different pragmatic phenomena that are indicative of such variation. In that sense, the broader project of understanding the pragmatics of Englishes is still only in its infancy. However, we believe that the importance of such an undertaking has been established through both this volume and other related works on pragmatic variation.

The study of the pragmatics of Englishes is, apart from its inherent value for understanding the English language itself, also important for pragmatics more broadly. Work in pragmatics using data and concepts from English has dominated much of the theorising in pragmatics to date. Given this theorisa-tion is more often than not grounded in the metalanguage and broad cultural worldview that is represented through the concepts and distinctions made in English, it is clearly helpful if we are to reach a better understanding of the meta-theoretical basis, and limitations therein, of pragmatics, for us to develop a more nuanced account of the pragmatics of English. In addition, the lessons that have been learnt can be applied, where useful, although not necessarily in a way that constrains analysts from asking other kinds of questions or proposing other forms of analysis, when analysing the pragmatics of other languages. Such lessons can also extend to other languages that are pluricentric in a manner similar to English, including many of the key world languages, such as Chinese, Spanish and Arabic, to name just a few.

To conclude, our explicit aim here has been to write a book about pragmatics and the English language. While much of the discussion in this book is naturally applicable in some way or another to other languages, in some cases it is not. We would suggest that a greater appreciation of taking such a position can only enrich our current understanding of pragmatics.

Bibliography

Corpora

The British National Corpus (BNC). The CQP-edition (Version 4.3) of BNCweb (Versions 3 and 4) developed by Sebastian Hoffmann (University of Trier) and Stefan Evert (Erlangen University). November 2013. Accessed at http://bncweb.lancs.ac.uk/

Oxford English Corpus (OEC). http://www.oxforddictionaries.com/words/the-oxford-english-corpus. Oxford University Press. July 2013. Accessed at http://www.sketch-engine.co.uk/

References

Abbott, Barbara (2000) Presuppositions as non-assertions. *Journal of Pragmatics*, 32: 1419–1437.

Aijmer, Karin (1996) *Conversational Routines in English: Convention and Creativity.* Harlow, Longman.

Allwood, Jens (1976) *Linguistic Communication as Action and Cooperation.* Gothenburg Monographs in Linguistics 2. Göteborg: Department of Linguistics.

Andersen, Richard C., Ralph E. Reynolds, Diane L. Schallert, and Ernest T. Goetz (1977) Frameworks for comprehending discourse. *American Educational Research Journal*, 14(4): 367–381.

Anderson, Stephen R. and Edward Keenan (1985) Deixis. In Timothy Shopen (ed.) *Language Typology and Syntactic Fieldwork*, Vol. III. Cambridge: Cambridge University Press, 259–308.

Andersson, Marta (2009) ' "I know that women don't like me!" ' Presuppositions in therapeutic discourse. *Journal of Pragmatics*, 41: 721–737.

Ariel, Mira (1988) The linguistic status of "here and now". *Cognitive Linguistics*, 9: 189–237.

Ariel, Mira (1990) *Accessing Noun Phrase Antecedents*. London: Croom Helm.

Arndt, Horst and Richard Wayne Janney (1987) *Intergrammar: Toward an Integrative Model of Verbal, Prosodic and Kinesic Choices in Speech*. Berlin: De Gruyter Mouton.

Arundale, Robert B. (2006) Face as relational and interactional: a communication framework for research on face, facework, and politeness. *Journal of Politeness Research*, 2(2): 193–217.

Arundale, Robert B. (2008) Against (Gricean) intentions at the heart of human interaction. *Intercultural Pragmatics*, 5(2): 229–258.

Atlas, Jay David (2004) Presupposition. In Laurence R. Horn and Gregory Ward (eds) *The Handbook of Pragmatics*. Oxford: Blackwell, 29–52.

Auden, W. H. ([1936]1976) *Funeral Blues*. *Selected Poems of W.H. Auden*. National Public Radio Website. http://www.npr.org/programs/death/readings/poetry/aude.html

Augustinos, Martha, Brianne Hastie and Monique Wright (2011) Apologizing for historical injustice: emotion, truth and identity in political discourse. *Discourse & Society*, 22: 507–531.

Austin, John L. ([1962] 1975) *How to do Things with Words* (2nd edn, edited by J. O. Urmson and Marina Sbisà). Cambridge, MA: Harvard University Press.

Bach, Kent (1999). The myth of conventional implicature. *Linguistics and Philosophy* 22: 327–366.

Bach, Kent (2001) You don't say? *Synthese*, 128(1/2): 15–44.

Bach, Kent (2004) Pragmatics and the Philosophy of Language. In Laurence R. Horn and Gregory Ward (eds) *The Handbook of Pragmatics*. Oxford: Blackwell, 463–487.

Bach, Kent (2006) The top 10 misconceptions about implicature. In Betty Birner and Gregory Ward (eds) *Drawing the Boundaries of Meaning: Neo-Gricean Studies in Pragmatics and Semantics in Honor of Laurence R. Horn*. Amsterdam: John Benjamins, 21–30.

Bach, Kent (2012) Saying, meaning, and implicating. In Keith Allan and Kasia M. Jaszczolt (eds) *The Cambridge Handbook of Pragmatics*. Cambridge: Cambridge University Press, 47–67.

Bach, Kent and Robert M. Harnish (1979) *Linguistic Communication and Speech Acts*. Cambridge, MA: MIT Press.

Bach, Kent and Robert M. Harnish (1992) How performatives really work: A reply to Searle. *Linguistics and Philosophy*, 15: 93–110.

Ballmer, Thomas and Waltraud Brennenstuhl (1981) *Speech Act Classification: A Study in the Lexical Analysis of English Speech Activity Verbs*. Berlin: Springer-Verlag.

Bara, Bruno G. (2010) *Cognitive Pragmatics*. Cambridge, MA: MIT Press.

Bargiela-Chiappini, Francesca (2003) Face and politeness: new (insights) for old (concepts). *Journal of Pragmatics*, 35(10–11): 1453–1469.

Barron, Anne (2005) Offering in Ireland and England. In Anne Barron and Klaus P. Schneider (eds) *The Pragmatics of Irish English*. Berlin: De Gruyter Mouton, 141–176.

Barron, Anne and Klaus P. Schneider (eds) (2005) *The Pragmatics of Irish English*. Berlin and New York: De Gruyter Mouton.

Bartlett, Frederick C. ([1932]1995) *Remembering: A Study in Experimental and Social Psychology*. Cambridge: Cambridge University Press.

Baxter, Leslie A. (1984) An investigation of compliance-gaining as politeness. *Human Communication Research*, 10: 427–456.

Beach, Wayne (1995) Conversation analysis: "okay" as a clue for understanding consequentiality. In Stuart J. Sigman (ed.) *The Consequentiality of Communication*. Hillsdale, NJ: Lawrence Erlbaum, 121–162.

Beaver, David (1997) Presupposition. In Johan van Benthem and Alice ter Meulen (eds) *The Handbook of Logic and Language*. Elsevier: Amsterdam, 939–1008.

Bertuccelli-Papi, Marcella (1996) Insinuating: the seduction of unsaying. *Pragmatics*, 6(2): 191–204.

Bertuccelli-Papi, Marcella (1999) Implicitness to whom? In Jef Verschueren (ed.) *Pragmatics in 1998. Selected Papers from the 6th International Pragmatics Conference*, Vol. 2. Antwerp, Belgium: International Pragmatics Association, 57–72.

Biber, Douglas, Susan Conrad and Randi Reppen (1998) *Corpus Linguistics: Investigating Language Structure and Use*. Cambridge, New York and Melbourne: Cambridge University Press.

Biber, Douglas, Stig Johansson, Geoffrey Leech, Susan Conrad and Edward Finegan (1999) *Longman Grammar of Spoken and Written English*. Harlow: Pearson Education.

Birner, Betty J. and Gregory Ward (1998) *Information Status and Noncanonical Word Order in English*. Amsterdam and Philadelphia: John Benjamins.

Blakemore, Diane (1987) *Semantic Constraints on Relevance*. Oxford: Blackwell.

Blakemore, Diane (2002) *Relevance and Linguistic Meaning*. Cambridge: Cambridge University Press.

Blommaert, Jan and Jef Verschueren (1998) *Debating Diversity: Analysing the Discourse of Tolerance*. London: Routledge.

Blum-Kulka, Shoshana (1987) Indirectness and politeness in requests: same or different? *Journal of Pragmatics*, 11: 131–146.

Blum-Kulka, Shoshana and Juliane House (1989) Cross-cultural and situational variation in requesting behavior. In Shoshana Blum-Kulka, Juliane House and Gabriele Kasper (eds) *Cross-Cultural Pragmatics: Requests and Apologies*, Vol. XXXI. Advances in Discourse Processes. Norwood, NJ: Ablex, 123–154.

Blum-Kulka, Shoshana, Juliane House and Gabriele Kasper (1989a) Investigating cross-cultural pragmatics: an introductory overview. In Shoshana Blum-Kulka, Juliane House and Gabriele Kasper (eds) *Cross-Cultural Pragmatics: Requests and Apologies*, Vol. XXXI. Advances in Discourse Processes. Norwood NJ: Ablex, 1–34.

Blum-Kulka, Shoshana, Juliane House and Gabriele Kasper (eds) (1989b) *Cross-Cultural Pragmatics: Requests and Apologies*, Vol. XXXI. Advances in Discourse Processes. Norwood, NJ: Ablex.

Bolinger, Dwight (1961) Contrastive accent and contrastive stress. *Language*, 37: 83–96.

Bousfield, Derek (2008) *Impoliteness in Interaction*. Philadelphia and Amsterdam: John Benjamins.

Bousfield, Derek and Miriam Locher (eds) (2008) *Impoliteness in Language: Studies on its Interplay with Power in Theory and Practice*. Berlin and New York: Mouton de Gruyter.

Bouton, Lawrence. 1988. A cross-cultural study of the ability to interpret implicatures in English. *World Englishes* 7: 183–196.

Bradac, James, J., Aaron Castelan Cargile and Jennifer S. Hallett (2001) Language attitudes: retrospect, conspect, and prospect. In W. Peter Robinson and Howard Giles (eds) *The New Handbook of Language and Social Psychology*. Chichester: John Wiley, 137–155.

Breheny, Richard, Napoleon Katsos and John Williams (2006) Are generalised scalar implicatures generated by default? An on-line investigation into the role of context in generating pragmatic inferences. *Cognition*, 100: 434–463.

Brennan, Susan E. and Herbert H. Clark (1996) Conceptual pacts and lexical choice in conversation. *Journal of Experimental Psychology: Learning, Memory, and Cognition*, 22: 1482–1493.

Breuer, Anja and Ronald Geluykens (2007) Variation in British and American English requests: a contrastive study. In Bettina Kraft and Ronald Geluykens (eds) *Cross-Cultural Pragmatics and Interlanguage English*. München: Lincom, 107–125.

Brinton, Laurel J. (1988) *The Development of English Aspectual Systems: Aspectualizers and Post-Verbal Particles*. Cambridge: Cambridge University Press.

Brown, Gillian (1995) *Speakers, Listeners and Communication: Explorations in Discourse Analysis*. Cambridge: Cambridge University Press.

Brown, Penelope and Stephen C. Levinson ([1978] 1987) *Politeness: Some Universals in Language Usage*. Cambridge: Cambridge University Press.

Brown, Roger and Albert Gilman (1960) The pronouns of power and solidarity. In Thomas A. Sebeok (ed.) *Style in Language*. Cambridge, MA: MIT Press, and New York and London: John Wiley & Sons, 253–276.

Burridge, Kate and Margaret Florey (2002) "Yeah-no he's a good kid'": a discourse analysis of *yeah-no* in Australian English. *Australian Journal of Linguistics*, 22(2): 149–171.

Burton-Roberts, Noel (2010) Cancellation and intention. In Belén Soria and Esther Romero (eds) *Explicit Communication: Robyn Carston's Pragmatics*. Basingstoke, Hampshire: Palgrave Macmillan, 138–155.

Butler, Clay (2007) From bite to nip: the dialogic construction of teases. *Texas Linguistic Forum*, 50: 22–34.

Candlin, Chris N. and Lucas, Jennifer (1986) Interpretations and explanations in discourse: modes of "advising" in family planning. In Titus Ensink, Arthur van Essen and Ton van der Geest (eds) *Discourse and Public Life: Papers of the Groningen Conference on Medical and Political Discourse*. Dordrecht: Foris Publications, 13–38.

Caffi, Claudia (1998) Metapragmatics. In Jacob Mey (ed.) *Concise Encyclopedia of Pragmatics*. Amsterdam: Elsevier, 581–586.

Carassa, Antonella and Marco Colombetti (2009) Joint meaning. *Journal of Pragmatics*, 41: 1837–1854.

Carston, Robyn (1996) Metalinguistic negation and echoic use. *Journal of Pragmatics*, 25: 309–330.

Carston, Robyn (1998) Negation, '"presupposition'" and the semantics/pragmatics distinction. *Journal of Linguistics*, 34: 309–350.

Carston, Robyn (2002) *Thoughts and Utterances: The Pragmatics of Explicit Communication*. Oxford: Blackwell.

Cavell, Stanley (1958) Must we mean what we say? *Inquiry*, 1(1/4): 172–212.

Chafe, Wallace L. (1976) Givenness, contrastiveness, definiteness, subjects, topics and point of view. In Charles N. Li (ed.) *Subject and Topic*. New York: Academic Press, 27–55.

Chang, Wei-Lin Melody and Michael Haugh (2011) Evaluations of im/politeness of an intercultural apology. *Intercultural Pragmatics*, 8: 411–442.

Chen, Rong (2010) Pragmatics east and west: similar or different? In Anna Trosborg (ed.) *Handbook of Pragmatics*, Vol. 7. Berlin: De Gruyter Mouton, 167–188.

Chomsky, Noam (1965) *Aspects of the Theory of Syntax*. Cambridge, MA: MIT Press.

Christie, Chris (2007) Relevance theory and politeness. *Journal of Politeness Research: Language, Behaviour, Culture*, 3: 269–294.

Clark, Herbert H. (1979) Responding to indirect speech acts. *Cognitive Psychology*, 11: 430–477.

Clark, Herbert H. (1996) *Using Language*. Cambridge: Cambridge University Press.

Clark, Herbert H. (1997) Dogmas of understanding. *Discourse Processes*, 23: 567–598.

Clark, Herbert H. and Catherine R. Marshall (1981) Definite reference and mutual knowledge. In Aravind K. Joshi, Bonnie L. Webber and Ivan A. Sag (eds) *Elements of Discourse Understanding*. Cambridge: Cambridge University Press, 10–63.

Clark, Herbert H. and Deanna Wilkes-Gibbs (1986) Referring as a collaborative process. *Cognition*, 22: 1–39.

Clark, Herbert H. and Peter Lucy (1975) Understanding what is meant from what is said: a study in conversationally conveyed requests. *Journal of Verbal Learning and Verbal Behaviour*, 14: 56–72.

Clift, Rebecca (1999) Irony in conversation. *Language in Society*, 28(4): 523–553.

Coleman, Linda and Paul Kay (1981) Prototype semantics: the English word "Lie"'. *Language*, 57(1): 26–44.

Cooke, Joseph R. (1968) *Pronominal Reference in Thai, Burmese, and Vietnamese*. University of California Publications in Linguistics, 52. Berkeley: University of California Press.

Coupland, Nikolas and Adam Jaworski (2004) Sociolinguistic perspectives on metalanguage: reflexivity, evaluation and ideology. In Adam Jaworski , Nikolas Coupland and Dariusz Galasiński (eds) *Metalanguage: Social and Ideological Perspectives*. Berlin: De Gruyter Mouton, 15–52.

Culpeper, Jonathan (1996) Towards an anatomy of impoliteness. *Journal of Pragmatics*, 25: 349–367.

Culpeper, Jonathan (2007) A new kind of dictionary for Shakespeare's plays: an immodest proposal. *SEDERI* (Yearbook of the Spanish and Portuguese Society for English Renaissance Studies) 17: 47–73.

Culpeper, Jonathan (2008) Reflections on impoliteness, relational work and power. In Derek Bousfield and Miriam Locher (eds) *Impoliteness in Language*. Berlin/New York: Mouton de Gruyter, 17–44.

Culpeper, Jonathan (2010) Historical sociopragmatics. In Andreas H. Jucker and Irma Taavitsainen (eds) *Historical Pragmatics*. Berlin/New York: Mouton de Gruyter, 69–94.

Culpeper, Jonathan (2011a) *Impoliteness: Using Language to Cause Offence*. Cambridge: Cambridge University Press.

Culpeper, Jonathan (2011b) "It's not what you said, it's how you said it!" Prosody and impoliteness. In Linguistic Politeness Research Group (ed.) *Discursive Approaches to Politeness*. Berlin: De Gruyter Mouton, 57–83.

Culpeper, Jonathan and Dan McIntyre (2010) Activity types and characterisation in dramatic discourse. In Jens Eder, Fotis Jannidis and Ralph Schneider (eds) *Characters in Fictional Worlds: Understanding Imaginary Beings in Literature, Film and Other Media*. Berlin: De Gruyter Mouton, 176–207.

Culpeper, Jonathan and Dawn Archer (2008) Requests and directness in Early Modern English trial proceedings and play-texts, 1640–1760. In Andreas H. Jucker and Irma Taavitsainen (eds) *Speech Acts in the History of English*, Amsterdam and Philadelphia: John Benjamins, 45–84.

Culpeper, Jonathan and Elena Semino (2000) Constructing witches and spells: speech acts and activity types in Early Modern England. *Journal of Historical Pragmatics*, 1(1): 97–116.

Culpeper, Jonathan and Jane Demmen (2011) Nineteenth-century English politeness: negative politeness, conventional indirect requests and the rise of the individual self. *Journal of Historical Pragmatics*, 12(1/2): 49–81.

Culpeper, Jonathan, Leyla Marti, Meilian Mei, Minna Nevala and Gila Schauer (2010) Cross-cultural variation in the perception of impoliteness: a study of impoliteness events reported by students in England, China, Finland, Germany and Turkey. *Intercultural Pragmatics*, 7–4: 597–624.

Culpeper, Jonathan and Merja Kytö (2010) *Speech in Writing: Explorations in Early Modern English Dialogues*. Cambridge: Cambridge University Press,

Curl, Traci S. and Paul Drew (2008) Contingency and action: a comparison of two forms of requesting. *Research on Language and Social Interaction*, 41: 129–153.

Davies, Bethan (2007) Grice's Cooperative Principle: meaning and rationality. *Journal of Pragmatics*, 39(12): 2308–2331.

Davis, Wayne (1998) *Implicature. Intention, Convention, and Principle in the Failure of Gricean Theory*. Cambridge: Cambridge University Press.

Dennett, Daniel C. (1991) *Consciousness Explained*. New York: Little, Brown and Co.

Deutschmann, Mats (2003) *Apologising in British English*. Umeå, Sweden: Umeå University.

Dickey, Stephen M. (2000) *Parameters of Slavic Aspect: A Cognitive Approach*. Stanford: CSLI Publications.

Diessel, Holger ([2005]2008) Distance contrasts in demonstratives. In Martin Haspelmath, Matthew S. Dryer, David Gil and Bernard Comrie (eds) *The World Atlas of Language Structures*. Oxford: Oxford University Press, 170–173. Republished in *The World Atlas of Language Structures Online*. Munich: Max Planck Digital Library, chapter 41. Available online at http://wals.info/chapter/41. Accessed on 1/7/10.

Dik, Simon C. (1980) *Studies in Functional Grammar*. London: Academic Press.

Donnellan, Keith S. (1966). Reference and definite descriptions. *Philosophical Review*, 75(3): 281–304.

Downing, Pamela (1996) Proper names as referential option in English conversation. In Barbara Fox (ed.) *Studies in Anaphora*. Amsterdam: John Benjamins, 95–143.

Dresner, Eli and Susan C. Herring (2010) Functions of the non-verbal in CMC: emoticons and illocutionary force. *Communication Theory*, 20: 249–268.

Drew, Paul (1984). Speakers' reportings in invitation sequences. In Maxwell J. Atkinson and John Heritage (eds) *Structures of Social Action*. Cambridge: Cambridge University Press, 129–151.

Drew, Paul (1998) Complaints about transgressions and misconduct. *Research on Language and Social Interaction*, 31(3/4): 295–325.

Dry, Helen Aristar (1992) Foregrounding: an assessment. In Shin Ja J. Hwang and William R. Merrifield (eds) *Language in Context: Essays for Robert E. Longacre*. Publications in Linguistics, 107. A Publication of The Summer Institute of Linguistics and The University of Texas at Arlington, 435–450.

Dunkling, Leslie (1995) *The Guinness Book of Names* (7th edn). London: Guinness Publishing.

Dynel, Marta (2011) Turning speaker meaning on its head: non-verbal communication and intended meanings. *Pragmatics and Cognition*, 19(3): 422–447.

Edwards, Derek (1999) Emotion discourse. *Culture & Psychology*, 5(3): 271–291.

Edwards, Derek. 2005. Moaning, whinging and laughing: the subjective side of complaints. *Discourse Studies* 7(1): 5–29.

Eelen, Gino (2001) *A Critique of Politeness Theories*. Manchester: St. Jerome Publishing.

Enfield, Nick (2003) The definition of what-d'you-call-it: semantics and pragmatics of recognitional deixis. *Journal of Pragmatics*, 35(1): 101–117.

Epstein, Richard (1999) *Roles, Frames and Definiteness*. In Karen van Hoek, Andrej A. Kibrik and Leo Noordman (eds) *Discourse Studies in Cognitive Linguistics*. Current Issues in Linguistic Theory, Vol. 176. Amsterdam and Philadelphia: John Benjamins, 53–74.

Ervin-Tripp, Susan M., Amy Strage, Martin Lampert and Nancy Bell (1987) Understanding requests. *Linguistics*, 25: 107–143.

Ervin-Tripp, Susan M., Jiansheng Guo and Martin Lampert (1990) Politeness and persuasion in children's control acts. *Journal of Pragmatics*, 14: 307–331.

Escandell-Vidal, Victoria (1996) Towards a cognitive approach to politeness. In Katarzyna Jaszczolt and Ken Turner (eds) *Contrastive Semantics and Pragmatics, Vol. 2: Discourse Strategies*. Oxford: Pergamon, 621–650.

Escandell-Vidal, Victoria (1998) Intonation and procedural encoding: the case of Spanish interrogatives. In Villy Rouchota and Andreas H. Jucker (eds) *Current Issues in Relevance Theory*. Amsterdam: John Benjamins, 169–203.

Eysenck, Michael W. and Mark T. Keane (2000) *Cognitive Psychology: A Student's Handbook*. 4th edn. Hillsdale, NJ: Lawrence Erlbaum.

Field, Margaret (1998) Politeness and indirection in Navajo directives. *Journal of Southwest Linguistics*, 17(2): 23–34.

Fillmore, Charles ([1971] 1997) *Lectures on Deixis*. Stanford: CSLI Publications.

Fiske, Susan T. and Shelley E. Taylor (1991) *Social Cognition* (2nd edn). Berkshire and New York: McGraw-Hill.

Fox, Barbara (1987) *Discourse Structure and Anaphora: Written and Conversational English*. Cambridge: Cambridge University Press.

Fox, Barbara (1996) *Studies in Anaphora*. Amsterdam: John Benjamins.

Fox, Kate (2004) *Watching the English: The Hidden Rules of English Behaviour*. London: Hodder and Stoughton.

Frajzyngier, Zygmunt (1996) On sources of demonstratives and anaphors. In Barbara Fox (ed.) *Studies in Anaphora*. Amsterdam: John Benjamins, 169–203

Fraser, Bruce (1990) Perspectives on politeness. *Journal of Pragmatics*, 14(2): 219–236.

Fraurud, Kari (1990) Definiteness and the processing of noun phrases in natural discourse. *Journal of Semantics* 7: 395–433.

Frege, Gottlob ([1892]1952) Über Sinn und Bedeutung. *Zeitschrift für Philosophie und Philosophische Kritik* (100: 22–50). Translated by Peter Geach and Max Black as "Sense and Reference". In Peter Geach and Max Black (eds) *Translations from the Philosophical Writing of Gottlob Frege*. Oxford: Blackwell, 56–78.

Fried, Mirjam (2009) Word order. In Frank Brisard, Jan-Ola Östman and Jef Verschueren (eds) *Grammar, Meaning and Pragmatics*. Handbook of Pragmatics Highlights 5. Amsterdam and Philadelphia: John Benjamins, 289–300.

Garfinkel, Harold (1967) *Studies in Ethnomethodology*. Englewood Cliffs, NJ: Prentice-Hall.

Garrett, Merrill and Robert Harnish (2009) Q-phenomena, I-phenomena and implicature: some experimental pragmatics. *International Review of Pragmatics*, 1(1): 84–117.

Gazdar, Gerald (1979) *Pragmatics: Implicature, Presupposition and Logical Form*. New York: Academic Press.

Geis, Michael (1995) *Speech Acts and Conversational Action*. Cambridge: Cambridge University Press.

Gibbs, Raymond W. Jr. (1981) Your wish is my command: convention and context in interpreting indirect requests. *Journal of Verbal Learning and Verbal Behavior*, 20: 431–444.

Gibbs, Raymond W. Jr. (1983) Do people always process the literal meanings of indirect requests? *Journal of Experimental Psychology: Learning, Memory and Cognition*, 9: 524–533.

Gibbs, Raymond W. Jr. (2002) A new look at literal meaning in understanding what is said and implicated. *Journal of Pragmatics*, 34(4): 457–486.

Gibbs, Raymond W. Jr. (2012) Are ironic acts deliberate? *Journal of Pragmatics*, 44: 104–115.

Givón, Talmy (1987) Beyond foreground and background. In Russell S. Tomlin (ed.) *Coherence and Grounding in Discourse*. Amsterdam: Benjamins, 175–188.

Goddard, Cliff (ed.) (2006) *Ethnopragmatics*. Berlin: De Gruyter Mouton.

Goddard, Cliff (2009) *Not taking yourself too seriously* in Australian English: semantic explications, cultural scripts, corpus evidence. *Intercultural Pragmatics*, 6(1): 29–53.

Goddard, Cliff and Anna Wierzbicka (2014) *Words and Meanings: Lexical Semantics across Domains, Languages, and Cultures*. Oxford: Oxford University Press.

Goffman, Erving ([1964] 1972) The neglected situation. In Pier P. Giglioli (ed.) *Language and Social Context*. Harmondsworth: Penguin, 61–66.

Goffman, Erving (1967) *Interaction Ritual: Essays on Face-to-Face Behavior*. New York: Pantheon Books.

Goffman, Erving (1981) *Forms of Talk*. Philadelphia: University of Pennsylvania Press.

Goodwin, Charles (1979) The interactive construction of a sentence in natural conversation. In Georg Psathas (ed.) *Everyday Language: Studies in Ethnomethodology*. New York: Irvington, 97–121.

Goodwin, Charles (2007) Interactive footing. In Elizabeth Holt and Rebecca Clift (eds) *Reporting Talk*. Cambridge: Cambridge University Press, 16–46.

Goodwin, Charles and Alessandro Duranti (1992) Rethinking context: an introduction. In Alessandro Duranti and Charles Goodwin (eds) *Rethinking Context: Language as an Interactive Phenomenon*. Cambridge: Cambridge University Press, 1–42.

Goodwin, Charles and Marjorie Harness Goodwin (1987) Concurrent operations on talk: notes on the interactive organization of assessments. *IPrA Papers in Pragmatics* 1(1): 1–54.

Goodwin, Charles and Marjorie Harness Goodwin (2004) Participation. In Alessandro Duranti (ed.) *A Companion to Linguistic Anthropology*. Malden, MA: Blackwell, 222–244.

Goodwin, Marjorie Harness (1990) *He-Said-She-Said: Talk as Social Organization among Black Children*. Bloomington: Indiana University Press.

Greenall, Annjo Klungervik (2009) Towards a new theory of flouting. *Journal of Pragmatics*, 41(11): 2295–2311.

Grice, H. Paul (1957) Meaning. *Philosophical Review*, 66(3): 377–388. Republished in Grice (1989), pp. 213–223

Grice, H. Paul (1967) *Logic and Conversation*. William James Lectures. Published in revised form in Grice (1989).

Grice, H. Paul ([1969] 1989) Utterer's meaning and intention. *Philosophical Review*, 78(2): 147–177. Republished in Grice (1989), pp. 86–116.

Grice, H. Paul (1975 [1989]) Logic and conversation. In Peter Cole and Jerry Morgan (eds) *Syntax and Semantics*, Vol. 3. Speech Acts. New York: Academic Press, 41–58. Republished in Grice (1989), 22–40.

Grice, H. Paul (1978 [1989]) Further notes on logic and conversation. In Peter Cole (ed.) *Syntax and Semantics*, Vol. 9. Pragmatics. New York: Academic Press, 113–127. Republished in Grice (1989), 41–57.

Grice, H. Paul (1981) Presupposition and conversational implicature. In: Peter Cole (ed.) *Radical Pragmatics*. New York: Academic Press, 183–198.

Grice, H. Paul (1987 [1989]) Retrospective epilogue. In H. Paul Grice (ed.) *Studies in the Way of Words*. Cambridge, MA: Harvard University Press, 339–385.

Grice, H. Paul (1989) *Studies in the Way of Words*. Cambridge, MA: Harvard University Press.

Gu, Yueguo (1990) Politeness phenomena in modern Chinese. *Journal of Pragmatics*, 14 (2): 237–257.

Gumperz, John (1982) *Discourse Strategies*. Cambridge: Cambridge University Press.

Gumperz, John (1992) Interviewing in intercultural situations. In Paul Drew and John Heritage (eds) *Talk at Work: Interaction in Institutional Settings*. Cambridge: Cambridge University Press, 307–327.

Gundel, Jeanette K. and Thorstein Fretheim (2004) Topic and focus. In Laurence R. Horn and Gregory Ward (eds) *The Handbook of Pragmatics*. Oxford: Blackwell, 175–196.

Gundel, Jeanette K., Mamadou Bassene, Bryan Gordon, Linda Humnick and Amel Khalfaoui (2010) Testing predictions of the Givenness Hierarchy framework: a crosslinguistic investigation. *Journal of Pragmatics*, 42(7): 1770–1785.

Gundel, Jeanette K., Nancy Hedberg and Ron Zacharski (1993) Cognitive status and the form of referring expressions in discourse. *Language*, 69(2): 274–307.

Halliday, Michael A. K. (1967) Notes on Transitivity and Theme in English, Part 2. *Journal of Linguistics*, 3: 199–244.

Halliday, Michael A. K. ([1970]2002) Language structure and language function. In John Lyons (ed.) *New Horizons in Linguistics*. Harmondsworth: Penguin Books, 140–165.

Republished in Jonathan Webster (ed.) (2002) *On Grammar: Collected Works of MAK Halliday*, Vol. 1. London: Continuum, 173–198.

Halliday, Michael A. K. (1973) *Explorations in the Functions of Language*. London: Edward Arnold.

Halliday, Michael A. K. (1978) *Language as Social Semiotic: The Social Interpretation of Language and Meaning*. London: Edward Arnold.

Halliday, Michael A. K. (1994 [1985]) *An Introduction to Functional Grammar* (2nd edn). London: Edward Arnold.

Halliday, Michael A. K. and Ruqaiya Hasan ([1976] 1997) *Cohesion in English* (English Language Series 9). London and New York: Longman.

Hanks, William F., Sachiko Ide and Yasuhiro Katagiri (2009) Towards an emancipatory pragmatics. *Journal of Pragmatics*, 41(1): 1–9.

Harris, Sandra (2001) Being politically impolite: extending politeness theory to adversarial political discourse. *Discourse and Society*, 12(4): 451–472.

Haugh, Michael (2002) The intuitive basis of implicature: relevance theoretic *implicitness* versus Gricean implying. *Pragmatics*, 12(2): 117–134.

Haugh, Michael (2003) Anticipated versus inferred politeness. *Multilingua*, 22(4): 397–413.

Haugh, Michael (2007a) The co-constitution of politeness implicature in conversation. *Journal of Pragmatics*, 39(1): 84–110.

Haugh, Michael (2007b) The discursive challenge to politeness research: an interactional alternative. *Journal of Politeness Research*, 3(7): 295–317.

Haugh, Michael (2008) The place of intention in the interactional achievement of implicature. In Istvan Kecskes and Jacob Mey (eds) *Intention, Common Ground and the Egocentric Speaker-Hearer*. Berlin: De Gruyter Mouton, 45–86.

Haugh, Michael (2009) Intention(ality) and the conceptualisation of communication in pragmatics. *Australian Journal of Linguistics*, 29(1): 91–113.

Haugh, Michael (2010) Co-constructing what is said in interaction. In Németh T. Enikő and Károly Bibok (eds) *The Role of Data at the Semantics-Pragmatics Interface*. Berlin: De Gruyter Mouton, 349–380.

Haugh, Michael (2011) Practices and defaults in interpreting disjunction. In Kasia M. Jaszczolt and Keith Allan (eds) *Salience and Defaults in Utterance Processing*. Berlin: De Gruyter Mouton, 193–230.

Haugh, Michael (2013a) Disentangling face, facework and im/politeness. *Sociocultural Pragmatics*, 1: 46–73.

Haugh, Michael (2013b) Implicature, inference and cancellability. In Alessandro Capone, Franco Lo Piparo and Marco Carapezza (eds) *Perspectives on Pragmatics and Philosophy*. New York: Springer, 133–151.

Haugh, Michael (2013c) Im/politeness, social practice and the participation order. *Journal of Pragmatics*, 58: 52–72.

Haugh, Michael (2013d) Speaker meaning and accountability in interaction. *Journal of Pragmatics*, 48: 41–56.

Haugh, Michael (in press 2014) *Im/politeness Implicatures*. Berlin: De Gruyter Mouton.

Haugh, Michael and Derek Bousfield (2012) Mock impoliteness, jocular mockery and jocular abuse in Australian and British English. *Journal of Pragmatics*, 44: 1099–1114.

Haugh, Michael and Kasia M. Jaszczolt (2012) Speaker intentions and intentionality. In Keith Allan and Kasia M. Jaszczolt (eds) *The Cambridge Handbook of Pragmatics.* Cambridge: Cambridge University Press, 87–112.

Heritage, John (1984a) A change of state token and aspects of its sequential placement. In Maxwell J. Atkinson and John Heritage (eds) *Structures of Social Action.* Cambridge: Cambridge University Press, 299–345.

Heritage, John (1984b) *Garfinkel and Ethnomethodology.* Cambridge: Polity Press.

Heritage, John (1998) Oh-prefaced responses to inquiry. *Language in Society*, 27: 291–334.

Heritage, John (2012) Epistemics in action: action formation and territories of knowledge. *Research on Language and Social Interaction*, 45: 1–29.

Heritage, John and Geoffrey Raymond (2012) Navigating epistemic landscapes: acquiescence, agency and resistance in responses to polar questions. In Jan P. de Ruiter (ed.) *Questions: Formal, Functional and Interactional Perspectives.* Cambridge: Cambridge University Press, 179–192.

Heritage, John and Marja-Leena Sorjonen (1994) Constituting and maintaining activities across sequences: and-prefacing as a feature of question design. *Language in Society*, 23: 1–29.

Holdcroft, David (1994) Indirect speech acts and propositional content. In Savas L. Tsohatzidis (ed.) *Foundations of Speech Act Theory: Philosophical and Linguistic Perspectives.* London and New York: Routledge, 350–364.

Holmes, Janet, Meredith Marra and Bernadette Vine (2012) Politeness and impoliteness in ethnic varieties of New Zealand English. *Journal of Pragmatics*, 44(9): 1063–1076.

Holtgraves, Thomas (1994) Communication in context: effects of speaker status on the comprehension of indirect requests. *Journal of Experimental Psychology: Learning, Memory and Cognition*, 20: 1205–1218.

Holtgraves, Thomas (1998) Interpersonal foundations of conversational indirectness. In Susan R. Fussell and Roger J. Kreuz (eds) *Social and Cognitive Approaches to Interpersonal Communication.* Mahwah, NJ: Lawrence Erlbaum Associates, 71–89.

Holtgraves, Thomas (1999) Comprehending indirect replies: when and how are their conveyed meanings activated? *Journal of Memory and Language*, 41(4): 519–540.

Holtgraves, Thomas (2005) The production and perception of implicit performatives. *Journal of Pragmatics*, 37: 2024–2043.

Hopper, Paul J. and Elizabeth Closs Traugott ([1993]2003) *Grammaticalization* (2nd edn). Cambridge, New York and Port Melbourne: Cambridge University Press.

Hopper, Paul J. and Sandra A. Thompson (1980) Transitivity in grammar and discourse. *Language*, 56 (2): 251–299.

Hopper, Paul J. and Sandra A. Thompson (1993) Language universals, discourse pragmatics, and semantics. *Language Sciences*, 159(4): 357–376.

Horn, Laurence (1984) Toward a new taxonomy for pragmatic inference: Q-based and R-based implicature. In Deborah Schiffrin (ed.) *Georgetown University Round Table on Languages and Linguistics. Meaning, Form, and Use in Context: Linguistic Applications.* Washington, DC: Georgetown University Press, 11–42.

Horn, Laurence (1985) Metalinguistic negation and pragmatic ambiguity. *Language*, 62: 121–174.

Horn, Laurence (1989) *A Natural History of Negation*. Chicago: University of Chicago Press.

Horn, Laurence (2004) Implicature. In Laurence Horn and Gregory Ward (eds) *Handbook of Pragmatics*. Oxford: Blackwell, 3–28.

Horn, Laurence (2009) WJ-40: implicature, truth, and meaning. *International Review of Pragmatics*, 1(1): 3–34.

Horn, Laurence (2012) Implying and inferring. In Keith Allan and Kasia M. Jaszczolt (eds) *The Cambridge Handbook of Pragmatics*. Cambridge: Cambridge University Press, 69–86.

Horn, Laurence and Samuel Bayer (1984) Short-circuited implicature: a negative contribution. *Linguistics and Philosophy*, 7: 397–414.

Hornby, Nick (1995) *High Fidelity*. London: Indigo.

Horvath, Barabara M. (1985) *Variation in Australian English: The Sociolects of Sydney*. Cambridge: Cambridge University Press.

Hua, Zhu, Li Wei and Qian Yuan (2000) The sequential organisation of gift offering and acceptance in Chinese. *Journal of Pragmatics*, 32: 81–103.

Huang, Yan (2000) *Anaphora: A Cross-Linguistic Study*. Oxford: Oxford University Press.

Hübler, Axel and Wolfram Bublitz (2007) Introducing metapragmatics in use. In Wolfram Bublitz and Axel Hübler (eds) *Metapragmatics in Use*. Amsterdam and Philadelphia: John Benjamins, 1–26.

Hymes, Dell (1974) *Foundations in Sociolinguistics. An Ethnographic Approach*. Philadelphia: University of Pennsylvania Press.

Irwin, Barry (1974) *Salt-Yui Grammar*. Pacific Linguistics, B-35. Canberra: ANU

Isaacs, Ellen A. and Herbert H. Clark (1987) References in conversation between experts and novices. *Journal of Experimental Psychology: General*, 116: 26–37.

Jakobson, Roman (1971) *Word and Language*. The Hague: Mouton.

Jary, Mark (1998) Relevance theory and the communication of politeness. *Journal of Pragmatics*, 30: 1–19.

Jaszczolt, Kasia M. (2005) *Default Semantics: Foundations of a Compositional Theory of Acts of Communication*. Oxford: Oxford University Press.

Jaszczolt, Kasia M. (2009) Cancellability and the primary/secondary meaning distinction. *Intercultural Pragmatics*, 6(3), 259–289.

Jaworski, Adam, Nikolas Coupland and Dariusz Galasiński (2004) Metalanguage: why now? In Adam Jaworski, Nikolas Coupland and Dariusz Galasiński (eds) *Metalanguage: Social and Ideological Perspectives*. Berlin: De Gruyter Mouton, 3–8.

Jucker, Andreas H. (2008) Politeness in the history of English. In Richard Dury, Maurizio Gotti and Marina Dossena (eds) *English Historical Linguistics 2006. Volume II: Lexical and Semantic Change*. Amsterdam and Philadelphia: John Benjamins, 3–29.

Jucker, Andreas H. (2009) Speech act research between armchair, field and laboratory: the case of compliments. *Journal of Pragmatics*, 41(8): 1611–1635.

Jucker, Andreas H. and Irma Taavitsainen (2000) Diachronic speech act analysis: insults from flyting to flaming. *Journal of Historical Pragmatics*, 1(1): 67–95.

Jucker, Andreas H. and Sara Smith (1996) Explicit and implicit ways of enhancing common ground in conversations. *Pragmatics*, 6(1): 1–18.

Kádár, Dániel Z. and Michael Haugh (2013) *Understanding Politeness*. Cambridge: Cambridge University Press.

Kallen, Jeffrey L. and John M. Kirk (2012) *SPICE-Ireland: A User's Guide*. Belfast: Queen's University Belfast, Trinity College Dublin and Cló Ollscoil na Banríona.

Kampf, Zohar (2009) Public (non-)apologies: the discourse of minimizing responsibility. *Journal of Pragmatics*, 41(11): 2257–2270.

Kant, Immanuel [1790] (1951) *Critique of Judgement*. New York: Hafner Publishing Company.

Karttunen, Lauri (1973) Presuppositions of compound sentences. *Linguistic Inquiry*, 4: 169–193.

Karttunen, Lauri and Stanley Peters (1979) Conventional implicature. In Choon-Kyu Oh and David A. Dineen (eds) *Syntax and Semantics*, Vol. 11. Presupposition. New York: Academic Press, 1–56.

Kasof, Joseph (1993) Sex bias in the naming of stimulus persons. *Psychological Bulletin*, 113(1): 140–163.

Katsos, Napoleon (2012) Empirical investigations and pragmatic theorising. In Keith Allan and Kasia M. Jaszczolt (eds) *The Cambridge Handbook of Pragmatics*. Cambridge: Cambridge University Press, 275–290.

Kecskes, Istvan (2002) *Situation-Bound Utterances in L1 and L2*. Berlin and New York: Mouton de Gruyter.

Kecskes, Istvan (2008) Dueling contexts: a dynamic model of meaning. *Journal of Pragmatics*, 40: 385–406.

Kecskes, Istvan (2010) The paradox of communication: socio-cognitive approach to pragmatics. *Pragmatics and Society*, 1(1): 50–73.

Kellerman, Kathy and Rodney Reynolds (1990) When ignorance is bliss: the role of motivation to reduce uncertainty in Uncertainty Reduction Theory. *Human Communication Research*, 17: 5–75.

Kennedy, Benjamin Hall (1985 [1962]) *The Revised Latin Primer* (edited and further revised by Sir James Mountford). Harlow: Longman.

Kesey, Ken ([1962] 2003) *One Flew over the Cuckoo's Nest*. Harmondsworth: Penguin Books.

Kiesling, Scott F. and Elka Ghosh Johnson (2010) Four forms of interactional indirection. *Journal of Pragmatics*, 42(2): 292–306.

Kiparsky, Paul and Carol Kiparsky (1970) Fact. In Manfred Bierwisch and Karl Erich Heidolph (eds) *Progress in Linguistics*. The Hague: Mouton, 143–173.

Klein-Andreu, Flora (1996) Anaphora, deixis, and the evolution of Latin *Ille*. In Barbara Fox (ed.) *Studies in Anaphora*. Amsterdam: John Benjamins, 305–331.

Krifka, Manfred (2009) Implicatures. In Uli Sauerland and Kazuko Yatsushiro (eds) *Semantics and Pragmatics: From Experiment to Theory*. New York: Palgrave Macmillan, 3–15.

Kripke, Saul (1972) Naming and Necessity. In Donald Davidson and Gilbert Harman (eds) *Semantics of Natural Language*. Dordrecht: Reidel, 253–355 and 763–769.

Kumatoridani, Tetsuo (1999) Alternation and co-occurrence in Japanese thanks. *Journal of Pragmatics*, 31: 623–642.

Kuno, Susumu (1973) *The Structure of the Japanese Language*. Cambridge, MA: MIT Press.

Kurtz, Victoria and Michael Schober (2001) Readers' varying interpretations of theme in short fiction. *Poetics*, 29: 139–166.

Labov, William (1972) *Language in the Inner City: Studies in the Black English Vernacular*. Oxford: Blackwell.

Lachenicht, L. G. (1980) Aggravating language. A study of abusive and insulting language. *International Journal of Human Communication*, 13(14): 607–687.

Lakoff, Robin Tolmach (1973) The logic of politeness, or minding your p's and q's. *Papers from the Ninth Regional Meeting of the Chicago Linguistic Society*, 292– 305.

Lakoff, Robin Tolmach (1989) The limits of politeness: therapeutic and courtroom discourse. *Multilingua*, 8(2–3): 101–129.

LaMarre, Heather L., Kristen D. Landreville and Michael A. Beam (2009) The irony of satire: political ideology and the motivation to see what you want to see in the Colbert report. *International Journal of Press/Politics*, 14(2): 212–231.

Lambrecht, Knud (1994) *Information Structure: Topic, Focus and the Mental Representations of Discourse Referents*. Cambridge: Cambridge University Press.

Laury, Ritva (2009) Definiteness. In Frank Brisard, Jan-Ola Östman and Jef Verschueren (eds) *Grammar, Meaning and Pragmatics*. Amsterdam: John Benjamins, 50–65.

Lee, Benny P.H. (2001) Mutual knowledge, background knowledge and shared beliefs: their roles in establishing common ground. *Journal of Pragmatics*, 33(1): 21–44.

Leech, Geoffrey N. (1983) *Principles of Pragmatics*, London: Longman

Leech, Geoffrey N. (1985) Stylistics. In Teun A. van Dijk (ed.) *Discourse and Literature*. Amsterdam: John Benjamins, 39–57.

Leech, Geoffrey N. (1999) The distribution and function of vocatives in American and British English conversation. In Hilde Hasselgård and Signe Oksefjell (eds) *Out of Corpora: Studies in Honour of Stig Johansson*. Amsterdam and Atlanta, GA: Rodopi, 107–118.

Leech, Geoffrey N. (2003) Towards an anatomy of politeness in communication. *International Journal of Pragmatics* 14:101–123.

Leech, Geoffrey N. (2007) Politeness: is there an East-West divide? *Journal of Politeness Research: Language, Behaviour, Culture*, 3(2): 167–206.

Leech, Geoffrey N., Paul Rayson and Andrew Wilson (2001) *Word Frequencies in Written and Spoken English: Based on the British National Corpus*. London: Longman.

Lerner, Gene H. (2004) Collaborative turn sequences. In Gene H. Lerner (ed.) *Conversation Analysis: Studies from the First Generation*. Amsterdam: John Benjamins, 225–256.

Levinson, Stephen C. (1979a) Activity types and language. *Linguistics*, 17(5–6): 365–399. Republished 1992 in Paul Drew and John Heritage (eds) *Talk at Work*. Cambridge: Cambridge University Press, 66–100.

Levinson, Stephen C. (1979b) Pragmatics and social dexis: reclaiming the notion of conventional implicature. *Berkley Linguistics Society*, 5: 206–223.

Levinson, Stephen C. (1983) *Pragmatics*. Cambridge: Cambridge University Press.

Levinson, Stephen C. (1988) Putting linguistics on a proper footing: explorations in Goffman's concepts of participation. In Paul Drew and Anthony Wootton (eds) *Erving Goffman: Exploring the Interaction Order*. Boston: Northeastern University Press, 161–227.

Levinson, Stephen C. (1995) Three levels of meaning. In F. Palmer (ed.) *Grammar and Meaning: Essays in Honour of Sir John Lyons*. Cambridge: Cambridge University Press, 90–115.

Levinson, Stephen C. (2000) *Presumptive Meanings: The Theory of Generalised Conversational Implicature*. Cambridge, MA: MIT Press.

Levinson, Stephen C. (2004) Deixis. In Lawrence R. Horn and Gregory Ward (eds) *The Handbook of Pragmatics*. Oxford: Blackwell Publishing, 100–121.

Lewis, David K. (1969) *Convention: A Philosophical Study*. Cambridge, MA: Harvard University Press.

Li, Charles N. and Sandra A. Thompson (1976) Subject and topic: a new typology of language. In Charles N. Li (ed.) *Subject and Topic*. New York: Academic Press, 457–489.

Littman, David C. and Jacob L. Mey (1991) The nature of irony: toward a computational model of irony. *Journal of Pragmatics*, 15(2): 131–151.

Locher, Miriam A. (2004) *Power and Politeness in Action: Disagreements in Oral Communication*. Berlin and New York: De Mouton Gruyter.

Locher, Miriam A. (2006) Polite behaviour within relational work: the discursive approach to politeness. *Multilingua*, 25(3): 249–267.

Locher, Miriam A. and Richard J. Watts (2005) Politeness theory and relational work. *Journal of Politeness Research: Language, Behaviour, Culture*, 1(1): 9–33.

Locher, Miriam A. and Richard J. Watts (2008) Relational work and impoliteness: negotiating norms of linguistic behaviour. In Derek Bousfield and Miriam Locher (eds.) *Impoliteness in Language*. Berlin: Mouton de Gruyter, 77–99.

Loftus, Elizabeth F. (1975) Leading questions and the eyewitness report. *Cognitive Psychology*, 7: 560–572.

Loftus, Elizabeth F. and John C. Palmer (1974) Reconstruction of automobile destruction: an example of the interaction between language and memory. *Journal of Verbal Learning and Verbal Behaviour*, 13: 585–589.

Long, Christopher (2010) Apology in Japanese gratitude situations: the negotiation of interlocutor role-relations. *Journal of Pragmatics*, 42: 1060–1075.

Lucy, John (2000) Reflexivity. *Journal of Linguistic Anthropology*, 9: 212–215.

Marmaridou, Sophia S. (2000) *Pragmatic Meaning and Cognition*. Amsterdam and Philadelphia: John Benjamins.

Matsumoto, Yoshiko (1988) Reexamination of the universality of face: politeness phenomena in Japanese. *Journal of Pragmatics*, 12(4): 403–426.

Mazzone, Marco (2011) Schemata and associative processes in pragmatics. *Journal of Pragmatics*, 43: 2148–2159.

McEnery, Anthony M. (2006) *Swearing in English: Bad Language, Purity and Power from 1586 to the Present*. London: Routledge.

Mercier, Hugo and Dan Sperber (2009) Intuitive and reflective inferences. In Jonathan Evans and Keith Frankish (eds) *In Two Minds: Dual Processes and Beyond*. Oxford: Oxford University Press, 149–170.

Mey, Jacob (2001) *Pragmatics. An Introduction* (2nd edn). Oxford: Blackwell.

Mey, Jacob (2010) Societal pragmatics. In Louise Cummings (ed.) *The Pragmatics Encyclopedia*. London and New York: Routledge, 444–446.

Miller, Jim (2006) Focus in spoken discourse. In Keith Brown (ed.) *Encyclopedia of Language and Linguistics* (2nd edn). Oxford: Elsevier, 511–518.

Mills, Sara (2003) *Gender and Politeness*. Cambridge: Cambridge University Press.

Mills, Sara (2009) Politeness and culture. *Journal of Pragmatics*, 41: 1047–1060.

Moeschler, Jacques (2012) Conversational and conventional implicatures. In Hans-Jorg Schmid (ed.) *Cognitive Pragmatics*. Berlin: De Gruyter Mouton, 405–433.

Mooney, Annabelle (2004) Co-operation, violations and making sense. *Journal of Pragmatics*, 36: 899–920.

Morgan, Jerry (1978) Two types of convention in indirect speech acts. In Peter Cole (ed.) *Syntax and Semantics*, Vol. 9. Pragmatics. New York: Academic Press, 261–280.

Morgan, Marcyliena (1996) Conversational signifying: grammar and indirectness among African American women. In Elinor Ochs, Emanuel Schegloff and Sandra Thompson (eds) *Grammar and Interaction*. Cambridge: Cambridge University Press, 405–434.

Morris, Charles W. (1938) *Foundations of the Theory of Signs*. In Otto Neurath (ed.) *International Encyclopedia of Unified Science*. Chicago: University of Chicago Press, 1–59.

Mosegaard-Hansen, Maj-Britt (2008) On the availability of ' "literal' " meaning: evidence from courtroom interaction. *Journal of Pragmatics*, 40(8): 1392–1410.

Mühlhäusler, Peter and Rom Harré (1990) *Pronouns and People: The Linguistic Construction of Social and Personal Identity*. Oxford: Blackwell.

Mukarovský, Jan (1970) Standard language and poetic language (edited and translated by Paul L. Garvin). In Donald C. Freeman (ed.) *Linguistics and Literary Style*. New York: Holt, Rinehart and Winston, 40–56.

Neisser, Ulric (1976) *Cognition and Reality: Principles and Implications of Cognitive Psychology*. San Francisco: W. H. Freeman.

Nevile, Maurice and Johanna Rendle-Short (2009) A conversation analysis view of communication as jointly accomplished social interaction: an unsuccessful proposal for a social visit. *Australian Journal of Linguistics*, 28(3): 75–89.

Niedzielski, Nancy and Dennis Preston (2009) Folk Pragmatics. In Gunter Senft, Jan-Ola Ostman and Jef Verschueren (eds) *Culture and Language Use*. Amsterdam: Benjamins, 146–155.

Nin, Anaïs (1990) *Henry and June: From the Unexpurgated Diary of Anaïs Nin*. Fort Washington, PA: Harvest Books.

Nwoye, Onuigbo G. (1992) Linguistic politeness and socio-cultural variations of the notion of face. *Journal of Pragmatics*, 18(4): 309–328.

Ogiermann, Eva (2009) *On Apologising in Negative and Positive Politeness Cultures*. Amsterdam and Philadelphia: John Benjamins.

Opp, Karl-Dieter (1982) The evolutionary emergence of norms. *British Journal of Social Psychology*, 21: 139–149.

Orvig, Anne Salazar, Haydée Marcosé, Aliyah Morgenstern, Rouba Hassan, Jocelyne Leber-Marin and Jacques Parès (2010) Dialogical beginnings of anaphora: the use of third person pronouns before the age of 3. *Journal of Pragmatics*, 42(7): 1842–1865.

Owen, Marion (1983) *Apologies and Remedial Interchanges: A Study of Language Use in Social Interaction*. Berlin, New York and Amsterdam: De Gruyter Mouton.

Pagliuca, William (1994) Preface. In William Pagliuca (ed.) *Perspectives in Grammaticalization*. Current Issues in Linguistic Theory, 109. Amsterdam: John Benjamins, i–xx.

Pan, Yuling and Dániel Z. Kádár (2011) *Politeness in Historical and Contemporary Chinese*. London: Continuum.

Panther, Klaus-Uwe and Linda Thornburg (1998) A cognitive approach to inferencing in conversation. *Journal of Pragmatics*, 30: 755–769.

Parret, Herman (1994) Indirection, manipulation and seduction in discourse. In Herman Parret (ed.) *Pretending to Communicate*. Berlin: De Gruyter Mouton, 223–238.

Peccei, Jean S. (1999) *Pragmatics*. London: Routledge.

Pérez Hernández, Lorena and Francisco J. Ruiz de Mendoza (2002) Grounding, semantic motivation, and conceptual interaction in indirect directive speech acts. *Journal of Pragmatics*, 34: 259–284.

Poesio, Massimo and Renata Vieira (1998) A corpus-based investigation of definite description use. *Computational Linguistics* 24: 183–216.

Potts, Christopher (2005) *The Logic of Conventional Implicatures*. Oxford: Oxford University Press.

Prince, Ellen (1981) Toward a taxonomy of given-new information. In Peter Cole (ed.) *Radical Pragmatics*. New York: Academic Press, 223–255.

Quirk, Randolph, Valerie Adams and Derek Davy (1975) *Old English Literature: A Practical Introduction*. London: Edward Arnold.

Quirk, Randolph, Sidney Greenbaum, Geoffrey Leech and Jan Svartvik (1985) *A Comprehensive Grammar of the English Language*. London and New York: Longman.

Recanati, François (2004) *Literal Meaning*. Cambridge: Cambridge University Press.

Rendle-Short, Johanna (2009) The address term *mate* in Australian English: Is it still a masculine term? *Australian Journal of Linguistics*, 29(2): 245–268.

Rendle-Short, Johanna (2010) ' "Mate' " as a term of address in ordinary interaction. *Journal of Pragmatics*, 42: 1201–1218.

Repp, Sophie (2010) Defining ' "contrast' " as an information-structural notion in grammar. *Lingua*, 120(6): 1333–1345.

Robinson, Jeffrey D. (2004) The sequential organisation of "explicit" apologies in naturally occurring English. *Research on Language and Social Interaction* 37(3): 291–330.

Rooth, Mats (1992) A theory of focus interpretation. *Natural Language Semantics*, 1: 75–116.

Rosaldo, Michelle Z. (1982) The things we do with words: Ilongot speech acts and speech act theory in philosophy. *Language in Society*, 11: 203–238.

Rosch, Eleanor (1975) Cognitive Representations of Semantic Categories. *Journal of Experimental Psychology: General*, 104(3): 192–233.

Rubin, Edgar (1915) *Synsoplevede Figurer* (visually experienced figures). Copenhagen: Gyldendal.

Ruhi, Şükriye (2008) Intentionality, communicative intentions and the implication of politeness. *Intercultural Pragmatics*, 5(3): 287–314.

Rühlemann, Christoph (2007) *Conversation in Context: A Corpus-Driven Approach*. London: Continuum.

Russell, Bertrand (1905) On Denoting. *Mind*, 14: 479–493.

Russell, Bertrand (1910–1911) Knowledge by acquaintance and knowledge by description. *Proceedings of the Aristotelian Society* (New Series), XI: 108–128.

Ryan, Marie-Laure (1991) *Possible Worlds, Artificial Intelligence and Narrative Theory*. Bloomington and Indianapolis: Indiana University Press.

Sacks, Harvey, Emanuel Schegloff and Gail Jefferson (1974) A simplest systematics for the organisation of turn-taking for conversation. *Language*, 50: 696–735.

Sadock, Jerrold (2004) Speech acts. In Laurence R. Horn and Gregory Ward (eds) *The Handbook of Pragmatics*. Oxford: Blackwell, 53–73.

Sandu, Roxana (2013) *Su(m)imasen* and *gomen nasai*: beyond apologetic functions in Japanese. *Pragmatics*, 23(4): 743–767.

Sarangi, Srikant (2000) Activity types, discourse types and interactional hybridity: the case of genetic counseling. In Srikant Sarangi and Malcolm Coulthard (eds) *Discourse and Social Life*. Longman: Harlow, 1–27.

Saul, Jennifer (2002a) Speaker meaning, what is said, and what is implicated. *Nous*, 36(2): 228–248.

Saul, Jennifer (2002b) What is said and psychological reality: Grice's project and relevance theorists criticisms. *Linguistics and Philosophy*, 25(3): 347–372.

Sbisà, Marina (1999) Ideology and the persuasive use of presuppositions. In Jan Verschueren (ed.) *Language and Ideology. Selected Papers from the Sixth International Pragmatics Conference*, Vol. 1. Antwerp, Belgium: International Pragmatics Association, 492–509.

Sbisà, Marina (2002) Speech acts in context. *Language and Communication*, 22: 421–436.

Schaffer, Deborah (2005) Can rhetorical questions function as retorts? Is the Pope catholic? *Journal of Pragmatics*, 37(4): 433–460.

Schank, Roger C. and Robert P. Abelson (1977) *Scripts, Plans, Goals, and Understanding: An Inquiry into Human Knowledge Structures*. Hillsdale, NJ: Lawrence Erlbaum.

Schegloff, Emanuel (2006) On possibles. *Discourse Studies*, 8(1): 141–157.

Schegloff, Emanuel (2007) *Sequence Organization in Interaction*. Cambridge: Cambridge University Press.

Schegloff, Emanuel, Elinor Ochs and Sandra Thompson (1996) Introduction. In Emanuel Schegloff, Elinor Ochs and Sandra Thompson (eds) *Interaction and Grammar*. Cambridge: Cambridge University Press: 1–51.

Schmid, Hans-Jörg (2001) ' "Presupposition can be a bluff' ": how abstract nouns can be used as presupposition triggers. *Journal of Pragmatics*, 33(10): 1529–1552.

Schneider, Klaus P. and Anne Barron (eds) (2008) *Variational Pragmatics*. Amsterdam: John Benjamins.

Schober, Michael F. and Herbert H. Clark (1989) Understanding by addressees and overhearers. *Cognitive Psychology*, 21: 211–232.

Scollon, Ronald and Suzanne Scollon (1995) *Intercultural Communication: A Discourse Approach*. Oxford: Blackwell.

Searle, John R. (1969) *Speech Acts: An Essay in the Philosophy of Language*. Cambridge: Cambridge University Press.

Searle, John R. (1975) Indirect speech acts. In Paul Cole and Jerry L. Morgan (eds) *Syntax and Semantics 3*. New York: Academic Press, 59–82.

Searle, John R. (1979) *Expression and Meaning*. Cambridge: Cambridge University Press.

Searle, John R. (2007) What is language: some preliminary remarks. In Istvan Kecskes and Laurence R. Horn (eds) *Explorations in Pragmatics: Linguistic, Cognitive and Intercultural Aspects*. Berlin: De Gruyter Mouton, 7–37.

Seidlhofer, Barbara (2001) Closing a conceptual gap: the case for a description of English as a lingua franca. *International Journal of Applied Linguistics*, 11(2): 133–158.

Semino, Elena (1997) *Language and World Creation in Poems and Other Texts*. London: Longman.

Seuren, Pieter A. M. (1985) *Discourse Semantics*. Oxford: Blackwell.

Siewierska, Anna (2004) *Person*. Cambridge: Cambridge University Press.

Silverstein, Michael (1976) Shifters, linguistic categories, and cultural description. In Keith H. Basso and Henry A. Selby (eds) *Meaning and Anthropology*. Alberquerque: The University of New Mexico Press, 11–56.

Silverstein, Michael (1993) Metapragmatic discourse and metapragmatic function. In John A. Lucy (ed.) *Reflexive Language: Reported Speech and Metapragmatics*. Cambridge: Cambridge University Press, 33–58.

Silverstein, Michael (2003) Indexical order and the dialectics of sociolinguistic life. *Language and Communication*, 23(3/4): 193–229.

Skovholt, Karianne and Jan Svennevig (2006) E-mail copies in workplace interaction. *Journal of Computer-Mediated Communication*, 12(1): 42–65.

Slobin, Dan Isaac (1975) The more it changes ... : on understanding language by watching it move through time. *Papers and Reports on Child Language Development*, 10: 1–30.

Smith, Sara W. and Andreas H. Jucker (2000) '"Actually'" and other markers of an apparent discrepancy between propositional attitudes of conversational partners. In Thorstein Fretheim and Gisle Andersen (eds) *Pragmatic Markers and Propositional Attitudes*. Amsterdam: Benjamins, 207–237.

Snow, Catherine E., Rivka Y. Perlmann, Jean Berko Gleason and Nahid Hooshyar (1990) Developmental perspectives on politeness: sources of children's knowledge. *Journal of Pragmatics*, 14: 289–305.

Spenader, Jennifer (2002) *Presuppositions of Spoken Discourse*. Unpublished doctoral dissertation. Department of Linguistics, Stockholm University.

Spencer-Oatey, Helen (1996) Reconsidering power and social distance. *Journal of Pragmatics*, 26: 1–24.

Spencer-Oatey, Helen (2002) Managing rapport in talk: using rapport sensitive incidents to explore the motivational concerns underlying the management of relations. *Journal of Pragmatics*, 34(5): 529–545.

Spencer-Oatey, Helen (2005) (Im)Politeness, face and perceptions of rapport: unpackaging their bases and interrelationships. *Journal of Politeness Research: Language, Behaviour, Culture*, 1(1): 95–119.

Spencer-Oatey, Helen (2008) *Culturally Speaking: Managing Rapport through Talk across Cultures* (2nd edn). London and New York: Continuum.

Sperber, Dan and Deirdre Wilson ([1986]1995) *Relevance: Communication and Cognition* (2nd edn). Oxford UK and Cambridge, USA: Blackwell.

Stalnaker, Robert C. (1972) Pragmatics. In Nicholas Rescher (ed.) *Studies in Logical Theory*. Oxford: Blackwell, 98–112.

Stalnaker, Robert C. ([1974] 1991) Pragmatic presuppositions. In Steven Davis (ed.) *Pragmatics*. New York: Oxford University Press, 471–481.

Starr, Kenneth (1998) The Starr Report. Unpublished report to the US House of Representatives. Available at http://www.washingtonpost.com/wp-srv/politics/special/clinton/icreport/icreport.htm.

Steffensen, Margaret S., Chitra Joag-Dev and Richard C. Andersen (1979) A cross-cultural perspective on reading comprehension. *Reading Research Quarterly*, 15: 10–29.

Stewart, Miranda (2005) Politeness in Britain: ' "*It's only a suggestion ...*' ". In Leo Hickey and Miranda Stewart (eds) *Politeness in Europe*. Clevedon, England: Multilingual Matters, 130–145.

Strawson, Peter F. (1950) On Referring. *Mind*, 52: 320–344.

Strawson, Peter F. (1952) *Introduction to Logical Theory*. London: Methuen.

Tanskanen, Sanna-Kaisa (2007) Metapragmatics utterances in computer-mediated communication. In Wolfram Bublitz and Axel Hübler (eds) *Metapragmatics in Use*. Amsterdam: John Benjamins, 87–106.

Taylor, Susan E. (1981) The interface of cognitive and social psychology. In John Harvery (ed.) *Cognition, Social Behavior and the Environment*. Hillsdale, NJ: Lawrence Erlbaum, 189–211.

Terkourafi, Marina (2001) *Politeness in Cypriot Greek: A Frame-Based Approach*. Unpublished PhD dissertation. Cambridge: University of Cambridge.

Terkourafi, Marina (2002) Politeness and formulaicity: evidence from Cypriot Greek. *Journal of Greek Linguistics*, 3: 179–201.

Terkourafi, Marina (2003) Generalised and particularised implicatures of politeness. In Peter Kühnlein, Hannes Rieser and Henk Zeevat (eds) *Perspectives on Dialogue in the New Millennium*. Amsterdam: John Benjamins, 151–166.

Terkourafi, Marina (2005a) Beyond the micro-level in politeness research. *Journal of Politeness Research: Language, Behaviour, Culture*, 1(2): 237–262.

Terkourafi, Marina (2005b) Pragmatic correlates of frequency of use: the case for a notion of "minimal context". In Sophia Marmaridou, Kiki Nikiforidou and Eleni Antonopoulou (eds) *Reviewing Linguistic Thought: Converging Trends for the 21st Century*. Berlin: De Gruyter Mouton, 209–233.

Terkourafi, Marina (2010) What-is-said from different points of view. *Language and Linguistics Compass*, 4(8): 705–718.

Tetreault, Chantal (2009) Reflecting respect: transcultural communicative practices of Muslim French youth. *Pragmatics*, 19(1): 65–84.

Thomas, Jenny A. (1983) Cross-cultural pragmatic failure. *Applied Linguistics*, 4(2): 91–112.

Thomas, Jenny A. (1995) *Meaning in Interaction: An Introduction to Pragmatics*. London: Longman.

Thornburg, Linda and Klaus-Uwe Panther (1997) Speech act metonymies. In Wolf-Andreas Liebert, Gisela Redeker and Linda Waugh (eds) *Discourse and Perspective in Cognitive Linguistics*. Amsterdam: Benjamins, 205–219.

Tracy, Karen and Sarah J. Tracy (1998) Rudeness at 911: reconceptualizing face and face attack. *Human Communication Research*, 25(2): 225–251.

Traugott, Elizabeth C. (1982) From propositional to textual and expressive meanings: some semantic-pragmatic aspects of grammaticalization. In Winfred P Lehmann and Ykov Malkiel (eds) *Perspectives on Historical Linguistics*. Amsterdam: John Benjamins, 245–271.

Trudgill, Peter and Jean Hannah (2002) *International English: A Guide to the Varieties of Standard English*. London: Arnold.

Tuggy, David (1996) The thing is that people talk that way. In Eugene Casad (ed.) *Cognitive Linguistics in the Redwoods: The Expansion of a New Paradigm in Linguistics*. Berlin: De Gruyter Mouton, 713–752.

van Dijk, Teun A. (1987) *Communicating Racism: Ethnic Prejudice in Thought and Talk.* Newbury Park: Sage Publications.

van Peer, Willie (1986) *Stylistics and Psychology: Investigations of Foregrounding.* London: Croom Helm.

Verschueren, Jef ([1995] 2010). Metapragmatics. In Jef Verschueren, Jan-Ola Ostman and Jan Blommaert (eds) *Handbook of Pragmatics Manual.* Amsterdam: John Benjamins. Republished 2010 in *Handbook of Pragmatics Online.*

Verschueren, Jef (1999) *Understanding Pragmatics.* London: Hodder Arnold.

Verschueren, Jef (2000) "Notes on the role of metapragmatic awareness in language use", *Pragmatics* 10, 4: 439–456.

Verschueren, Jef (2012) *Ideology in Language Use.* Cambridge: Cambridge University Press.

Wales, Katie (1996) *Personal Pronouns in Present-Day English.* Cambridge: Cambridge University Press.

Walker, Traci, Paul Drew and John Local (2011) Responding indirectly. *Journal of Pragmatics*, 43(9): 2434–2451.

Ward, Gregor and Betty Birner (2004) Informational structure and non-canonical syntax. In Laurence R. Horn and Gregory Ward (eds) *The Handbook of Pragmatics.* Oxford: Blackwell, 153–174.

Watts, Richard J. (1988 [1993]) A relevance-theoretic approach to commentary pragmatic markers: the case of actually, really and basically. *Acta Linguistica Hungarica*, 38: 235–260.

Watts, Richard J. (2003) *Politeness.* Cambridge: Cambridge University Press.

Watts, Richard J. (2005) Linguistic politeness research: *Quo vadis?* In Richard J. Watts, Sachiko Ide and Konrad Ehlich (eds) *Politeness in Language: Studies in Its History, Theory and Practice* (2nd edn). Berlin and New York: De Gruyter Mouton, xi–xlvii.

Weigand, Edda (2009) The dialogic principle revisited: speech acts and mental states. In Edda Weigand (ed.) *Language as Dialogue.* Amsterdam: John Benjamins, 21–44.

Weizman, Elda (1985) Towards an analysis of opaque utterances: hints as a request strategy. *Theoretical Linguistics*, 12: 153–163.

Wierzbicka, Anna (1985) A semantic metalanguage for a crosscultural comparison of speech acts and speech genres. *Language in Society*, 14: 491–514.

Wierzbicka, Anna (1987) *English Speech Act Verbs: A Semantic Dictionary.* New York: Academic Press.

Wierzbicka, Anna ([1991] 2003) *Cross-Cultural Pragmatics: The Semantics of Human Interaction* (2nd edn). Berlin and New York: De Gruyter Mouton.

Wierzbicka, Anna (2010) Cultural scripts and intercultural communication. In Anna Trosborg (ed.) *Pragmatics Across Languages and Cultures.* Berlin: De Gruyter Mouton, 43–78.

Wilkes-Gibbs, Deanna and Herbert H. Clark (1992) Coordinating beliefs in conversation. *Journal of Memory and Cognition*, 31: 183–194.

William F. Hanks, Sachiko Ide and Yasuhiro Katagiri (2009) Towards an emancipatory pragmatics. *Journal of Pragmatics*, 41(1): 1–9.

Wilson, Deirdre (2000) Metarepresentation in linguistic communication. In Dan Sperber (ed.) *Metarepresentations: A Multidisciplinary Perspective.* Oxford: Oxford University Press, 411–448.

Wilson, Deirdre and Dan Sperber (1981) On Grice's theory of conversation. In Paul Werth (ed.) *Conversation and Discourse*. London: Croom Helm, 155–178.

Wilson, Deirdre and Dan Sperber (1992) On verbal irony. *Lingua*, 87: 53–76.

Wilson, Deirdre and Dan Sperber (1993) Linguistic form and relevance. *Lingua*, 90: 1–25.

Wilson, Deirdre and Dan Sperber (2004) Relevance theory. In Gregory Ward and Laurence Horn (eds) *Handbook of Pragmatics*. Oxford: Blackwell, 607–632.

Wittgenstein, Ludwig (1953) *Philospohical Investigations*. Oxford: Basil Blackwell.

Woods, John. 2010. Inference. In Louise Cummings (ed.), *The Pragmatics Encyclopedia*, pp. 218–220. London: Routledge.

Index